Reading Heliodorus' *Aethiopica*

Reading Heliodorus' *Aethiopica*

Edited by

IAN REPATH AND TIM WHITMARSH

OXFORD
UNIVERSITY PRESS

Great Clarendon Street, Oxford, OX2 6DP,
United Kingdom

Oxford University Press is a department of the University of Oxford.
It furthers the University's objective of excellence in research, scholarship,
and education by publishing worldwide. Oxford is a registered trade mark of
Oxford University Press in the UK and in certain other countries

© Oxford University Press 2022

The moral rights of the authors have been asserted

First Edition published in 2022

Impression: 1

All rights reserved. No part of this publication may be reproduced, stored in
a retrieval system, or transmitted, in any form or by any means, without the
prior permission in writing of Oxford University Press, or as expressly permitted
by law, by licence or under terms agreed with the appropriate reprographics
rights organization. Enquiries concerning reproduction outside the scope of the
above should be sent to the Rights Department, Oxford University Press, at the
address above

You must not circulate this work in any other form
and you must impose this same condition on any acquirer

Published in the United States of America by Oxford University Press
198 Madison Avenue, New York, NY 10016, United States of America

British Library Cataloguing in Publication Data

Data available

Library of Congress Control Number: 2021951891

ISBN 978–0–19–879254–3

DOI: 10.1093/oso/9780198792543.001.0001

Printed and bound in the UK by
TJ Books Limited

Links to third party websites are provided by Oxford in good faith and
for information only. Oxford disclaims any responsibility for the materials
contained in any third party website referenced in this work.

For John Morgan, in admiration and affection

Contents

List of Contributors	ix
1. Introduction: Reading Heliodorus *Tim Whitmarsh*	1
2. Odyssean and Herodotean Threads in the *Tainia* of Heliodorus' Opening Chapters (1.1–5) *Ewen Bowie*	7
3. Visualizing Assemblages: Demaenete, Thisbe's Bed-Trick, and the Creation of Charicleia (1.15–17) *Helen Morales*	20
4. Thisbe's Intrigue: A Plot between Deception and Illusion (1.15–17) *Jonas Grethlein*	39
5. Theagenes' Second Lament (2.4) *Stephen M. Trzaskoma*	52
6. Cnemon Meets Calasiris (2.21–2) *Alain Billault*	70
7. Allegory, Recognition, and Identity: The Egyptian Homer in Context (3.11.5–15.1) *Lawrence Kim*	80
8. The Mustering of the Delphians (4.19–21) *Tim Whitmarsh*	102
9. Calasiris on Zacynthus and His Dream of Odysseus (5.17–22) *Michael Paschalis*	116
10. Life, the Cosmos, and Everything (5.26–34) *Ken Dowden*	129
11. On the Road Again (6.1–4) *Silvia Montiglio*	146

12.	Chariclea's Dark Night of the Soul (6.8–11) *David Konstan*	161
13.	Epic into Drama (7.6–8) *Richard Hunter*	174
14.	Enter Arsace and Her Entourage! Lust, Gender, Ethnicity, and Class at the Persian Court (Books 7 and 8) *Froma I. Zeitlin*	186
15.	Sending the Reader Round the Bend (8.14–17) *Ian Repath*	203
16.	The Siege of Syene: Ekphrasis and Imagination (9.3) *Ruth Webb*	221
17.	Sphragis 1: To Infinity and Beyond (10.41.4) *Tim Whitmarsh*	246
18.	Sphragis 2: The Limits of Reality and the End of the Novel (10.41.3–4) *Ian Repath*	256

References 271
Index Locorum 289
General Index 299

List of Contributors

Alain Billault is Professor of Greek Emeritus at Sorbonne Université.

Ewen Bowie is Professor Emeritus at the University of Oxford and a Fellow Emeritus of Corpus Christi College.

Ken Dowden is Professor of Classics Emeritus at the University of Birmingham.

Jonas Grethlein is Professor of Greek Literature at Heidelberg University.

Richard Hunter FBA is Regius Professor of Greek Emeritus and Fellow of Trinity College, University of Cambridge.

Lawrence Kim is Professor of Classical Studies at Trinity University.

David Konstan is Professor of Classics at New York University.

Silvia Montiglio is Gildersleeve Professor of Classics at Johns Hopkins University.

Helen Morales is Argyropoulos Professor of Hellenic Studies at the University of California, Santa Barbara.

Michael Paschalis is Professor Emeritus at the University of Crete.

Ian Repath is Senior Lecturer at Swansea University.

Stephen M. Trzaskoma is Professor and Director of the Center for the Humanities at the University of New Hampshire.

Ruth Webb is Professor of Greek Language and Literature at the University of Lille.

Tim Whitmarsh FBA is A. G. Leventis Professor of Greek Culture at the University of Cambridge, and a Fellow of St John's College.

Froma I. Zeitlin is Ewing Professor of Greek Language and Literature Emerita at Princeton University.

1
Introduction

Reading Heliodorus

Tim Whitmarsh

There was a time when scholars of Greek literature used to dismiss the Greek romances as easy reading to fatten up the intellectually moribund as they languished under the *pax Romana*.[1] A low estimation of the literary quality of the romances was accompanied by cavalier assumptions about the demographic make-up of the readership, summed up in Ben Edwin Perry's notorious assessment that the romance was 'melodrama for the edification of children and the poor-in-spirit...adapted to the taste and understanding of uncultivated or frivolous-minded people'.[2] That model has not been sustainable for many years: particularly since the 1990s, scholars have demonstrated how many intellectual demands these texts place upon their readers.[3] The romances, which themselves vary enormously in terms of sophistication and style, no doubt attracted a diverse readership; but there is no reason whatsoever to doubt that women and men of the highest intellectual sophistication found richness and depth in these texts. As Stephen M. Trzaskoma's contribution to this volume shows, we are only now beginning to comprehend just how extensively the romance-writers shaped the world-view of those around them.

---

[1] 'When, as an undergraduate in the 1970s, I first declared my interest in doing my doctoral research in the area of the Greek novel, I was reassured, in all kindness, by a very senior Oxford classicist that I need not feel downhearted at the prospect of spending three whole years reading silly love stories, because there were some very interesting uses of the optative to be discovered in Heliodoros' (Morgan 1996: 63).

[2] Perry 1967: 5 (the phrase 'the poor in spirit' alludes to Matt. 5:3).

[3] On the social contexts for the production and reception of the Greek romances see Bowie 1994; Stephens 1994; Morgan 1995; Cavallo 1996. For an insightful discussion of the relationship scholars have assumed between the alleged low quality of the literature and the low standing of the readership, with an emphasis on gender, see Egger 1999: 108–12.

There are five romances that survive in full: Xenophon's *Ephesian Adventures of Anthia and Habrocomes* and Chariton's *Callirhoe* (both probably first century CE), Achilles Tatius' *Leucippe and Clitophon* (second century), Longus' *Daphnis and Chloe* (second or third century), and Heliodorus' *Ethiopian Adventures of Charicleia and Theagenes* (probably fourth century).[4] In the case of the first four of these (chronologically speaking), it is just about possible to see how earlier generations of scholars might have misread them as simple tales for simple souls. Take *Daphnis and Chloe*, the tale of two young rustics who fall in love, but in their hopeless naivety lack the intellectual resources to consummate their desire. This story was idolized by Europeans Romantics, who found in it a perfect depiction of pure innocence; this has given Longus' tale a singular prominence among the romances, which brought it to the attention of creative artists as diverse as Ravel, Chagall, and Mishima. Recent scholars, however, have emphasized that pastoral, romantic charm is only one aspect of an infinitely more complex text, a parable, alternately comic and religiose, about the relationship between urban wealth and rustic poverty, the (gendered) violence of socialization, the play of nature and nurture, and literary self-reflexivity.[5]

To read Longus' text as a simple, sweet tale is an act of gross simplification, for sure; but history shows that it is quite possible to do so. To read Heliodorus' *Ethiopian Adventures of Charicleia and Theagenes* (conventionally shortened to 'the *Aethiopica*') in this way, however, would be impossible. This is a labyrinthine text composed in arguably the most challenging prose of any ancient Greco-Roman literary writer. As Otto Mazal noted, Heliodorus' extravagant syntax and bejewelled lexis mirror the complexities of his narrative.[6] In fact one early reader, and one alone, seems to have claimed it to be an easy read. Photius, the tirelessly bibliophagic ninth-century bishop of Constantinople, described it as 'brimming with sweet simplicity' (ἀφελείᾳ καὶ γλυκύτητι πλεονάζει); Heliodorus' clauses, he commented, are balanced, compact, and brief (περίοδοι σύμμετροι καὶ πρὸς τὸ βραχύτερον οἷα δὴ συστελλόμεναι).[7] At first sight this is inexplicable: the only possible reason might be that Photius may have found Heliodorus mildly easier than the tortuous intricacies of Byzantine theology. In fact, however, Photius' assessment is probably based not on a hard-nosed stylometry but on a moral judgement of the *Aethiopica*'s sexual character: when

---

[4] For general introductions see Morgan and Stoneman eds 1994; Schmeling ed. 2003; Whitmarsh ed. 2008; Cueva and Byrne eds 2014.
[5] Morgan 2004a; Bowie 2019.   [6] Mazal 1958.   [7] Phot. *Bibl.* Cod. 73 50a.

he writes of the 'purity' of Heliodorus' expression (λέξεσί τε εὐσήμοις καὶ
καθαραῖς), for example, he borrows an epithet used in the text itself of
Charicleia, the virtuous heroine.[8] Stylistic and moral assessments have
become entangled here. Correspondingly, Photius saw a contrast between
the purity of the *Aethiopica* and 'the excessively disgraceful, impure nature'
(τό γε λίαν ὑπέραισχρον καὶ ἀκάθαρτον) of Achilles Tatius.[9]

Other ancient readers clearly shared modern readers' impressions of
Heliodorus as a challenging but rewarding stylist.[10] In the eleventh century,
in the early years of the Comnenian revival of the Byzantine Empire (which
inspired a literary renaissance and a recovery of classical learning), the historian and philosopher Michael Psellos returned to the comparison between
Heliodorus and Achilles. Like Photius, Psellos preferred Heliodorus on
moral grounds, but he also observed the greater complexities. The
Aethiopica, thought Psellos, 'is of loftier design, thanks to its innovative
phrasing' (τῇ καινοτομίᾳ τῆς φράσεως πρὸς τὸ ὑψηλότερον συγκεκρότηται);
Heliodorus uses the arts of Isocrates and Demosthenes, famously grandiose
writers (presumably the implication here is that Achilles, by contrast, follows the 'simple style' of Lysias). But it is not just a question of style. Psellos
also acknowledges (in colourful language) the narrative sophistication that
recent scholars have done so much to expose:

> At first the reader thinks that there is a lot of excess material; but as the
> story unfurls, he will marvel at the author's organization of his text (τὴν
> οἰκονομίαν τοῦ συγγεγραφότος). The beginning of the text looks like coiled
> snakes, concealing their heads inside the nest while the rest of the body
> pokes out.

It is not just that Heliodorus begins *in medias res*, confusing the reader by
withholding crucial information; it is also that multiple, unresolved plot
lines appear almost simultaneously. Charicleia, Theagenes, Thyamis,
Cnemon, Thisbe, Calasiris, and Nausicles are all introduced in the opening
two books, and all have interesting backstories that are either partially or
completely obscured at this early stage. Conversely, Psellos notes, Heliodorus
makes the middle of the story into a beginning (ἀρχὴν πεποίηται τὴν
μεσότητα). As with the *Odyssey*, to which the *Aethiopica* repeatedly looks,

---

[8] Phot. *Bibl.* Cod. 73 50a.   [9] Phot. *Bibl.* Cod. 88 66a.
[10] In general on Heliodorus' Byzantine reception, see Gärtner 1969; Agapitos 1998; Nilsson
and Zagklas 2017; and Trzaskoma in this volume.

the narrative falls into two halves, a complex first one (with multiple plot lines and flashback narrative) and a more linear second one, during which the organization (οἰκονομία) becomes clear.

Ancient readers found Heliodorus fascinating for another reason. There are hints in the *Aethiopica* itself that invite an allegorical reading.[11] At least one ancient reader accepted the invitation, and read Charicleia's story as a disguised parable of the journey of the soul through life. 'Philip the Philosopher' is thought by many to have been a *nom de plume* of the twelfth-century Philagathos of Cerami,[12] and his reading reflects the way the text provokes multi-layered readings, of a kind which feature prominently in this volume.

For modern readers, the text's complexity takes its cue from its portrayal of character, particularly that of the priest Calasiris, who seems to combine high-minded virtue and duplicitousness in equal measure.[13] Since Calasiris is a major narrator, the question of his moral probity is inseparable from that of the trustworthiness of the stories he tells—especially since he notoriously tells two conflicting tales of how he discovered the truth of Charicleia's origins.[14] Calasiris emerges from much modern scholarship as an Odyssean figure whose ambiguities model those of the text itself.

The endeavour to make sense of this extraordinary author is an ongoing one. In 1982, Jack Winkler wrote that 'the *Aithiopika* is an act of pure play, yet a play which rehearses vital processes by which we must live in reality—interpretation, reading, and making a provisional sense of things'.[15] In 1998, Richard Hunter asked whether it is 'beyond interpretation'.[16] This emphasis upon the lability of the text, its stubborn refusal to yield any final meaning, might be thought characteristic of the postmodern phase of literary criticism, and thus perhaps even obsolescent. Yet there is no sign of any slowdown; indeed, readers are currently unearthing ever deeper layers of sophistication. Heliodorus' handling of narrative,[17] fictionality,[18] allusion,[19]

---

[11] Most 2007.
[12] The text is printed in Colonna 1938 and Bianchi 2006. See further Trzaskoma in this volume.
[13] Especially since Winkler 1982; see also Sandy 1982b; de Temmerman 2014: 250–7; and Kim 2019.
[14] The starting point for Winkler 1982; see further Baumbach 1997, 2008; Billault 2015.
[15] Winkler 1982: 158.   [16] Hunter 1998a.
[17] Morgan 1998, 2004b, 2007a, 2007b, 2012a; Montiglio 2013a; Andreadakis 2016; Kruchió 2018a, 2018b; Palone 2020.
[18] Jackson 2016.
[19] Elmer 2008; Telò 2011; Tagliabue 2015, 2016; Castrucci 2017: 93–9; Kasprzyk 2017; Ciocani 2018; Lefteratou 2018; Zanetto 2018; Krauss 2021 (exploring 'horizontal' intertexts in the fourth-century world).

aesthetic experience,[20] and ethics[21] have all come under ever-more intense scrutiny.

Modern readers have also discovered new depths in Heliodorus' treatment of identity, and in particular what we have come to call 'race'. A text that focuses on a white girl born of black parents has an obvious allure in an age in which skin pigmentation has been scrutinized as (arguably) never been before. Already in the early years of the twentieth century, the celebrated African-American novelist Pauline Hopkins cited the *Aethiopica* as an early instance of Afrocentrism.[22] More recently, however, Charicleia's colouring has been seen more as a paradox or a conundrum: something that calls, once again, for close interpretation, and turns the act of reading identity from skin colour into a puzzle.[23] And a highly politicized puzzle, what is more: in the *Aethiopica* Charicleia's implausible acceptance as an Ethiopian in spite of her white skin takes place in front of the Ethiopian populace, and catalyses a revolution in religious practice (the abolition of human sacrifice). 'The parallel between a social and legal scandal and the scandal of narrative credibility', writes Terence Cave, 'is all but explicit here'.[24] Heliodorus' treatment of gender too has been subjected to scrutiny: some have found his handling of the resourceful and energetic Charicleia indicative of a constructive gynocentrism;[25] others have disputed this appraisal, pointing instead to his stereotyped presentation of sexually appetitive older women,[26] the creation of Charicleia as a complex, enigmatic figure from the cloth of earlier literature,[27] and her reduction to the status of tradeable commodity.[28] His relationship to Christianity too has been much disputed: some see points of continuity,[29] others sharp differentiation.[30]

Each generation finds new treasure in the *Aethiopica*, a text that seems never to stop giving to those prepared to dig new mines. This volume brings together an international team of Heliodorean specialists to explore the pleasures, subtleties, nuances, and difficulties of reading the *Aethiopica* at

---

[20] Grethlein 2017: 74–130. [21] Bird 2017, 2019, 2020.
[22] Hopkins 1905: 16, with Selden 1998: 204–8. For a comparative reading of Hopkins's *Of One Blood* and the *Aethiopica*, see Harris 2001.
[23] Whitmarsh 1998; Perkins 1999; Stephens 2008; Lye 2016; Derbew 2022 (I am grateful to the author for advance sight of a version of her Heliodorus chapter); D'Alconzo 2019.
[24] Cave 1988: 19. [25] e.g. Johne 1987; Egger 1999: 134–6.
[26] See Zeitlin in this volume, with further literature.
[27] Papadimitropoulos 2017; Capettini 2018; Lefteratou 2018; Morales in this volume.
[28] Lefteratou 2019 (and more generally on Heliodorus' use of the trade theme Sánchez Hernández 2018).
[29] e.g. Ramelli 2002; Andújar 2013; Krauss 2021.
[30] e.g. Bargheer 1999; Morgan 2005.

the level of detail. Each contributor has chosen a specific passage on which to focus; each of the ten books is covered. The aim has been not to define a single methodology for reading this text but to showcase the exuberant range of reading practices adopted by scholars. Some contributors have selected shorter passages, some longer; some have focused narrowly on the passages in question, others have ranged more freely. Indeed, to underline both the richness of the text and the variety of approaches, on two occasions, two contributors (Morales and Grethlein; Whitmarsh and Repath) read the same passage, coming to instructively different conclusions.

In commissioning these chapters, the editors have sought out a distinguished, international cast list. The omission of one name from the contents list, however, will strike all who know the field as an obvious absence. Despite the inevitable cost to the volume, that omission was quite intentional: this volume is dedicated to John Morgan by his friends, colleagues, collaborators, and students, in boundless gratitude for over forty years of Heliodorean inspiration and insight. One need only see how often his work is referred to over the course of the following chapters to appreciate his deep and lasting influence on the scholarship on the *Aethiopica*: the editors hope this volume will manage to repay some small part of the debt that all the contributors, and many others, feel.

2
Odyssean and Herodotean Threads in the *Tainia* of Heliodorus' Opening Chapters (1.1–5)

Ewen Bowie

On an Egyptian beach, brigands encounter a mysterious and beautiful young woman, holding a bow, but wholly absorbed in tending a handsome, wounded youth, and surrounded by dead men variously slaughtered. The bandits' plundering of the nearby ship's high-value cargo is interrupted by another, larger group of robbers. These use their only two horses to convey the young people to their community, living in huts or boats in lake-edge marshland, their babies fed on sun-roasted fish and tethered to prevent drowning.[1]

Unlike the other four members of the famous five, Heliodorus opens with no indication of his couple's origins or identity, though by 1.3 his description of the unmanageably beautiful κόρη and the handsome ephebic youth whom she tends has at least disclosed to readers that this *is* a couple.[2] He also offers only a brief, albeit precise indication of *where* the scene is set: 'at the outpouring of the Nile and its mouth that is called that of the Heracleion' (κατ' ἐκβολὰς τοῦ Νείλου καὶ στόμα τὸ καλούμενον Ἡρακλεωτικόν, 1.1.1). The reason for its name, as will have been known to readers of Herodotus'

---

[1] For discussions of 1.1 and its ekphrastic dimension, see inter alia Feuillâtre 1966; Winkler 1982: 95–114; Bartsch 1989: 47–50; Morgan 1991; Birchall 1996b; Winkler 2000–1; Whitmarsh 2002: 116–19; Webb 2009: 181; Telò 2011; Whitmarsh 2011: 108–9; Tagliabue 2015; Lefteratou 2018; Zanetto 2018. For comparisons with cinematographic technique, see Bühler 1976; Morgan 1991: 86; Winkler 2000–1; Fusillo 2007: 131–2. On the representations of the scene in modern art, see Stechow 1953.
[2] Despite the identification of the κόρη as a goddess attributed to some of the bandits I think the term κόρη and the description of the gravely wounded and barely conscious Theagenes excludes the suggestion of Wasdin 2019: 388 that for a reader the two may be taken to be 'divine siblings or romantic partners'.

version of the story of Helen's time in Egypt (a story that is one of the many ancestors of that of Charicleia),[3] was a temple of Heracles. The temple and associated city, Thonis–Heracleion, and its close links with another city that will turn out to be important for the *Aethiopica*, Naucratis, are now much better understood after the spectacular results of Franck Goddio's underwater archaeology.[4] As was noted by John Morgan in his introduction to his translation,[5] the Nile's Heracleotic mouth is very close to the site of Alexandria. The fact that Heliodorus' chosen mode of reference here says nothing of the city of Alexandria and that as the story unfolds we encounter brigand-ridden marshlands and lakescapes but no city until the mention of Memphis (1.18.4) together allow the reader to infer that the novel's action is imagined to precede Alexandria's foundation. At the same time the references to the institutions of democratic Athens in Cnemon's inset narrative—the Areopagus (1.9.1) and the *ekklēsia*, albeit anachronistically functioning as a court (1.13.1)—point her to the period after the end of the Peisistratid tyranny in 511–510 BC.[6] But throughout *Aethiopica* Book 1, and for most of Book 2, the events narrated are compatible with any date between the late sixth century and the conquests of Alexander of Macedon in the 330s BC, a temporal frame that receives final confirmation, but no further precision, from the reader's discovery (at 2.24.2) that Egypt is currently ruled by a Persian satrap, Oroondates.[7]

For a reader familiar with Herodotus—and much in the *Aethiopica* suggests that Heliodorus envisaged such a reader[8]—the earlier part of that period is a time at which Egypt was part of the Persian Empire (as of course it still was after the years covered by Herodotus' *Enquiries*). Even before the mention of Oroondates' position as satrap, then, and indeed as early as Cnemon's *logos* set in 'classical' Athens, a reader may expect that the *dramatis personae* will include not simply pirates, Egyptian *boukoloi* and brigands,

---

[3] For the reworking of major myths by the novelists, see Lefteratou 2018.
[4] See Robinson and Goddio 2015. The mouth was sometimes called Naucratitic: Plin. *HN* 5.64.
[5] Morgan 1989c: 350.
[6] The *Panathenaea* festival (1.10.1) is not similarly diagnostic since its foundation happened no later than the 560s BC.
[7] Oroondates (if correctly transmitted, which with sixty-three instances in the text is surely the case) is not a bad shot at a Persian name: cf. the previously unattested Iranian name Ὀροντοδάτης from Xanthos in Lycia, first century AD, reported by *SEG* 46.1723. The editors compare Ὀροντοβάτης and Ὀροντοπάτης, all these based on Orontes, of which a few cases are attested in the Greek world (one in Cyprus; six in northern Greece and Pontus in *LGPN* vol. 4). I am grateful to Andrej Petrovic for directing me to this item.
[8] Cf. Elmer 2008.

and young Greek prisoners, but also representatives of the occupying power, Persians.

This bears upon a reader's interpretation of the opening scene. Mario Telò has demonstrated in detail that Odysseus' slaughter of the suitors (μνηστηροφονία) is an important intertext for this tableau, and Aldo Tagliabue has convincingly argued that the visual qualities of Heliodorus' ekphrasis suggest that he himself possessed, and expected some of his readers to possess, some knowledge of the treatments of this scene in painting and sculpture.[9] Tagliabue may be right to think that sarcophagi will have been one channel by which some readers might know visual representations of the story, but the paintings on classical vases that he also mentions, albeit important for our modern reconstruction of iconographic traditions, are very unlikely to be known in this period. Moreover, as Tagliabue points out, both these media regularly present the slaughter of the suitors in progress, and only one ancient treatment is so far known which portrayed Odysseus *after* the conflict had ended, just as Charicleia is presented after the slaughter on the beach has ceased. To me that treatment seems to be highly relevant to the opening of the *Aethiopica*. This was a painting by Polygnotus, probably painted soon after 479 BC, and displayed in the temple of Athena Areia at Plataea which was constructed with the proceeds of the Plataean spoils from the battle of Marathon:[10]

Πλαταιεῦσι δὲ Ἀθηνᾶς ἐπίκλησιν Ἀρείας ἐστὶν ἱερόν· ᾠκοδομήθη δὲ ἀπὸ λαφύρων ἃ τῆς μάχης σφίσιν Ἀθηναῖοι τῆς Μαραθῶνι ἀπένειμαν. τὸ μὲν δὴ ἄγαλμα ξόανόν ἐστιν ἐπίχρυσον, πρόσωπον δέ οἱ καὶ χεῖρες ἄκραι καὶ πόδες λίθου τοῦ Πεντελησίου εἰσί· μέγεθος μὲν οὐ πολὺ δή τι ἀποδεῖ τῆς ἐν ἀκροπόλει χαλκῆς, ἣν καὶ αὐτὴν Ἀθηναῖοι τοῦ Μαραθῶνι ἀπαρχὴν ἀγῶνος ἀνέθηκαν, Φειδίας δὲ καὶ Πλαταιεῦσιν ἦν ὁ τῆς Ἀθηνᾶς τὸ ἄγαλμα ποιήσας. γραφαὶ δέ εἰσιν ἐν τῷ ναῷ Πολυγνώτου μὲν Ὀδυσσεὺς τοὺς μνηστῆρας ἤδη κατειργασμένος, Ὀνασία δὲ Ἀδράστου καὶ Ἀργείων ἐπὶ Θήβας ἡ προτέρα στρατεία. αὗται μὲν δή εἰσιν ἐπὶ τοῦ προνάου τῶν τοίχων αἱ γραφαί, κεῖται

---

[9] Telò 2011; Tagliabue 2015; cf. Zanetto 2018. For the importance of comparisons to works of art in Heliodoran writing, see Whitmarsh 2002: esp. 112–18, and for the possibility that Charicleia's posture may recall a well-known statue of Penelope (the Vatican 'Penelope'), see ibid. 116; see however Lefteratou 2018.

[10] Roscino 2010: 15. Zanetto 2018: 219–20 notes that this painting described the 'outcome of the slaughter' but does not emphasize enough how that and its description by Pausanias make it a prime candidate for Heliodoran intervisuality, nor does he note the possible relevance of the context of its display at Plataea.

δὲ τοῦ ἀγάλματος πρὸς τοῖς ποσὶν εἰκὼν Ἀριμνήστου· ὁ δὲ Ἀρίμνηστος ἔν τε τῇ πρὸς Μαρδόνιον μάχῃ καὶ ἔτι πρότερον ἐς Μαραθῶνα Πλαταιεῦσιν ἡγήσατο.

The Plataeans have a sanctuary of Athena with the cult-title Warlike. It was built from the spoils which the Athenians apportioned to them from the battle at Marathon. The cult-statue is a wooden image, gilded, but the face, hands and feet are of Pentelic stone. In size it is not much smaller than the bronze Athena on the acropolis, which the Athenians likewise dedicated as first-fruits of the conflict at Marathon, and Pheidias was the one who made the cult-statue of Athena for the Plataeans too. In the temple are paintings, one, by Polygnotus, of Odysseus when he has already killed the suitors; the other, by Onasias, is the earlier expedition of the Argives, under Adrastus, against Thebes. These paintings are on the walls of the *pronaos*, while at the feet of the cult-statue is a portrait of Arimnestus. It was Arimnestus who commanded the Plataeans at the battle against Mardonius and even before that for Marathon.

Pausanias 9.4.1–2

Similarly Charicleia (as we later, at 1.8.4, discover she is called) is described at 1.1–2 in the immediate aftermath of her slaughter of the pirates (she is totally engrossed in tending the wounded Theagenes).

If a reference by Heliodorus to this painting is accepted—to a painting about which he, like modern scholars, could know from reading Pausanias—then the fact that Polygnotus' painting was located at Plataea acquires considerable importance, not least because its location was in a sanctuary built from the share of the spoils of Marathon that had been allocated to the Plataeans by Athens. The Athenian dimension is further reinforced by Pausanias' mention of Arimnestus as the leader of the Plataean force both at Marathon in 490 BC and at the battle of Plataea in 479 BC.[11] Two of the three great Greek victories over the Persians are evoked for any reader of Heliodorus who knows, whether from Pausanias or from another periegetic writer now lost (e.g. Polemo of Ilium) that Polygnotus' painting of the *mnēstērophonia* was displayed in the temple of Athena Areia at a prime *lieu de mémoire* of the fifth-century Greeks' conflict with Persia, Plataea.

At a point when Persians have not yet been explicitly mentioned, but at which the narrator's silence about Alexandria suggests that the temporal

---

[11] Mentioned briefly, but without these details, in Herodotus' account of Plataea, 9.72.1.

context of his narrative precedes 331 BC, this evocation of the Greco-Persian wars of 480–479 BC invites readers to be alert to the Greek–barbarian polarity that had acquired its developed form during and after these wars,[12] and within that polarity to look out for the *aretē* of Athenians and the *kakia* of Persians. What in due course the reader encounters is considerable *kakia* in classical Athens, with even the narrator of the New Comedy hanky-panky, Cnemon, only a little better than the duplicitous Athenians whose misdeeds he narrates,[13] and a set of Persians who display a mixture of moderately good and very bad qualities.

The evocation of the *mnēstērophonia*, moreover, by its reference via Polygnotus' painting to the Persian wars, strengthens the impression that Herodotus is an important intertext for the *Aethiopica*. It also, by drawing attention to its own ekphrastic virtuosity, recalls and invites comparison with two of Heliodorus' novelistic predecessors who had placed a description of a painting at or near the opening of their work, Longus (in his preface) and Achilles Tatius (at 1.1.2–13).[14] Furthermore it sets up the expectation—an expectation that will be repeatedly and amply fulfilled—that Heliodorus' descriptions of scenes and events will compete with painting in the way that the work of such poets as Simonides was reckoned to compete by literary critics of the imperial period.[15]

A similar incentive to ponder the relationship between the text and the visual arts is offered in Book 4 during Calasiris' narrative of events at Delphi, when Charicles discloses to Calasiris, as they discuss Charicleia's apparent illness, the name of the nephew to whom he had betrothed her (he was mentioned first at 2.33.4):

ηὐχόμην δὲ Ἀλκαμένους αὐτὴν ἐρᾶν ἢ πάντα χρήματα, τοῦ τῆς ἀδελφῆς παιδὸς τῆς ἐμῆς, ὃν πάλαι αὐτῇ νυμφίον ὅσα γε εἰς βούλησιν ἧκει τὴν ἐμὴν κατηγγύησα.

---

[12] Hall 1989.   [13] See Morgan 1989b.
[14] For Heliodorus inviting comparison of his work with Longus, see Bowie 1995. I find it hard to accept that Heliodorus asks readers to see his opening ekphrasis *as a* γραφή in the sense 'painting', as argued by Zanetto 2018: 212–13, as opposed to *like* a γραφή.
[15] e.g. Simonides in Longinus 15.7. See also Plutarch's quotation of Simonides' apophthegm 'Painting is…poetry': πλὴν ὁ Σιμωνίδης τὴν μὲν ζωγραφίαν ποίησιν σιωπῶσαν προσαγορεύει, τὴν δὲ ποίησιν ζωγραφίαν λαλοῦσαν. ἃς γὰρ οἱ ζωγράφοι πράξεις ὡς γινομένας δεικνύουσι, ταύτας οἱ λόγοι γεγενημένας διηγοῦνται καὶ συγγράφουσιν ('But Simonides calls painting "silent poetry" and poetry "talking painting": for the actions painters represent as they are happening are those which words narrate and recount as having happened'), Plut. *De glor. Ath.* 346f. For the signals given by the resemblance of Heliodorus' opening to a painting such as those in Achilles Tatius and Longus see van Mal-Maeder 1991: 18–23; Zanetto 2018.

More than anything I used to pray that she would be in love with Alcamenes, my sister's son, whom long ago I betrothed to her to be her husband, as far as this falls within my volition. (4.7.9)

Though not especially uncommon, the name Alcamenes is not run-of-the-mill.[16] It was borne by one of the most important fifth-century BC sculptors, a pupil of Pheidias with half a dozen mentions in Pausanias. The first of these refers to a sculptural group dedicated by Alcamenes himself on the Athenian acropolis and representing Procne and her son Itys: Pausanias explains that she is contemplating Itys' murder:

Πρόκνην δὲ τὰ ἐς τὸν παῖδα βεβουλευμένην αὐτήν τε καὶ τὸν Ἴτυν ἀνέθηκεν Ἀλκαμένης.

Alcamenes dedicated Itys and Procne herself when she had resolved what she will do to her child.   Pausanias 1.24.3

If we may suppose that some of Heliodorus' expected readers knew of this sculpture and that it might be brought to mind by his use of the name Alcamenes, then Heliodorus, as so often, seems to be hitting two birds with one stone. The mention of any painter or sculptor—and this is the only name of a painter or sculptor used in the *Aethiopica*—would re-activate the opening scene's invitation to contemplate the written work's relation to the visual arts. The choice of Alcamenes in particular might have two consequences. First, the learned reader would think of the myth of Tereus, Procne, and Itys, in which an outraged wife took revenge on her husband by the extreme act of killing their child.[17] Such a myth offers a provocative foil to the story of Persinna's decision to expose her child, Charicleia, and to conceal her very existence from her father Hydaspes, an exposure that for all she knew would lead to the baby's death. That is clear from the words read by Calasiris on the band (ταινία), which revealed to him the secret of Charicleia's origins in a scene narrated less than a couple of columns after the character named Alcamenes had been introduced:

ὡς μὲν οὐδὲν ἀδικοῦσα, παιδίον, οὕτω σε γενομένην ἐξεθέμην οὐδὲ πατέρα τὸν σὸν Ὑδάσπην τὴν σὴν θέαν ἀπεκρυψάμην, ἐπικεκλήσθω μάρτυς ὁ γενεάρχης ἡμῶν Ἥλιος· ἀλλ' ὅμως ἀπολογοῦμαι πρός τε σέ ποτε, θύγατερ,

---

[16] *LGPN* vol. 2 has sixteen cases from Attica, vol. 3b has six from Delphi; other areas have only twos and threes, Macedonia just one.
[17] For the standard version in imperial Greece, see Apollodorus 3.3.8.

εἰ περισωθείης, πρός τε τὸν ἀναιρησόμενον, εἴ τινά σοι θεὸς ἐπιστήσειε, πρός τε αὐτὸν ὅλον τὸν τῶν ἀνθρώπων βίον, ἀνακαλύπτουσα τὴν αἰτίαν τῆς ἐκθέσεως.

That I was not doing any wrong, my child, in exposing you in this way when you were born or in concealing the sight of you from Hydaspes, may our family's ancestor the sun be called as witness. But nevertheless I at last set out my defence to you, daughter, if you should survive, and to the person who will pick you up, if god should send some such person to you, and to the whole community of mankind itself, revealing the reason for your exposure. (4.8.2)

Unlike the characters of traditional myth, and unlike some characters in the Athens of Cnemon's narrative, Persinna is keen to escape the charge of acting unjustly; but, as with Procne, her mode of dealing with her husband, whom she expected to assume her to be an adulteress because she had given birth to a white child, risks that child's destruction. As I have suggested for Longus' exploitation of traditional mythology in his inset tales,[18] so too Heliodorus implicitly juxtaposes with his own story a traditional myth with which it has significant elements in common, and he encourages us to conclude that *his* sort of narrative is one which eschews the killing of the innocent—a conclusion that is emblematized in Book 10, when Hydaspes' cliff-hanging *volte-face* saves the couple from their apparently inevitable sacrifice.

But Heliodorus has yet another trick up his sleeve. The myth of Tereus, Procne, Philomela-Chelidon, and Itys was told at some length by Achilles Tatius' Clitophon to Leucippe (5.5.2-9)—mentioning the women came from Athens—after Clitophon had already described to his narratee its depiction in painting that he happened to see in an artist's studio (5.3.4-8). The appearance of Alcamenes' name in Calasiris' narrative, evoking the sculptor's famous work on the Athenian acropolis, may recall the double appearance of the Tereus myth in Achilles Tatius, including a narration set in Alexandria, and prepare the reader for the return of Heliodorus' own narrative to the Egyptian territory where in Book 1 it began—a narrative whose modes of handling things and people Egyptian is so very different from that of Achilles, perhaps himself Alexandrian. Heliodorus' own narrative in Book 4 has no explicit mention of swallows, of nightingales, or of the unfortunate Itys, but the Procne myth flies momentarily before the reader's attention in

---

[18] Bowie 2007.

Book 5 when the lamenting Charicleia is compared to a nightingale: ᾔσθετο γυναικὸς λαθραῖόν τι καὶ γοερὸν οἷον ἠρινῆς ἀηδόνος αἴλινον ἐν νυκτὶ μυρομένης ('he heard a woman wailing a secret and mournful lament in the night, like a nightingale in spring', 5.2.6). The myth of the nightingale and Itys that may lurk beneath Heliodorus' text in Book 4, with its introduction of an Alcamenes, and in Book 5, with its comparison of the lamenting Charicleia to a nightingale,[19] could have taken its ancient readers to the first appearance of that story (though in a slightly different form) in Penelope's long speech to the disguised Odysseus at *Odyssey* 19.509–53. Here Penelope compares her own continual lamentations to those of the nightingale for her child Itylus whom she has killed (*Od.* 19.518–23). The two passages in Heliodorus triggering thoughts of Procne and Itys thus have a role—as have so many other nuanced details—in reminding the reader that the most important ancestor of the *Aethiopica* is the *Odyssey*, and that the most important model for Charicleia is Penelope.

The myth of Procne and Itys is not the only direction, however, in which the name Alcamenes might take a reader. The historical sculptor's most important work in Athens, according to Pausanias, was that of 'Aphrodite in the Gardens':

τὸ δὲ ἄγαλμα τῆς Ἀφροδίτης <τῆς> ἐν [τοῖς] Κήποις ἔργον ἐστὶν Ἀλκαμένους καὶ τῶν Ἀθήνησιν ἐν ὀλίγοις θέας ἄξιον.

The statue of 'Aphrodite in the Gardens' is the work of Alcamenes, and of the things in Athens it is especially worth looking at.   Pausanias 1.19.2

Modern identification of the work mentioned by Pausanias with a surviving sculptural type is still not certain: the strongest candidate is a well-draped and demure version of the goddess of *erōs*,[20] very different from the highly erotic, naked 'Crouching Aphrodite' of Doedalses or from the similarly provocative Aphrodite of Cnidus (probably by Praxiteles). As a prospective

---

[19] For the association of the nightingale's song with a lament for Itys, cf. Longus 3.12.4 with Bowie 2019: 233 ad loc., and for the nightingale's association with the swallow 2.5.1. Generally it is the swallow rather than the nightingale that is linked with spring (e.g. Ar. *Peace* 799–801, reworking Stesichorus fr. 174 Finglass; cf. Bowie 2015: 113–15).

[20] Schuchhardt 1977: 9–27, with bibliography on p. 59; Stewart 1990: 267–9 with figures. Rosenzweig 2004: 29–44, following the argument of Delivorrias 1968 that the cult statue at Daphni was a copy of that of 'Aphrodite in the Gardens', favours the leaning, well-draped figure known from a Roman copy in the Museo Nazionale, Naples (no. 6396), illustrated by her fig. 35. That there were copies in the imperial period is important for judging whether the statue-type would be familiar to Heliodorus and his readers.

husband for the priestess Charicleia, whose dress is always modest and who is strongly committed to retaining her chastity, a young man whose name Alcamenes might evoke not these sensuous versions of Aphrodite but the restrained 'Aphrodite in the Gardens' is a palmary candidate.

The effects explored above show the extent of Heliodorus' possible exploitation of canonical works of Greek art, and may be seen as some support for my interpretation of the opening scene of Book 1 as acquiring part of its meaning from its relation to Polygnotus' *Mnēstērophonia* at Plataea.

I now return to that opening scene. It is set on a beach, which as a boundary between sea and land appropriately symbolizes the frontier zone of the vast text of the *Aethiopica* into which the readers now take their first steps. For this shoreline Heliodorus uses the word αἰγιαλός. As was noticed by Mario Telò, the opening of Book 1 is indeed the only place he uses αἰγιαλός, and there it appears four times, thrice in the accusative (1.1.1, 1.3.3., 1.5.1)[21] and once in the nominative (1.1.3).[22] It reappears in the nominative plural in his cameo ethnography of the marsh-dwellers at 1.5.2:

ὃ γὰρ ταῖς θαλάτταις αἰγιαλοί, τοῦτο ταῖς λίμναις τὰ ἕλη γίνεται.

For what beaches are to seas, that is what marshes are to lakes.

Elsewhere the word Heliodorus uses is not αἰγιαλός but ἀκτή: he does this both at three places unrelated to his opening sequence (2.30.3, 5.18.3, 5.20.2) and at two where reference is being made to precisely the same situation and same beach (1.22.3, 5.27.7). αἰγιαλός does not appear in *Daphnis and Chloe*—for 'beach' Longus uses either ἀκτή (2.15.2) or, in Daphnis' discovery of the dead dolphin, the more vivid word κυματωγή (3.28.1), a recherché term he undoubtedly takes from Herodotus (4.196, 9.100).[23] κυματωγή is not used at all by Heliodorus, and is not among the synonyms offered by Pollux, whose list of 'places by the sea at which a boat can put in' (χωρία ἐπιθαλαττίδια, οἷς ἔστι προσσχεῖν) comprises ἀκτή, ᾐών, αἰγιαλός,

---

[21] ὡς οὐδὲν ἄγρας λῃστρικῆς ἐπηγγέλλετο μὴ πλεόμενον, ἐπὶ τὸν πλησίον αἰγιαλὸν τῇ θέᾳ κατήγοντο ('since nothing in the way of piratical prey was registered as under sail, they put in with their observation to the nearby beach', 1.1.1); τὴν λείαν ἐπὶ τὸν αἰγιαλὸν καταθέντες εἰς φορτία καὶ μοίρας κατενέμοντο ('they deposited the plunder on the beach in loads and distributed portions among themselves', 1.3.3); παραμείψαντες οὖν ὅσον δύο στάδια τὸν αἰγιαλόν ('they made their way along the beach for about two stades', 1.5.1).
[22] ὁ δὲ αἰγιαλός, μεστὰ πάντα σωμάτων νεοσφαγῶν ('as for the beach, everywhere was full of newly slain corpses', 1.1.3).
[23] See Bowie 2019: 252 ad loc.

χηλὴ ὕφορμος, ὅρμος, λιμήν ('shore, strand, beach, mole with an anchorage, anchorage, harbour').[24]

αἰγιαλός had indeed been used by three of Heliodorus' novelistic predecessors—once by Chariton (3.4.2), twice by Xenophon of Ephesus (2.11.10 and, unless emended away, 2.12.2), and once by Achilles Tatius (1.18.4, in Clitophon's paradoxographic story of the viper's lust for the eel). But in none of these places do we find the heavy concentration that is so striking in the opening of the *Aethiopica*. Since that opening is Odyssean, and since many incidents in the *Odyssey* involve boats and their occupants putting in to land, one might expect to find a number of instances of αἰγιαλός in the *Odyssey*. But no, in the *Odyssey* αἰγιαλός is a *hapax*—a *hapax* that is found precisely in the *mnēstērophonia*:[25]

> πάπτηνεν δ' Ὀδυσεὺς καθ' ἑὸν δόμον, εἴ τις ἔτ' ἀνδρῶν
> ζωὸς ὑποκλοπέοιτο, ἀλύσκων κῆρα μέλαιναν.
> τοὺς δὲ ἴδεν μάλα πάντας ἐν αἵματι καὶ κονίῃσι
> πεπτεῶτας πολλούς, ὥς τ' ἰχθύας, οὕς θ' ἁλιῆες
> κοῖλον ἐς αἰγιαλὸν πολιῆς ἔκτοσθε θαλάσσης
> δικτύῳ ἐξέρυσαν πολυωπῷ· οἱ δέ τε πάντες
> κύμαθ' ἁλὸς ποθέοντες ἐπὶ ψαμάθοισι κέχυνται·
> τῶν μέν τ' ἠέλιος φαέθων ἐξείλετο θυμόν·
> ὣς τότ' ἄρα μνηστῆρες ἐπ' ἀλλήλοισι κέχυντο.

Odysseus peered about his house to see if one of the men was still alive, hiding himself and trying to escape black death. But he saw that absolutely all of them lay fallen in the blood and dust, in huge numbers, like fish which sea-folk have pulled up out of the white-flecked sea onto the curving shore with their many-meshed net: and they are all piled on the sands, longing for the waves of the sea, and their life has been taken from them by the blazing sun. So it was that then the suitors had been piled on each other.

Odyssey 22.381–9

Heliodorus' choice of αἰγιαλός, then, reinforces the passage's credentials as a reworking of the *mnēstērophonia*. He may also be distributing the situation

---
[24] Pollux 1.99–100, cf. 1.115, 9.28.
[25] There are four Iliadic cases: *Iliad* 2.210, 4.422, 14.34, 22.385.

of Odysseus between more than one of his characters. Charicleia without doubt contests with Calasiris the title of his Odysseus-figure *par excellence*, and it will not be long before we have evidence of her Odyssean μῆτις. But the *boukoloi* who pop their heads over the brow of the hill and scan the sea—τὴν ὑποκειμένην θάλατταν ὀφθαλμοῖς ἐπήρχοντο ('they ranged with their eyes over the sea that lay beneath them')—also owe something to the Odysseus whose eyes rove about his house (πάπτηνεν δ' Ὀδυσεὺς καθ' ἑὸν δόμον) as has been superbly argued in detail by Telò.

The passage also, however, gives another signal. By contrast with its sporadic appearance in earlier novels—and with just a single appearance in the much-read *oeuvre* of Xenophon the Athenian, at *Anabasis* 6.4.2—there are no fewer than sixteen appearances of αἰγιαλός in Herodotus, eleven in Book 7 and five in Book 9.[26]

The Herodotean colour thus given by αἰγιαλός is one that especially evokes his Persian-War books, to which his use of the word is limited, and that point of reference is reinforced by the association of Polygnotus' *mnēstērophonia*, as argued above, with both Marathon and Plataea. The *Enquiries* of Herodotus remained throughout antiquity the classic narrative of the Persian Wars. Their Book 2 was also a foundation text for later Greek accounts of Egypt, as is exemplified in the imperial period by Aelius Aristides' *Egyptian Oration* (36 Keil). Thus the reader of the opening paragraphs will be alerted to expect a work in which both the *Odyssey* and the *Enquiries* of Herodotus are to be important intertexts: and of course the reader is not disappointed in either of these expectations.

There may admittedly be little else that is Herodotean in 1.1–4, but at 1.5–6 the description of the *politeuma* of the marsh-dwellers draws heavily, as has been observed,[27] on Herodotus' account of lake-dwelling Paeonians (5.16). That passage is linked to Heliodorus' opening sentences by two significant details. First, as noted above, at 1.5.2 the geographical paradox ὃ γὰρ ταῖς θαλάτταις αἰγιαλοί, τοῦτο ταῖς λίμναις τὰ ἕλη γίνεται ('for what beaches are to seas, that is what marshes are to lakes') reactivates the associations of αἰγιαλός in the opening sentences. That reactivation is corroborated by another ethnographic detail: the children once weaned (and likewise, by implication, the adults) are fed on fish which have been baked in the sun: τὰ δὲ ἀπὸ τούτου τοῖς ἀπὸ τῆς λίμνης ἰχθύσι πρὸς ἥλιον ὀπτωμένοις ἐκτρέφει ('and after this the bandit feeds them with fish from the lake that have been

---

[26] Hdt. 7.59.1, 2, 3; 100.3 (×2); 115.1; 176.1; 183.3; 188.1 (×2), 3; 9.98.2 (×2), 99.1, 102.1, 106.1.
[27] e.g. Morgan 1989c: 357 n. 6.

baked in the sun', 1.5.4). These fish roasted by the Egyptian sun are literary descendants of the fish in the simile at *Odyssey* 22 (discussed above) which the sun's heat has killed: τῶν μέν τ' ἠέλιος φαέθων ἐξείλετο θυμόν (22.388). That these fish—and only they—are mentioned as elements in the lake-dwellers' diet—which we must imagine to have been somewhat more varied—is surely because Heliodorus wants to remind us of the *Odyssey*'s fish-simile and with it of the power of the eponymic sun which in the Heliodoran text can cook for nourishing and pleasing consumption those creatures that in Homer's poem it merely kills.

The sun-given fish eaten by the lake-dwellers may have another role too. Herodotus' Egypt had a people whom he calls 'Fish-eaters', Ἰχθυοφάγοι. Herodotus introduces them not in his extensive Egyptian λόγος that we know as Book 2 but early in what we know as Book 3, in his account of Cambyses' expedition against the Ethiopians (3.19.1). These 'Fish-eaters', Ἰχθυοφάγοι, live in the *polis* of Elephantine, and it is because they understand the Ethiopian language that Cambyses decides to send them to Ethiopia as spies. For a reader brought up on Herodotus, then, fish-eating will generate thoughts of Ethiopia, thoughts presumably already latent in the mind of any reader whose copy of the *Aethiopica* had a title either preceding its text or (more likely since titles are more often attested at the end of papyrus rolls) written on a tag (*syllabē*) identifying the roll.[28] That in his narrative of events at Syene and Elephantine Heliodorus has nothing at all about Ἰχθυοφάγοι may be an indication that he was as sceptical as some modern scholars have been about the historicity of this group. But his familiarity with Herodotus' account of Cambyses' exploitation of the Ichthyophagoi is suggested, albeit not formally proved, by his brief digression on the use of scouts and spies who know the language of local inhabitants and of enemies, a digression prompted by the capture of Theagenes and Charicleia by Ethiopian special forces on the borders of Egyptian and Ethiopian territory where Herodotus locates his Ichthyophagoi.[29]

---

[28] Neither Ethiopia nor Ethiopians are mentioned by name before 2.28.2: ἐμοῦ δὲ…διελθόντος ὡς τὰς μὲν ἀρχὰς ἐκ τῶν ἄκρων τῆς Αἰθιοπίας ἐσχάτων δὲ τῆς Λιβύης λαμβάνει ('and when I…recounted how it (sc. the Nile) has its beginnings in the mountains of Ethiopia and the furthest reaches of Libya').

[29] Οἱ γὰρ ὀπτῆρές τε καὶ σκοποὶ λεγομένων τε καὶ πραττομένων ἀποσταλέντες ὁμογλώσσους τε καὶ ὁμοφώνους τοῖς τε ἐγχωρίοις καὶ πολεμίοις ἐπάγεσθαι ὑπὸ τῆς χρείας ἐδιδάχθησαν, Hld. 8.17.2. Herodotus' term for the spying function of the Ichthyophagoi, κατάσκοποι (3.19.2, 23.2 and 3, 25.1), is avoided here, but then used twice at the beginning of Book 9 (9.1.3 and 5) just before the couple's iron chains are replaced by chains of gold, another detail drawn from Herodotus (3.23.4). For the functions of Herodotus' Ichthyophagoi story in his Cambyses narrative, see Irwin 2014.

Finally one further detail concerning the brigands' life on boats or on swamp-girt patches of land deserves attention. They have to tether their children by the ankle to prevent them drowning in the marsh (1.5.4). This and other details have been taken from Herodotus' account of lake-dwelling Paeonians near Mount Pangaeon, but Heliodorus sets it in the context of women working and giving birth, thereby foregrounding (in a way it is not foregrounded by Herodotus) the theme of mothers' attachment to their children—an attachment which operates so differently in the case of the Ethiopian queen Persinna and her daughter Charicleia,[30] and which, as I have argued above, will later be evoked by the introduction of the name Alcamenes.

I hope that these proposals may add some useful threads to the vast web of Heliodoran intertextuality to whose understanding John Morgan has contributed so much.

[30] On the importance of the bond between Persinna and Charicleia, see Whitmarsh 2013a: 134.

3
Visualizing Assemblages
Demaenete, Thisbe's Bed-Trick, and the Creation of Charicleia (1.15–17)

Helen Morales

This chapter focuses on an episode within the story told by the young Athenian Cnemon to Theagenes and Charicleia.[1] The three of them have been taken prisoner by Egyptian bandits, and, ostensibly in order to console his fellow captives, Cnemon recounts how he has ended up in Egypt. His story takes up a substantial section of the first book of the novel (1.9.1–1.18.1), and is resumed in Book 2 and again in Book 8. Readers have been drawn to Cnemon's tale because of its scandalous account of incestuous lust, adulterous betrayal, and suicide.

In a ground-breaking 1989 article, John Morgan showed the many ways in which 'Cnemon's novella is, by reason of its programmatic position and its contents, a vital part of the moral economy of the whole novel'.[2] Morgan argues that Cnemon's tale operates as a subplot that explores destructive ways of loving, in contrast to the main narrative that celebrates chastity, loyalty, spirituality, and marriage. For example, the seductive scheming of Cnemon's stepmother, Demaenete, prefigures the sexually predatory behaviour of the Persian princess Arsace towards Theagenes in Book 7: moreover, 'Demaenete and Arsace are connected through the mythical figure of Phaedra and are intended to stand jointly as the antitype of the

---

[1] Parts of this research were presented at the University of Uppsala, and the Postclassicisms workshop at UC Berkeley. I am especially grateful to Ingela Nilsson, Dimitrios Iordanoglou, Glenn Most, Emilio Capettini and the editors of this volume. It is a pleasure to honour John Morgan who, many years ago, was the external examiner of my Cambridge PhD thesis. I appreciated his kindness as well as his intellectual generosity. Translations in this chapter are from his excellent translation of Heliodorus. All other translations are my own unless otherwise indicated.
[2] Morgan 1989b: 113.

Helen Morales, *Visualizing Assemblages: Demaenete, Thisbe's Bed-Trick, and the Creation of Charicleia (1.15–17)* In: *Reading Heliodorus' Aethiopica*. Edited by: Ian Repath and Tim Whitmarsh, Oxford University Press.
© Oxford University Press 2022. DOI: 10.1093/oso/ 9780198792543.003.0003

sexual morality of the central pair'.[3] He concludes that '[t]he novella is a paradigm, of an inverse kind, that provides a scale against which the significance of the central plot can emerge. Good and bad are two sides of the one coin: they cannot exist apart. Between them, the negative love of the novella and the positive love of the novel form a framework of moral values, the expression and reinforcement of which is the fundamental *raison d'être* of the *Aethiopica*'.

My analysis takes Morgan's interpretation as its starting point. This chapter has three sections. The first extends and enlarges upon Morgan's analysis of Demaenete's incestuous desire. The second explores the nature and function of the bed-trick, the ploy whereby Demaenete's slave Thisbe, fearing her mistress's reprisal after Thisbe's role in Cnemon's exile, contrives Demaenete's downfall. According to Cnemon, who is told of Demaenete's fate by a friend of his named Charias, Thisbe arranges for Demaenete to substitute for Cnemon's lover and thus trick him into sleeping with his stepmother. This is, however, a set-up and Thisbe alerts Aristippus (Cnemon's father) to his wife's adulterous intentions, prompting Demaenete to commit suicide. This section will also read Heliodorus' bed-trick scene through and against other literary bed-tricks. My third section takes as its starting point the slave Thisbe, and the prevalent interpretation of her character, following Morgan's article, as 'an anti-Charicleia'.[4] I will argue that, although at one level Thisbe is clearly portrayed as the antithesis of Charicleia, the dynamics of characterization, and the attendant sexual politics, are more complicated than a simple opposition. Drawing on assemblage theory first outlined by Gilles Deleuze and Félix Guattari, I will advance a reading of Charicleia's character as an assemblage of female figures whose visibility is established in Roman imperial society: the prostitute, the priestess, and the martyr. Charicleia is created as a *visualizing assemblage* of these female roles, 'visualizing' in the sense that the component parts of the assemblage make her character visible. Heliodorus, I will argue, portrays Charicleia through, and at times as, these female figures in the public gaze, with shifting intensities and moral affects, and thereby creates a new model of womanhood: the elite and upright betrothed woman whose visibility is socially sanctioned. In this reading, Thisbe functions not as the antithesis of Charicleia's character, but as a constituent component of it.

---

[3] Morgan 1989b: 112.   [4] Morgan 1989b: 111.

All three sections feature the figure of the prostitute. Readers ancient and modern often overlook prostitutes in the ancient romances, a perspective that is complicit with the novels' celebration of nobility and *eugeneia*.[5] One of the broader aims of this chapter is to foreground prostitutes in Heliodorus, including the resplendent Thracian hetaera Rhodopis who is described in the second book of the *Aethiopica*.

3.1 Demaenete's Incestuous Desire

At Book 1.15.4–5, Cnemon relates Demaenete's impassioned expression of her desire for him (as if quoting what Thisbe, his confidante and Demaenete's slave, had reported):

Νῦν δὲ ὁρᾶν φαντάζομαι, παρόντος ἀκούειν ἀπατῶμαι, ὀνειδίζοντα τὴν ἄδικον ἐπιβουλὴν αἰσχύνομαι· συντεύξεσθαί ποτε ὑπελθόντι καὶ ἀπολαύσειν, ἢ καὶ αὐτὴ παρ' ἐκεῖνον φοιτήσειν ὅπου ποτ' ἂν ᾖ γῆς ὑποτίθεμαι. Ταῦτα ὑπεκκαίει, ταῦτα ἐκμαίνει. Δίκαια μὲν ὦ θεοὶ πάσχω· τί γὰρ οὐ περιεῖπον ἀλλ' ἐπεβούλευον; Τί δὲ οὐχ ἱκέτευον ἀλλ' ἐδίωκον; Ἠρνήσατο τὴν πρώτην ἀλλὰ προσηκόντως· ἀλλοτρίαν μὲν ἀλλ' οὖν γε πατρῴαν εὐνὴν ᾐσχύνετο· τυχὸν ἂν μετεπείσθη χρόνῳ πρὸς τὸ ἡμερώτερον καὶ πειθοῖ μεταπλαττόμενος. Ἀλλ' ἡ θηριώδης ἐγὼ καὶ ἀνήμερος ὥσπερ οὐκ ἐρῶσά τινος ἀλλ' ἄρχουσα....

I fancy I see him; I delude myself[6] that can hear his voice; I blush to hear him rebuke my wicked scheme. I dream that one day I shall find him come to me by stealth and take my pleasure of him, or that I shall go to him, wherever in the world he may be. These thoughts fan the flames of desire and drive me mad with longing. Oh, gods! I deserve my torment! Why did I not use gentle persuasion instead of underhand schemes against him? Why did I not cast myself on his mercy instead of hounding him? He repelled my first advances—but so he ought: he was shrinking not merely from adultery, but from adultery with his own father's wife. But perhaps in time he might have been induced to soften; perhaps gentle handling might have brought him round. Instead, I behaved like a savage beast, more like a tyrant than a lover.

---

[5] A couple of examples: Photius, in his summary of the *Aethiopica*, omits any reference to Rhodopis or Thisbe. In his important book on characterization in the novels, Koen de Temmerman makes no mention of Rhodopis, and refers to Thisbe only once in a footnote (de Temmerman 2014: 111).

[6] For the connotations of *apatē* here, see Jonas Grethlein's chapter in this volume.

It is important to remember that the internal and external audiences of Cnemon's account have already been told that Demaenete is now dead (1.14.3), having met the punishment that she deserved (1.14.4). We do not yet know how she died, and Cnemon has teased Theagenes and Charicleia (and the reader) by attempting to prolong the denouement of the story so that he can get some sleep. Demaenete's desires and actions in this and the following section comprise, therefore, further grounds for her miserable end, and some pleasure for the audience lies in finding out exactly how justice was served.

Demaenete's fantasies drive her 'mad' with longing (ταῦτα ἐκμαίνει) and *ekmainō* here echoes the same verb used earlier to describe her erotic hold over Aristippus (ἐφ᾽ ἑαυτὴν ἐκμῆναι 1.9.4). Her association with erotic madness, both being driven mad herself, and driving others mad, may prompt us to read her name as 'motivated', with *-main-* understood as deriving from the root denoting madness.[7] Her desire is incestuous ('adultery with his own father's wife').[8] Demaenete, we are reminded, had previously used her position as stepmother to gain physical access to Cnemon: she 'pretended to look on me as a son', he recalls, and 'she showed a mother's affection towards me' (1.9.3). Her behaviour alternated between maternal and seductive, and thus perverted the maternal:

νῦν μὲν παιδίον νῦν δὲ γλυκύτατον ὀνομάζουσα καὶ αὖθις κληρονόμον καὶ μετ᾽ ὀλίγον ψυχὴν ἑαυτῆς ἀποκαλοῦσα καὶ ἁπλῶς τὰ καλὰ τῶν ὀνομάτων τοῖς ἐπαγωγοῖς παραμιγνῦσα καὶ οἷστισι μᾶλλον προστρέχω περισκοποῦσα, ὡς ἐν μὲν τοῖς σεμνοτέροις μητέρα ἑαυτὴν ἀναπλάττουσα ἐν δὲ τοῖς ἀτοπωτέροις τοῦτο ἐκεῖνο λαμπρῶς ἐρωμένην ὑποφαίνουσα.

Sometimes she would call me her child, at others her darling. She would address me as her son and heir, and then, a minute later, as her beloved. In short, she intertwined decent names with seductive ones and observed carefully which I responded to best. With the more respectable names she masqueraded as a mother, but with those unnatural endearments she revealed all too plainly that she was aflame with desire. (1.9.4)

---

[7] As Meriel Jones suggests: Jones 2006: 559. She also notes the literal meaning of the name Demaenete: 'Praised by the People', an ironic touch for a character who earns public condemnation.

[8] Sexual relations between stepmother and stepson were explicitly forbidden in Roman law, as the imperial edict of 295 CE emphasized: Corcoran 2000; Evans Grubbs 2015.

Eventually, she stopped trying to hide her desire, and embraced Cnemon, calling him 'My young Hippolytus!' thereby casting herself as Greek tragedy's paradigm of an immoral, incestuous, stepmother: Phaedra.[9]

Demaenete is characterized so as to have a strong affinity with Arsace, whom she foreshadows: another intemperate woman who schemes to commit adultery, and who abuses her position of power (she attempts to seduce and then coerce Theagenes into a sexual relationship with her). Both women display their carnality through their gaze, a characteristic conveyed in similar terms: Cnemon says of Demaenete 'Her gaze went beyond the chaste' (τὸ βλέμμα τοῦ σώφρονος ἐξιστάμενον 1.9.3), and Arsace looks at Thyamis with unchaste eyes (ὀφθαλμούς τε ἐπέβαλλεν οὐ σώφρονας 7.2.2). Arsace's intemperate and appetitive gazing on Theagenes is repeatedly and emphatically described.[10] Like Demaenete, Arsace becomes maddened through her desire.[11] Both are associated with tyranny: Demaenete regrets behaving like a tyrant towards Cnemon (because a gentler approach might have been more successful, 1.15.5), and Arsace literally enslaves Theagenes (7.24.4). Both have female slaves who machinate to facilitate their adultery. Both women commit suicide: Demaenete jumps from the Pit in the Academy when her adulterous behaviour has been revealed to her husband,[12] and Arsace hangs herself when her adultery is about to be revealed to her husband. Most striking, however, is the connection of Demaenete and Arsace through the tragic figure of Phaedra. As has already been noted, Demaenete casts herself as Phaedra when she calls Cnemon her 'young Hippolytus'. The language used to describe Arsace hanging herself strongly alludes to the description in Euripides' *Hippolytus* of Phaedra's suicide by hanging.[13]

---

[9] ὁ νέος Ἱππόλυτος (1.10.2). The text immediately after this may refer to Theseus, but appears corrupt: see Rattenbury's note in the apparatus of his Budé text. At the very beginning of Cnemon's tale he characterizes it as a tragedy and quotes from Euripides' *Medea* (1.8.7, quoting *Medea* 1317), a drama about another paradigmatic 'bad mother'. Later, Demaenete is described as being pursued by Furies (1.14.6), a striking motif from tragedy.

[10] See 7.6.1, 7.8.6, and 7.12.7 with Morales 2005: 11–12.

[11] 'Her desire was degenerating imperceptibly into insanity' (εἰς μανίαν λοιπὸν ἐλάνθανεν ὁ ἔρως ὑποφερόμενος 7.9.4), and 7.20.5 where Cybele begs Theagenes to have pity on her mistress whose 'behaviour is the consequence of her insane infatuation with you' (εἰς τἄδικα διὰ τὸν σὸν πόθον οὕτως ἐκμεμηνυῖα).

[12] On the significance of the location, see Schwartz 2012: 178: 'As with the trial of Cnemon, the arrest of Demaenete is set within the Athenian legal landscape. Demaenete's place of punishment has suitably archaic connotations, a conflation of the *barathron*, the site in Athens where criminals were executed, and the Tarpeian Rock in Rome'.

[13] τέθνηκεν Ἀρσάκη βρόχον ἀγχόνης ἁψαμένη (8.15.2) echoes Eur. *Hipp.* 802: βρόχον κρεμαστὸν ἀγχόνης ἀνήψατο. See also Morgan 1989b: 112, and MacAlister 1996: 65 who notes that a crucial difference between the death of Demaenete and that of Phaedra is that Phaedra was motivated by shame, whereas Demaenete is motivated by loss of hope, and the desire to

Demaenete and Arsace are both portrayed as having characteristics commonly associated with prostitutes.[14] Cnemon says of Demaenete that she was 'extraordinary well versed in the arts of allurement' (τέχνην τὴν ἐπαγωγὸν ἐκτόπως 1.9.2). The word *tekhnē* is significant here: such skill is the province of a sex-worker, and not a wife.[15] Arsace also behaves like a prostitute: she uses cosmetics, and is distinguished by her perverted hedonism (7.2.1).[16] More pointedly, Demaenete and Arsace share traits with the hetaera Rhodopis. Demaenete ensnares Aristippus, just as Rhodopis ensnares men (the same verb is used of both).[17] Rhodopis is described as surrounding herself with luxury and extravagance (2.25.1) and as being a frequent visitor to the temple of Isis where Calasiris was high priest, 'performing constant devotions to the goddess with hugely expensive sacrifices and dedications' (2.25.2). Arsace's wealth and splendour are similarly emphasized, for example at 7.19.1: '[Theagenes] found her enthroned on high, resplendent in a gown of purple shot with gold, flaunting the conspicuous value of her jewelry and the majesty of her crown', and she too makes expensive dedications at the temple of Isis (7.9.1). Rhodopis is a figure through whom female predation is imbricated and triangulated, and the associations between Demaenete and Arsace more strongly forged.[18]

Demaenete also shares an affinity with Arsace's scheming slave, Cybele: both are false mothers, using a pretence of maternal love in order to seduce or procure their young charges. Cybele calls Theagenes and Charicleia her

---

escape punishment. More generally on Heliodorus' use of Euripides, see Pletcher 1998, and on 'the Phaedra model' vs 'the Phaedrus model' (slavery vs self-mastery) throughout the novel, see Morgan and Repath 2019.

[14] Of course, adultery and prostitution were linked in Roman law. 'Under the *lex Iulia*, the penalty for an adulteress was to be degraded to the status of prostitute and a husband who failed to take action against the adulterer was liable under the charge of *lenocinium*, pimping' (Schwartz 2012: 178). See further *Digest* 44.37.1, 48.5.9.

[15] See Jones 2006: 559 n. 79 on the possibility that the *dēm*-prefix also connotes prostitution.

[16] Cosmetics: 7.19.1. Arsace also behaves like a brothel owner, and like a client, arranging for many young men to minister to her sexual appetite.

[17] Of Demaenete, Cnemon says, 'By all this my father was ensnared: he lived for her, had eyes for her alone': οἷς ἅπασιν ὁ πατήρ μου σαγηνευθεὶς ὅλην ἐκείνην καὶ ἔπνει καὶ ἔβλεπεν (1.9.2). Of Rhodopis, Calasiris says, 'any man who crossed her path was trapped, for there was no escaping or resisting the net of sensuality that she trailed from her eyes': οὐ γὰρ ἦν ἐντυχόντα μὴ ἡλωκέναι, οὕτως ἄφυκτόν τινα καὶ ἀπρόσμαχον ἑταιρίας σαγήνην ἐκ τῶν ὀφθαλμῶν ἐπεσύρετο (2.25.1).

[18] One effect of designing Demaenete as akin to Arsace, is, as Steven Smith points out, to show that there is little to distinguish Athens from Persia (and, we might add, if we take into account Rhodopis, from Thrace); it is one way in which Heliodorus challenges Hellenocentrism: Smith 2007b.

'darling little children' (7.12), just as Demaenete calls Cnemon her 'child'.[19] This language is a perversion of *oikeiōsis*, the Stoic view whose practitioners advocated treating all human beings like family, and using familial names like 'father' and 'brother' to refer to non-kin.[20]

Furthermore, while it has been noted that 'the opposition of natural and artificial parentage' is a 'persistent theme in this text',[21] the disparity between artificial mothers and artificial fathers has been less well observed. The father figures Charicles and Calasiris care for and protect Charicleia. They are 'real' fathers in all but blood relationship, as Theagenes (who is at the time posing as Charicleia's brother) indicates when he describes Calasiris as 'my apparent, indeed my real, father' (τὸν δοκοῦντα καὶ ὄντα πατέρα 7.13.1).[22] The contrast is striking: substitute fathers are paternal and supportive, whereas substitute mothers are dangerous and corrupting. Moreover, the father figures co-opt tropes of romantic love in the service of parental care; for example Charicles and Calasiris wander in search of their adopted daughter, as Chaereas does in search of Callirhoe, and Clitophon in search of Leucippe,[23] in contrast to the mother figures who *literally* behave like romantic lovers. This marked and misogynist asymmetry is one aspect of the *Aethiopica* that upholds the patriarchal. Persinna, once united with her daughter, may be a loving mother to Charicleia, but in general mother figures, unlike their male counterparts, are monstrous.

3.2. The Bed-Trick

The outline of the bed-trick is as follows: Thisbe deceives Demaenete into believing that Cnemon is still in Athens, staying at the house of the prostitute Arsinoe, with whom he has been sleeping. Thisbe tells Demaenete that she will arrange for Demaenete to take Arsinoe's place in Cnemon's bed, but on the sly informs Demaenete's husband, Aristippus, that she will

---

[19] This echoes Ovid's unwittingly incestuous father Cinyras, who calls his lover 'daughter' before he realizes she is indeed his daughter, Myrrha: *Met.* 10.467.
[20] See Hierocles, quoted in Stobaeus 4.671–3, Cicero *De fin.* 3.62. Montiglio 2013a: 129 discusses *oikeiōsis* in relation to the 'call of blood' in *Aethiopica*.
[21] Whitmarsh 1998: 107.
[22] See also Calasiris' words to Charicleia at 4.5.7: 'Am I not old enough to be your father? And, more important, do I not love you like a father?'
[23] Charicles and Calasiris: 10.34.3; 2.22.3–4. See Lalanne 2006: 248–9, and Montiglio 2013a: 135 who also notes that the language and imagery used in other novels for romantic relationships is employed by Heliodorus to describe Hydaspes' love for Charicleia.

reveal her mistress's adultery to him. Lying to Arsinoe about her reasons for doing so, Thisbe borrows Arsinoe's house, encourages Demaenete to get into bed in anticipation of tricking her stepson into sleeping with her, and then ushers in Aristippus. Her deception discovered, Demaenete escapes Aristippus and kills herself rather than face judicial punishment.[24] This is a threefold trick by Thisbe: she deceives Demaenete into believing that Cnemon is not in exile, but at his lover's house in Athens; she lies to Arsinoe, telling her that she wants the house so that she, Thisbe, can meet her lover Teledemos; and she lies to Aristippus, pretending that she wants an audience with him to confess to her wrongdoings.

Had Demaenete succeeded in tricking Cnemon into having sex with her, she would have committed a form of rape (in our terms at least). However, the bed-trick, whether consummated or, as here, interrupted, is a privileged and highly theatrical moment in a narrative; it is a type scene that is 'rare in life but very common in texts'.[25] Demaenete's bed-trick imports the literary baggage of previous bed-tricks, but these are not confined to any single genre or tone. The defining characteristic of the bed-trick is that the duped party does not know the identity of their lover. The most famous example of this is in the tale of Cupid and Psyche in Book 5 of Apuleius' Latin novel *Metamorphoses*, where Cupid forbids his Psyche to look upon her husband, and disasters ensue when she disobeys him and unmasks his identity.

Some bed-tricks in ancient literature are played for laughs. In Ovid's *Fasti* Anna Perenna, who has just been deified, substitutes herself for Minerva, and thus protects the virgin goddess from the lust of Mars (3.675–96). Mars, 'on the verge of a kiss', realizes he has been fooled and is ashamed and angry at being the object of ridicule. The joke is also on the would-be lovers in Plautus' *Casina*, where Lysidamus and his slave Olympio are duped by Lysidamus's wife Cleostrata into having sex not, as they think, with the nubile Casina, but with Cleostrata's hairy male slave Chalinus, masquerading as Casina in a darkened room. The humour comes from the gap between the lovers' expectations, and the hairy, muscular reality, with plenty of obscene jokes about parts of the body.

---

[24] Schwartz 2012 is a valuable analysis of the connections between four episodes: the bed-trick, Demaenete's scheme (1.9.1–1.14.2), and the scenes involving Charicleia in the cave (1.28.1–1.31.1 and 2.2.1–2.9.5) and Thisbe in the cave (2.10.1–2.14). She observes that 'the conclusion of each episode is cast in judicial language, or in the form of a trial scene': Schwartz 2012: 177.
[25] Doniger 2000: 3.

Other bed-tricks are more tragic than comic. Demaenete's bed-trick is in some ways an aborted version of the bed-trick of Crateia, mother of Periander, the tyrant of Corinth, as told in the *Romantic Sufferings* of Parthenius (17), and a curtailed inversion of that of Myrrha and Cinyras in Ovid's *Metamorphoses* 10. Periander's mother had a strong desire for him when he was a young man and satisfied it at first through hugging him. When that no longer sufficed, she told him that a woman was in love with him and persuaded him to consent to sleeping with her, despite his reluctance to corrupt a married woman. She instructed her son not to look at the woman, and their union was committed in darkness and silence. However, he began to fall in love with her and one night brought in a lamp to reveal her identity. Horrified, he tried to kill his mother but was stopped by a divine force. Periander became mad and killed many of his citizens. In Orpheus' tale in the *Metamorphoses*, Myrrha falls in love with her father Cinyras and, with the help of her old nurse, tricks him into having sex with her by substituting herself for a fictional girl of her age said to be in love with him. Their trysts take place in the dark, and, the poet tells us, with Cinyras perhaps calling his lover 'daughter', and Myrrha replying 'father', there is a darkly ironic blending of the language of romantic and parental love that we also see Demaenete use with Cnemon. Eventually Cinyras discovers Myrrha's deceit and attempts to kill her. Orpheus absolves Cupid of any blame for Myrrha's crime, and accuses instead 'one of the Furies'. This is echoed in Cnemon's tale, when he introduces the bed-trick episode by saying 'As for Demaenete, the Furies were on her trail...' (2.14.6).

Sexual masquerades were sometimes used to test the chastity or fidelity of a spouse or relative. Ovid's story of Cephalus and Procris is one of testing a wife's fidelity (and later, her husband's).[26] Cephalus goes home in disguise and tests his wife by attempting to seduce her and promising her gifts of money. In the end she hesitates, and is caught out. The anonymous second-century CE Greek text *The Life of Secundus the Philosopher* also features an interrupted bed-trick whose aim is to test a woman's chastity. Here, however, it is a mother who is tested by her son. Secundus, who has spent many years away from home studying, desires to test the maxim 'every woman is a whore', and so returns home and, with a maid's help, persuades his mother who does not recognize him, to have sex in exchange for money. He spends the night with her, but they do not have intercourse. When she questions

[26] *Met.* 7.690–862.

him in the morning, Secundus reveals that he is her son, and his mother, ashamed, kills herself. Both Secundus and Heliodorus' Thisbe take one woman's behaviour as a measure of women's behaviour *in general*. Thisbe assures Demaenete that 'it is more than likely that your passion will abate; for most women one consummation is enough to dowse the fires of their desire' (1.15.8), and Secundus assumes that a saying about women can be proven or disproven by testing his mother.

The bed-trick puts into relief questions about sameness and difference. An anecdote in Plutarch's *Advice to the Bride and Groom* tells how an unnamed woman, in order to talk a man named Philip out of raping her, argues that 'all women are the same when the lights are out' (πᾶσα γυνὴ τοῦ λύχνου ἀρθέντος ἡ αὐτή ἐστι 144e).[27] While he acknowledges that this is a good answer in desperate circumstances, Plutarch is worried by the implications of the woman's response. A wife ought not to be same as any other woman, he urges, but 'when her body is not visible, her virtue (τὸ σῶφρον), her private relationship with her husband (ἴδιον τῷ ἀνδρί), her loyalty (τεταγμένον), and her affection (φιλόστοργον) ought to be most evident' (144f). The bed-trick commonly relies on the understanding that women are all the same when the lights are out. It relies on a Cnemon not noticing the difference between an Arsinoe and a Demaenete; in a sense, by reducing her to her sexual function and erasing any sense of individuality when the lights are out, the bed-trick *makes* every woman a whore. Only very occasionally does a narrative admit that substituting one woman for another might not be easy. In the *Acts of Andrew* the Christian wife Maximilla arranges for her slave Euclia to take her place in the marriage bed, so that Maximilla can avoid 'filthy intercourse', but considerable coaching is needed before Euclia is ready to substitute for her mistress.[28]

A further observation: it is a trope of bed-trick tales that a female slave plays a crucial role in arranging the bed-trick.[29] This happens in *The Life of Secundus*, in Ovid's Myrrha tale, in the *Acts of Andrew*, and in Cnemon's story. We do not know what becomes of the interfering servants in *The Life of Secundus* and Ovid, but the torture and killing of Euclia upon discovery of her masquerade is a gruesome forewarning of Thisbe's death: bed-tricks are dangerous for slave women.

---

[27] See also Ov. *Ars am.* 1.249–50.
[28] *Acts of Andrew* 17–22; see further Schwartz 2007 and Nilsson 2009.
[29] On Thisbe's status as a slave, and her relations within the household of Aristippus, see Morgan and Repath 2019.

The very same questions that are posed by literary bed-tricks animate the *Aethiopica* as a whole, from Persinna's worry that she will be accused of adultery, to Theagenes' failure to recognize a bedraggled Charicleia: How well do you know your beloved? How do we come to know them? Are you sure that you will recognize him or her in different circumstances? Can you trust them? Moreover, we might wonder, as we will with Calasiris' storytelling later in the novel, whether or not Cnemon is a reliable narrator of the account that he claims that Charias told him; in other words, whether the form as well as the content of the story is a masquerade. If form and content here converge, then we are presented with the destabilizing possibility that we might have got the hierarchy of the levels of representation within the narrative wrong: can we be certain (in the novel, as in real life) whether we are in a minor drama or the main narrative, whether we are a bit player, or star of the show, and whether we are reading from the same script as our fellow actors?

Scholars have recognized that Cnemon's story is of a different generic order to the surrounding narrative, an observation that is intensified by the wildly varying generic qualities associated with bed-trick scenes (some are tragic, others comic, some moralizing, others not). The cunning slave and the comedy of mistaken identity are reminiscent of New Comedy,[30] and perhaps of the comic scenarios in mime.[31] The interweaving of tragedy and comedy or mime is significant for Demaenete because (as it is reported by Cnemon) she has cast herself as a tragic protagonist through the reference to Euripides' *Hippolytus*, but from her husband's perspective, she is playing the role of an adulteress from a comedy or mime. Demaenete's suicide can thus be interpreted as a reclamation of her role: 'she reinstates her tragic role at the end of the story by committing suicide to avoid being taken to court, a resolution that would have belonged to mime rather than tragedy.'[32] In terms of narrative dynamics, Cnemon's story inaugurates a meta-narrative awareness that an audience can choose to view a scene through one dramatic and generic lens or another. It acknowledges and opens up the

---

[30] Paulsen 1992: 96, 209. See also Montiglio 2013a: 109–10 who notes that a key difference between Thisbe and cunning slaves in New Comedy is that the latter aim to help the lovers, whereas Thisbe plots her mistress's downfall.

[31] Webb 2013: 293: 'In the case of Cnemon's tale, reminiscences of the Phaedra plot co-exist with elements that certainly seem to be more in keeping with mime than with tragedy. These latter include the complex chain of substitutions that lead to Demaenete's downfall.... The use of the door, the comedy of mistaken identity and the figure of the cunning slave girl all point to a mimic inspiration in this section of Cnemon's tale.'

[32] Webb 2013: 294.

possibility of renegade reading, of refusing the generic frame offered and choosing another instead.

Thisbe may be a character from a comedy or a mime, albeit one whose name is associated with doomed romance,[33] but Charicleia is not: in Richard Hunter's words, 'Thisbe and Charicleia belong to different fictional worlds'.[34] I want now to explore two insights that are implicated in this observation, and that may be in tension with each other. The first is that Thisbe and Charicleia are substitutes for each other, and the second is that they are polar opposites.

At the level of plot, Thisbe 'substitutes' for Charicleia on several occasions. Both while dead and alive Thisbe is mistaken for, and treated as if she were, Charicleia. The first book ends with Thyamis, the captain of the robbers, killing 'the Greek woman', whom he thinks is Charicleia but is in fact Thisbe: the first time she 'substitutes for' Charicleia. At the beginning of the following book, Theagenes clasps to him the dead body of the woman he believes to be Charicleia and, grief-stricken, contemplates suicide. He is delighted when he learns that the corpse is that of Thisbe. He exclaims, 'I was weeping for her in another's body, for I thought that the dead woman was she' (ἣν ἐθρήνουν ἐν ἀλλοτρίῳ σώματι, ταύτην εἶναι τὴν κειμένην ἡγούμενος 2.7.2), disconcerting phraseology that conjoins Thisbe and Charicleia, as the latter is momentarily (experienced as being) in the body of the former, a dynamic similar to that of a bed-trick, which could be glossed as sleeping with a woman in another's body. In Book 5, Nausicles thinks he has Thisbe in his protection, when it is really Charicleia. Cnemon listens to the woman lamenting and calling herself Thisbe and, convinced that his lover has come back to life, faints with terror (5.3.1). It is not a surprise to learn that 'the woman he had heard lamenting was not Thisbe, but Charicleia!' A while later we hear how Nausicles persuaded Charicleia to masquerade as Thisbe in order to outwit Mitranes (5.10.2). The question first raised in the bed-trick scene when Demaenete substitutes herself for Arsinoe—how substitutable is one woman for another?—is dramatized repeatedly through the narrative, with Thisbe being substituted for Charicleia, and vice versa.

The substitutability of Charicleia for Thisbe relies on Thisbe's concomitant importance and expendability. Like the unnamed prostitute who is beheaded instead of Leucippe in *Leucippe and Clitophon* (see 8.16), Thisbe

---

[33] The tale of Pyramus and Thisbe is told in Ovid *Met*. 4.55–92, possibly influenced by a lost Hellenistic version. On this, and the associations of the name Thisbe, see Bowie 1995: 273–6.
[34] Hunter 1998a: 56.

is both essential to saving the life of the heroine, and rendered disposable through her lower social status as a slave, together with her lower fictional status as a mimic or comedic character. Thisbe's disposability is part of the novel's elite ideology, and also enacts on the level of plot what happens on the poetic level: the character, like the inset story of the bed-trick, is a type, and ultimately removable from the teleological sweep of the main narrative.

The fact that Thisbe is a substitute for Charicleia may be in tension with a further observation that is frequently made about the relationship between the two characters, that Thisbe is the polar opposite of Charicleia. The next section will explore this issue, and the role of Thisbe and others in the fashioning of the character of Charicleia, in more depth.

3.3. Visualizing Charicleia

John Morgan argued that Thisbe is constructed as an 'anti-Charicleia', as Charicleia's 'antitype'. This is part of his broader tracing of the 'antithesis between Athenian and Charicleian love'.[35] Katherine Haynes elaborates: 'Even when the narrative apparently focuses on female characters, such interest may in fact function as a photographic negative of the heroine: talking about Thisbe and Demaenete, the author is in fact determining what the heroine is not'.[36] While I agree with the broader argument, that the emotions and relationships in Cnemon's tale provide a negative contrast to the spiritual desire and chaste love of Theagenes and Charicleia, the more specific contention that Thisbe is the 'antithesis' of Charicleia seems to me reductive. It is (largely) true that in terms of their expressed moral stances, moral behaviour, and social statuses, Charicleia and Thisbe are poles apart. However, moral choice (*proairesis*) and social status comprise only one index of characterization.

It may be more productive to understand Charicleia's characterization not in terms of opposition, and as part of a structure of polarities, but as an assemblage. The French philosophers Gilles Deleuze and Felix Guattari first articulated the concept of the assemblage, or *agencement*,[37] and Deleuze's definition is as follows:

---

[35] Morgan 1989b: 111. [36] Haynes 2003: 68.
[37] The original French term conveys a greater sense of agency than does the English word 'assemblage'.

It is a multiplicity which is made up of many heterogeneous terms and which establishes liaisons, relations between them.... Thus, assemblage's only unity is that of co-functioning: it is a symbiosis, a 'sympathy'. It is never filiations which are important but alliances, alloys; these are not successions, lines of descent, but contagions, epidemics, the wind.[38]

In other words, assemblage is a way of ordering heterogeneous elements (whatever these may be) so that they work together in some way for a certain amount of time. Assemblages function as a whole, but are made up of constituent parts that can be extracted from one system and plugged into another. Assemblage thinking (a better term than assemblage *theory* because, as Martin Müller explains, 'the concept of the assemblage is a provisional analytical tool rather than a system of ideas geared towards an explanation that would make it a theory')[39] is a perspective that privileges the relations between elements and how they come together and produce new expressions. It prioritizes what something *does*, over what it *is*.[40] It seeks to understand the world as consisting of sets of connections between things, processes, relations, and intensities that are in flux.[41]

It is striking that Charicleia (like Theagenes) is not described in detail. It would be hard for a reader to recall what she looked like, beyond appearing white, with blonde hair, despite her Ethiopian ethnicity, and having a ring of black skin pigment around one arm.[42] Instead she is presented primarily in terms of her *affect*, her impact on other characters. Lack of detailed physical description is part of the idealization of Charicleia, but it also facilitates viewing her not through the lens of realism, but as an assemblage of female roles and associations. I propose that Charicleia comprises figures, and facets of figures, of the prostitute, goddess (and image of a goddess), priestess, and martyr. I will briefly discuss each of these in turn, paying most attention to the prostitute because this has not so far been recognized as playing more than an oppositional role.

Charicleia is explicitly called a 'little prostitute' (*hetairidion*) by Cybele (7.10.5). Charicleia shows some of the qualities associated with Thisbe and prostitutes in general. She is deceitful, and feigns agreeing to marriage to a

---

[38] Deleuze and Parnet 1987: 69.   [39] Müller 2015: 28.
[40] A caveat: using assemblage to understand characterization is not what Deleuze and Guattari intended: they are rather dismissive of the 'signifier enthusiast' (Deleuze and Guattari 1987: 66), focusing instead on the book as an exterior object and its relationship to other objects.
[41] See Grosz 1993.
[42] See 3.4.5–6 and 10.15.2 for Charicleia, and 2.35.1 for Theagenes.

series of men: to Charicles' nephew, Alcamenes (4.13), to the pirate captain, Trachinus (5.26), and to the bandit chief, Thyamis (1.22). Charicleia's sexual scheming and the association with different men characterize her as a prostitute, even if she and the reader know that she has, in fact, remained chaste. Her reaction to Trachinus' taking her as his wife shows Thisbe-like resourcefulness and dissimulation: 'Charicleia, the clever little minx, ever quick to turn a situation to her advantage...discarded the downcast expression that her ordeals had brought to her face, and composed her features into an alluring smile' (5.26.2.2-6). Her deception of Thyamis is described with the following image: 'her words worked a siren spell on him and compelled his assent' (ὑπὸ δὲ τῶν λόγων ὥσπερ τινὸς σειρῆνος κεκηλημένος καὶ πρὸς τὸ πείθεσθαι κατηναγκασμένος 1.23.2).[43] The simile both links her to Calasiris who is also said to speak 'like a Siren' (5.1), and characterizes her as a prostitute, as Sirens were sometimes associated with prostitutes.[44]

Charicleia's voice may be potent, but it is her beauty that has the most impact on other characters. One of the first descriptions of Charicleia, when she and Theagenes have been taken prisoners by the bandits, couches her affect in terms of its ability to overturn power relations:

> Καὶ ἦν δόξης οὐκ ἐκτὸς τὸ γινόμενον· δουλεύειν ὁ ἄρχων ἐφαίνετο καὶ ὑπηρε τεῖσθαι ὁ κρατῶν τοῖς ἑαλωκόσιν ᾑρεῖτο. Οὕτως εὐγενείας ἔμφασις καὶ κάλλους ὄψις καὶ ληστρικὸν ἦθος οἶδεν ὑποτάττειν καὶ κρατεῖν καὶ τῶν αὐχμηροτέρων δύναται.
>
> There was something remarkable in the sight: the master appeared as a servant; the captor chose to minister to his captives. Thus may nobility of appearance and beauty of countenance vanquish even a brigand heart, and triumph over the harshest of natures. (1.4.3)

This motif is repeated later in the novel, with the lovers' beauty functioning as a weapon (and providing the opportunity for the narrator's sententiousness about social status):

> Τῶν δὲ ἐπελθόντων ἐπανετείναντο μέν τινες ὡς πατάξοντες· ὡς δ' ἐπιβλέψαντες οἱ νέοι κατηύγασαν τοὺς ἐπιφερομένους ὤκλαζεν αὐτοῖς ὁ

---

[43] On Charicleia's deception of Thyamis, see further de Temmerman 2014: 258-69.
[44] e.g. in a passage attributed to Anaxilas' *Neottis* in which hetaerae are compared to mythical monsters, including Sirens (*Ath.* 13.558 a–b, c), and Heraclitus' *Peri Apistōn* in which the Siren is rationalized as a hetaera. On Charicleia as Odysseus *and* as Siren, see Brethes 2007.

θυμὸς καὶ παρεῖντο αἱ δεξιαί, τοὺς γὰρ καλοὺς καὶ βάρβαροι χεῖρες ὡς ἔοικε δυσωποῦνται καὶ πρὸς τὴν ἐράσμιον θέαν καὶ ἀπρόσφυλος[45] ὀφθαλμὸς ἡμεροῦται.

A couple of attackers raised their arms to strike them dead, but when the young lovers turned their eyes towards them, their beauty so dazzled their assailants that their anger subsided and their arms dropped to their sides; for even the hand of a savage, it seems, is overawed by beauty; even the eye of a heathen is subdued by something so love-worthy. (5.7.3)

Still later, Charicleia ensures that the safety of Calasiris and Theagenes by looking at Trachinus: 'her glances reduced him to abject slavery' (ὑπὸ τῶν βλεμμάτων πρὸς τὸ ὑπήκοον ἐδουλοῦτο 5.26.4).

Achieving dominance through beauty is a capacity that Charicleia shares with Callirhoe, the heroine of Chariton's novel, and Anthia, the heroine of Xenophon of Ephesus' novel, all demythologized descendants of Helen of Troy.[46] However, there is a crucial difference in how the characters are represented in this regard. Callirhoe disavows the power that her beauty affords her; it empowers her *despite herself*.[47] When Anthia's beauty 'captivates' Habrocomes, he becomes a prisoner of *eros*, not of Anthia (1.3.2).[48] Charicleia, in contrast, owns and manipulates her beauty. In portraying her thus, the narrative aligns Charicleia with women who are repeatedly represented as achieving mastery through their beauty: hetaerae. In the second book of the *Aethiopica* the hetaera Rhodopis is described as capturing men: 'Any man who crossed her path was trapped, for there was no escaping or resisting the net of sensuality that she trailed from her eyes' (οὐ γὰρ ἦν ἐντυχόντα μὴ ἡλωκέναι, οὕτως ἄφυκτόν τινα καὶ ἀπρόσμαχον ἑταιρίας σαγήνην ἐκ τῶν ὀφθαλμῶν ἐπεσύρετο 2.25.1), a common metaphor for the hetaera's gaze,[49] which resonates with Demaenete's 'ensnaring' of Aristippus, Charicleia's subduing of men with her gaze, and Charicleia's affinity with Artemis the huntress.

---

[45] A neologism, literally 'from outside the tribe' (like the commoner ἔκφυλος).
[46] For Callirhoe as Helen, see Laplace 1980, Morales 2005: 6–7. Euripides' *Helen* is alluded to at *Aeth.* 2.8 and 2.11, with Thisbe envisaged as Helen: 'It is not possible', says Charicleia, '... How can someone suddenly be spirited away by a sort of theatrical special effect, out of Greece to the remotest parts of Egypt?' and a short while later Cnemon and Theagenes continue the allusion. Cnemon says '... Even dead I regard you with suspicion, and am haunted by the fear that... you have come across the sea to make me the victim of another Attic tragedy, but in an Egyptian setting!' and Theagenes responds 'Enough... of your dread of ghosts and phantoms!', both strong evocations of Helen and her *eidōlon* in Euripides' play.
[47] At 2.3.7 and 5.4.3: Morales 2004: 162–3.   [48] See further Morales 2005: 6, 12–13.
[49] See the description of Theodote in Xenophon's *Memorabilia* (3.11.10–14).

Thisbe and Rhodopis are different kinds of prostitute. Rhodopis is a wealthy hetaera, of exceptional beauty. Thisbe is not explicitly called a prostitute, but it is implied, and, in any case, the demarcations between the 'street' prostitute and the slave or lower-class women who may also have been exploited sexually were unclear. Charicleia is compared to both Thisbe and Rhodopis—the only two occasions in the novel where she is compared to other characters—and it is significant that the point of the comparison in both cases is not morality, but beauty. Rhodopis, according to Calasiris, was 'second only to Charicleia in beauty' (2.25.1), whereas Thisbe, in Nausicles' view, is nowhere in her league: οὐ γὰρ μικρὸν εἶναι τὸ διάφορον ἀλλ᾽ ὅσον ἄν τι γένοιτο θεοῦ πρὸς ἄνθρωπον, οὕτως οὐκ εἶναι τοῦ κάλλους ὑπερβολὴν οὐδὲ αὐτῷ δυνατὸν εἶναι τῷ λόγῳ φράζειν... ('there was a vast difference between the two, a difference as great as that between man and god. Her [i.e. Charicleia's] beauty was beyond compare and beyond his power to describe in words' 5.10.2). Both Thisbe and Rhodopis are used to emphasize the pre-eminence of Charicleia's beauty.

Even Charicleia's name may evoke sexual availability. In an important study of the significance of names in Heliodorus, Meriel Jones notes that Charicleia is a rare name in ancient literature, but does appear in Lucian's *Toxaris*, as the name of a hetaera.[50] In Deinias' tale within *Toxaris* (13), Charicleia is a woman who gives herself 'to anyone who happened to meet her', a sophisticated, seductive prostitute who shares characteristics with, and is described using some of the same vocabulary as, Heliodorus' Demaenete. Jones reads Heliodorus' allusion to Lucian's Charicleia as 'ironic': 'for although the two share many traits, our Charicleia is infinitely superior from a moral viewpoint, and consequently her nobility is thrown into relief.'[51] Aldo Tagliabue, who has argued that Heliodorus deliberately defines his novel in relation to this episode in Lucian's *Toxaris*, sees the point as one of contrast: 'through his engagement with Lucian's *Toxaris* Heliodorus gives a characterization of both his female protagonist and his novel by means of opposition.'[52]

My approach is to see Lucian's Charicleia as part of a swirl of elements— declaration, metaphor, affect, behaviour, and affinity—that territorialize or

---

[50] Jones 2006: 552. The Delphic oracle in Book 2 places great emphasis on the etymology of the protagonists' names. 2.35 puns on the names Charicleia and Theagenes, with Charicleia comprising *charis* (grace) and *kleos* (glory) and Theagenes *the-* (divinity) and *genos* (birth). On hyper-significance and allegory, see Most 2007.
[51] Jones 2006: 553.
[52] Tagliabue 2016: 18. For the 'erotic ambivalence' afforded Charicleia through intertextual play with Bion of Smyrna's *Epitaph on Adonis*, see the forthcoming work of Emilio Capettini.

congeal (to use the imagery of assemblage thinking) to imagine Heliodorus' Charicleia as a prostitute. This image is not sustained in a concerted way throughout the novel, but deterritorializes and reterritorializes at particular moments. This fluid, and open aspect of the novel, what Roman Brethes has called an 'espace brouillé', 'ou les identités sont très confusés avant de se fixer, et sa position multiplie les interférences entre plusieurs traditions littéraires et morales',[53] is in tension with the teleological progression of the narrative, especially in the second half, and the simplified moral interpretations encouraged by focusing on marriage as the *telos* of the novel.[54] The prostitute is one component of Charicleia that operates in relation to several others, and it is to these that I will now turn.

Other images and similes are used to portray Charicleia as a goddess, and as a statue of a goddess, as a priestess, and as a Christian martyr. At the very beginning of the novel she is likened to Artemis and Isis, 'a creature of such indescribable beauty that one might have taken her for a goddess'; others take her to be priestess (1.2). A little later we are told that the bandits wondered 'had they carried off the priestess... or was this girl the statue of a goddess, a living statue?' (1.7.2). Sisimithres remembers seeing something 'godlike' about the light in the 7-year-old Charicleia's eyes (2.31.1), and Charicles describes the adult Charicleia as 'like a statue of ideal beauty' who has 'dedicated herself to the sacred service of Artemis' (2.33.3–4).[55] Indeed, Charicleia served ten years of life as a priestess of Artemis at Delphi. In the final paragraph of the novel she becomes the priestess of Selene who, like Artemis, is a moon goddess. During the scene where Arsace attempts to burn Charicleia on a pyre, however, it is not a priestess who is envisaged, but a martyr, more precisely, Thecla. As Rosa Andújar has shown, in the scenes where Charicleia is placed on a pyre that is set alight, and tested on the gridiron, there are strong evocations of the second-century Christian work *The Acts of Paul and Thecla*.[56] She comments that the effect of this intertextual engagement is to import a particular tableau, one in which Charicleia is a 'desexualized erotic object'. The emphasis is on Charicleia as a different kind of spectacle.

---

[53] Brethes 2007: 227.   [54] See Whitmarsh 2011: 156–7.
[55] She is described by Calasiris as 'Artemis herself' (5.31.1).
[56] Andújar 2013. The most striking illustration of this is at 8.9.13 where Charicleia 'seemed like a bride in the nuptial chamber of fire'. The metaphor of fire as a *thalamos* appears in only one other place, the rewritten version of the Acts of Thecla from 470 CE (1.12.57–62): see Andújar 2013: 147–8.

In conclusion, all of these elements—the priestess, the prostitute, the living work of art, the Christian martyr, and the earthly analogue of a goddess—form an assemblage that visualizes Charicleia.[57] Typically, upper-class women in the Roman Empire were not visible. Good women were invisible, which is one reason that Chariton's Callirhoe must disavow her beauty and the advantages it brings. Women with public presences were prostitutes, slaves, priestesses, and martyrs.[58] What is significant, innovative, bold, and brilliant about the visualizing assemblage in the *Aethiopica* is that it makes visible a woman who is an elite young woman, and betrothed to become a wife. Some of these elements are imbricated in the broader visual field, for example, the hetaera and the living work of art (as in Lucian's *Eikones*), and the hetaera and the priestess (as in the description of Phryne's exposure in the lawcourt),[59] but their collocation in a single character that is not a hetaera, or a morally ambiguous mythological figure like Helen, is remarkable.[60] The components of Charicleia shift and thereby create different intensities, with different, and sometimes conflicting, sexual and moral personae.[61]

On a simple level of moral behaviour and values, Thisbe contrasts with Charicleia. On a more complicated level of character construction, in which Heliodorus is creating a new model of womanhood, in which a morally good wife-to-be can be visible, Thisbe is part of an assemblage of spectacular female roles—prostitute, actress, martyr, priestess—through whose shifting aspects and images Charicleia is fashioned as a new kind of heroine. The relationship between prostitute and Charicleia may be one of contrast on the explicit moral level, but it is one of entailment and co-option in the visual sphere. In turn, of course, this subtly affects the reception of Charicleia as a moral character; Charicleia *as an assemblage* can never escape the contagion of Thisbe, Rhodopis, and Lucian's Charicleia because they constitute her, even as Charicleia *as a subject* attempts to live in a very different moral universe.

---

[57] A more detailed analysis of her visuality would of course include the circumstances of her conception, and the importance to her identity of the image of Andromeda, on which see Olsen 2012.

[58] Is it telling that when Charicleia is abducted, the Delphians decide to prevent the priestess of Artemis from appearing in public in the future: see further Tim Whitmarsh's chapter in this volume.

[59] Hermippus F68 = Athenaeus 590e, on which see Morales 2011. On the interplay of the categories of prostitute, wife, and priestess in the Athenian writings of the classical period, see Gilhuly 2009.

[60] And, in its complexity, unparalleled, although Xenophon of Ephesus' Anthia and Achilles Tatius' Leucippe share some similarities with Charicleia.

[61] My reading here is in tune with scholarship that has seen greater moral ambiguity in the character of Charicleia than is often allowed, especially Brethes 2007, and Ormand 2010.

4
Thisbe's Intrigue
A Plot between Deception and Illusion (1.15–17)

Jonas Grethlein

This chapter considers the same passage as the previous chapter, from a different angle.

Heliodorus' virtuoso juggling of genres has been duly praised. He not only plays with epic, lyric, historiography, and drama, but also pits their generic conventions against each other. It has been noted, for example, that Cnemon's attempt to stylize himself as a tragic hero is undercut by the comic elements of his own story.[1] One of the characters that seems to come straight out of a comedy by Menander is Thisbe, the servant of Cnemon's stepmother Demaenete. Her scheming skills easily match that of Daos in *Aspis* and the *servi callidi* populating the works of Plautus. Thisbe's masterpiece is the intrigue in which she sends her mistress to her doom. It is also a masterpiece of literary sophistication, forming part of an embedded story within an embedded story: Cnemon recounts a friend's report to Theagenes and Charicleia (1.15–17). I shall analyse the artful orchestration of the plot and then explore the reflexivity of the episode.

In one of his ground-breaking papers on Heliodorus, John Morgan alerted us to the role of narrative doublets in the *Aethiopica*.[2] As he demonstrated, repetition is 'one of the engines of Heliodorus' plotting.... Apart from differentiating a plot from a mere series of occurrences and hence functioning as an implicit guarantee of a controlling intelligence and literary meaningfulness, symmetries are intellectually and aesthetically satisfying in their own right'.[3] While some of the doublets explored by Morgan bring together passages that are separated from each other by several books, others follow closely upon another. Thisbe's scheme at 1.15–17 can be read as a re-run of

---

[1] Paulsen 1992: 82–141.   [2] Morgan 1998.   [3] Morgan 1998: 78.

Jonas Grethlein, *Thisbe's Intrigue: A Plot between Deception and Illusion (1.15–17)* In: *Reading Heliodorus' Aethiopica*. Edited by: Ian Repath and Tim Whitmarsh, Oxford University Press. © Oxford University Press 2022.
DOI: 10.1093/oso/9780198792543.003.0004

something just narrated, namely Demaenete's intrigue that brought about Cnemon's exile (1.11.3–12). I would first like to tease out the intellectual and aesthetic satisfaction granted by this micro-doublet and then argue that the narration is imbued with reflexivity, shedding light on an aspect that went unnoticed in John Morgan's and Jack Winkler's seminal investigations of the Cnemon episode.[4] What may seem to be merely a delightful plot design also effectively questions the reader's control over the text.

Unlike the *servus callidus* of comedy, Thisbe employs her scheming skills not only on behalf of her mistress, but also for her own interests and against her mistress.[5] It is a nice twist that the intrigue resulting in the death of Demaenete is modelled on the intrigue that Demaenete herself had struck up to take revenge on Cnemon. Enraged by Cnemon's rejection of her desire, she had Thisbe enter into an intimate relationship with him and gain his trust. Thisbe, following Demaenete's instructions, alerted Cnemon that his stepmother was having an affair, and informed him about a night which Demaenete would spend with her lover. When, however, Cnemon forced his way into the paternal bedroom with his sword in his hand, he found his father beside Demaenete. Now Thisbe stages another chase of an adulterer, again having an interloper storm into a bedroom where there is no adulterer. In both scenes, there is a light that guides the invader: in the first there is a torch (1.12.2), in the second the moonlight, since Thisbe has taken away the torch (1.17.2–3). Aristippus' statement 'I have the very criminal I most wanted' (τὴν ἀλιτήριον καὶ ἣν μάλιστα ἐβουλόμην ἔχω, 1.17.4) echoes Cnemon's cry 'Where is the criminal?' (ποῦ ποτε ὁ ἀλιτήριος; 1.12.2).

While reprising Demaenete's stratagem, Thisbe's scheme is far more complex and delicately reassigns the roles. Demaenete's set-up requires the deception of only one person, namely Cnemon. Thisbe, however, lies to all protagonists involved, besides Demaenete also Aristippus and Arsinoe. She multiplies the pretences and in one case even nests one lie within another. Cunningly she pretends to Demaenete that she will fool Arsinoe into thinking that she is in love with Cnemon. Instead of herself, however, she suggests it will be Demaenete who will pretend to be Arsinoe when she shares Cnemon's bed. The careful imbrication of lies on which Thisbe's plot is built outperforms Demaenete's own machination, evil though that is. The ultimate result of the intrigue, Demaenete's death, is also more drastic than the exile of Cnemon, the outcome of Demaenete's scheming.

---

[4] Winkler 1982; Morgan 1989b.   [5] Montiglio 2013a: 109–10.

Demaenete's and Thisbe's schemes thus alert us to a point that can be added to Morgan's analysis of doublets. Morgan masterfully teases out the nuances of the comparison invited by repetition, showing how their contemplation 'leads the reader, in some cases at least, through back-ways to the moral and ethical issues with which the novel concerns itself'.[6] Another noteworthy aspect is the climactic arrangement of some doublets. Two of Morgan's examples may serve as further illustrations. First the doublet of the Delphic foot-race and the wrestling match at Meroe: as Morgan notes, whereas Theagenes 'asserts himself as the truest of Hellenes' in Delphi, the competition at Meroe casts him as 'the champion of the Ethiopian crowd' and thereby prepares his transformation into an Ethiopian.[7] At the same time, there is an *auxēsis*: the foot-race has become an *agōn* in wrestling, the Greek athlete has been replaced with an Ethiopian man who is so tall that 'even as he knelt to kiss the king's knee he was almost as tall as those sitting on elevated thrones' (τὸ γόνυ τοῦ βασιλέως φιλῶν μικροῦ φανῆναι τοῖς ἐφ' ὑψηλοῦ προκαθημένοις ἐξισούμενος, 10.25.1). At Meroe, Theagenes braves not only the giant, but also a bull frenzied by the unfamiliar sight of the giraffe (10.28–10.30.6). He chases the bull on a horse and finally jumps on it to force it to the ground. Prefiguring and paralleling the wrestling, the rodeo show adds emphasis to the final contest. The situation is incomparably more serious: in Delphi he had been the proud head of an embassy in charge of sacrifices; now Theagenes is about to be sacrificed himself. The crown he receives as victor in Meroe is, as Hydaspes notes bitterly, at the same time the adornment of the sacrificial victim (10.32.3). Whereas in Delphi Theagenes receives the crown from Charicleia, he now asks for the favour of being executed by her (10.32.4). The wrestling contest corresponds with the foot-race and simultaneously outshines it.

A second doublet on which Morgan touches only in passing, Trachinus and Thyamis (the two robber-captains who claim Charicleia as their own part of the booty), is worth mentioning as the amplification operates only in the discourse and not in the story. The very name Trachinus indicates the rough nature of its bearer. Thyamis, at the same time, is, as Cnemon puts it, 'not at all a savage but has a gentle side to his character, and comes from a distinguished family and has taken up his present way of life only out of necessity' (οὐ παντάπασι βάρβαρον εἶναι τὰ ἤθη τὸν λῄσταρχον ἐγγυώμενος, ἀλλ' ἔχειν τι καὶ ἥμερον γένος τε ὄντα τῶν ἐπὶ δόξης καὶ πρὸς ἀνάγκης τὸν

---

[6] Morgan 1998: 78.   [7] Morgan 1998: 74–5.

παρόντα βίον ἑλόμενον, 1.19.2). Trachinus claims to 'love (Charicleia) maniacally after seeing her once' (αὐτῆς...ἐρῶ μανικῶς ἅπαξ θεασάμενος, 5.20.6), Thyamis' wish to marry her is triggered by a miraculous dream in which Isis entrusts her to him (1.18.4–5). Trachinus simply claims Charicleia for himself, whereas Thyamis deems it right to ask his men for their approval (1.19–20). Likewise, Thyamis' decision to ask Charicleia for her hand contrasts with the roughness of Trachinus, who makes it clear that he will take Charicleia with or without the permission of Calasiris (1.21.2, 5.28.1–2).

Not only are the characters of the two suitors different, but also the threats posed to Charicleia and the plot of the *Aethiopica* vary in their intensity. The marriage with Thyamis is postponed until they come to Memphis. Trachinus, by contrast, after the interlude of a storm, tells Calasiris that he will marry Charicleia 'today' (τήμερον, 5.28.1). The urgency is thrown into relief by the long that time Trachinus was lying in wait for Charicleia just as Thyamis grants a postponement of the wedding after bumping into her unexpectedly. Now the protagonists are captured first by the pirates under Trachinus, then by Thyamis and the buccaneers. Through the distorted presentation of events in the *Aethiopica*'s first half, however, the two episodes are narrated in reversed order. The achronological narration creates a climactic structure for the reader: first the captivity by a considerate man, then the greater threat from a barbarian.

Let us return to Thisbe's scheme. Besides the amplification, the recasting of the players renders the episode intellectually and aesthetically appealing. Thisbe involves the same characters as Demaenete does, but reshuffles their roles drastically. Cnemon, who violently invaded the paternal bedroom, is now expected as lover by Demaenete—yet he does not turn up. Aristippus, whom Cnemon mistook for an adulterer, now figures as the invader. Thus Cnemon, who confronted Aristippus in the first instance, is the character whom in the second scene Aristippus would catch were Demaenete's expectation to be fulfilled. However, Demaenete, after being the master of the first intrigue, now becomes the primary victim of the second. Now it is not the interloper but the one surprised by him who is punished. The repetition of Demaenete's intrigue with the same characters in a radically altered constellation is an exhilarating *tour de force*. The impression given is that the scheme alone is fixed, and the characters are variables that can be assigned any role arbitrarily.

The reader of the *Aethiopica* is free to relish these narrative acrobatics, as Cnemon, recounting his friend's report, assumes the perspective of an omniscient narrator. While the characters are deceived by Thisbe's pretences, readers, following her preparations step by step, enjoy full insight into the set-up. A closer look, however, reveals a deeper level of significance in Thisbe's intrigue, and this ultimately leads readers to question the control that they exert over the *Aethiopica*. Thisbe's intrigue is twice called an *apatē* ('deception', 1.17.5; 2.8.4).[8] At the beginning of the episode, the stem *apat-* appears in a different context when Demaenete complains:

Νῦν δὲ ὁρᾶν φαντάζομαι, παρόντος ἀκούειν ἀπατῶμαι, ὀνειδίζοντα τὴν ἄδικον ἐπιβουλὴν αἰσχύνομαι· συντεύξεσθαί ποτε ὑπελθόντι καὶ ἀπολαύσειν, ἢ καὶ αὐτὴ παρ' ἐκεῖνον φοιτήσειν ὅπου ποτ' ἂν ᾖ γῆς ὑποτίθεμαι. Ταῦτα ὑπεκκαίει, ταῦτα ἐκμαίνει.

But, as it is, I fancy I see him; I delude myself that I can hear his voice in person; I blush to hear him rebuke my wicked scheme. I dream that one day I shall find him come to me by stealth and take my pleasure of him, or that I shall go to him, wherever in the world he may be. These thoughts fan the flames of desire and drive me mad with longing. (1.15.4)

Here, it is not guile that deceives, but the imagination that makes Demaenete hear the voice of somebody not present. There is subtle irony in that Demaenete, who talks about an *apatē*, fails to sense the *apatē* to which she is about to fall prey. The deception crafted by Thisbe supplants the deceptive images of Demaenete's mind. While promising to give flesh to these images, Thisbe's plot ultimately fails to substantiate them. The smooth transition from imagination to delusion proves lethal for Demaenete.

There is another passage in which Heliodorus uses *apatē* in order to juxtapose a literal deception with images produced by the imagination. When Calasiris describes lavishly the Delphian procession at which Theagenes and Chariclea fall for each other, Cnemon interrupts him, exclaiming (3.4.7): 'There they are, Chariclea and Theagenes!' (Οὗτοι ἐκεῖνοι Χαρίκλεια καὶ Θεαγένης). Now Calasiris believes that Chariclea and Theagenes are around the corner, fulfilling Cnemon's promise that he will be reunited with them before the night. As I argue elsewhere, this carefully wrought passage contains a nuanced comment on aesthetic illusion.[9] Whereas Cnemon's exclamation showcases the strong responses that narratives can elicit, the juxtaposition with delusion, namely Calasiris' expectation of the heroes' arrival, throws into relief the limits of aesthetic illusion. As immersed as Cnemon is in Calasiris' narration, he remains aware of attending to a story.

---

[8] For a full exploration of the poetics of *apatē* in the *Aethiopica*, see Grethlein 2021: ch. 10.
[9] Grethlein 2015a: 317–20. For further thoughts on aesthetic experience in the *Aethiopica*, see Grethlein 2015b.

For my argument here, it is Calasiris' deployment of the stem of *apat-* that is of interest. Before complaining that Cnemon has deceived (ἐξαπατᾶν) him with his promise that Charicleia and Theagenes will show up, he moans: 'Such a sweet deception (ὢ τῆς ἡδείας ἀπάτης), such a pleasant mistake, Cnemon! My heart was all aflutter when I thought you could see my beloved children and were telling me they were here' (3.4.9). Here *apatē* refers not to the treachery of which Calasiris accuses Cnemon, but to his delusion that Theagenes and Charicleia have just arrived. As in the episode of Thisbe's intrigue, Heliodorus harnesses the word *apatē* to juxtapose a wrong impression generated by guile with a phantasy proliferating from the imagination. Heliodorus does not conflate the two; rather, he lets them resonate against each other. The use of the same word prompts the reader to ponder the similarities and differences, to what extent mental images are a form of deception.

The 'sweet deception' invoked by Calasiris carries, I think, a special connotation. Calasiris does not speak of an image evoked by a story, but the focus of the passage on narrative and its immersive capacity cannot fail to conjure up *apatē*'s meaning of aesthetic illusion. In a long tradition reaching back to the classical era, *apatē* is used for the beguiling effect of words as well as paintings on their recipients. Gorgias, for example, notes that in tragedy 'he who deceives is more just than he who does not deceive, and he who is deceived is wiser than he who is not deceived' (ὅ τ' ἀπατήσας δικαιότερος τοῦ μὴ ἀπατήσαντος καὶ ὁ ἀπατηθεὶς σοφώτερος τοῦ μὴ ἀπατηθέντος, 82 B 23 DK = Plut. *Mor.* 348c).[10] Strikingly, Gorgias, like Heliodorus, marshals the word *apatē* to blur the boundary between ethics and aesthetics. As the ekphraseis by Philostratus and Callistratus illustrate, the use of *apatē* to denote aesthetic illusion was particularly popular in imperial literature on art.[11] The very phrase ἡδεῖα ἀπάτη figures in a comment on the illusionistic capacity of pictures that introduces the *Imagines* of the younger Philostratus (*proem* 4). When Calasiris speaks of ἡδεῖα ἀπάτη in a dialogue that features a piercing reflection on the absorption of an audience into narrative it is hard not to hear the aesthetic connotation of *apatē*.[12] Heliodorus hence uses the word *apatē* to entwine a literal deception with

---

[10] See also Gorg. *Hel.* 9–11. For similar references to *apatē*, see *Dissoi Logoi* 3.10; Ephorus FGrH 70 F8; *Vita Aeschyli* 7. Cf. Pohlenz 1920; Segal 1962: 112–15, 130–2; Lanata 1963: 204 n. 2; Buchheim 1989: XIX n. 38; Halliwell 2002: 20–2 with n. 49. On the aesthetics of *apatē* from the classical to the imperial eras, see Grethlein 2021.

[11] Cf. Webb 2006; Squire 2013: 110–17. See also Squire and Grethlein 2014: 301–9 for the thesis that the *Tabula Cebetis* plays with *apatē*'s meaning of aesthetic illusion and thereby comments on its own ekphrasis.

[12] Whitmarsh 2002: 121.

the phenomenon of aesthetic illusion. The significance of this entwinement in a text which itself is highly immersive is obvious.

When Demaenete speaks of deception, she only refers to the images her desire conjures up in her mind. That being said, it is not unlikely that also in her speech the sense of aesthetic illusion is activated. There are other critical terms that help to evoke this connotation of *apatē*. Demaenete describes her mental images of Cnemon as multi-sensorial: besides 'being deceived' (ἀπατῶμαι) she can hear Cnemon, she 'imagines' (φαντάζομαι) she can see him.[13] Since Plato, *phantasia* is linked to artistic representations and then, particularly under Stoic influence, becomes a central term for the verbal representation and evocation of images.[14] The author of *De sublimitate*, for instance, notes (15.1): 'The term *phantasia* is used generally for anything which in any way suggests a thought productive of speech. But nowadays the word is predominantly used when through inspiration and emotion you seem to see what you say and bring it before the eyes of the audience' (καλεῖται μὲν γὰρ κοινῶς φαντασία πᾶν τὸ ὁπωσοῦν ἐννόημα γεννητικὸν λόγου παριστάμενον· ἤδη δ' ἐπὶ τούτων κεκράτηκε τοὔνομα, ὅταν ἃ λέγεις ὑπ' ἐνθουσιασμοῦ καὶ πάθους βλέπειν δοκῇς καὶ ὑπ' ὄψιν τιθῇς τοῖς ἀκούουσιν.)[15] The distinction that the author of *De sublimitate* draws between rhetorical and poetic *phantasia* need not concern us here. What matters is the use of *phantasia* as a term for the capacity to express images verbally and to transform these expressions into images again. The numerous references to *phantasia* in the ancient scholia attest its salience in ancient criticism.[16]

Demaenete further says that she fancies, literally 'puts herself under the impression' (ὑποτίθεμαι), that she will be united with Cnemon when he returns or she goes to him. ὑποτίθεσθαι is another term that occurs frequently in ancient criticism.[17] To give an example which combines ὑποτίθεσθαι with *phantasia*: commenting on Homer's description of how Achilles drives the Trojans apart (*Il*. 21.3), the scholion notes: 'he gives the impression of a marvellous image' (θαυμαστήν τινα τὴν φαντασίαν ὑποτίθεται).[18] In countless other scholia, ὑποτίθεσθαι describes the activity of the

---

[13] For a different interpretation, see Whitmarsh 2011: 173, who argues that appetitive visualization 'is particularly associated with lustful, barbarian and low-class figures'.
[14] Cf. Manieri 1998: 17–94; Otto 2009: 91–101; Sheppard 2014.
[15] On this passage, see Manieri 1998: 51–60 with further literature on 51 n. 145 and, more recently, Halliwell 2011: 347–50.
[16] Cf. Meijering 1987: 67–71; Nünlist 2009: 154.   [17] Cf. Meijering 1987: 107–33.
[18] For a discussion of this scholion, see Meijering 1987: 70, who considers it in light of Σ 14.342–51, which adduces, as one of three *tropoi* of poetry: ὁ καθ' ὑπέρθεσιν τῆς ἀληθείας καὶ

author who presents something. By no means are *apatē, phantasia*, and ὑποτίθεσθαι confined to criticism. *Apatē* signifies any kind of deception, *phantasia* applies to imagination in general, and ὑποτίθεσθαι has a wide range of meanings. And yet, used together in a single sentence as in Heliodorus 1.15.4, they cannot fail to evoke the language of criticism. In a work that brims with self-reference it is not too fanciful to assume that this accumulation of critical terms triggers *apatē*'s meaning of aesthetic illusion that is so dear to the writers of the imperial era. Like in 3.4.7, Heliodorus aligns deception, here triggered by Thisbe, with mental images, especially those that the representative arts evoke. The deception of Thisbe's victims is thus brought close to the spell that the *Aethiopica* strives to cast on its readers.

There is one other meta-narratively charged sentence that deserves our attention: Thisbe hopes that intercourse with Cnemon will alleviate her suffering for 'performance of the act satiates desire' (κόρος γὰρ ἔρωτος τῶν ἔργων τὸ τέλος, 1.15.8). Not only *telos*, here iconically standing at the end of the sentence, but also *koros* are terms that figure prominently in the vocabulary of ancient critics.[19] In fact, Heliodorus employs both meta-narratively, for example when Cnemon says to Calasiris 'bring the tale to an end' (εἰς τέλος ἄγε τὴν διήγησιν, 3.4.10) and when in response Calasiris calls Cnemon 'eager to listen...and insatiable when it comes to beautiful stories' (φιλήκοός...καὶ καλῶν ἀκουσμάτων ἀκόρεστος, 3.4.11). In a novel which has the satiation of love as its *telos*, the meta-narrative dimension of Thisbe's comment is palpable. It blurs the boundary between scheming and the act of narrating.

The implicit entwinement of erotics and poetics in Thisbe's words becomes explicit in a later comment by Cnemon:

Ἐγὼ καὶ Ὁμήρῳ μέμφομαι, ὦ πάτερ, ἄλλων τε καὶ φιλότητος κόρον εἶναι φήσαντι, πράγματος ὃ κατ' ἐμὲ κριτὴν οὐδεμίαν φέρει πλησμονὴν οὔτε καθ' ἡδονὴν ἀνυόμενον οὔτε εἰς ἀκοὴν ἐρχόμενον· εἰ δέ τις καὶ τοῦ Θεαγένους καὶ Χαρικλείας ἔρωτος μνημονεύοι, τίς οὕτως ἀδαμάντινος ἢ σιδηροῦς τὴν καρδίαν ὡς μὴ θέλγεσθαι καὶ εἰς ἐνιαυτὸν ἀκούων; ὥστε ἔχου τῶν ἑξῆς.

I cannot agree with Homer, Father, when he says that there is satiety of all things and especially love. In my estimation, one can never have a surfeit of love, whether one is engaged in its pleasures or listening to tales of it.

φαντασίαν (φαντασίας b). See also Philostratus *VA* 6.19, for a passage that makes *phantasia* the subject of ὑποτίθεσθαι.
[19] See, for example, Dionysius of Halicarnassus *Pomp.* 3.11; Σ *Il.* b. 1.8–9; Σ Soph. *Aj.* 38a.

And if somebody recalls the love of Theagenes and Charicleia, who could be so steely and iron-hearted that he would not be spell-bound, even if he had to listen for an entire year? So please continue. (4.4.3)[20]

Cnemon's comment is diametrically opposed to Thisbe's assertion, and yet both blend together love and narrative, if in inverse directions: while Cnemon marshals the semantics of *erōs* for his reflection on narrative, Thisbe's *gnōmē* on erotic desire is couched in the vocabulary of narrative and its reception. Neither claim fully chimes with the plot of the *Aethiopica*. Heliodorus, after the long deferral of desire, does grant satiation in the ending of his novel; however, it is not brought about by the kind of love that Thisbe envisages. Thisbe's claim not only invites the reader to think about her scheme as a form of narration, but also more specifically underscores the discrepancy between the Athenian novella and the *Aethiopica*'s main plot.

It is not the use of critical language alone that suggests a meta-narrative interpretation of Thisbe's scheme. Morgan pointed out that Thisbe has significance beyond her role in the plot, that she 'seems deliberately written up as a sort of Doppelgänger to the heroine'.[21] While Thisbe is mistaken for Charicleia at the beginning of Book 2, in Book 5 Cnemon believes he hears Thisbe when he is in fact listening to Charicleia. I suggest that there is yet another facet to Thisbe. Heliodorus presents Thisbe unmistakably as an 'author'. Thisbe does not herself get to tell Demaenete's story, as she offers to Cnemon on the tablet found with her corpse (2.10.1),[22] but her scheming is explicitly compared with authoring a story: 'poetess of the plan against him [i.e. Cnemon] and Demaenete' (τὴν τῶν εἰς αὐτὸν ἐπιβουλῶν καὶ Δημαινέτην ποιήτριαν, 2.8.2). Promoting his own image as tragic character, Cnemon labels Thisbe more precisely as tragedian:

Ὡς κἀγώ σε καὶ κειμένην ἔχω δι' ὑποψίας καὶ σφόδρα δέδοικα μὴ καὶ πλάσμα ἐστὶν ἡ Δημαινέτης τελευτὴ κἀμὲ μὲν ἠπάτησαν οἱ ἐξαγγείλαντες

---

[20] For a reading of this passage in the light of Peter Brooks's *Reading for the Plot*, see Hardie 1998: 30–1. In his illuminating discussion of the erotics of reading in the *Aethiopica*, Whitmarsh 2011: 150–5, 168–76 surprisingly does not refer to this passage. It contains an intertextual reference to Pindar fr. 123.1–6 as well as an intratextual link to 7.9.5.
[21] Morgan 1989b: 111. On Thisbe see also Hunter 1998a: 42–6, who challenges the common condemnation of Thisbe beginning with Philip the Philosopher (p. 368.67–8) and highlights the bias of Cnemon from whom we learn about her.
[22] Hunter 1998a: 45 thus speaks of 'Thisbe's silence'.

σὺ δὲ καὶ διαπόντιος ἥκεις ἑτέραν καθ' ἡμῶν σκηνὴν Ἀττικὴν καὶ ἐν Αἰγύπτῳ τραγῳδήσουσα.

Even dead I regard you with suspicion, and I am haunted by the fear that the story of Demaenete's death is untrue, that the friends who brought me the news were deceiving me, and that you have come across the sea to make me the victim of another Attic tragedy, but in an Egyptian setting!

(2.11.2)

As already noted, Thisbe's intrigue is comic rather than tragic, and yet Cnemon's comment further blends together scheming with writing.

In English, the word 'plot' nicely captures the similarity that Heliodorus exploits: both schemer and author set up a plot. Indeed, the dexterity of her intrigue makes Thisbe a match for Heliodorus and his artful story-telling. Just as Heliodorus has crafted a plot in which various strands of action are carefully sown together, leaving no loose ends, the lies of Thisbe are like cogs that smoothly interlock to propel the wheel of her plot. That being said, Thisbe's *gnomē* on the satiation of love just discussed highlights the gap that separates her plotting from Heliodorus' plot. Thisbe's scheming skills may equal Heliodorus' literary sophistication, but her understanding of love is a far cry from the love envisaged by Heliodorus.[23]

The comparison of Thisbe with an author highlights the mastery with which she directs the action. Like a story-teller, who resides on a different plane from the characters, Thisbe seems to be in full control of the plot. In the end, however, she is stabbed to death by Thyamis, who mistakes her for Charicleia in the dark of the cave. Silvia Montiglio notes the irony: Thisbe finally falls victim to the very device she wields so brilliantly: misrecognition.[24] I would like to spell out the discomforting questions that the casting of Thisbe as an author raises for the readers. As already mentioned, Thisbe's scheme is delightful to the readers of the *Aethiopica*, who fully see through the intrigue. The net of lies, however, in which Thisbe entangles the other characters in her plot illustrates the capacity of an author to lead her readers astray. As Heliodorus' pun on *apatē* drives home, the same term signifies aesthetic illusion and deception. The case of Demaenete alerts us to the possibility that aesthetic illusion is coupled with deceit. Authors not only strive to immerse the reader in the worlds of their narrations, they also have the power to deceive her.

---

[23] On the *Aethiopica* as a reflection on love, see especially Morgan 1989b.
[24] Montiglio 2013a: 109–10.

This danger is highly pertinent to the reader of the *Aethiopica*. While fully comprehending Thisbe's plot and Cnemon's story at large, the reader is left disturbingly uncertain about the main plot or, more precisely, the strand of the action which those familiar with the conventions of the genre are likely to identify as the main plot. The narrator has given us the names of Charicleia and Theagenes without revealing their identity. The appearance of Cnemon affords an opportunity to unveil who they are, but instead we get the Athenian story of Cnemon. In the further course of Book 1, Charicleia will tell Thyamis that they are priests from Ephesus and siblings. The latter sits uncomfortably with generic conventions and is soon proven a lie, but the reader is still waiting for positive evidence. Her curiosity is titillated further until Calasiris' narration will provide the story of Charicleia and Theagenes. It is only at the end of Book 5, halfway into the novel, that the reader will fully understand the scene with which the novel begins....[25]

The delusion of the characters in the novella not only contrasts with the reader's clear grasp of the Cnemon story, it also underscores the danger of wrong interpretations which the reader faces in trying to come to grips with the main plot. This is a new aspect of the reflexivity inherent in the Cnemon story that has received so much scholarly attention. On the one hand, Morgan showed that the Athenian novella serves as a thematic foil to the main story line.[26] The depraved forms of love in Athens cast into relief the pure love between Charicleia and Theagenes. On the other hand, Winkler demonstrated the meta-narrative function of Cnemon's account. The—at least at the beginning—straightforward narration contrasts with the—at least in the first half—more complex plot of the *Aethiopica* and thereby turns the spotlight on the sophistication of Heliodorus as story-teller.[27] According to the reading advanced here, the Cnemon story sheds light not only on the narrator, but also on the reader of the *Aethiopica*. The hermeneutic errors within the embedded story illuminate the situation of the reader trying to follow the story of Charicleia and Theagenes. In the same way that the characters are duped, the reader can easily be deceived by wrong leads.

The case of Aristippus underscores how slippery the line between truth and delusion is. After the suicide of Demaenete, Aristippus says: 'Now I have justice from you even before the laws took their course' (ἔχω παρὰ σοῦ καὶ πρὸ τῶν νόμων τὴν δίκην, 1.17.6). This is true, but not in the intended sense, for

---

[25] On the ending of Book 5 and the beginning of Book 6, see Grethlein 2016.
[26] Morgan 1989b.
[27] Winkler 1982. For the added qualification, see Morgan 1989b: 104–6.

Aristippus' view of his wife's treachery is skewed. Thisbe's self-revelation to him is itself another scheme, for which she freely blends truth with lie (1.16.2–5): Demaenete in fact intends to cheat on her husband, but Thisbe does not mention that Cnemon is the object of her desire. Thisbe also blurs her own role. She was indeed aware of Demaenete's adulterous aspirations, but Cnemon's assault on his father was part of Demaenete's scheme and not the result of Thisbe's misfired attempt to betray her mistress.

'Attention, master, do not be deceived a second time' (ὅρα, δέσποτα, μὴ καὶ τὰ δεύτερα σφαλῇς, 1.17.4), Thisbe exclaims when Aristippus is about to arrest Demaenete after her non-existing lover has turned the corner. The exclamation is not only itself deceptive, but also draws the attention of the reader to the fact that Aristippus, without knowing, participates in a ruse for the second time. There is no sign that Aristippus finally learns the truth: he seems to remain in thrall to his delusion. Even those who are sure of having uncovered a deception may still be deceived. What, we are invited to ask, guarantees that the reader who is struggling to grasp what is going on in the main plot will gain full comprehension and, if she finally has the feeling of understanding the action, will not have been misled?

The figure of Thisbe intimates that the deception ruling in the novella can also affect the reader. In the Cnemon story, Thisbe's manipulation is transparent to the reader. Her sudden appearance in the main plot, though, surprises the reader as well as the characters. After the raid on the village of the buccaneers, Theagenes and Cnemon return to the cave where Thyamis had hidden Charicleia. When they find a female corpse, they automatically assume that Charicleia has been killed, but as it turns out, Charicleia is hidden further down in the cave and the corpse is...Thisbe. Charicleia wonders (2.8.3): 'How can someone suddenly be spirited away by a sort of theatrical special effect, out of the heart of Greece to the remotest parts of Egypt?' (πῶς ἦν εἰκός...τὴν ἐκ μέσης τῆς Ἑλλάδος ἐπ' ἐσχάτοις γῆς Αἰγύπτου καθάπερ ἐκ μηχανῆς ἀναπεμφθῆναι;). A critic notes: 'As if by magic, Thisbe emerges from the pre-history and unexpectedly turns out to be directly involved in the main action.'[28]

Thisbe's scheming power has wandered from the tertiary to the primary narrative, and while not literally deceiving the reader, she surprises her in a way that she did not do with her actions in the novella. In the novella the reader knows that Cnemon will face not an adulterer in the bedroom, but

[28] Futre Pinheiro 1998: 3157.

his father. In the main story, however, she does not know that the corpse in the cave is not Charicleia, but Thisbe. Familiar with the conventions of the novel, the reader may expect that the corpse is not Charicleia, but nothing leads her to suspect that it is Thisbe. The clear grasp of identities within the novella has given way to insecurity. Figuring in Cnemon's narration of a friend's report, Thisbe's intrigue is safely framed and distanced; the unexpected move of Thisbe to the primary narrative brings her destabilizing force closer to the reader. That she keeps some of her force even in death comes to the fore in Cnemon's words (2.11.2): 'Even dead I regard you with suspicion, and I am haunted by the fear that the story of Demaenete's death is untrue...' ('Ὡς κἀγώ σε καὶ κειμένην ἔχω δι' ὑποψίας καὶ σφόδρα δέδοικα μὴ καὶ πλάσμα ἐστὶν ἡ Δημαινέτης τελευτή...).

To conclude, the narration of Thisbe's intrigue is multi-faceted, showing Heliodorus' art at its best. The reconfiguration of the chase of the adulterer is intellectually and aesthetically appealing. Thisbe not only tricks her mistress, she also outperforms her with a scheme that, while modelled on Demaenete's, is far shrewder. Granted full access to the set-up, the reader can indulge in Thisbe's manipulations that fit together like the pieces of a jigsaw puzzle. At the same time, critical vocabulary and the presentation of Thisbe as author-like endow the episode with a significance that is disconcerting. The deception of the characters by Thisbe illustrates the danger to which the reader of the *Aethiopica* is exposed. While the Cnemon novella is fully transparent, the reader is struggling to comprehend what is going on in the main story line. The novella thus not only alerts us to the sophistication of the *Aethiopica*'s narrator but also highlights the hermeneutic challenges its reader is facing: *apatē* signifies both deceit and aesthetic illusion, and the latter may morph into the former when the plotting infects the plot.... The *Aethiopica* is a chameleonic novel that can be read in many ways and at different levels. The narration of Thisbe's intrigue is emblematic in that it furnishes a meta-narrative reflection as well as a gripping story. Its entwinement of the two qualities is particularly delicate: what grants the reader a superior view of the characters' misapprehensions simultaneously questions her control over the text.

5
Theagenes' Second Lament (2.4)

Stephen M. Trzaskoma

In comparison with many portions of the first two books of the *Aethiopica*, Theagenes' brief lament delivered at 2.4 is at first sight unremarkable (which is not to say that it has been neglected in modern scholarship).[1] Pre-modern readers, however, responded to this passage to a surprising degree, as I will demonstrate. I will also follow their lead to tease out patterns built upon the interplay the lament has with other portions of the novel, with the aim of uncovering some of its important structural and thematic functions. A study of the lament gives us insight into the construction of the narrative of Theagenes and Charicleia in the early books of the novel, especially with reference to the figure of Cnemon. As with almost any section of Heliodorus' remarkable narrative, close attention is rewarded, a point that has been demonstrated by this volume's *honorandus* repeatedly over his distinguished career.

The context: Book 2 opens with the brigands' island in flames. The bandit Thyamis has been captured by his brother's soldiers (1.33) but not before he has rushed to the island cave, where he had Charicleia stashed, and killed the woman he encounters in the dark (1.30–1). Theagenes and Cnemon go after Charicleia. They see the flames and Theagenes laments, assuming that the inferno has killed her (2.1). He attempts suicide but Cnemon stops him and tells him Charicleia is safe in the cave (2.2). They kindle torches, enter the cave, and stumble upon a woman's body, which Cnemon assumes is Charicleia's (2.3). He drops his torch, preventing certain identification of the body. He takes Theagenes' sword to forestall another suicide attempt and rushes outside to relight his torch. Theagenes then delivers a second lament:

---

[1] Notable treatments are Jones 2012: 126–8, who productively considers the lament and its aftermath in terms of the construction of masculinity in the novel; Winkler 2014, who pays close attention to it as part of a larger structure of almost cinematic suspense and revelation in the *Aethiopica*, and especially Paulsen 1992: 60–2, 134–5, who compares it with Cnemon's outburst in 6.7.3 and considers the passages' tragic (or paratragic) tones.

Stephen M. Trzaskoma, *Theagenes' Second Lament (2.4)* In: *Reading Heliodorus'* Aethiopica. Edited by: Ian Repath and Tim Whitmarsh, Oxford University Press. © Oxford University Press 2022.
DOI: 10.1093/oso/9780198792543.003.0005

1. κἂν τούτῳ τραγικόν τι καὶ γοερὸν ὁ Θεαγένης βρυχώμενος 'ὦ πάθους ἀτλήτου' φησὶν 'ὦ συμφορᾶς θεηλάτου. τίς οὕτως ἀκόρεστος Ἐρινὺς τοῖς ἡμετέροις κακοῖς ἐνεβάκχευσε φυγὴν τῆς ἐνεγκούσης ἐπιβαλοῦσα, κινδύνοις θαλασσῶν κινδύνοις πειρατηρίων ὑποβαλοῦσα, λῃσταῖς παραδοῦσα, πολλάκις τῶν ὄντων ἀλλοτριώσασα; 2. ἓν μόνον ἀντὶ πάντων ὑπελείπετο καὶ τοῦτο ἀνήρπασται· κεῖται Χαρίκλεια καὶ πολεμίας χειρὸς ἔργον ἡ φιλτάτη γεγένηται, δῆλον μὲν ὡς σωφροσύνης ἀντεχομένη καὶ ἐμοὶ δῆθεν ἑαυτὴν φυλάττουσα· κεῖται δ' οὖν ὅμως ἡ δυστυχής, οὐδὲν μὲν αὐτὴ τῆς ὥρας ἀποναμένη, εἰς οὐδὲν δὲ ὄφελος ἐμοὶ γενομένη. ἀλλ' ὦ γλυκεῖα, πρόσφθεγξαι τὰ τελευταῖα καὶ εἰωθότα· ἐπίσκηψον εἴ τι καὶ κατὰ μικρὸν ἐμπνεῖς. 3. οἴμοι, σιωπᾷς καὶ τὸ μαντικὸν ἐκεῖνο καὶ θεηγόρον στόμα σιγὴ κατέχει καὶ ζόφος τὴν πυρφόρον καὶ χάος τὴν ἐκ τῶν ἀνακτόρων κατείληφεν· ὀφθαλμοὶ δὲ ἀφεγγεῖς οἱ πάντας τῷ κάλλει καταστράψαντες, οὓς οὐκ εἶδεν ὁ φονεύσας, οἶδα ἀκριβῶς. ἀλλ' ὦ τί ἄν σέ τις ὀνομάσειε; νύμφην; ἀλλ' ἀνύμφευτος· γαμετήν; ἀλλ' ἀπείρατος. τίνα οὖν ἀνακαλέσω; τίνα προσφθέγξομαι λοιπόν; ἢ ἄρα τὸ πάντων ὀνομάτων ἥδιστον Χαρίκλειαν; 4. ὦ Χαρίκλεια, θάρσει· πιστὸν ἔχεις τὸν ἐρώμενον· ἀπολήψῃ με μικρὸν ὕστερον· ἰδοὺ γάρ σοι χοὰς ἐπάξω τὰς ἐμαυτοῦ σφαγὰς καὶ σπείσομαι τὸ σοὶ φίλον αἷμα τοὐμόν· ἕξει δὲ ἡμᾶς αὐτοσχέδιον μνῆμα τόδε τὸ σπήλαιον. ἔξεσται πάντως ἀλλήλοις συνεῖναι μετὰ γοῦν θάνατον εἰ καὶ ζῶσιν ὁ δαίμων οὐκ ἐπέτρεψε.'

While Cnemon was doing that, Theagenes gave a tragic, mournful wail: 'Unbearable calamity! Divinely sent catastrophe! What Fury is insatiable enough to revel in our troubles after inflicting upon us exile from our native land, after subjecting us to dangers at sea, dangers among pirates, after delivering us to bandits, after time and again cutting us off from what we had? In place of it all only a single thing remained, and that has now been snatched away. Charicleia lies dead. The one I love most has ended up the victim of an enemy's hand. It's clear she was clinging to her chastity and must have been saving herself for me! All the same, the unfortunate girl lies dead as a result. She derived no joy from her beauty and, in the end, gave me none either. Sweetheart, speak to me for the last time in that way of yours. Tell me what to do if you have left even a bit of breath. Alas! You are quiet! Silence grips that prophetic and divinely inspired mouth. Gloom shrouds the one who carried the sacred fire, and abysmal darkness holds the one who emerged from the god's shrine. Dark are the eyes that dazzled everyone with their beauty. The man who murdered you didn't see them, that I know for certain. But, oh, what's the right thing to call you? Bride? But you had no groom. Wife? But you never married. So what will I call you? How will I refer to you now? By the sweetest of all names—Charicleia? Charicleia! Have no fear! Your beloved remains faithfully yours. In a little while you'll have me back. Look! I'm going to use my own slashed throat to make an offering. As a libation I'll pour out my blood, which is dear to you. This cave will hold us as an improvised tomb. I'm certain we'll be able to be together after death, even if divine will did not allow it while we lived'.[2] (2.4)

This brief paragraph is surrounded by some of the most memorable parts of the novel: on the one side, the cinematic opening of the novel, the first part of Cnemon's story, and the action-packed events that fill out the remainder of Book 1, and, on the other side, the continuation of the story of Cnemon, the interlude with Thermouthis and, not least, the introduction of Calasiris and his narrative. The immediate aftermath of the lament has drawn more interest than the lament itself, because the mistaken belief that the body is Charicleia's and the revelation that it is actually that of Thisbe, a woman from Cnemon's past, are important in that they provide the narrative hinge between what precedes and what follows.[3] More importantly, the intertwined identities and fates of Thisbe and Charicleia have been a crucial tool in many interpretive assays since at least the medieval period.[4] For the moment, I want to consider the lament in isolation and trace its reception.

5.1. Theagenes' Lament and the Reception of Heliodorus

Late antique and Byzantine readers found Theagenes' lament intensely interesting, to judge by their imitations of it.[5] It is convenient to start with the twelfth-century Philagathos of Cerami, since I have already mentioned him under his alias 'Philip the Philosopher'. Philagathos' authorship of the interpretive essay on Heliodorus has been firmly established by recent

---

[2] This translation and most others are my own. I sometimes refer to or use Morgan 1989c.
[3] Montiglio 2013a: 107–10.
[4] Already in Philip the Philosopher's *Hermeneuma* (this portion of the text at Bianchi 2006: 53, lines 92–6 and Colonna 1938: 368 lines 67–70). 'Philip' is the twelfth-century cleric Philagathos of Cerami discussed just below.
[5] Gärtner 1969 remains the classic study of Heliodorus' reception in Byzantium, but a large amount of evidence has been subsequently uncovered. Agapitos 1998 and Roilos 2005: 40–50 are valuable and more recent studies that treat rhetorical and aesthetic aspects.

work,[6] but that text is not our concern here. What is significant is that in discussing it scholars have demonstrated knowledge of the *Aethiopica* in other works of Philagathos.[7] Colonna initiated this inquiry with the thought that Heliodorus' novel inspired a passage in Philagathos' sixth *Homily* (6.8–9),[8] a sermon that treats the story of the widow's son raised from the dead by Jesus (Luke 7:11–17).[9] Colonna did not adduce any evidence for this connection but more recent investigators have found corroboration for his claim of intertextuality with Heliodorus in other homilies,[10] and quite recently Corcella and Duluş discovered an imitation close to Colonna's initial guess.[11] Additional examples have been uncovered in this homily, revealing a deep engagement with Heliodorus.[12] Our lament comes into play because Philagathos closely imitates a sentence from 2.4 in *Hom.* 6.12.8–10, the

---

[6] The identification, first made by Colonna 1938, has been challenged, most notably by Tarán 1992, but is widely upheld: see, among others, Gärtner 1969: 60–4 and, most definitively, Cupane 1978 and Bianchi 2006: 27–47. Cf. also Bianchi 2011a: 32 with n. 13.

[7] For Philagathos' considerable knowledge of earlier Greek literature, see Corcella 2011 and Torre 2011. Cf. Duluş 2011: 59 n. 41 for bibliography and 61: 'His use of classical sources is not simply ornamental but…accomplish[es] surprisingly consistent superposition of narrative and existential contexts'.

[8] Colonna 1960: 27: 'significativa mi sembra, ad esempio, la scena tratteggiata nell'*Omilia* VI, col. 225, che ricorda molto da vicino, per le espressioni e per il colorito stilistico, il quadro di eccidio sanguinoso, con cui si apre il romanzo delle *Etiopiche*'.

[9] Philagathos imitates at least one other piece of novelistic prose in this homily, namely ps.-Nilus' *Narrationes* (composed between the fifth and ninth centuries). For this work's novelistic connections, see Conca 1983, Caner 2010, and, with a more literary focus, Morgan 2015. In *Hom.* 6.8.12–13 (ἐνατενίζουσα τῷ παιδὶ ἀσκαρδαμύκτῳ καὶ κεχηνότι τῷ βλέμματι—'looking only at her son with eyes unblinking and wide open') Philagathos imitates *Narr.* 6.1 (ἀλλ' ἀτενῶς ἔβλεπον πρὸς αὐτὸν ἀσκαρδαμυκτῶν κεχηνότι τῷ βλέμματι—'but I stared at him unblinkingly, with eyes wide open'). Caner 2010: 117 n. 163 feels the passage in the *Narrationes* owes something to Achilles Tatius 3.15.5, making for an interesting chain of influence in the history of Greek prose. Also, compare Philagathos, *Hom.* 31.23.2 (ὧν γὰρ ἡ ὅρασις τοὺς χαρακτῆρας ταῖς μνήμαις οὐ παραδέδωκε, τούτων αἱ μορφαὶ πάντάπασιν ἀνεπίγνωστοι— 'because viewing them does not pass their characteristics into our memories, their appearances are not at all known distinctly') with *Narr.* 1.8 (ὧν γὰρ ἡ ὅρασις τοὺς χαρακτῆρας τῇ μνήμῃ οὐ παρέδωκε, τούτων αἱ μορφαὶ ἄστατοι καὶ ἀόριστοι—'because viewing them does not pass their characteristics into one's memory, their shapes are unstable and unclear').

[10] See Zaccagni 1998 for connections between *Hom.* 37 and the novel. See Bianchi 2006: 35–7 for a clear imitation in *Hom.* 79 Scorso of 9.22.6. Bianchi 2011a: 33–5 sums up identified borrowings of the *Aethiopica* in the *Homilies* and discusses other possible echoes.

[11] Corcella 2010: 29 and Duluş 2011: 60–2 note the dependence of the simile in *Hom.* 6.9.9–11 (Philagathos comparing the widow with a bird whose chicks have been eaten by a snake) on Heliodorus 2.22.4 (Calasiris making the same comparison about himself).

[12] Cf. Lavagnini's 1974: 6 prediction regarding the potential of a close study of the *Homilies* for Heliodorean influence. Further study is required. Cf. Bianchi 2006: 41 n. 109 on the shortcomings of the edition of Rossi Taibbi 1969 in this regard.

mother's lament over her son: σιωπᾷς καὶ τὸ γλυκὺ στόμα κατέσχε σιγῇ καὶ ζόφος περικέχυται ταῖς λαμπάσι τῶν ὀφθαλμῶν.[13]

This citation is preceded by other imitations of the *Aethiopica*,[14] and, strikingly, Philagathos concludes the widow's lament with the verb ἐπετραγῴδει (6.12.14 'she was lamenting tragically'), the very word that Heliodorus uses for Charicleia's outburst in 1.3.2. Theagenes' second lament is also marked as 'tragic' (2.4.1 τραγικόν). We can note that Philagathos' imitations come from some of the most memorable passages of the novel, especially from Books 1 and 2, and usually (though not always) from emotionally charged episodes and utterances such as laments. In other words, Theagenes' speech in 2.4 was for Philagathos a purple passage and one worthy of emulation in combination with other such passages when he was constructing his own atmosphere of lamentation.

In another part of the Mediterranean, and perhaps contemporaneously with Philagathos' activity in Southern Italy and Sicily, one of the writers in the *Digenes Akrites* tradition also read this same lament of Theagenes and was similarly moved to imitate it. This author places the fictional lover's words, only slightly altered, into his hero's mouth as he mourns the passing of his father (Grottaferrata 7.126): οἴμοι, σιγᾷ τὸ μαντικὸν ἐκεῖνο καὶ θεηγόρον στόμα.[15] The words of a fictional lover could instantiate grief for these two very different Byzantine imitators so purely that the form of expression could be transferred to a homily or an epic, to the mouth of a mother or a son, all without apparent concern for the changed contexts and relationships. Of course, the twelfth century is the time of the so-called revival of the Greek romance, and perhaps we would expect to find imitations in this period. However, the *Digenes* poet and Philagathos were not the first to find inspiration in this scene or to effect such a transference of

---

[13] 'You are quiet and silence holds your sweet mouth and gloom pours around the lights of your eyes'. Compare in our passage σιωπᾷς—ἀφεγγεῖς (2.4.3). This is noted by Corcella 2010: 29.

[14] Corcella 2010: 29 rightly connects *Hom.* 6.12.4–5 with Heliodorus 7.7.5. It seems to me that *Hom.* 6.12.8 (οἴκτειρον μητρὸς πολιάν—'pity a mother's grey hair') reflects Heliodorus 1.12.3 (οἴκτειρον τὸν γεννήσαντα, φεῖσαι πολιῶν—'pity your father; spare his grey hairs'). Also, compare the general resemblance of Charicleia's treatment of the wounded Theagenes with the widow's reaction to regaining her son (*Hom.* 6.16), including at least one verbal echo in ἠπίστει κατέχουσα (6.16.12, 'unable to believe that she was holding him'; cf. the same phrase in Heliodorus 1.2.6).

[15] 'Alas! That prophetic and divinely inspired mouth is silent!' Heliodorus' influence on *Digenes* is known, but this instance does not appear to have been noticed. For the list of passages supposedly dependent on Heliodorus, see Mavrogordato (1956) 265, where he does list an obvious imitation in the Grottaferrata (3.284) of a passage in Heliodorus (2.6.4) very close to Theagenes' lament. On Heliodorus and *Digenes*, see Jeffreys 1998: xlvi–xlvii.

language and thought to a new object of lamentation. Already in the mid-eleventh century, Michael Psellos, a known admirer of the *Aethiopica*,[16] had recalled this very lament.

In Psellos' early poem on the death of Maria Skleraina, the mistress of Konstantinos IX Monomachos, the narrator laments over the dead woman (*In Mariam Sclerenam* 131-2): τὸ μουσικὸν δὲ καὶ θεηγόρον στόμα | σιγῇ κατέσχεν.[17] This echoes the sentence of Theagenes' lament that would later reappear in both the Grottaferrata *Digenes* and Philagathos' *Homily* 6.[18] This specific case also confirms and illuminates another allusion to the same passage in one of Psellos' later works; for we can now reject decisively Criscuolo's identification of the phrase θεηγόρον στόμα (*Encomium* 1526) in the funeral oration he wrote for his mother about a decade later[19] as an imitation of John of Damascus (*Trans.* 6, θεηγόρῳ στόματι). Heliodorus is the source for Psellos (and, for that matter, for the Damascene, as well),[20] as is perhaps more obvious when we look at the content and form of the entire sentence (*Encomium* 1525-6): κέκλεισται δέ σου τὸ θεηγόρον στόμα καὶ σεσίγηκέ σοι ἡ θεοφόρητος γλῶσσα ('Your divinely inspired mouth has been closed and your God-inspired tongue has fallen silent').

To stay with the *Encomium*, the Heliodorean colouring is actually considerably more extensive than a single citation, and that influence is connected intimately with the wider scene of lamentation in the hypotext.[21] In other words, it is not just that the Byzantine writer imitates the *Aethiopica* by putting into his own mouth a few words uttered by Theagenes. We have additional

---

[16] For Psellos' essay on Heliodorus and Achilles Tatius, in which he favours the *Aethiopica* over *Leucippe and Clitophon*, see the text and translation in Dyck 1986.

[17] 'Silence has gripped her musical and divinely inspired mouth'. Agapitos 2008: 562-3 suggests a date very close to Skleraina's death in 1045.

[18] The twelfth-century writers could have got their Heliodorus indirectly (from intermediaries like Psellos or florilegia), but the exact nature and variety of the various imitations makes that unlikely in these particular cases.

[19] Or perhaps later. See Walker 2004: 64-8 on the date of the *Encomium*.

[20] John of Damascus echoes Heliodorus elsewhere in the saints' prayer to Mary in his *Second Homily on the Dormition of Mary* 8.26: σοὶ καὶ ζώσῃ συζῆν καὶ θνῃσκούσῃ συνθνῄσκειν μακάριον ('It is a blessing to live with you while you live and die with you when you die')— behind which lies Heliodorus 10.19.2 'ὅτι' ἔφη 'ἐμοὶ καὶ ζῶντι συζῆν καὶ θνῄσκοντι συντεθνάναι τῷ ἀνδρὶ τῷδε πρὸς τοῦ δαιμονίου καθείμαρται' ('Because', she replied, 'it is fated by divine will for me to live with this man while he lives and die with him when he dies').

[21] In addition to the examples given in the notes below, Criscuolo finds Heliodorus' influence on Psellos in the *Encomium* at 936 and 940 (from 1.12.3, clearly an imitation) and at 594-5 (from 1.21.1, which would be too slight a resemblance to be certain of on its own). Additionally, πλάνητα... βίον (1192 'life of wandering'), which occurs in Psellos' lament for his father, is more likely to come from Heliodorus (cf. 5.6.2 and 7.12.2) than from Plut. *Brutus* 33.6, as Criscuolo suggests.

verbal echoes, but the imitation occurs also on the level of episodes and scenes. Psellos is supposedly recording at this point his own lament for his mother after arriving too late to see her final moments, just as Theagenes believes he has got to the cave too late to find Charicleia alive. Both Theagenes and Psellos also want last words from the deceased (cf. *Encomium* 1523–4). The resemblance extends further to the following paragraphs of the novel, as can be seen quite clearly in the description of Psellos' emotional collapse and his subsequent revival. Here is the moment in the *Aethiopica* after Theagenes' second lament when he realizes that Charicleia is alive and the lovers are reunited:

3... τέλος εἰς τοὔδαφος ἀθρόον καταφέρονται καὶ εἴχοντο ἀλλήλων ἄναυδοι μὲν ἀλλ' ὥσπερ ἡνωμένοι καὶ μικροῦ ἔδει ἀποθνῄσκειν αὐτούς. **4**. Οὕτως ἄρα καὶ τὸ χαρᾶς ὑπερβάλλον εἰς ἀλγεινὸν περιέστη πολλάκις καὶ τῆς ἡδονῆς τὸ ἄμετρον ἐπίσπαστον λύπην ἐγέννησεν. Ὡς δὴ κἀκεῖνοι παρ' ἐλπίδα σωθέντες ἐκινδύνευον, ἕως ὁ Κνήμων πίδακά τινα διαμώμενος καὶ τὴν συρρυεῖσαν κατὰ βραχὺ νοτίδα κοίλαις ταῖς χερσὶν ὑδρευσάμενος τὸ πρόσωπόν τε αὐτῶν ἐπέρραινε καὶ αἰθάλῃ[22] τῶν ῥινῶν ἐπαφώμενος ἐπὶ τὸ φρονεῖν ἐπανήγαγεν.

αἰθάλῃ scripsi : θαμά codd.

...they finally collapsed together to the ground. Wordlessly, but virtually uniting into a single person, they clung to each other and very nearly died. So it is both that the surfeit of joy often gives rise to pain and the immensity of pleasure, feeding on itself, becomes grief. They were thus in danger after having been saved beyond any expectation, until Cnemon scraped out a sort of seep hole. Gathering the water that slowly trickled in with his cupped hands, he sprinkled their faces with it and, daubing some soot to their nostrils, brought them back to consciousness. (2.6.3–4)

By contrast with the lovers, Psellos' mother truly has departed this life, and her son weaves together both Theagenes' lament, as we have seen, and this reaction of the lovers to their reunion. More broadly, Psellos nicely picks up on Heliodorus' exploration of the fine line between joy and grief, a synthesis

---

[22] Using a substance with a strong odour is a traditional method of revival (see below for perfume being used in a derivative scene in Psellos), and while soot is not normally that substance, it is the only thing available. θαμά would be a scribal correction for θαλη once the αι- fell out after καί, a natural enough guess (cf. θαμά in 1.28.2, 2.20.4, 2.25.2, 3.3.4, and 7.9.1), since the change makes the sentence intelligible with minimal intervention. αἰθάλη is used by Heliodorus at 10.24.2.

that he plays with in the larger context of his grief over his mother's bodily death intertwined with his joy at the eternal life she now enjoys. For our present purposes, however, we can concentrate closely on Psellos' swoon over her corpse, which is obviously and thoroughly modelled on Heliodorus' scene and has as its central conceit the same near-death experience and revival (1499-1506):

ἐπ' αὐτοῦ τοῦ ἱεροῦ καὶ θείου σώματος καὶ ζῶντος ὡς ἀληθῶς[23]—'ἀψευδὴς γὰρ ὁ εἰπών'[24]—καταπεσὼν ἐκείμην νεκρός, οὐδὲν ὧν ἐπεποιήκειν ἢ ἐπεπόνθειν εἰδώς, ἕως με οἱ παρόντες οἰκτείραντες καὶ διειληφότες, εἶτα δὴ διαναστήσαντες καὶ ψυχρῷ ὕδατι καταρράναντες, εἶτα δὴ καὶ δακτύλοις εὐωδιάζουσι τῶν ῥινῶν ἐπαφώμενοι,[25] συνήγαγόν τέ μοι τὸν νοῦν καὶ τὰς δυνάμεις ἀνεκαλέσαντο.

Collapsing right onto her body, sacred, divine and living in truth—'For the one who said it is without falsehood!'—I lay there a corpse, aware of nothing that I did or suffered, until those around me took pity and supported me in their arms, and then roused me and sprinkled me with cold water, and then also daubed perfumed fingers on my nostrils, and restored my mind to me and summoned my faculties back to life.

Suggestive coincidences abound throughout the surrounding scene in Psellos, which has a wider resonance with novelistic narrative and romance characters' laments, particularly Theagenes'. To limit ourselves to the language of *Aethiopica* 2.4, we can note that while it is the beauty of Charicleia's *eyes* that were dazzling (2.4.3 τῷ κάλλει καταστράψαντες [sc. ὀφθαλμοί]), it is the light of Theodote's *virtues* that dazzled Psellos (1519 τῷ τῶν σῶν ἀρετῶν φωτὶ καταστράψασα).[26] In each case the light of an exemplary woman is now imagined as having been extinguished by death.

---

[23] For the phrase, cf. Heliodorus 1.2.4.

[24] We can see from this quote of Basil (*Ep.* 236.2.15) how Heliodorus' influence is combined in Psellos closely and seamlessly with that of other authors.

[25] Rather than with Heliodorus 2.6.4, Criscuolo connects this with Hipp. *Mul. Morb.* 2.118 (= Littré 8.254.7) ἐπαφώμενος τῷ δακτύλῳ—touching lightly with the finger. The splashing with cold water from Heliodorus may also be behind a scene in *Digenes Akrites* (Grottaferrata 3.277-87 and Escorial 583-4). See Jeffreys 1998: xlvi-xlvii.

[26] Criscuolo connects this instead with Acts 9:3 (περιήστραψε φῶς, of Paul on the road to Damascus) but elsewhere he does identify κάλλει κατήστραψεν (*Encomium* 605-6, in this case the beauty of Theodote's words) as deriving from Heliodorus' τῷ κάλλει καταστράψασα (1.21.3, Charicleia's effect on Thyamis). The collocation of dazzling (καταστράπτω) and beauty (κάλλος) is a favourite of Heliodorus. All in all, he uses it four times (again in 10.9.3 of Charicleia and in 7.10.3 of Theagenes). It occurs in no Greek literature before the *Aethiopica*.

60 THEAGENES' SECOND LAMENT (2.4)

All of this seems to represent a particular interest on the part of Psellos specifically in lamentation in Heliodorus and on using what he found to enrich his own representations of lament.[27] It is worth noting that many of the imitations of Heliodorus in the *Encomium* fall into two broad groups: (1) imitations of Book 1 and particularly 1.12.3, a passage related to Cnemon's father, localized in the narrative about the death of Psellos' father and the lament it occasions (*Encomium* 1142-1202); (2) imitations of the present passage and its surrounding context (2.4-6), which are localized in the narrative about the death of Psellos' mother and his lament over her (*Encomium* 1493-1558). To conclude this section, then, I will give a couple of examples of the former category: first, Psellos cites Cnemon's words from 1.12.3 about the Athenian youth's reaction to his father's pleas (ἐγὼ δέ, ὥσπερ τυφῶνι βληθείς, αὖος ἀπόπληκτος εἰστήκειν—'and I, as if struck by a whirlwind, stood trembling, incapacitated') to characterize his reaction to his own father's imminent death (*Encomium* 1156 αὖος οὖν καὶ ἀπόπληκτος εἰστήκειν—'so I stood, trembling and incapacitated');[28] second, he uses language describing Theagenes when, though gravely wounded, he draws breath to speak his first words in the novel (1.2.4 πνεῦμα συλλεξάμενος καὶ βύθιόν τι ἀσθμήνας—'gathering his breath and sighing deeply'), just a little later when he is about to begin his lament for his father (*Encomium* 1170-1 συλλέξας καὶ βύθιόν τι ἀσθμήνας).[29]

---

[27] Cf. *Charicleia and Leukippe* 40-1, where he comments specifically on the nature and style of laments delivered by Charicleia. For a brief discussion, see Agapitos 1998: 136-7.

[28] This is noted by Criscuolo in his *apparatus fontium* and marked with quotation marks. The word εἰστήκειν, however, ought also to be printed as part of the quotation. Psellos imitates the same sentence differently in a later work (*Chron.* 5.40): ὥσπερ δὲ τυφῶνι βληθεὶς αὖος εἰστήκειν καὶ ἀχανής ('I stood trembling and speechless as if struck by a whirlwind', with which cf. *Chron.* 7.17). This more complete echo allows us to be certain that Psellos is thinking of Heliodorus rather than Achilles Tatius' description of Clinias' reaction to Charicles' death in 1.12.2 (ὥσπερ τυφῶνι βεβλημένος τῷ λόγῳ—'struck by the message as if by a whirlwind'). By contrast, Theodoros Prodromos, *R&D* 7.259 (βεβλημένη γὰρ ὡς τυφῶνι τῷ λόγῳ—'struck by the message as if by a whirlwind') is clearly dependent on Achilles Tatius. I would not place a bet as to whether Heliodorus or Psellos is the proximate source of Anna Komnene's αὖος ἐφ' ἱκανὸν εἱστήκει ὥσπερ ὑπὸ κεραυνοῦ βληθείς (*Alex.* 6.5.1 'He stood trembling for a while, as if struck by a thunderbolt'), but her citation of Heliodorus' opening sentence (1.1.1) at *Alex.* 1.9.1 and 8.5.4 should make us unwilling to discount the possibility that her knowledge comes directly from one of the novels widely read at the time in the imperial court. As a matter of curiosity, it may be worth mentioning that the unknown author of the ps.-Libanian *Declamation* 40, although we cannot date him with any precision (see Foerster 1913: 317-19), seems to be the earliest writer to have picked up on Heliodorus' phrase (*Dec.* 40.2.20 ἀλλ' εἰστήκειν αὖος ὅλος, ἀπόπληκτος).

[29] This instance is not noted by Criscuolo, but he does believe the similar βαρύ τι στενάξασα (*Encomium* 1362-3) derives from Heliodorus 2.14.5 βαθύ τι καὶ βύθιον στενάξας. It is perhaps worth noting in passing that ps.-Nilus earlier took similar phrasing also from Heliodorus (cf. *Narr.* 7.1.1 στενάξας βύθιον καὶ βαρύ).

5.2. Theagenes' Second Lament in Context

These Byzantine readers are reacting to the lament in 2.4 qua lament, that is, they are responding to the emotional content and the circumstances in which the speech is delivered. They are interested, too, in finding stylistic inspiration, particularly but not always where rhetoric and emotion are complementary.[30] There are many ways to explore this further, but in the space remaining to me I would like to take up one aspect of Psellos' reception of the lament and focus our attention back on Heliodorus. My subject is the layering of lamentation and, more generally, the layering of narrative. As we have seen, Psellos incorporates into his *Encomium* two laments quite close to each other, one for his father and one for his mother, and he seems to have two distinct portions of Heliodorus in mind during each, Book 1 (father) and the start of Book 2 (mother), each full of expressions of strong emotion.

In fact, such repetition of lament is typical for most Greek novels, and so passages of lamentation are regularly taken as concentrations of generic markers[31] and sites of intra- and intertextuality.[32] But Psellos found in portions of Heliodorus a more dense matrix of lamentation than in other potential ancient models.[33] And *typicality* is exploited by Heliodorus in untypical ways. We are apt, if we are looking for Heliodorus' distinctiveness, to pass over the lament in 2.4 too quickly as simply an expected feature of the genre with stereotyped language and content: a catalogue of woes, lament for the loss of the beloved, the themes of death and marriage, threatened

---

[30] One final observation about the influence of the language of 2.4. While the idiom ἔργον γίγνομαι with a genitive in the sense 'become a victim of' is attested a few times before Heliodorus (LSJ s.v. ἔργον IV.3), our author uses it several times in the *Aethiopica*, including at 1.1.5 and 6.13.5. In 2.4, however, we have the earliest recorded instance of a very distinctive form of the expression, namely, πολεμίας χειρὸς ἔργον... γεγένηται (2.4.2 'she has ended up the victim of an enemy's hand'). This afterwards appears in Choricius (*Op*. 42.2.101 ἂν... γένωμαι πολεμίας ἔργον χειρός 'if I might end up the victim of an enemy's hand'), Psellos (*Theologica* 25 τῆς πολεμίας χειρὸς ἔργον γενήσονται 'they will end up the victim of an enemy's hand') and no fewer than three times in Anna Komnene's *Alexiad* (1.5.9, 1.13.9, and 14.6.4).

[31] See Birchall 1996a generally (esp. 14–16); for Heliodorus, Fusillo 1989: 33–42; Webb 2007: 529–31; Whitmarsh 2011: 224–6.

[32] Regarding Heliodorus' laments, see Paulsen 1992: 56–66 for their tragic intertextuality. Note in particular his judgement on their typicality (62): 'Seine Monologe werden durch die traditionellen Inhalte in traditioneller Form anläßlich einer typischen Situation gekennzeichnet'. Paulsen, however, does not at all mean by this that Heliodorus' monologues lack interest or distinctiveness.

[33] Roilos 2005: 79–112 discusses lamentation in the Byzantine romances but not without relevance to a consideration of the ways in which laments in ancient novels were read in Byzantium more generally.

suicide, and a concern with burial. But Psellos and others did not pass over the second lament; they lingered on it.

This lament does not exist as a free-standing or self-contained section of Heliodorus' narrative.[34] Rather, it achieves its prominence not just by its individual virtues but by being worked into a larger structure of lamentation that patterns the first and second books. That structure, in turn, is itself part of the larger edifice of the intricately mingled narratives of the protagonists and Cnemon. The young Athenian's role in responding to this lament reflects the complexity—and unfolding uncertainty—of his function in the wider whole. He does not witness the second lament, but he is both its cause and its eventual solution by misidentifying the body as Charicleia's and then identifying it correctly as Thisbe's. Even in his absence his influence is felt; for his surreptitious theft of Theagenes' sword (2.3.4) prevents the hero from carrying out his suicide until Cnemon can return to prove to him in person why it would be a mistake. What is *a*typical of all this is that much of this has happened before, and only a page or so earlier (2.1.2–3), when Theagenes laments Charicleia, Cnemon knocks his sword out of his hand and then gives him reasons for why his lamentation is performed mistakenly and he should not commit suicide. In other words, Cnemon need not be present for the second lament because he has already heard it.

In an important paper, John Morgan has drawn attention to doublets and repetition in Heliodorus, a prominent but still incompletely analysed narrative feature.[35] He notes that repetitions 'generate comparisons, contemplation of which leads the reader, in some cases at least, through back-ways to the moral and ethical issues with which the novel concerns itself'.[36] Theagenes' lament in 2.4 is just such a doublet and is consciously framed as one.[37] 'Typicality' denotes a generalized idea, i.e. that this is just the sort of thing that novelistic heroes do. But the doubling of lamentation by the same character over the same not-really-dead woman in such a brief compass of narrative amounts to a manoeuvre by which it becomes *overly* typical and thereby more marked.[38] No other novelist attempts anything like this. The

---

[34] For brief remarks on how Heliodorus, unlike the other novelists, uses laments 'to advance the plot', see Birchall 1996a: 14–16.
[35] Morgan 1998.   [36] Morgan 1998 78.
[37] For the *Doublettencharakter* of the two laments, see the remarks of Paulsen 1992: 60, who sees the variation in content between them as a sign that Heliodorus is trying to tone down the sense of repetition.
[38] On the other hand, modern readers frequently tend to collapse them into a single lament or skip over one when discussing this portion of the novel casually. Webb 2007: 530 remarks that 'the apparent death of Charicleia prompts Theagenes to pronounce *a lament* at the beginning

multiple laments by Clitophon over the not-really-dead Leucippe in Achilles Tatius are spaced out and set the tempo of narrative quite differently, although this is precisely the model that Heliodorus is invoking (multiple laments for multiple *Scheintode*) and playing with. Heliodorus' doubling, however, is doubly—triply, quadruply, and more—marked.

By this I mean that it is not just that Theagenes laments twice or that Charicleia 'dies' twice or that Cnemon prevents Theagenes' suicide by sword twice. Both 'deaths' occasion laments that contain indictments of supernatural powers (the options are doubled: an unspecified daemon in 2.1.3 and a Fury in 2.4.1), wedding imagery and regret for the lack or loss of physical intimacy. Both times, Cnemon assures Theagenes that Charicleia is alive on the basis of his knowledge of how she came to be in the cave. Both times Theagenes disbelieves him. Throughout the two passages attention is drawn by the characters themselves to this multiplication. Theagenes upbraids Cnemon twice, the second time saying: 'And you have done Charicleia *too* an additional wrong, having deprived her *now a second time* of the companionship she most craves' (2.5.1 προσηδίκησας δὲ καὶ Χαρίκλειαν τῆς ἡδίστης αὐτὴν κοινωνίας ἤδη δεύτερον ἀποστερήσας). Theagenes, after his second lament, when he hears the voice of Charicleia call his name (for the second time), offers two reasons why her spirit might haunt the earth:[39] 'It is quite obvious that you are still wandering the earth, unable to bear it because of the separation from that wonderful body you were driven out of by violence, or perhaps shut out by the phantoms of the underworld because of your unburied state' (2.5.2 εὔδηλος εἶ περὶ γῆν ἔτι φερομένη, τὸ μὲν διὰ τὸ[40] τοιούτου σώματος οὗ πρὸς βίαν ἐξηλάθης ἀποστατεῖν οὐ φέρουσα, τὸ δὲ διὰ

---

of the *Aethiopica*'. Cf. the summary of the novel in Morgan 2003: 428, where the first lament is omitted: 'Book 2: Next Cnemon takes Theagenes to the cave, only to stumble over a corpse. As Theagenes laments...'. Konstan 1994: 21–2 notes the repeated suicide attempt but not the double lament.

[39] On the so-called 'amphibolies' in Heliodorus, see Winkler 1982: 121–9. His list of instances is, as Hilton 2012: 205 notes, incomplete and it omits this example, which somewhat complicates Winkler's categories because the first explanation is not straightforwardly naturalistic. Contrast Morgan 1982: 229–32 and note, in particular, his salutary emphasis at 232 on distinguishing between alternate explanations provided by the omniscient narrator and his characters.

[40] 2.5.2 τὸ μὲν διὰ τὸ scripsi: τὸ μὲν διότι (vel ὅτι) codd.: secl. Koraes. The two versions of the paradosis are garbled (*neutrum tolerabile* is the judgement of Rattenbury and Lumb) but the sense is obvious. My minor change presumes that the infinitive ἀποστατεῖν is not the object of οὐ φέρουσα but the participle is modified by a prepositional phrase syntactically parallel to that in the δέ clause (for the late and admittedly rare usage of φέρω with διά see LSJ s.v. φέρω III.2). The sort of parallelism I am restoring here is common in later Greek, e.g., John Chrys. *Ad Stag.* MPG 47.442, τὸ μὲν διὰ τὸ θνητοὺς εἶναι, τὸ δὲ διὰ τὸ ταχέως εἰς ἀπόνοιαν αἵρεσθαι.

τὸ ἄταφον ἴσως ὑπὸ νερτερίων εἰδώλων εἰργομένη).[41] Even the setting reveals the same echo-chamber effect: there are two swords in the cave; torches have to be lit twice; Cnemon enters the cave twice. And beyond the laments, the effect lingers: when Cnemon revives the lovers, it is the second such revival; for Theagenes has already earlier revived Cnemon (2.6.1). And, on a more important level, there are two Charicleias in the cave, the real one and Thisbe, and Cnemon makes two identifications of the corpse and has two different reactions. Equally significantly, there are two *stories* in the cave, one belonging to Theagenes and Charicleia and the other to Cnemon, and it is here that the two stories become tied inexorably together into one, through the unexpected presence of the unfortunate Thisbe.

This crossover in story extends and responds to an extended pattern that ties this doubled scene to portions of Book 1. My contention is that the speech at 2.4 is meant not only to draw increased attention to itself through the oddity of the rapid repetition of content but to make us retrospectively cast our thoughts both back over the previous lament and to Charicleia's emotional speeches in the first book.[42] This is the effect, anyway, that it seems to have had on Psellos. In this light, Theagenes' second lament is part of a distinct armature around which the story is being shaped, the function of which at least to some degree is to achieve strong mechanical connections between the main narrative and Cnemon's. Through sophisticated play with romance tropes, episodes, and characters from other novels, it also allows Heliodorus to create resonances in his readers as he presents them with the radically different mechanisms that he uses in the construction of the narrative of the *Aethiopica*, as Jack Winkler and John Morgan in

---

[41] Itself a variation on 1.2.4, when Theagenes comes out of his first near-death experience and offers alternate explanations for Charicleia's presence. Additional repetition between these scenes: Theagenes' question to Charicleia in 1.2.4 (σώζῃ μοι ὡς ἀληθῶς;—'are you really alive?') is repeated as a positive statement in 2.6.3 (ζῇς μοι, Χαρίκλεια—'you are alive, my Charicleia') and, for that matter, will be repeated again later about Thisbe/Chariklea in 5.3.3 (ζῇ γὰρ ὡς ἀληθῶς—'she is truly alive'); Charicleia threatens suicide with a sword if Theagenes dies (matching Theagenes' later attempts at suicide by sword when he believes she is dead); Charicleia throws herself across Theagenes' body and weeps (1.2.6, matching Theagenes throwing himself across the body of Thisbe). I will outline some additional repetitions linking the events of Book 1 and the first part of Book 2 below.

[42] Such connections and repetitions are propagated prospectively into later portions of the novel, but more space would be required to explore this. I will mention here only the well-known moment in Book 5 where Cnemon is again the audience for a supposedly private lament, this time one by Charicleia, but he mistakes her voice and identity as Thisbe's; this forms a complex with the laments and events of 2.1–7, most notably in repeating the interchanged identities of the two women and in the emphasis on Cnemon's inability to recognize Charicleia's voice as he does in 2.5.3. For this see, most recently, Montiglio 2013a: 110–12.

their different ways have definitively and influentially shown. By modulating these resonances, Heliodorus can play with adherence and divergence, conformity and diversity—in effect training readers of fiction to read his particular fiction by recalibrating their expectations against generic norms. There is obviously too much to be said about all of this here, so I would like to stay within the confines of Heliodorus' narrative and consider intratextual rather than intertextual readings.

The very first articulated lament in the *Aethiopica* belongs not to Theagenes but to Charicleia (1.8.2-3). Ken Dowden has, in discussing the religiosity of Heliodorus, connected this lament loosely with part of the beginning of Book 2.[43] Here I have nothing much to contribute to the subject of religious belief, but it seems quite right to me that these parts of the novel are meant to be read together. As Dowden notes, in the case of Charicleia's lament, which consists of an accusatory catalogue of woes directed at the god Apollo—peppered with the threat of suicide and a pledge of allegiance to chastity—Theagenes tells her to stop, and she does, and he cautions her to 'beseech, not reproach' even if she has just cause to complain. Dowden's point of connection is Theagenes' rejection of blame directed at the divine, and he contrasts this with his apparently abrupt acceptance of 'random' divine intervention in 2.6.2 when he gets Cnemon to focus on the task at hand (reunion with Charicleia) and to hurry 'in case even now some malign power is making fun of us' (trans. Morgan). In Dowden's initial analysis this was 'a surprising view' for Theagenes to have, but it should not surprise us at all at this point because he has already expressed it not once but twice before—in his two laments that just precede, in which he blames the envy of a *daimon* and an insatiable Fury for the lovers' tribulations.[44]

So, Charicleia laments (1.8) and blames Apollo while threatening suicide; Theagenes stops her lament and tells her not to criticize the god but acknowledges that she has valid cause to lament. Having lost Charicleia, Theagenes laments (2.1) and blames an invidious divine power while threatening suicide, and Cnemon stops him but makes no mention of the nature of the lament, only the reason (the cause of lament is invalid). Then, having lost Charicleia again, Theagenes laments a second time (2.4), again blaming a divine power, again threatening suicide, and again Cnemon stops him, again because his reason is invalid. Cnemon has an emotional reaction to the revelation of Thisbe's identity, but Theagenes stops him from learning

---

[43] Dowden 1996: 271-3 and Dowden 2010: 373-4.
[44] As Dowden 2010: 373 recognizes and emphasizes.

the truth of his own story by drawing Cnemon's and our attention back to his and Charicleia's story through the insistence that a divine power (although obviously one was not responsible for the death of Charicleia in his laments) could still give him reason to lament. We can see here how repetition and variation create pattern and texture.

Theagenes' shift in his view of divine power is not really so radical. When Charicleia makes her lament in 1.8, Theagenes corrects her not because it is not right to lament or because divine powers are not responsible for hardships in this world or because it is wrong to blame a divine power. Instead, he cautions her that to criticize such a power is to *provoke* it (1.8.2 παροξύνεις). They are in the middle of a story and the ending is unclear, but for the moment, after all, they are both alive and they are together, so provocation could have awful consequences. When he comes to his own laments in 2.1 and 2.4, however, in his view there is no longer any danger in such provocation, and so no reason not to blame a divine power. Still, he carefully switches from Charicleia's target Apollo to more generic and clearly malignant forms of divinity. Charicleia is dead and his intention is to join her, so their story is over.

The scene of lament in Book 1 is tied to those in Book 2 through still further mechanisms. What happens after Charicleia's lament in 1.8 is weighty for several reasons. This is the moment when we first encounter the names Charicleia and Theagenes, a revelation long delayed. We find out that these two young people have been separated from family, captured by pirates and faced trouble at sea before ending up with the bandits. It is here, we might say, that first-time readers can clarify whatever suspicions they have about the place of the work they are reading within a genre and about the nature and identity of the main characters. This is actually the first place such a reader can confirm that the couple *are* the protagonists through the use of their names and through the disclosure that the past events of their story, however little we may have learned of it at this point, have, though unnarrated, nevertheless conformed in broad strokes to a clichéd romance itinerary.[45] Both Winkler and Morgan consider it possible to read 1.8 without identifying Theagenes and Charicleia as the hero and heroine—Winkler even confesses (I suspect not entirely truthfully) that he himself missed it as a first-time reader. In combination with the generic clues of the passage it seems unlikely to me that readers would not recognize the pair as romance protagonists. On the other hand, such confusion is quite reasonable even

---

[45] Cf. Winkler 1982: 106 with n. 19 and Morgan 1989b: 99 with n. 4 on recognizing the protagonists and the possible importance of the novel's varying title on readers' experiences.

for alert readers if they are uncertain that they are dealing with a *romance*; for how can we have romance protagonists in something other than a romance? But if, as Winkler asserts, 'the opening tableau leaves us...certain *that* this is a romance'[46] then what alternative protagonists do we have?

We do have one, as it happens, and he enters the picture at precisely this moment; for it is here that we also have the introduction of Cnemon as a speaking character, and not just any speaking character, but a young man with a story to tell, and a woeful tale at that, one that he prefers not to tell. This recalls—and perhaps we can go so far as to say is meant to recall—the introduction of Clitophon in Achilles Tatius' novel. Could Cnemon be our hero? The suspicion that he may turn out to be the narrator of an entirely different novel can throw a reader off balance as they attempt to 'locate and connect the two narratives with which he [sic] is being compelled to juggle'.[47] Has Heliodorus been reeling out an elaborate and extended frame narrative, one-upping Achilles Tatius in complexity and length? This potential is dispensed with quickly. There is almost nothing about Cnemon's story besides his initial biographical data (young, Greek, well-born, and handsome) that could make him a romance hero, and his story diverges from any such expectations quite quickly.

Still, his story remains in competition with the main narrative, and here too we have repetition with variation between the same two portions of the novel that I have been considering. We should note that after Charicleia's lament Cnemon tries to avoid telling his story and does so in clearly metaliterary terms: 'This is no time to introduce a new theme into your own tragedy in the form of my misfortunes' (1.8.7, trans. Morgan). Cnemon does narrate it, but only at their insistence; but they insist specifically because *they believe his story will be like theirs* (1.9.1). It turns out not to be very like theirs at all, not least because Cnemon's tale, although we will not have a complete accounting of it until later, is cast retrospectively while Theagenes and Charicleia's is still unfolding. Cnemon seems to be living on after the end of his story. Then, with the discovery that the corpse in the cave is Thisbe's, Cnemon's story becomes a potentially active one again. In response, Theagenes, in contrast to his earlier demand for narration, refuses to allow Cnemon to pursue it, instead insisting that he delay his story to allow the main narrative to continue until a more suitable moment.

---

[46] Winkler 1982: 101. The full context: 'The opening tableau leaves us both certain *that* this is a romance and quite uncertain as to *how*' (original emphasis).
[47] Morgan 1989b: 99.

Although Winkler and Morgan provide very different answers to the question of how Cnemon's narrative relates to that of Charicleia and Theagenes, they share the same impulse in reading the Athenian's story in counterpoint to that of the lovers'. What I want to note here is that the intertwining of the two tales is begun and made explicit first with the lament in 1.8 and then reasserted and confirmed in the aftermath of the lamentations in Book 2. Both of these passages are marked by repetition, as we have seen, since the laments in Book 2 are a doublet and together form a doublet with Charicleia's earlier one, especially through Cnemon's presence.

The scene of Charicleia's lament actually contains another, subtler doublet that conveys a sense of the oddity. Cnemon's Greek ethnicity and speech are mentioned in 1.7.3, but we have no indication of his importance, and he remains an anonymous Greek youth for the time being. Charicleia's lament at first seems to be a private one, one that no one else should be able to hear because Heliodorus emphasizes that her bed is well apart from the others, so that her sighs and speech will be inaudible (1.8.2). When Theagenes interrupts her in 1.8.4, then, it comes as a surprise to the reader, who is aware only at this moment that her lover has not only noticed her lamentation but has heard its every word. How much more surprising it is, then, when in this emotionally charged and extremely private exchange, Heliodorus immediately does the same exact thing by having Cnemon join in. It is a brief repetition of the revelation but one that attaches Cnemon immediately and irrevocably to the story of the two lovers; for he enters the conversation just as Theagenes did, first as an unobserved and silent audience member, then as a participant who we realize has overheard the whole of the preceding conversation. Heliodorus heightens the effect through a neat trick. Charicleia asks Theagenes how he feels, and he says that he is feeling better now that it is evening and because of the care that the young man has given him (1.8.4). Then the reply (1.8.5): "'Well, you'll feel even better at dawn,' said *the young man to whom their care had been entrusted*'. Until we get to the masculine article '*the*' in the Greek—that is, until the eighth word of the sentence—we have had no idea that Cnemon has heard anything or that these are not the words of Charicleia herself. It is as if a cinematographer has jarringly widened the shot to reveal the presence of a completely unexpected third character in a scene we thought contained only two (and which a moment before we thought contained only one).[48]

---

[48] It also should cause us to consider witnessed laments and how they may differ from unwitnessed ones. The latter are the norm in novels generally and in Heliodorus (cf. Birchall 1996a: 15).

There is far more to be said about Theagenes' lament in 2.4, as well as the patterns and repetitions into which Heliodorus incorporates it. My purpose here, however, has not been to provide a complete discussion but to suggest new ways of thinking about this passage. In fact, no treatment could ever be exhaustive when dealing with an author of Heliodorus' sophistication and continuing appeal. Just as a thousand years ago readers such as Psellos and Philagathos were bringing their particular concerns to the novel and coming away with valuable inspiration, so we will always be able to find new ways of approaching the *Aethiopica* and admiring its author's skill.

6
Cnemon Meets Calasiris (2.21–2)

Alain Billault

After the island where they were prisoners of the Herdsmen has been stormed by enemies of the latter, Theagenes, Charicleia, and Cnemon manage to get away with Thermouthis, a shield-bearer of Thyamis. As they do not trust this man who is a Herdsman and suspects them of the murder of Thisbe, they try to get rid of him and send him away to seek information about Thyamis (2.17.5). But Thermouthis comes back immediately and declares he is afraid of searching by himself. He needs someone to accompany him. Cnemon is afraid of travelling with Thermouthis, but Theagenes persuades him to set out with the Herdsman and then to drop him as soon as possible. They agree to meet in Chemmis, a village upon a hill on the banks of the Nile (2.18). Cnemon contrives to leave Thermouthis, who is later bitten by a snake and dies (2.19.3–20.2). When Cnemon was a captive of the Herdsmen, he had grown long hair to look like them. Now he cuts it short and heads for Chemmis. As he reaches the Nile, he sees a man walking by the riverside.

The passage starts with this surprising encounter. Other surprises follow as Cnemon starts talking to the man, whose replies and questions prove false every guess he has made (2.21). Then Cnemon accepts the man's invitation to join him in a house nearby where he will be enjoying unexpected hospitality and start to learn something, but not all about the man's life (2.22). In these chapters, Calasiris, who will be a most important character in the novel, appears for the first time. Heliodorus introduces him by referring to Homer, but also to Plato and to Achilles Tatius. He portrays him in a paradoxical light and depicts him first as an elusive personality. The passage provides a good illustration of Heliodorus' skills in using literary tradition and creating a narrative replete with narratological paradoxes and suspense.

6.1. The Literary References

Homer is the main literary reference-point in these chapters. These allusions are a good example of the importance of the Homeric pattern in the novel.[1] Calasiris first quotes Homer when Cnemon asks him to tell him his misfortunes. He replies 'It is an *Odyssey* of woe' (2.21.5). This is John Morgan's ingenious translation[2] of the Greek Ἰλιόθεν με φέρεις, which means literally 'you are carrying me from Ilion'. The old man's words are a modified quotation of Odysseus' first words when he starts telling his adventures to Alcinous: Ἰλιόθεν με φέρων ἄνεμος Κικόνεσσι πέλασσεν, 'a wind carrying me from Ilion led me close to the land of the Cicones' (*Od.* 9.39). Calasiris thus compares his own story to the adventures of Odysseus from the moment he left Ilion to come back to Ithaca; he considers himself a new Odysseus. His words are surprising and may arouse suspicion of overstatement. But they are justified later when Calasiris reveals that Odysseus announced to him in a dream that he would have to experience sufferings like his own (5.22.3). For the moment, Calasiris plainly confesses he went through hard times and deliberately situates his future narrative under the sign of Homer.

Then he finds himself in a genuinely Homeric situation when he invites Cnemon to come with him to the house where he is staying. Hospitality is a major Homeric theme. It is a high and sacred principle that kings live by in the *Iliad* and the *Odyssey*. It entails certain duties that they must perform.[3] Odysseus' treatment by Alcinous, the king of the Phaeacians, in the *Odyssey* (6–8)[4] provides a good example of its importance. Heliodorus handles the theme in his own way. He reverses the roles, and modifies the elements of the Homeric pattern. Alcinous and Odysseus were kings, which Calasiris and Cnemon are not. Odysseus was Alcinous' guest; Calasiris, who compared himself to Odysseus, wants to be Cnemon's host. Alcinous entertained Odysseus in his own palace; Calasiris invites Cnemon to join him in another man's house in Chemmis. This is where they will tell their adventures to each other. Cnemon accepts this unforeseen arrangement because he remembers

---

[1] Whitmarsh 1998; Elmer 2008. [2] Morgan trans. 1989c.
[3] Finley 1964: 115–20; Thalmann 1998: 141–6; Bakkert 2013: 54–5. [4] Garvie 1994.

he has an appointment with Theagenes in the village (2.21.7), but he soon forgets about it as he enjoys Calasiris' paradoxical hospitality.

He is in fact treated as if he were his guest. Heliodorus carefully describes the situation. He emphasizes that the genuine master of the house is absent, but he specifies that his daughter is there and that she has reached the age of marriage. This was also the case in the *Odyssey*, with Alcinous' daughter Nausicaa. The king even offered Odysseus the opportunity to marry her (*Od.* 7.311–16). Even though he compared himself to Odysseus, the old Calasiris is unlikely to marry his friend's young daughter. But her father will offer her to Cnemon, and he will marry her.[5] Thus Cnemon will also become a new kind of Odysseus, an Odysseus who accepts the offer to settle down. After Calasiris, he will fit the Odyssean type in his own way.

For now, Calasiris is treated by the girl and the servants as if he were their father (αἳ τὸν ξένον ἴσα καὶ πατέρα ἦγον, 2.22.1). But this is not the case. Calasiris does not even seem at this stage to have children of his own (later we shall discover that his sons are Petosiris and Thyamis); nevertheless, he is referred to as the 'father' of another man's children. It will soon be discovered that he is a sort of father of others too. Even Cnemon calls him 'father' when he wonders at the hospitality they are enjoying as if they were in the house of Zeus Xenios, the god of hospitality (2.22.2). Calasiris replies by sketching a portrait of their absent host, whose worshipping of Zeus Xenios he emphasizes. He explains that the man leads the wandering life of a merchant and 'knows by experience many cities and the way of life and thinking of many men', πολλαὶ μὲν πόλεις πολλῶν δὲ ἀνθρώπων ἤθη τε καὶ νοῦς εἰς πεῖραν ἥκουσιν (2.22.3). These words call to mind the portrait of Odysseus at the beginning of the *Odyssey* (1.3): πολλῶν δ' ἀνθρώπων ἴδεν ἄστεα καὶ νόον ἔγνω, 'he saw the hometowns and knew the way of thinking of many men.' After Calasiris and prior to Cnemon, their absent host is another Odysseus. This is the reason why, according to Calasiris, he recognized him as a fellow-traveller and opened his house to him when he saw he was roaming erratically. Just as Odysseus himself was traveling widely, so the allusions to Odysseus wander over the novel, from one character to another. Every time such an allusion appears, it does not contradict or cancel out any former occurrences, for the Odyssean identity is not exclusive to any one character. Because of the Odyssean nature of his life, Calasiris could seek help from the merchant, this new Odysseus; and Cnemon, in turn, wants to hear about Calasiris' Odyssean life.

But there is no telling of that tale quite yet. Calasiris simply summarizes his misfortunes without fully recounting them: his children, he says, have

---

[5] For the idea that the name Nausicleia evokes the Homeric Nausicaa, see Bowie 1995: 278.

been kidnapped by bandits. He knows who the latter are, but he cannot avenge himself on them. To emphasize his miserable plight, he resorts once more to Homer. He refers to the frightful omen of which Odysseus reminds the Achaeans in the *Iliad* (2.301–3): as they were offering victims to the gods in Aulis, a snake appeared and swallowed down a brood of eight young sparrows nested upon a plane tree. Their helpless mother witnessed and lamented their death flying around the nest and was finally devoured too by the snake. The Achaeans were terrified, but Calchas swiftly explained to them the meaning of the sign: they had to fight at Troy for nine years and, in the tenth year, they were going to take the city. Odysseus reminds them of this episode to revive their morale as they are about to give up and go back to Greece. This is supposed to be an energizing story. Calasiris transforms it into a pathetic one, by omitting the context and the end of the story. He compares himself to the mother of the sparrows in order to highlight his helplessness and his anxiety about his children's fate (2.22.3). Cnemon is clearly moved by his words, but when he wants to know more, Calasiris once again delays his telling. He justifies this new delay by quoting once more Homer who, in the *Odyssey* (17.286–7) called the stomach hateful (οὐλομένην), because it always wants its desire to be fulfilled immediately. This is, clearly, another Homeric motif.[6] Calasiris uses it as a device to hold back for a while the story of his life, on the grounds it is dinner-time. But dinner-time is precisely the moment when Odysseus starts telling his story to Alcinous (*Odyssey* 9.1–18).[7] This is the fourth and last reference to Homer in the passage. Calasiris does not quote the poet just to display his knowledge and impress Cnemon. He uses him to steer the conversation in the direction he wants, and to describe his own situation in his own way. By referring to Homer, he sketches his own self-portrait. But the first image of him which is provided by these chapters is not made of only Homeric elements. Heliodorus also uses other literary references to paint it.

When Cnemon first sees Calasiris, the latter is walking by the side of the Nile. This activity has seen him compared to a peripatetic philosopher and to an orator of the Second Sophistic.[8] But we also know of another philosopher who famously took a stroll with a friend along a river under the sun at noon: Socrates in Plato's *Phaedrus*. Socrates meets Phaedrus by chance as he is getting out of Athens to take a walk in the nearby countryside and he decides to accompany him (227a–d). They turn to the Ilissus river and

---

[6] See the list of references provided at Morgan trans. 1989c: 395 n. 51.
[7] On Heliodorus' evocation of the nocturnal setting of the *apologoi*, see Hardie 1998: 38–9.
[8] Baumbach 2008: 174.

walk in its shallow water until they reach the place Phaedrus considers appropriate to read and discuss the speech by Lysias he has listened to in the house of Epicrates (229a–230a). Plato carefully gives many topographical indications to make the scene of his dialogue lively and realistic.[9] Heliodorus partly rewrites it. Of course, the Nile is certainly not the Ilissus, and Cnemon and Calasiris have never met before. Calasiris asks Cnemon: 'But where are you going to, young man? Where do you come from?' (Ἀλλὰ ποῖ δὴ πορεύηι καὶ πόθεν, ὦ νεανία; 2.21.5). This question shows strong similarities to the first question of Socrates to Phaedrus in the *Phaedrus*: ὦ φίλε Φαῖδρε, ποῖ δὴ καὶ πόθεν; (227a1). Calasiris then invites Cnemon to join him in the shade of a house 'for a spot under the scorching midday sun is not the most agreeable of places for listening to long tales' (2.21.6). His words sound like a reversed reference to Plato's *Phaedrus* where the dialogue takes place outdoors in the heat of noonday. Calasiris, who is older than Cnemon, will turn out to have a story to tell him; this inverts the Platonic model, where it is the younger Phaedrus who has a speech to disclose to Socrates. Heliodorus gives a Platonic colouring to their dialogue.

Yet this is a novel, not a philosophical treatise; this is why he alludes also to Achilles Tatius. After he has compared his misfortunes to the adventures of Odysseus, he says to Cnemon: 'You are disturbing a swarm of sufferings (σμῆνος κακῶν), and drive their endless buzz towards yourself' (2.21.5). Near the beginning of Achilles Tatius' novel, Clitophon uses almost the same words to reply to the man who wants to know what he has suffered from Eros: 'You are waking up a swarm of narratives' (σμῆνος ἀνεγείρεις…λόγων, 1.2.2). Similarly, the claim (discussed above) that 'a spot under the scorching midday sun is not the most agreeable of places for listening to long tales' (2.21.6) refashions and inverts the claim of Achilles' narrator that 'a spot like this is agreeable and just the place for erotic tales' (1.2.3). Heliodorus does not just allude to Plato; he alludes to Plato through the lens of Achilles Tatius, in order to highlight the literary genre within which he is working. He emphasizes that, with all his Homeric and Platonic features, Calasiris' story will be part of a novel. And this will be a very paradoxical novel.

6.2. Narratological Paradoxes

The first paradox of the episode is the meeting of Cnemon with Calasiris. Cnemon had fixed an appointment with Theagenes in Chemmis, but the

[9] Yunis 2011: 86.

two will in fact never meet again. In Heliodorus' novel, nothing ever happens according to the plans formed by the characters. When Cnemon gets close to Chemmis, he meets another man instead. As soon as he sees him, the focus of the narrative shifts. It concentrates on the stranger whose look and demeanour immediately attract Cnemon's attention:

...πρεσβύτης τις ἀνὴρ ἐναλύων ταῖς ὄχθαις ἐφάνη καὶ δόλιχόν τινα τῷ ῥείθρῳ πολλάκις ἄνω καὶ κάτω παραθέων καὶ ὥσπερ τῷ ποταμῷ φροντίδων τινῶν κοινούμενος· ἡ κόμη πρὸς τὸ ἱερώτερον καθεῖτο καὶ ἀκριβῶς ἦν λευκή, τὸ γένειον λάσιον καὶ σεμνότερον βαθυνόμενον, στολὴ καὶ ἐσθὴς ἡ ἄλλη πρὸς τὸ ἑλληνικώτερον βλέπουσα.

He saw an old man wandering erratically along the riverbank, pacing many times to and fro beside the stream like a runner engaged in a long-distance race, and seeming to confide his cares to the river. His hair was long in a priestly way and entirely white; his beard grew thick and deep with an air of dignity, while his cloak and the rest of his clothes looked rather Greekish. (2.21.2)

The description of the man is highly paradoxical. Cnemon, who has recently cut his hair, sees a man with long hair. The scene takes place in Egypt where, according to Herodotus (2.36), the priests shave their heads. Therefore, the man does not look like an Egyptian priest. But his long hair and beard are nevertheless considered possible signs of his priestly condition, because they give him the look of a Greek priest.[10] This supposition would fit the story if this episode were narrated by the Athenian Cnemon. The narrator here, however, is Heliodorus' primary narrator, and the focalization is ambiguous, at least for a first-time reader: who exactly, readers wish to know, is saying that he looks like a Greek priest, and with what authority? This uncertainty increases when Cnemon comes into contact with him.[11]

Again paradoxically, this meeting takes some time to enact. Cnemon draws near to the man, who does not seem to be aware of his presence. In the end, he stands in front of him. He decides to address him and wishes him 'rejoice' (χαίρειν), i.e. have a good day. The old man replies, over-literally, that he is incapable of being happy. To this Cnemon exclaims: Ἕλλην...ὁ ξένος; ('Is this stranger a Greek?'). But the other answers: 'Not a

---

[10] Baumbach 2008: 171.
[11] There is also a subtle echo in this passage of Achilles' distress at the start of *Iliad* 24: with Calasiris' ἐναλύων ταῖς ὄχθαις compare Achilles' ἀλύων παρὰ θῖν' ἁλός (*Il.* 24.12).

Greek; I am from here, I am an Egyptian' (2.21.3).[12] The dialogue between the two men starts with a word-play. Cnemon uses the verb χαίρειν to salute the man, who decides to understand it as an invitation to be joyful, which he says is impossible for him. Thus, he reveals he can speak Greek, which is why Cnemon thinks he is a Greek. His exclamation echoes a previous one in the novel. When Theagenes and Charicleia are taken prisoner by the Herdsmen, they are entrusted to a young man, who helps them to heal their wounds, treats them like friends, and sympathizes with them in their sad plight. This man is Cnemon who eventually confesses he is a Greek himself just like them: 'A Greek! O Gods!' exclaimed the youngsters happily. 'A Greek truly, by birth and speech!' (1.8.6).

In this dialogue between Cnemon and Calasiris, Heliodorus seems to create a new version of that scene; in fact, however, he reverses everything. Cnemon was a providential Greek for Theagenes and Charicleia, who were pleasantly surprised by his revelation. Now he is himself astonished to discover that the old man he has just met is a Greek. But the latter immediately undeceives him by replying that he is not a Greek, but an Egyptian. This is a new paradox: he can speak Greek, but he is an Egyptian, an Egyptian who nevertheless looks like a Greek priest.[13] There is another difference from the former scene. Cnemon had immediately given his name to Theagenes and Charicleia and specified he was Athenian by birth. In the later scene, the man does not disclose his name to him. Nor does Cnemon reveal his own identity. This mutual reticence is mysterious. It seems to announce a relationship of distrust between the two men. The mystery gets deeper when Cnemon asks the old man why he is wearing Greek clothes, and the latter explains his dress by his misfortunes. Cnemon is astonished by his reply and wants to know what these misfortunes are (2.21.4–5).[14] He reacts as if he were a reader of Heliodorus. This is metaphorically what he wants to become since he asks the man to tell him his story. He will listen to it as the reader will read it. Heliodorus uses the encounter of his characters to establish the scene of the reading of his book inside the book itself.[15] Just like the reader, Cnemon has seen his suppositions proved false so far. He has already discovered many paradoxes in the situation. But the priest-like man still has

---

[12] This passage borrows from Philostr. *Her.* 1.1.
[13] Similarly, among the three παράδοξα claimed by Favorinus was the fact that though a Gaul he spoke Greek (Γαλάτης ὢν ἑλληνίζειν, Philostr. *VS* 489).
[14] Another echo of the opening of Achilles Tatius (1.2.1–2).
[15] On this theme in Heliodorus, see Winkler 1982; Morgan 1991.

more in store for him as, for the first time, he seems to be about to start to tell his story.

One paradox, as we have seen, is that he does not tell it and prefers to warn Cnemon against the length and the violence of his story which he compares to the adventures of Odysseus. Another is that he seems suddenly to change his mind: he wants Cnemon instead to tell him his story. The young man declines his request and underscores the paradox of the situation: the man has told him nothing about himself and wants to know his story (2.21.5). The paradox is in fact bigger than Cnemon tells it, since Cnemon has already told his story to Theagenes and Charicleia when they were captives of the Herdsmen (1.9–18.1). Theagenes had asked to hear it, and Cnemon's first reply was not dissimilar to Calasiris':

'Παῦε' ἔφη· 'τί ταῦτα κινεῖς κἀναμοχλεύεις;' τοῦτο δὴ τὸ τῶν τραγῳδῶν. Οὐκ ἐν καιρῷ γένοιτ' ἂν ἐπεισόδιον ὑμῖν τῶν ὑμετέρων τἀμὰ ἐπεισφέρειν κακά.

'Stop! Why do you try to push these stories and lever them open?', to quote these words from the tragedians? This is no time to introduce my misfortunes as a new episode into your own tragedy. (1.8.7)

Cnemon too had misfortunes to tell, but felt reluctant to tell them. He quoted not from Homer but from Euripides' *Medea* (1317), where Medea ironically asks Jason (who wants to open the doors of the house where she has murdered his children) 'why are you trying to push these doors and lever them open?' (τί τάσδε κινεῖς κἀναμοχλεύεις πύλας;). Cnemon was thus comparing his own adventures to a tragedy that would only add to his new friends' woes. Theagenes and Charicleia, however, were so insistent that he had to give up and tell them his story.[16] In the earlier scene, Cnemon played with the young lovers the role that Calasiris now assumes with him. But he will not tell his own story again. On the contrary, he will press Calasiris to tell his story, and so will copy the attitude Theagenes and Charicleia adopted towards himself. Heliodorus thus reverses the roles he had established in a previous scene and reveals once more his fondness for dramatic paradox (with some help from Calasiris).

After Cnemon has refused to tell him his story, Calasiris once again seems to change his mind. He now seems ready to comply with the young man's wish, but the reasons for his acceptance are surprising. He first

---

[16] The function of which in the novel has been convincingly explained by Morgan 1989b.

recognizes that Cnemon is a Greek who has been obliged by a misfortune to disguise himself. He therefore feels a kinship with him (2.21.6). We may surmise that Cnemon has not properly cut his hair, and so still looks like a stranger in the disguise of a herdsman. Calasiris also sees that he is eager to listen to his story and acknowledges that his desire coincides with his own. He confesses he too wants to tell his story to someone. Eventually, as the legend goes, he would have confided it to the reeds by the river had he not met with Cnemon (2.21.6). Thus, he compares himself to a well-known figure of a legend, the barber of Midas who knew that the king had donkey ears. He was not permitted to disclose this secret, but could not keep it and had to confess it into a hole he dug into the ground; some reeds grew up there, and repeated the secret every time the wind blew. This is a funny story and a revealing one. As he refers to it, Calasiris shows he still maintains a sense of humour, which comes as a surprise after he has mentioned he has gone through many misfortunes. At the same time, Heliodorus uses Calasiris' confession to emphasize that the telling of a story is an urgent activity for both parties: Calasiris the story-teller is just as keen to tell his story as Cnemon, the listener, is to hear it.

6.3. Suspense

Jacques Amyot observed that the suspense in the *Aethiopica* derives from the singular construction of the novel, which begins in the middle of the story.[17] Theagenes and Charicleia have been left alone among the dead and the remains of a previous battle. They are taken prisoner by the Herdsmen. For readers, this is the beginning of the couple's adventures; but they soon want to know what happened to them previously. This desire will lie at the root of the suspense in the first part of the novel, until all is finally revealed in Book 5. Thereafter the reader will want to know what will happen to the protagonists until the end of their story.[18] The appearance of Calasiris intensifies the suspense in the first part. Questions about him inevitably arise: who is this man who looks like a Greek priest but is in fact an Egyptian priest (he proclaims his respect for his religious duties at the end of the passage: 2.22.5)? What misfortunes has he gone through? Did they really resemble Odysseus' adventures? And how are they related to the story of

[17] Plazenet 2008: 45–7, 160–1.   [18] Cave 1988.

Theagenes and Charicleia, who may be the children whose fate Calasiris is lamenting? These are questions Heliodorus raises in the reader's mind as Calasiris is introduced. Others will arise later, about the activity and the moral status of the man, when the story of his life is disclosed.[19] They will not be easy to answer either. From the very start, Heliodorus presents Calasiris as an elusive personality whose adventures are modelled on several literary patterns, while his attitude constantly gives the lie to every guess which may be made about him. As the curtain rises up on Calasiris, we already see him as the mysterious character he will remain until the end of the novel.

[19] Sandy 1982b; Winkler 1982; Billault 2015.

7
Allegory, Recognition, and Identity
The Egyptian Homer in Context (3.11.5–15.1)

Lawrence Kim

It has long been recognized that Homer is Heliodorus' most important classical literary model: one thinks not only of the *Aethiopica*'s Odyssean narrative structure and thematization of *nostos*, wandering, and marriage, but also of Theagenes' purported descent from Achilles and the appearance of Odysseus in Calasiris' dream, not to mention the numerous quotations, allusions, and reminiscences of Homeric poetry in the novel.[1] The most explicit 'Homeric' moment in the *Aethiopica*, however, is Calasiris' unorthodox account of the poet's origins (3.14), which has understandably attracted a great deal of scholarly attention: its parallels with aspects of Calasiris' own life (Egyptian from Thebes, sexual scandal, exile) and especially those of Charicleia's (controversial paternity, recognized by a birthmark, 'passing' as Greek) have long been noticed, and Tim Whitmarsh has influentially interpreted the episode as Heliodorus' sophisticated, meta-poetic reflection on the *Aethiopica*'s own literary filiation.[2]

My aim in this chapter is to offer a slightly different perspective on Calasiris' *vita Homeri* by reading it as an intrinsic part of the extended digression in which it is embedded: the four-page (in the Budé edition) stretch of text from 3.11.5–15.1. The section begins with Calasiris telling

---

[1] 'Heliodorus' greatest debt is to Homer': Morgan 2003: 436. See Keyes 1922; Hefti 1950: 98–103; Feuillâtre 1966: 105–14; Sandy 1982a: 85–8; Fusillo 1991: 24–31; 2006: 290–5; Whitmarsh 1998: 97–9; 1999: 21–3; 2011: 112–15; Morgan 2003: 436–7; 2016: 267–8; Hunter 2004: 251–3; Elmer 2008: 413–16. For studies of particular Homeric reminiscences: Garson 1975; Fusillo 1990; Paulsen 1992: 143–50, 161–4; Whitmarsh 1998: 101–4; Robiano 2000; Hilton 2001; Telò 2011; Tagliabue 2015; Peigney 2017.

[2] Whitmarsh 1998: 105–6 on Calasiris' Homer as a stand-in for the *Aethiopica* itself. On Calasiris' life of Homer (including parallels with the novel's characters), see also Kerényi 1927: 256; Merkelbach 1962: 296–8; Winkler 1982: 102–3; Fusillo 1991: 28; Paulsen 1992: 176–7; Whitmarsh 1998: 104–7; Perkins 1999: 209; Morgan 2013: 231–4. Less useful are Most 2007; Pitcher 2016.

Lawrence Kim, *Allegory, Recognition, and Identity: The Egyptian Homer in Context (3.11.5–15.1)* In: *Reading Heliodorus'* Aethipica. Edited by: Ian Repath and Tim Whitmarsh, Oxford University Press.
© Oxford University Press 2022. DOI: 10.1093/oso/9780198792543.003.0007

Cnemon how Apollo and Artemis had visited him at night in Delphi and commanded him to take Charicleia and Theagenes away (3.11.5); Cnemon interrupts to ask how he knew the gods had really appeared (3.12.1), and Calasiris responds by enigmatically quoting *Il.* 13.71-2 (3.12.2). The conversation that ensues touches upon not only divine epiphany, but also Homeric exegesis (3.13), before veering off into the celebrated account of Homer's Egyptian origins (3.14). Afterwards, Cnemon urges Calasiris to return to the point in his narrative where he had left off: 'But now, Calasiris, having detected the gods by the Homeric method (ὁμηρικῶς), tell me what happened next' (3.15.1)—a clear signal that the 'digression' from 3.12.1-15.1 is envisioned as a single cohesive unit.[3]

In what follows, I argue that the three separate topics discussed in this digression—the 'Homeric' identification of gods in divine epiphanies, the 'symbolic' interpretation of Homer's verses, and the description of Homer's life—are intimately linked, not just by the continued reference to Homer, but also by the allegorical logic Calasiris ascribes to each of them: one that posits a reality hidden under the veil of appearances and accessible only by symbols and hints. In such a context, Homer himself, and not just his poetry, is constituted as an allegorical text to be deciphered, the 'truth' of which Calasiris discovers and reveals by reading the symbols found on Homer's very own person. Calasiris' biography of Homer thus illustrates how closely allegorical thinking maps onto the concerns of the novel—disguised appearances, recognition through signs, and revelations of true identities. The point, however, is not that the *Aethiopica* should be read allegorically, as hiding sacred truths to be revealed only to the clever reader, but that one's 'true' or 'real' identity is indeed the most important mystery, the revelation of which is as surprising and wonderful as any theological knowledge.

7.1. Appearance and Reality in Calasiris' Vision (3.11.5–12.1)

The event that precipitates the digression occurs at a point in Calasiris' narrative after he has heard the oracle that alludes to Charicleia and Theagenes, witnessed them falling in love during the Delphic procession, and finally confirmed his suspicions in separate meetings with each of the

---

[3] The Greek text of the *Aethiopica* is cited from Rattenbury and Lumb 1935-43. Unless otherwise noted, translations are those of Morgan 1989c.

lovers. Calasiris tells Cnemon that, as he was lying in bed, trying to figure out the meaning of the oracle, Apollo and Artemis appeared to him in the middle of the night (ἤδη δὲ μεσούσης τῆς νυκτός: 3.11.5) and ordered him to take Charicleia and Theagenes to his homeland, Egypt, and from there to 'wherever . . . it please the gods' (ὅποι . . . τοῖς θεοῖς φίλον: 3.12.1). At first glance, the scene is unremarkable, a typical literary example of a divine epiphany: the gods appear to Calasiris at night, tell him what to do, and then depart.[4] All that was left for Calasiris to ascertain was the identity of the unnamed land to which the gods were referring. But just as the priest is about to continue the narrative, Cnemon interrupts, intrigued by a different aspect of the vision:

ἀλλὰ τίνα δὴ τρόπον ἔφασκες ἐνδεδεῖχθαί σοι τοὺς θεοὺς ὅτι μὴ ἐνύπνιον ἦλθον ἀλλ' ἐναργῶς ἐφάνησαν;
But you said that the gods demonstrated to you that they had not come *in a dream*, but had *manifested themselves in physical form*. How? (3.12.1)

Cnemon is referring to the enigmatic sentence with which Calasiris concluded his description of the epiphany:

Ταῦτα εἰπόντες οἱ μὲν ἀπεχώρησαν ὅτι μὴ ὄναρ ἦν ἡ ὄψις ἀλλ' ὕπαρ, ἐνδειξάμενοι.
With these words they [the gods] departed, and in so doing they demonstrated that my vision had been *real* and *no mere dream*. (3.12.1)

Calasiris' statement and Cnemon's rephrasing both establish an important conceptual contrast that will resonate throughout the rest of our passage: that between *reality* ('my vision . . . real': ἡ ὄψις . . . ὕπαρ; gods 'manifested in physical form': ἐναργῶς ἐφάνησαν)[5] and the *semblance of reality* (in this case, dreams: ὄναρ, ἐνύπνιον).[6] The specific phrase that Calasiris uses to express this distinction, μὴ ὄναρ . . . ἀλλ' ὕπαρ ('no mere dream, but real'), is almost

---

[4] Harris 2009: 36–7 on epiphanic dreams and visions. On divine dream epiphanies in the novel, see Hägg 2002: 57; Whitmarsh 2011: 193–4; Harrisson 2013: 130–1.

[5] On ἐναργῶς as a technical term in epiphanic contexts, see Kerényi 1927: 96 n. 16; Versnel 1987: 48; Heliodorus also uses it at 8.11.2 and, playfully, 3.4.7. The combination of ἐναργής and φαίνεσθαι could be an allusion to Homer, in whose descriptions of divine epiphanies it often appears: e.g. *Il.* 20.131; *Od.* 3.420, 7.201, 16.161; cf. the similar usage at Chariton 3.6.4.

[6] The opening sentence of Calasiris' narrative articulates a similar distinction: 'if indeed I did *imagine* [the gods] and not see them *for real*' (εἴ γε ᾤμην ἀλλὰ μὴ ἀληθῶς ἑώρων: 3.11.5).

certainly an allusion to a verse from Penelope's account of her dream in *Odyssey* 19.[7] She describes how an eagle, after killing twenty of her geese, first declares to her that '... this is *no mere dream, but real*, a good thing, which will come to pass' (οὐκ ὄναρ, ἀλλ' ὕπαρ ἐσθλόν, ὅ τοι τετελεσμένον ἔσται: *Od.* 19.547),[8] and then goes on to explain that the geese represent the suitors, and that he, the eagle, is actually Odysseus.[9]

At a basic level, this allusion prefigures the explicitly Homeric focus of the remainder of the digression, thematically binding Calasiris' vision more tightly to what comes afterward.[10] But the parallels between the two passages are more than just linguistic. The narrative context is remarkably similar: in both, a character describes a vision he or she has seen to a third party (the disguised Odysseus, Cnemon), and in both visions, the epiphanic figure(s) indicate(s) that the vision is 'real' (Odysseus explicitly, Apollo and Artemis implicitly). Moreover, in the subsequent discussions of the visions with their interlocutors, both narrators behave in a manner that has led scholars to characterize them as artful, cunning, and even untrustworthy;[11] in fact, each has been suspected of fabricating their vision—another indication of how cleverly Heliodorus has modelled his devious narrator upon his Homeric counterpart.[12]

---

[7] While the adverbs ὄναρ ('in a dream') and ὕπαρ ('in waking life' or 'in reality') are often contrasted in ancient prose (especially under the influence of Plato, e.g. *Resp.* 382e, 476c, etc. (Kessels 1978: 236–42 for discussion); examples in the novels include Charit. 5.5.6; *Aeth.* 8.11.1), the particular expression μή/οὐκ ὄναρ ... ἀλλ' ὕπαρ is very rare, found twice in Homer and twice in Heliodorus (see n. 10), but otherwise only in Ael. Arist. *Or.* 2.400, 48.18, Max. Tyr. 9.7 (the last two instances regarding divine epiphanies; all three are likely quotations of Homer).

[8] On the common misinterpretation of ὄναρ and ὕπαρ in this line as 'deceptive dream' vs. 'dream that will come true', see Kessels 1978: 186–9.

[9] Cf. Rattenbury and Lumb 1935–43: vol. 1, 114 n. 2. The other Homeric occurrence of the phrase is also spoken by Penelope, at the beginning of the following book. Upon waking from a dream in which Odysseus was by her side, she says: 'and my heart was glad, since I believed it was *no mere dream, but* already *real*' (ἐπεὶ οὐκ ἐφάμην ὄναρ ἔμμεναι, ἀλλ' ὕπαρ ἤδη: *Od.* 20.90). Heliodorus probably alludes to this line at 2.16.3, where Charicleia uses the phrase in an almost identical way, when she says *apropos* of the nightmare (ὄναρ) in which she loses an eye: 'if only the vision had been *real* and *no mere dream*': καὶ εἴθε γε ὕπαρ ἦν καὶ μὴ ὄναρ ... τὸ φανέν.

[10] See Hilton 2001 for another Heliodoran allusion (4.14.2) to Penelope's dream.

[11] Cnemon's question, which precipitates the entire digression, has been artfully elicited by Calasiris, who casually mentions that the gods 'demonstrated' that they were 'real' without indicating *how* they did so. On Calasiris' persistent teasing and manipulation of Cnemon throughout their conversation: Anderson 1982: 33–5; Sandy 1982b: 143–4; Winkler 1982: 139–47; Morgan 1991: 97; Paulsen 1992: 175–7.

[12] I owe this observation to Tim Whitmarsh. On Penelope's invention of her dream, see Büchner 1940: 149 n. 1; Harsh 1950: 16; Kessels 1978: 97–100. Winkler 1990: 154. On Calasiris, see Bretzigheimer 1998: 111–13, who argues that he both invents the epiphany to justify his decision to take the lovers away from Delphi (so Hefti 1950: 55–6; Levin 1992: 501) and orchestrates the ensuing digression in order to draw attention away from the inconsistencies in the

Although Penelope is describing a predictive dream and Calasiris a night-time epiphany, they both employ the phrase μή/οὐκ ὄναρ, ἀλλ' ὕπαρ to the same end—to articulate a contrast between a vision without significance (a *mere dream*), and one linked to truth and *real* life.[13] The allusion to the *Odyssey* thus expands the narrow question of whether the gods in Calasiris' vision were actually present or not to the more general issue that will occupy the rest of the digression—that of differentiating reality and the truth from the merely apparent or imagined. Finally, the evocation of Penelope's dream prepares the ground for a subtle yet significant shift in the topic of the conversation with Cnemon. While both Calasiris' vision and Penelope's dream are of the 'epiphanic' or 'message' variety, where a god or other figure delivers instructions or a prophecy, Penelope's dream, or rather its first part, is also 'symbolic', i.e. purporting to predict the future and requiring interpretation.[14] For Calasiris' immediate purposes this discrepancy is not terribly important, since he is concerned with establishing a general contrast between mere appearance and reality, one that underlies both types of visions. But the ensuing discussion, while still centring on epiphanies, will adopt a hermeneutic model in which 'reality' is uncovered by the deciphering of signs—an interpretative method associated with symbolic, rather than epiphanic dreams. The allusion to Penelope's dream thus hints delicately toward what will turn out to be the primary theme of the digression.

7.2. Recognizing the Gods and Reading Homer

Calasiris' answer to Cnemon's question about the epiphany—how had the gods shown that they 'had manifested themselves in physical form'?—explicitly moves the conversation in this symbolic direction:

---

account of his motives. The unusual nature of Calasiris' 'vision' also hints at the possibility of invention: every other epiphany in the *Aethiopica* occurs in a dream (Isis to Thyamis, 1.18.3–4; Odysseus to Calasiris, 5.22.1; Calasiris to Charicleia, 8.11.1: ὄναρ is used each time), but Calasiris curiously insists that his vision is *not* a dream (μὴ ὄναρ).

[13] The valence of ὕπαρ and ὄναρ is slightly different in each passage: the eagle claims that what Penelope saw *will be* 'real' (ὕπαρ) *in the future*, i.e. prophetic, as opposed to a *mere dream* (ὄναρ) that will not come true. Calasiris, however, asserts that he was seeing a 'real' vision (ὕπαρ) *at that moment*. With the allusion, Calasiris is thus collapsing two different distinctions between appearance and reality, the first relating to prophetic dreams—was it 'real' (i.e. will it come true) or just a dream—the second to epiphanic visions: were the gods 'real' (i.e. present) or just a dream (only imagined).

[14] For the terminology, see Harrisson 2013: 65–6. Penelope's dream is first symbolic, then epiphanic when the eagle arrives and delivers his message (Harris 2009: 50). But the eagle's words 'no mere dream but real' refer to the symbolic, not the epiphanic, part of the dream.

"Ὃν τρόπον . . . καὶ ὁ σοφὸς Ὅμηρος αἰνίττεται, οἱ πολλοὶ δὲ τὸ αἴνιγμα παρατρέχουσιν· 'ἴχνια γὰρ μετόπισθεν', ὡς ἐκεῖνός που λέγει, 'ποδῶν ἠδὲ κνημάων || ῥεῖ' ἔγνων ἀπιόντος, ἀρίγνωτοι δὲ θεοί περ.'

In the way . . . that also Homer, the *wise* man, *hints at*; but the *masses* miss the *hint*. As he says somewhere [*Il.* 13.71–2], 'For from behind as he went away, I easily *recognized* the tracks [or '*traces*'] of his feet and legs; the gods are *recognized without difficulty*'.[15]   (3.12.2)

The quotation comes, appropriately enough, from a divine epiphany episode in the *Iliad*: the speaker is Oilean Ajax, who explains to his Telamonian namesake how he had known that it was Poseidon who had just appeared before them. There is nevertheless a significant difference between the Homeric and Heliodoran episodes: in the *Iliad* Poseidon had come disguised as the prophet Calchas, while in Calasiris' vision, Apollo and Artemis were not disguised, but immediately identifiable.[16] The two accounts are similar insofar as their respective revelations occur as the gods in question 'depart' (ἀπεχώρησαν: *Aeth.* 3.12.1; ἀπιόντος: *Il.* 13.72), but Ajax realizes that what he saw was a real god, *not a human*, while Calasiris realizes that what he saw were real gods, *not imaginary gods*. The slight incongruity is important: in the narration of his vision Calasiris was concerned with the *ontological* question of distinguishing a real god from a mere illusion, but the Homeric quote is concerned rather with *hermeneutics*—recognizing the real identity of a disguised god by reading the visible 'traces' that allow one access to that identity. As we shall see, in the remainder of our passage Calasiris loses interest in the former concern and devotes his attention solely to the latter.

The emphasis laid upon the proper interpretation of signs *within* the Homeric verses is paralleled in Calasiris' remarks on reading Homer that introduce the quotation: 'Homer the wise man *hints*' (ὁ σοφὸς Ὅμηρος αἰνίττεται), but 'the masses miss the *hint*' (οἱ πολλοὶ δὲ τὸ αἴνιγμα παρατρέχουσιν). Cnemon's response presents a more detailed model of the kind of Homeric interpretation to which Calasiris is alluding:

Ἀλλ' ἦ καὶ αὐτὸς ἔοικα τῶν πολλῶν εἶναι καὶ τοῦτο ἴσως ἐλέγχειν, ὦ Καλάσιρι, βουλόμενος τῶν ἐπῶν ἐμνημόνευσας, ὧν ἐγὼ τὴν μὲν ἐπιπολῆς

---

[15] My translation.
[16] This is a significant difference between divine epiphanies in Homer and in the Greek novel; as Hägg 2002: 57 notes, 'there is in the novels . . . no instance of a god appearing incognito, in the guise of an ordinary mortal, as in Homer'.

> διάνοιαν ὅτε περ καὶ <u>τὴν λέξιν</u> οἶδα ἐκδιδαχθεὶς τὴν δὲ ἐγκατεσπαρμένην αὐτοῖς <u>θεολογίαν</u> <u>ἠγνόηκα</u>.
>
> I seem to be one of the *masses* then, and perhaps, Calasiris, your purpose in referring to those verses was to prove that! I know that I was taught the *surface meaning* of the lines when the text was first expounded to me, but I am totally *unaware* of the *religious teaching* embedded within them.[17]   (3.12.3)

Cnemon, then is one of the 'masses' (οἱ πολλοί) referred to by Calasiris, who 'miss' the 'hint' (τὸ αἴνιγμα) in Homer's verses, only understanding the 'surface meaning' (τὴν ἐπιπολῆς διάνοιαν) and therefore remaining 'totally unaware of the religious teaching' (τὴν . . . θεολογίαν ἠγνόηκα) hidden therein. Put in a more general way, the unenlightened *hoi polloi* may be familiar with Homeric poetry's literal meaning (cf. τὴν λέξιν, 'the text')—that is, with its *appearance*—but they are completely unaware of its deeper meaning—that is, its *reality*.

Note the striking similarity between this description and that of recognizing the gods in the *Iliad* verses: 'the traces of his legs and feet' by which Ajax successfully identifies Poseidon correspond to the 'hints' that Homer has inserted into his poem. Both are signs that need to be properly read in order to discover the 'truth'—the identity of Poseidon or the method of recognizing the gods. The Homeric quotation and the comments about reading Homer thus conceive of the relation between appearance and reality in a new way: whereas before, Calasiris had posed the question in terms of *differentiating* between reality ('real' gods) and appearances ('mere dreams'), now he is interested in *uncovering* the reality (the identity of Poseidon, 'religious teaching') that lies hidden underneath the appearances (the Calchas-disguise, 'the surface meaning').

This basic correspondence between reading Homer and recognizing the gods is taken to another level in the following section, where Calasiris finally answers both of Cnemon's questions: how to identify the gods as gods, and how to properly interpret Homeric poetry:[18]

> <u>Τοὺς</u> μὲν δὴ <u>βεβήλους</u> κἂν <u>διαλάθοιεν</u> τὴν δὲ <u>σοφοῦ γνῶσιν</u> οὐκ ἂν διαφύγοιεν, ἀλλὰ τοῖς τε ὀφθαλμοῖς ἂν <u>γνωσθεῖεν</u> ἀτενὲς διόλου βλέποντες

---

[17] Morgan's translation, slightly modified ('masses' and 'surface meaning' are my translations).
[18] As Bretzigheimer 1998: 111–12, n. 36, notes, the following discussion no longer addresses Cnemon's initial question of how the gods showed that they were really manifest as opposed to mere dreams, but instead answers the question posed by the Homeric quotation—how to distinguish a god who has come disguised in human form (cf. 3.13.1: θεοὶ καὶ δαίμονες . . . εἰς ἀνθρώπους . . . ἑαυτοὺς εἰδοποιοῦσι, 'gods and *daimones* give themselves the form of humans').

καὶ τὸ βλέφαρον οὔποτε ἐπιμύοντες καὶ τῷ βαδίσματι πλέον, οὐ κατὰ διάστασιν τοῖν ποδοῖν οὐδὲ μετάθεσιν ἀνυομένῳ ἀλλὰ κατά τινα ῥύμην ἀέριον καὶ ὁρμὴν ἀπαραπόδιστον τεμνόντων μᾶλλον τὸ περιέχον ἢ διαπορευομένων. Διὸ δὴ καὶ τὰ ἀγάλματα τῶν θεῶν Αἰγύπτιοι τὼ πόδε ζευγνύοντες καὶ ὥσπερ ἑνοῦντες ἱστᾶσιν· ἃ δὴ καὶ Ὅμηρος <u>εἰδώς</u>, ἅτε Αἰγύπτιος καὶ <u>τὴν ἱερὰν παίδευσιν</u> ἐκδιδαχθείς, <u>συμβολικῶς</u> τοῖς ἔπεσιν ἐναπέθετο <u>τοῖς δυναμένοις συνιέναι γνωρίζειν</u> καταλιπών....

[Gods and *daimones* in human form] might *pass unperceived by the uninitiated*, but they *cannot escape the knowledge* of the *wise* [man], and will *be recognized* firstly by their eyes, which have an extraordinary intensity and never blink,[19] but more especially *by their method of locomotion*, which is not accomplished by the displacement or transposition of their feet but by a sort of smooth, gliding motion and without touching the ground, so that they cleave rather than walk through the circumambient air. This is why the Egyptians make their statues of the gods with the two feet connected and carved virtually as one form. And Homer, *was well aware of* this too, for he was an Egyptian, and well versed in our *holy lore*. So he included references to these phenomena *symbolically* into his epics, leaving them to be *recognized* by *those who were capable of understanding* them....[20] (3.13.2-3)

The following table highlights the conceptual model linking this passage's descriptions of Homeric exegesis and the method of recognizing the divine (3.13) to those expressed previously by Ajax (in Homer), Calasiris, and Cnemon (3.12):

Identifying the Gods (Ajax and Calasiris)

	Reality	Know/Recognize	Signs	Do not Know
Ajax 3.12.2	θεοί gods	ἔγνων I recognized (knew)	ἴχνια traces	
Calas. 3.13.2	[θεοί] [gods]	τὴν γνῶσιν, γνωσθεῖεν knowledge, be recognized	τῷ βαδίσματι by the gait	διαλάθοιεν τοὺς βεβήλους pass unperceived by the uninitiated

---

[19] In Homer, gods are recognized by their eyes at *Il.* 1.104, 3.396-7, 21.415. As Jones 2005: 96 notes, Charicleia's eyes are described in a similar way at 2.31.1; are we meant to treat her as divine?

[20] Morgan's translation except for my modifications: 'escape the knowledge of', 'and will be recognized', and the entire last sentence.

Reading Homer (Calasiris and Cnemon)

	Reality	Know/Recognize	Signs	Do not know
Calas. 3.12.2			αἰνίττεται hints at τὸ αἴνιγμα the hint	οἱ πολλοὶ παρατρέχουσιν the masses miss
Cn. 3.12.3	θεολογίαν religious teaching	–	–	ἠγνόηκα I was totally unaware τὴν ἐπιπολῆς διάνοιαν the surface meaning
Calas. 3.13.3	τὴν ἱερὰν παίδευσιν holy lore	συνιέναι, γνωρίζειν to understand, to recognize	συμβολικῶς symbolically	τινες ἠπάτηνται[21] some, who are deceived

The last row in each table sets out the complete 'theory' of interpreting Homer or recognizing the gods as expressed by Calasiris in 3.13, to which the partial references made earlier in 3.12 correspond. Combining them, we are presented with the following: the *Reality* of the first column—the gods, religious teaching, or holy lore—is only known, recognized, or understood by those in the second column, the wise who *Know* or *Recognize* reality because they are able to read the *Signs* of that reality listed in the third column—traces, hints, symbols, or, specifically, the divine gait. In contrast to the wise are those who *Do not know* in the fourth column: the unperceiving masses, the uninitiated, the unaware, and the deceived who merely know the surface meaning. Both activities thus operate within the same conceptual frame: the wise are opposed to the ignorant masses, and only the former can recognize the hints, traces, or symbols that point to a hidden reality or truth, while the latter just see the apparent truth: the human disguises of the gods or the surface meaning of Homer's poetry.

7.3. Neoplatonism, Calasiris, and Allegorical Logic

Although some of the language used in Calasiris' description of Homeric exegesis echoes that of allegorical critics throughout antiquity (e.g. συμβολικῶς

---

[21] For this phrase, see the concluding sentence of 3.13.3, quoted below, pp. 89–90.

and αἰνίττεσθαι),[22] the conceptual frame as a whole, as Gerald Sandy observes, is strongly reminiscent of that employed by Neoplatonic philosophers, like Porphyry of Tyre (third century CE), Iamblichus (third-fourth century CE), Synesius of Cyrene (fourth century CE), and Proclus of Athens (fifth century CE).[23] These critics operated on the presumption, in Sandy's words, 'that Homer made use of enigmas and riddles and that only the intelligent were capable of discerning what he has intentionally made obscure. The general public and the profane must remain oblivious of ἡ θεολογία enshrined in the poet's verses'.[24] Moreover, the Neoplatonists also associated 'symbols', sacred wisdom, and 'hinting' with Egypt, providing a fitting context for Calasiris' linking of Homer's allegorical methods to the poet's Egyptian heritage.[25]

In our passage, then, Heliodorus exploits the fact that a Neoplatonist-inspired allegorical logic underlay the contemporary exegesis both of Homer, which Calasiris discusses, and Egyptian lore, mentioned only in passing. But as we have seen, Calasiris also applies the language of allegory—of visible 'surface' phenomena, 'hints', 'symbolically' concealed wisdom, those in the know, the uninitiated masses—to an intellectual activity, viz. identifying the gods in epiphanies, that operates in a fundamentally different way. This can be seen more clearly if we analyse Calasiris' explanation of how the identification works, his long-awaited revelation of the secret hidden under the surface of *Il.* 13.71–2, that is, the so-called 'sacred teaching' that Homer had 'inserted symbolically (συμβολικῶς) into his poetry, leaving it to be recognized by those able to understand' (3.13.3):

ἐπὶ μὲν τῆς Ἀθηνᾶς 'δεινὼ δέ οἱ ὄσσε φάανθεν' εἰπών, ἐπὶ δὲ τοῦ Ποσειδῶνος τὸ 'ἴχνια γὰρ μετόπισθε ποδῶν ἠδὲ κνημάων ‖ ῥεῖ' ἔγνων ἀπιόντος', οἷον ῥέοντος ἐν τῇ πορείᾳ· τοῦτο γάρ ἐστι τὸ 'ῥεῖ' ἀπιόντος' καὶ οὐχ ὡς τινες ἠπάτηνται, 'ῥᾳδίως ἔγνων' ὑπολαμβάνοντες.

---

[22] For συμβολικῶς, cf. Heraclit. *All.* (first century CE) 26.10, 66.3, 74.1; for αἰνίττεσθαι 39.6 and [Plut.] *Vit. Hom.* (second–third century CE) 100, 101, 102, 126, 201.

[23] Sandy 1982b: 154–7; cf. Lamberton 1986: 150–2. For Neoplatonism in the *Aethiopica* more generally, Sandy 1982b: 154–67; Mecella 2014: 647–54. Neoplatonic elements are associated almost exclusively with Calasiris; the only exception is the allegorical account of the Nile floods in 9.9–10, related by the novel's narrator (on which, see Sandy 1982b: 157–60; Whitmarsh 2011: 129–32).

[24] Sandy 1982: 157.

[25] Sandy 1982: 159–61, with selected quotations (cf. also Synes. *De prov.* 1.1 = 89a–b). Cf. also the interest in fictional Egyptian priests among the Neoplatonists reflected in Porphyry's *Letter to Anebo*, addressed to one fictional Egyptian priest, and Iamblichus' *Reply of Master Abamon* (*De mysteriis Aegyptiorum*), written in the voice of another.

Thus he says of Athena, 'her eyes shone terribly' [*Il.* 1.200] and of Poseidon, 'for from behind, as he went away easily I recognized the tracks of his feet and legs', as if he were flowing in his gait (ῥέοντος ἐν τῇ πορείᾳ); for this is the [way to understand] 'as he went away easily' (ῥεῖ' ἀπιόντος) and not as some, who are *deceived*, construe [the line], as 'easily I recognized' (ῥᾳδίως ἔγνων).[26] (3.13.3)

The tell-tale sign of divinity that Calasiris had just described, namely that gods depart by gliding through the atmosphere without moving their feet, is shown to have been familiar to and hinted at by Homer. Calasiris manages to simultaneously 'solve' a Homeric problem—what does 'tracks of his feet and legs' mean?[27]—and adopt Homer as an authority for his own method of divine recognition.

But in what sense has Homer introduced this knowledge into his poem 'symbolically' (συμβολικῶς: 3.13.3)? Traditionally, allegorical exegetes presume that Homer operated according to a principle of substitution, in which gods or other divinities 'symbolize' something else. For instance, in Heraclitus' *Homeric Allegories* (first century CE), Hephaestus is the earthly fire, which is 'symbolically' (συμβολικῶς) called 'lame' by Homer because it is not as powerful as the celestial fire (*Hom. All.* 26.10). Elsewhere, Homer 'philosophizes the [rivers] in Hades *symbolically*' (συμβολικῶς)—i.e. they are not real rivers, but stand for characteristics associated with death (74.1). Neoplatonic Homeric allegoresis is often even more removed from the text— the poetic episode in question invariably illustrates Platonic metaphysical principles: e.g. Proclus' reading of the Sirens as 'souls, life principles, that animate the spheres' (*In Rep.* 2.238.7) or of Hephaestus as the demiurge-created world (because the former is lame and the latter described as 'legless' in Plato's *Timaeus: In Rep.* 1.126–7).[28] Calasiris' exegesis is markedly different, interpreting Homer's words in a *philological* or *grammatical* manner. He takes the adjective ῥεῖα ('easily') with ἀπιόντος ('as [the god] departed')

---

[26] My translation.
[27] A mystery also to modern commentators: cf. Janko 1992: 52, 'Aias' recognition of a god from the ἴχνια of his "feet and shins" is odd'; Platt 2011: 58–9: 'what, after all, do the *ichnia* of Poseidon's feet actually look like?'; Purves 2019, 51: 'the unusual nature of Poseidon's feet and legs as he walks away'. Dietrich 1983: 68 suggests that the god was identified 'by his presumably outsize legs and feet'; so too Petridou 2016: 37 'simply too big to have belonged to a human being' (further discussion at 81; 76–81 on divine footprints in general). Ameis and Hentze 1905 ad *Il.* 13.71: 'ἴχνια hier in der ursprünglichen Bedeutung (ἰκνεῖσθαι) Bewegungen'; similarly West 1998–2000 ad *Il.* 13.71 reads ἴθματα (LSJ: 'step', 'motion') for ἴχνια, following Σ A ad *Il.* 13.71. Cf. Vernant 1991: 43.
[28] Examples taken from Lamberton 1986: 180–232, on Proclus' Homeric exegesis.

instead of with ἔγνων ('I recognized'), so that the line reads 'as [the god] departed easily', and then claims that Homer, when he uses ῥεῖα (an epic adverbial form of ῥάδιος: 'easy', 'light') wants the reader to recall the verb ῥέω ('to flow'): ῥεῖα ἀπιόντος should be thus taken to mean 'as [the god] departed easily', or, 'flowing', that is, as gliding away without moving his feet.[29]

Modern scholars have generally found this solution ridiculous.[30] For Thomas Paulsen, it is another instance of Calasiris' mocking of Cnemon's gullibility, part of Heliodorus' generally sardonic characterization of the Egyptian priest as a deceptive, roguish, yet sympathetic figure.[31] For Sandy, the passage forms a crucial element of his argument that the allegorical, Neoplatonic ambience of the novel, and of this conversation in particular, is primarily 'decorative overlay rather than . . . thematic underpinning' (1982: 165). Sandy suggests that we are meant not only to laugh *with* Calasiris, as he toys with Cnemon, but also *at* him; the absurdity of his Homeric exegesis contributes to his portrayal as an intellectually and ethically dubious Egyptian priest, whose claims to divine knowledge and arcane wisdom are shown to be without substance.

Parallels for at least a part of Calasiris' interpretation, however, have been found in ancient sources: as Mario Telò has noted, the Homeric scholia to these lines also suggest taking ῥεῖα with ἀπιόντος, and further explain that Ajax realized that the gods 'do not leave tracks' (μὴ ἀπομαξαμένας ἴχνος), which, while not exactly what Calasiris says, does not contradict it.[32] So

---

[29] On the specific steps in Calasiris' argument, see Fusillo 1990: 44–5; Paulsen 1992: 176; and Telò 1999: 72–3; all three correct the interpretation of Colonna 1987: 209 n. 4 (which is also followed, curiously, by Palone 2020, 55).

[30] Paulsen 1992: 176: 'Diese Herleitung ist ohne Zweifel absurd'. So Sandy 1982b: 165: 'only the ignorant would be fooled by Calasiris' interpretation'.

[31] Paulsen 1992: 172–89, whose reading of Calasiris' character is probably closest to my own (cf. Kim 2019). Calasiris' interpretation is reminiscent of Socrates' similarly playful readings of Homer and other poets: cf. Pl. *Alc.* 2, 147b, where αἰνίττεται is used during a non-allegorical reading of a verse of Homer's *Margites*; and *Prt.* 380a–88e, where Socrates twists the meaning of a Simonides poem by means of the same grammatical operation that Calasiris uses here.

[32] Sch. bT ad *Il.* 13.71-2: ἀναχωροῦντος αὐτοῦ τὰς ἀποχαράξεις τῶν ποδῶν ἔγνων, φησί, μὴ ἀπομαξαμένας ἴχνος. τὸ δὲ 'ῥεῖα' πρὸς τὸ 'ἀπιόντος'· ῥαδίως γὰρ ἀπηλλάγη ὡς θεός. καὶ συνῳδὸν τὸ τάχος τῷ 'αὐτὸς δ' ὥς τ' ἴρηξ' ('[Ajax] says, "As he departs, I recognized the marks of his feet, that they didn't leave a track". The 'ῥεῖα' goes with the 'ἀπιόντος'; for since he was a god, he departed easily. And his speed is echoed in the phrase "he, like a hawk" [*Il.* 13.62]).' Eustathius (ad *Il.* 13.71) also sees 'speed' as relevant, claiming that Poseidon was recognized 'by his departing *speedily* and running lightly' (ἐν τῷ ταχὺ ἀπιέναι καὶ κοῦφα θέειν). He repeats the theory that Poseidon left no footprints, but also offers two other alternatives: the much larger distance between strides as seen by prints, or excessive speed to the limits of imperceptibility (which also links to the scholium's mention of 'speed' (τάχος)). As Telò says (1999: 75), the scholium's reading is *fortemente consonante* with Calasiris' since both take ῥεῖα with ἀπιόντος rather than ἔγνων; neither the scholium nor Eustathius, however, repeats Calasiris' theory about gliding gods, cleaving through the air without moving their feet.

while I agree that the interpretation plays a part in Heliodorus' use of Neoplatonic 'décor' to portray Calasiris in an ironic and slightly detached way, I would put less emphasis on the absurdity of the interpretation itself, and more on its comic juxtaposition with the extended, dramatic, and mystical build-up that precedes.[33] By means of his references to Neoplatonist allegoresis and his secretive, suggestive statements, Calasiris has positioned himself as an initiate into divine mysteries that he will, in turn, reveal to Cnemon. Before his explanation, he is described by the narrator as having 'achieved the exalted state of mind appropriate to the contemplation of *holy mysteries*' (τὸν νοῦν πρὸς τὸ μυστικώτερον ἀνακινήσας: 3.13.1); afterwards Cnemon expresses his gratitude in similar language: 'you have *initiated* me into one *mystery, reverend sir*' (ταυτά με, ὦ θειότατε, μεμύηκας: 3.14.1). Calasiris speaks of lofty objectives: knowing the gods, gaining knowledge of 'religious teaching', acquiring 'sacred learning'. But in the end, despite all the talk of concealed theology, arcane symbols, and hints that only the wise can read, we are left with a rather strained 'reading' of Homer's verses based on ordinary grammar and etymology. This comic discrepancy between heightened expectation and banal result helps to portray Cnemon, who fails to notice it, as gullible, and Calasiris, who perpetrates it, as playfully deceptive.

But it is not just the particular *method* of 'allegorical' exegesis of Homer that is revealed as less exalted than advertised; the *content* too, the 'sacred learning' unknown to the 'uninitiated' that Homer has hidden in his verses turns out to be rather pedestrian too: the gods are recognized by their unusual gait. In other words, no esoteric Egyptian knowledge or training in Platonic cosmology is required to uncover the gods' true identity; one need only observe their feet. Calasiris has re-described the profane procedures of recognition and careful observation in the lofty, mystical language of allegory. Words like *ainittesthai* and *sumbolikōs*, which could be understood in the neutral sense of 'to be enigmatic' and 'figuratively', take on an allegorical and cosmic air when Calasiris couples them with terms like *theologia*, *gnōsis*, and *bebēloi*. But the act of recognition that is at issue here functions not according to the substitutive logic of allegory—the name 'Hephaestus' is replaced by the concept 'fire'—but by an inferential or evidentiary logic, in which a particular feature like a scar, or in this case, a gliding mode of locomotion, is read as an index of a subject's true, but hidden and disguised, *identity*.[34]

---

[33] So Bretzigheimer 1998: 111 n. 46 against Sandy 1982b: 155–7 and Paulsen 1992: 176.
[34] Allegorical interpretation can seize on 'hints' that something lies beneath the surface, but there is no direct connection between the sign or symbol and the 'truth' that it conceals.

Calasiris' 'inferential' answer to Cnemon's question about the gods thus shows us that we are no longer in the cryptic and enigmatic world of allegory and the ineffable. The broader world-view of false appearances and true realities still holds, as does the emphasis on properly reading signs to access the truth. But now instead of profound religious wisdom, the truth is an individual's 'real' *identity*, concealed under the 'surface' of a disguise or a deceptive physical appearance, and the means by which the observer recovers the former from the latter is by reading a sign—that is, by an act of *recognition*. These themes, as we shall see, are central to the portrait of Homer that Calasiris sketches in the remaining section of the digression.

7.4. Homer's Biography

Cnemon's initial question about identifying the gods has now finally been answered, but Calasiris' casual reference to Homer's being 'Egyptian' (the second time in his narrative, as Cnemon notes)[35] piques his curiosity, especially since it strikes him as something that, 'it may well be, no one in the whole world has heard made before today' (ὃ τῶν πάντων ἴσως οὐδεὶς ἀκήκοεν εἰς τὴν σήμερον: 3.14.1). The remarkable account of Homer's birthplace, origin, and name that follows deserves to be quoted in full (3.14.2–4):[36]

"Ὅμηρος, ὦ φίλος, ὑπ᾽ ἄλλων μὲν ἄλλοθεν ὀνομαζέσθω καὶ πατρὶς ἔστω τῷ σοφῷ πᾶσα πόλις· ἦν δὲ <u>εἰς ἀλήθειαν</u> ἡμεδαπὸς Αἰγύπτιος καὶ πόλις αὐτῷ Θῆβαι, 'αἳ ἑκατόμπυλοί εἰσι᾽ κατ᾽ αὐτὸν ἐκεῖνον. Πατὴρ δὲ <u>τὸ μὲν δοκεῖν</u> προφήτης <u>τὸ δὲ ἀψευδὲς</u> Ἑρμῆς, οὗπερ ἦν ὁ δοκῶν πατὴρ προφήτης· τῇ γὰρ τούτου γαμετῇ τελούσῃ τινὰ πάτριον ἁγιστείαν καὶ κατὰ τὸ ἱερὸν καθευδούσῃ συνῆλθεν ὁ δαίμων καὶ ποιεῖ τὸν Ὅμηρον φέροντά τι τῆς ἀνομοίου μίξεως <u>σύμβολον</u>. Θατέρῳ γὰρ <u>τοῖν μηροῖν</u> αὐτόθεν ἐξ ὠδίνων πολύ τι μῆκος τριχῶν <u>ἐπεπόλαζεν</u>, ὅθεν παρ᾽ ἄλλοις τε καὶ οὐχ ἥκιστα παρ᾽ Ἕλλησιν ἀλητεύων καὶ τὴν ποίησιν ᾄδων <u>τοῦ ὀνόματος</u> ἔτυχεν, αὐτὸς μὲν <u>τὸ ἴδιον</u> οὐ λέγων ἀλλ᾽ οὐδὲ πόλιν ἢ γένος ὀνομάζων <u>τῶν δὲ ἐγνωκότων</u> τὸ <u>περὶ τὸ σῶμα</u> πάθος <u>εἰς ὄνομα</u> κρατησάντων.'

'Τί δὲ σκοπῶν, ὦ πάτερ, ἐσιώπα τὴν ἐνεγκοῦσαν;'

---

[35] Cnemon's comment (Αἰγύπτιον δὲ Ὅμηρον ἀποκαλοῦντός σου πολλάκις: 'several times you have referred to Homer as an Egyptian': 3.14.1) refers to Calasiris' earlier mention of 'the works of the Egyptian poet Homer' (ἡ . . . Ὁμήρου τοῦ Αἰγυπτίου ποίησις: 2.34.5).
[36] My translation.

"Ήτοι τὸ φυγὰς εἶναι καταιδούμενος, ἐδιώχθη γὰρ ὑπὸ τοῦ πατρὸς ὅτε ἐξ ἐφήβων εἰς τοὺς ἱερωμένους ἐνεκρίνετο, ἀπὸ τοῦ <u>κηλῖδα</u> φέρειν <u>ἐπὶ τοῦ σώματος</u> νόθος εἶναι <u>γνωρισθείς</u>, ἢ καὶ τοῦτο <u>σοφίᾳ</u> κατεργαζόμενος κἀκ <u>τοῦ τὴν οὖσαν ἀποκρύπτειν</u> πᾶσαν ἑαυτῷ πόλιν μνώμενος.'

[Cal.] 'Let Homer, my son, be named by others from other places, and for the wise man, let every city be considered home; but *in truth* he was a fellow Egyptian and his city was Thebes, 'of a hundred gates' [*Il.* 9.383] according to his very words. His *apparent* father was a priest, but his *real* father was Hermes, whom the *apparent* father served as priest; for the god came to the priest's wife as she was sleeping in the temple during the celebration of some ancestral ritual and fathered Homer, who bore a *symbol* of this unequal liaison. For on the very day he was born a great mass of hair *spread over the surface* of one of his *thighs*; whence he acquired his name, as he wandered among other peoples and especially the Greeks, singing his poems. He never mentioned his *own* name, nor named his city or ethnicity, but those who *knew of* the condition of his body prevailed in their use of *this name* [*ho mêros*: 'the thigh'].'

[Cn.] 'Why was he silent about his homeland?'

[Cal.] 'It could be that he was ashamed to be an exile, for he had been driven out by his father after he was *recognized* as a bastard from the *mark* he carried *on his body* (when he was selected from the ephebes for the priesthood); or perhaps he *wisely* contrived this and by hiding his *true* homeland courted every city as his own.' (3.14.2–4)

The revelations expressed here concern three issues that recur in most ancient Homeric biographies—his place of birth and native land, his parentage, and the origin of his name—and it is worth assessing the singularity of Calasiris' claims against this backdrop. First of all, despite Cnemon's exclamation, Homer's Egyptian origins are the story's least surprising element. Several ancient authors mention the possibility that Homer was Egyptian, with a further group identifying Thebes as the city of his birth.[37] Indeed, the fact that Calasiris, an Egyptian priest from Thebes,

---

[37] On the tradition of Homer as an Egyptian, see Sinko 1906 and Quack 2005. Homer as Egyptian: Gell. *NA* 3.11.6; Clem. Al. *Strom.* 1.66; Epiphanius, *Adv. Haer.* 1.3, the *Vita Romana*, and Hesychius of Miletus (preserved in the *Suda* s.v. Ὅμηρος). Homer as Egyptian, born in Thebes: ps.-Luc. *Dem. Enc.* 9; *Anth. Pal.* 7.7, Olympiodorus of Thebes (see following note); the *Vita Scorialiensis* II. Pitcher 2016: 295–301 considers Calasiris' certainty as to Homer's birthplace unusual, compared with the agnosticism of the *Vitae*. But individual authors, as these examples and those that follow show, often put forward claims with as much confidence as Calasiris.

sees Homer as sharing his ethnicity (ἡμεδαπὸς Αἰγύπτιος) and place of birth conforms to a well-attested ancient practice.[38] Another typical procedure that Calasiris employs is the 'ethnographic method', occasionally used by authors to support their claims for Homeric origins. For instance, the *Vita Romana* preserves the claim that Homer was Egyptian 'because he portrays heroes kissing one another, which is an Egyptian custom' (2).[39] Calasiris' version of this argument is expressed slightly differently, but essentially adheres to the pattern. Earlier he had mentioned that Egyptians represent the gods with their feet connected based on their knowledge of the divine manner of movement; Homer, being Egyptian, naturally knew this as well and inserted it into his poetry (3.13.3). But the same information could be reconfigured as evidence for Homer's nationality: Homer portrays the gods in the same way that the Egyptians do; therefore, Homer was Egyptian. In his self-serving identification of Homer's homeland and his use of ethnographic evidence to back it up, Calasiris is very much playing by the rules of Homeric biography.

As Calasiris fills out the details of Homer's Egyptian origins, however, a less orthodox portrait begins to emerge. For example, while many different identities and names were proposed in antiquity for Homer's parents (including the occasional divinity),[40] and the circumstances surrounding his birth are often very complicated (usually to explain why so many cities claimed him as their own),[41] Calasiris' account of an adulterous liaison between the wife of an Egyptian priest and Hermes is otherwise unattested.[42] Similarly exceptional is Calasiris' explanation of the name 'Homer'. Customarily, ancient biographers derived the name Ὅμηρος from ὅμηρος,

---

[38] E.g. Antimachus of *Colophon* (F 130 Wyss); Ephorus of *Cyme* (*FGrH* 70 F 1); Meleager of Gadara (Homer is *Syrian*: Ath. 4.157b); perhaps Lucian (*Babylonian*: *VH* 2.20) as argued by Nesselrath 2002: 155 (but see Ní-Mheallaigh 2009: 25–6). In the following century, the historian Olympiodorus follows Calasiris in identifying his own home city of Egyptian Thebes as Homer's birthplace (Phot. 80.61b). For more on the practice, Kim 2010: 162–8, with bibliography.

[39] Heath 1998, 30 notes that Homer never depicts heroes kissing each other, nor is the practice attested elsewhere as an Egyptian custom; on the ethnographic method, see Heath 1998: 29–30; Kim 2010: 165–7.

[40] Arist. fr. 20.1 Gigon = [Plut.] *Vit. Hom.* 1.3 (father: *daimōn*); *Suda* o 251 = *Vit. Hom.* 6.1 West (parents: Apollo and Calliope); *Vit. Scor. I* = 8.1 West (mother: Calliope); *Certamen* 3 (Metis, Calliope); *Anth. Pal.* 16.296 (Calliope).

[41] e.g. [Hdt.] *Vit. Hom.* 1–3; Arist. fr. 20.1 Gigon = [Plut.] *Vit. Hom.* 1.3.

[42] Egyptian parents are mentioned only in the *Certamen* ('the Egyptians say that his father was Menemachus, a temple scribe': 3) and by Eustathius (*Od.* 1713.17–28) who, on the authority of the otherwise unknown Alexander of Paphos, names them as Dmasagoras and Aethra, and notes that the daughter of Horus, an Isiac priest, was his wet-nurse.

adopting one of two interpretations: either as 'hostage' (the standard meaning of ὅμηρος) or else as a dialectal variant for 'blind' (e.g. from ὁμηρεύειν, 'to guide', because the blind need someone to 'guide' them).[43] The first alternative is more popular; and the fact that Homer was a 'hostage' could also be used to account for his multiple origins, e.g. he could be born in Smyrna, but given as a hostage to Colophon.[44] The second, although requiring an extra step of etymological explanation, has the benefit of deriving Homer's name from one of his most characteristic features—his blindness (cf. ὁ μὴ ὁρῶν, 'he who does not see').

Calasiris, however, is more adventurous, deriving Homer's name from the words ὁ μηρός ('the thigh').[45] At first glance, this solution seems outlandish. While the words closely match the name Ὅμηρος, they do not evoke any of Homer's traditional biographical details (as 'hostage' and 'blind' do); in fact, the explanation of how Homer came by the name requires the invention of a new and peculiar fact—that Homer was born with one extremely hairy thigh.[46] As modern scholars have pointed out, however, there is a certain logic to Calasiris' argument. Thighs play a fairly significant role in Homer, particularly in the *Odyssey*. One thinks immediately of Odysseus— not only from the famous episode where Eurycleia recognizes him from the scar on his thigh caused by a boar's tusks ('above the knee', γουνὸς ὕπερ: *Od.* 19.450), but also from Book 18, where a glimpse of his muscular 'thigh' (ἐπιγουνίδα) poking through his rags arouses the suitors' amazement and hints at his true identity.[47] In fact, both of these episodes are alluded to in the dream that Calasiris has in Book 5, where they also serve as clues to Odysseus' identity:

---

[43] On the various etymologies for Homer's name, see the list in Witte 1913: cols. 2199–200 and the discussion in Graziosi 2002: 79–82.

[44] This ploy works well for claims of non-Greek origins: Lucian, for instance, employs it to explain how the poet, born Tigranes of Babylon, ended up in Greece with the name Homer (*VH* 2.20); Paulsen 1992: 177 argues that Heliodorus alludes to Lucian here.

[45] Anderson 1979: 149, followed by Paulsen 1992: 176-7 and Whitmarsh 1998: 105, see Heliodorus as parodying Euripides' *Bacchae*, 286–97, where Dionysus' birth from Zeus' thigh (ὁ μηρός) is rationalized as a misunderstanding of his role as a *hostage* (ὅμηρος). Since these lines establish a connection between 'the thigh' and 'hostage', but not between 'the thigh' and 'Homer', I see no necessary reason why Heliodorus would be alluding to them.

[46] Why is the thigh *hairy*? And why a sign of divine parentage? Excessive hair could signify courage (cf. the hairy heart of Aristomenes of Messene: Plin. *HN* 70.11.183; Dio Chrys. *Or.* 35.3) or sexual depravity (Plin. *HN* 11.94.229; Adam. *Physiogn.* B37). Winkler 1982: 102 connects the hair with Hermes, whose other son, Pan, was covered in hair. I remain mystified.

[47] *Od.* 18.74: οἵην ἐκ ῥακέων ὁ γέρων ἐπιγουνίδα φαίνει; cf. 18.67–8: φαῖνε μηροὺς|καλοὺς τε μεγάλους τε. For the reception of this episode in imperial Greek literature, see Pernot 2004.

Age had withered him almost to a skeleton, except that his cloak was hitched up to reveal a *thigh* (ἐπιγουνίδα) that retained some vestige of the strength of his youth ... he was lame in one leg ['*thigh*': μηρόν], as if from a wound of some kind. (5.22.1)

When one considers the fact that Theagenes also has a scar 'above his knee' (ἐπὶ τοῦ γόνατος: 5.5.2), inflicted by a wild sow, which he and Chariclea agree to use as the ultimate proof of his identity, John Morgan is surely right to comment that 'wounds and marks on thighs are part of an extensive game' in the *Aethiopica* centring on two of its most important themes—recognition and identity.[48] The final touch in this rich intertextual play is the proof of Charicleia's Ethiopian identity, the birthmark on her upper arm, which is described as 'a black ring *staining the ivory* of her arm' (ἔβενος περίδρομος ἐλέφαντα τὸν βραχίονα μιαίνων: 10.15.2)—an allusion to *Il.* 4.141, 'just as when some woman *stains ivory* with crimson' (ὡς δ' ὅτε τίς τ' ἐλέφαντα γυνὴ φοίνικι μιήνῃ) where Homer describes the blood from Menelaus' wound on his *thighs* (μηροί: *Il.* 4.146).[49]

This intertextual connection between Calasiris' Homer and Charicleia reinforces the often-observed similarities between the two that I alluded to at the beginning of this chapter.[50] Charicleia is also born of a priestly family, suspected of being the offspring of an adulterous liaison (in her case incorrectly), goes into exile because of a physical defect (in her case, being white-skinned), and is identified by a birthmark.[51] She too passes as Greek, is given a Greek name, and like Homer, becomes more Greek than the Greeks themselves; one might add that just as Calasiris never mentions Homer's original, Egyptian name, so we never learn Charicleia's Ethiopian one (if ever given). The fanciful explanation of 'Homer' as 'the thigh' is thus the means by which Calasiris' biography of Homer is intimately bound up with the novel in which it is embedded, reflecting the lives of two of its main characters and wittily confirming the *Aethiopica*'s debts to its most illustrious and influential predecessor.

---

[48] Morgan 2013: 232 n. 25.
[49] As Morgan 2013: 231–2 cleverly observes, Heliodorus may also be playing on the word φοῖνιξ, which means 'crimson' in the Iliadic verse, but also 'Phoenician', as in the author's *sphragis* at the novel's conclusion: ἀνὴρ φοῖνιξ. For other Heliodoran allusions to this simile, see Bowie 1998: 2–3 (and the article in general for more 'Phoenician games').
[50] See the works cited in n. 2.
[51] Montiglio 2013a: 139 notes that the use of Charicleia's birthmark as a token of recognition has 'no literary precedent'.

7.5. Reading the Figure of Homer

One aspect of the biography that has not been sufficiently examined, however, is its relation to the preceding discussions about identifying gods and reading Homeric poetry. Of course, the passage is explicitly linked to the previous discussion—Calasiris' casual reference to 'Egyptian Homer' both inspires Cnemon's request for the biographical digression and provides information that helps to 'prove' his Egyptian origins. And after Calasiris has finished, Cnemon associates Homer's newly revealed Egyptian identity with his propensity toward the 'hinting' that had been so prominent in an earlier phase of the conversation:[52]

> Ταῦτα μὲν εὖ τε καὶ ἀληθῶς μοι λέγειν ἔδοξας, τεκμαιρομένῳ τῆς τε ποιήσεως τοῦ ἀνδρὸς <u>τὸ ἠνιγμένον</u> τε καὶ ἡδονῇ πάσῃ σύγκρατον, ὡς <u>Αἰγύπτιον</u>. . . .
>
> I find what you have to say completely convincing, bearing in mind not only the typically *Egyptian* combination of *concealed meanings* and enjoyment in his poetry. . . . (3.15.1)

Within the biography itself, however, Calasiris makes no explicit reference to this 'allegorical' aspect of Homer's Egyptian identity. But if we probe a little more deeply below the surface, we can see that the same concerns that animated Calasiris' and Cnemon's conversation about epiphanic visions and Homeric poetry are repeated and reflected here in the very person of Homer himself. Calasiris applies to the person of Homer both the 'allegorical' language that informed the foregoing conversation (especially regarding Homeric exegesis) and its thematic focus on recognition and identity (of the gods).

The opposition between appearance and reality, illusion and truth, that so strongly coloured the previous discussion is highlighted in the very first lines of Calasiris' biography, where an immediate dichotomy is established between the false beliefs of the many (ὑπ' ἄλλων . . . ἄλλοθεν) who claim Homer for their own, and the 'truth' (εἰς ἀλήθειαν) that he was Egyptian (3.14.2). Homer has two fathers—an *apparent one* and a *true one* (πατὴρ δὲ <u>τὸ μὲν δοκεῖν</u> προφήτης <u>τὸ δὲ ἀψευδὲς</u> Ἑρμῆς: 3.14.2); he has an apparent

---

[52] Because τὸ ἠνιγμένον ('concealed meanings') is only Rattenbury and Lumb's conjecture, albeit an attractive one, for the manuscripts' τὸ ἀνηγμένον ('sublimity', retained by Colonna 1987), I do not put too much weight on this point.

name, Homer, and a *true* one ('his own', τὸ ἴδιον: 3.14.3); he is apparently Greek, but *hides his true* homeland, Egypt (τοῦ τὴν οὖσαν ἀποκρύπτειν: 3.14.4). Homer, just like gods disguised as humans, or his own double-layered poetry, boasts a false appearance that conceals a true, underlying reality.

But there is more. Just as the true identity of the gods or the sacred wisdom sprinkled in Homer's poetry is only recognized by those able to decipher the 'traces' left by the gods or the 'hints' left by Homer, so too is Homer's identity and origin only recognized by 'those who *knew* of the *condition* of his body' (τῶν δὲ ἐγνωκότων τὸ περὶ τὸ σῶμα πάθος: 3.14.3); 'he was *recognized* as a bastard from the *mark* he carried on his body' (ἀπὸ τοῦ κηλῖδα φέρειν ἐπὶ τοῦ σώματος νόθος εἶναι γνωρισθείς: 3.14.4). In both of these phrases, the act of knowing and recognizing, so familiar from the earlier discussion, is focused on the 'mark' (κηλῖδα) or 'condition' (πάθος) on his 'body' (τὸ σῶμα; τοῦ σώματος), the notorious hairy thigh. But compare how Calasiris describes Homer's unusual birthmark—'a great mass of hair *spread over the surface* of one of his thighs' (ἐπεπόλαζεν: 3.14.3), 'a *symbol* of this unequal liaison' (σύμβολον: 3.14.2)—to Cnemon's earlier reference to 'the *surface* meaning' (τὴν ἐπιπολῆς διάνοιαν: 3.12.3) of Homer's poetry and Calasiris' mention of the sacred learning *symbolically* (συμβολικῶς: 3.13.3) embedded therein. For both Homer *and* his poetry, the 'symbols' on the 'surface' permit access to the truth hidden in the depths. And let us not forget that both Homer *and* Homer's gods are 'recognized' by the 'traces of their feet and legs'.

In the sections prior to the biography, Calasiris had carefully established that the uninitiated, the ignorant, and the masses see only the surface appearances of the world, while the wise man who can read the hints, the traces, the symbols can access the reality beneath. Homer himself was referred to by Calasiris as 'the wise man' (ὁ σοφός: 3.12.2), a notion that undergirds the Neoplatonic allegorical tradition. But Calasiris now reveals that this allegorical world-view is etched onto the body of Homer himself and defines his very being: Homer too is not what he seems to be, and his hairy thigh, which *appears* to be merely a mark on his body, is actually a 'symbol' hinting at who he *really* is: a semi-divine, Egyptian bastard.[53] In fact, even his name is not what it appears to be; 'Homer' (Ὅμηρος) is not a

---

[53] Cf. Pernot 2004: 249–50 on the symbolic function of Odysseus' thigh at *Od.* 18.74, and its relation to the general theme of appearance vs reality that dominates *Od.* Books 17 and 18.

name, but a different word altogether, 'the thigh' (ὁ μηρός), that has been *mistaken* for a name. The name 'Homer' too is thus a sign, which, when read properly, points the way to the physical sign, his thigh, that reveals the truth of his birth, genealogy, *and* ethnic identity.

With his fanciful tale of Homer's origins and his absurd etymology of the poet's name, Calasiris is surely poking fun at and parodying the biographical tradition, much as Lucian had centuries earlier with his tale of a Babylonian Homer, born with the name of Tigranes. Seen from this perspective, the story is the crowning example of Calasiris' playing on Cnemon's credulity and desire for secret 'wisdom'.[54] But, despite its joking tone, the narrative also resonates with the major themes of the digression in which it is embedded: one needs not only to recognize the traces of the gods to know their true identity and to interpret the symbols of Homer's verses to know the true wisdom therein, but also to be able to properly 'read' Homer himself. Homer, it turns out, does not just *compose* symbolic, enigmatic verses, but *is himself* an enigma, who seems to be one thing—a Greek—to the masses who look only to his outward appearance, but whose *true* identity—an Egyptian—is recognized as such by those who can read the enigmatic symbol on his body. The various elements of the digression are intricately intertwined—Calasiris' epiphany, the lines of Homer he quotes, the way Homer composes, the way Calasiris reads him, and now, in a final touch, the very person of Homer himself. Calasiris shows us first how to read 'Homer', that is, *his poetry*, and then how to read 'Homer', that is, *the poet himself*—to look beyond the surface appearance, recognize the symbols and hints, and uncover its true *meaning*, and his true *identity*.

It is important, however, to remember that this 'reading' of Homer's body is *not* allegorical, but, like Calasiris' previous interpretation of Homer's verses, only cloaked in the mystical and esoteric language of allegory.[55] For readers like Reinhold Merkelbach and others, the allegorical rhetoric that so strongly informs this part of the *Aethiopica*, comic as it may seem, was evidence that Heliodorus had concealed cosmological and theological content in what seemed a mere romance to the casual reader.[56] But just as

---

[54] Paulsen 1992: 176–7, 180.

[55] That this satirical attitude toward Neoplatonic interpretation is not confined to Calasiris can be seen at 8.11.4, where 'Theagenes' "allegorical" (almost neo-Platonic) reading of his dream prophecy proves amusingly wrong' (Hunter 2005b: 136).

[56] Merkelbach 1962: 295–8, who sees the absurdity of Calasiris' portrayal of Homer as a 'hint' to read it allegorically, as reflecting Charicleia, who represents the soul; cf. Papadimitropolous 2013: 110–13 on Charicleia as 'the symbol of the soul and of the mind that adorns it' (113), following the identification of Philip the Philosopher. For 'softer' allegorical readings of the *Aethiopica*, see Most 2007; Whitmarsh 2011: 129–35; more generally, Dowden 2005.

Calasiris' purely philological reading of Homer's poetry was described as 'symbolic', so too is his revelation of Homer's identity strewn with terms like 'surfaces', 'symbols', 'appearance', and 'truth'—not only to poke fun at and parody Neoplatonic allegory, but also to suggest that a person's 'real' identity, unknown to the unperceiving masses and accessible only to the privileged few skilled enough to observe and interpret the signs, is just as sublime and sacred a 'truth' as that promised by allegorical critics. After all, there is something astonishing, miraculous, and holy about the revelation and proof of identity that lies at the heart of all literary recognition scenes, but especially those at the endings of the *Aethiopica* and of its literary model, the *Odyssey*.[57]

---

[57] Earlier versions of this chapter were delivered at the University of Washington, Transylvania University, and the Virtual Humboldt Kolleg, *Things Have Changed*. Many thanks to the audiences at those venues for their comments, to the volume editors for their helpful suggestions, to Sira Schulz for her improvements of the chapter's style and arguments, and of course to John Morgan for his groundbreaking and inspiring work on Heliodorus.

8
The Mustering of the Delphians (4.19–21)

Tim Whitmarsh

These chapters, which close the fourth book, treat the aftermath of Charicleia's and Theagenes' escape from Delphi. Calasiris—the narrator of these events—records how he approached Charicles, Charicleia's adoptive father and (disingenuously, we are to assume) enjoined him to pursue the miscreants. The latter then summoned a nocturnal assembly in the theatre. With the support of the general Hegesias a decision was taken to go after Theagenes and the Thessalians, to seek to deprive their descendants of civic status, and to prevent the priestess of Artemis from appearing in public in the future. The passage closes with the mustering for war of the entire city, including women and the old.

The passage plays three distinct but interrelated roles. First, it serves as the point of departure for a new phase in the plot, and thus both engages with and remodels traditional stories of narrative origination. Secondly, it injects new life into the questions around female abduction and genesis of war that overhang so much of the Greek literary tradition. Thirdly, it explores a legal question that was of demonstrable interest in Heliodorus' own day, that of female consent in cases of seduction.[1] As we shall see in conclusion, all of these strands ultimately converge.

8.1. Beginning Again

The *Aethiopica* takes the complexity of beginnings as one of its central themes. The memorable opening 'in the middle', at daybreak on the

[1] In this third section I have sought to discuss the issues in a way that is at once historically honest and sensitive to the moral issues; but it is only fair to warn the reader in advance that some difficult topics are covered.

Egyptian coast, is more than a gesture of affiliation to Homer's *Odyssey*[2] and a dramatization of readerly *aporia*.[3] By dislocating the conventional narrative order, this beginning also foregrounds issues of origination—in a novel that will prove to be centrally about where people come from. In part these are hermeneutic questions for the reader: who are these two young people, and how did they come to be in this position? But they also relate self-reflexively to the novel's own genesis. What kind of a text is this? Where should we locate it on the generic and geo-cultural map? To what sources can we trace it?[4]

Heliodorus expects his readers to be practised interpreters of the romance as genre, familiar with established conventions. In particular, he expects them to know how novels start: with an encounter at a festival between girl and boy. This is the pattern at the start of Chariton's *Callirhoe* and Xenophon's *Anthia and Habrocomes*. The latter in particular seems to operate for Heliodorus as a kind of template for the romance in its most primitive form.[5] Calasiris' embedded narrative, of which our episode forms a part, supplies this generically conventional narrative of beginning, in a chronologically linearized form. A beautiful young girl and boy meet at a Greek festival, fall in love, and depart on their travels. This is the beginning that we would have been expecting—but not where we would have expected it. Heliodorus' narrative is designedly preposterous.[6]

This is thus one of a series of concatenated episodes within Calasiris' narrative that explore the question of where the story begins. The Delphic episode as a whole provides one answer—although it will prove ultimately to have been a misleading one, a Hellenocentric bait to the unwary reader reared on conventional romances. This is not an *Ephesian* but an *Ethiopian Story*. In the course of the novel, readers will learn that this romance narrative is only one type of narrative, and not necessarily the most

---

[2] The *Odyssey* is of course Heliodorus' primary narrative model, and the canonical example of 'beginning in the middle' (though it is the *Iliad* that prompts Horace's phrase *in medias res*: A.P. 148). Telò 2011 argues that Heliodorus' scene of bloodshed also references the Odyssean *mnēstērophonia*. See also Bowie in this volume, with full references.

[3] For this now well-established line of interpretation, see esp. Bühler 1976 and Winkler 1982: 95–9.

[4] Whitmarsh 1998; Elmer 2008.

[5] See Whitmarsh 2011: 117 on Heliodorus' generically self-aware rewriting at 3.4 of Xenophon's relatively bald account of the Ephesian procession near the start of *Anthia and Habrocomes*. The issue of Heliodorus' relationship to Xenophon (and indeed to Achilles Tatius) calls for a longer study.

[6] See Goldhill 2020 on 'preposterous' (i.e. temporally dislocated) themes in late antique literature.

important: the deeper, older, and more exotic starting-point is the wondrous myth of the Ethiopian princess born white.[7]

The Delphic episode has already provided us with one beginning point, in the form of the story of the falling-in-love and elopement of Charicleia and Theagenes. Our passage, however, activates a set of *topoi* that are differently coded, in generic terms. Our passage looks to the origins of epic conflict in the abduction of women. As will transpire, the war fizzles out immediately, once the fugitives have boarded the Phoenician ship. As with the hostilities between the Methymnaeans and the Mytilenaeans in Books 2 and 3 of Longus' *Daphnis and Chloe* (where the dominant military hypotext is Thucydides),[8] the anticipation of conflict is frustrated, as if the romance genre after Chariton were reluctant to host these alien elements.[9] First-time readers, however, will not know this. By the end of Book 4 they have been set up to expect a major conflict; they may well even be expecting the impending Delphian war to supply the explanation for the carnage on the Egyptian shore described in the opening of Book 1.

In metanarrative terms, this passage is all about the generation of urgency, the need to shake off the sloth and get things moving. Calasiris, who is pretending to be on the side of Charicles and the Delphians, addresses his exhortatory speech to Charicles 'with a bellow' (ἐμβοήσας), a participle that often presages violent engagement with an enemy.[10] The oration begins 'Wretches, for how long (ἄχρι τίνος) will you sit there looking like fools, silent and inactive…?' (4.19.2) The hackneyed ἄχρι τίνος opening is characteristic of emotive, rhetorically charged appeals for immediate action;[11] the accusation of excessive 'sitting around' recalls Demosthenes;[12] the combined charge of being 'silent and inactive' (ἄναυδοι καὶ ἄπρακτοι), meanwhile, may carry an implicit suggestion of the alleged feckless indolence of the ill-educated.[13] Not for the first time, Calasiris proves that he knows how to work a Greek audience: he successfully provokes Charicles into action. In response to Charicles' own impassioned address to the assembled Delphians, the

---

[7] On the romancers' heavy dependence on mythological themes, see Lefteratou 2018.
[8] Longus and Thucydides: Trzaskoma 2005, with further literature.
[9] At least, in Heliodorus' case, until Book 9.
[10] e.g. Thuc. 2.92.1, 4.34.1; Dion. Hal. *Ant.* 1.80.2, 3.25.1, 7.35.4, 11.38.4.
[11] e.g. Duris *FGrH* 76 F3 = Theopompus *FGrH* 115 F280; Cic. *In Cat.* 1.1; Philo *Leg. ad Gaium* 1.1; Jos. *Ant.* 11.162; *Epistula Heracliti* 9.1. Such phrases are found in other rhetorical contexts in the romances: see e.g. *Ninus*, fr. A 68, Ach. Tat. 2.5.1, and Hld. 5.6.2; and in general Whitmarsh 2020: 197.
[12] Heliodorus' specific form καθεδεῖσθε is found at *De Chers.* 77; *In Aristog.* 1.12.
[13] Luc. *De dom.* 1. On 'the silence of the masses', see Schmitz 1997: 91–6.

general Hegesias ('Mr Leader') is so whipped up that he interrupts him ἔτι λέγοντα (4.20.1), and urges the people to pursue without delay (cf. μελλήσει, 4.20.2). The result is an 'irresistible surge' (δρόμος ἀκάθεκτος, 4.21.2) from the theatre and to war. The passage as a whole, then, promises a rapid transition from the placidity of the festival to a frenetic fervour.[14]

8.2. How Do Wars Start?

Going to war on behalf of an abducted woman is of course a narrative *topos* in Greek literature, rooted ultimately in the mythical mustering of the Achaean forces to recover Helen.[15] The Paris and Helen story hovers in the background of Heliodorus' episode: Theagenes, who had arrived in Delphi as a descendant of Achilles, is now cast in the role of Paris. There was, however, in Greek literature a substantial secondary tradition exploring the relationship between abduction and warfare. As is well known, fifth-century Athens saw Herodotus' *Histories* and several dramas exploring the idea that ἁρπαγή might be a legitimate *casus belli*.[16] Athenian literature's androcentrism is reinforced by the sense of a male community gathering around to observe the 'problem'[17] of female betrayal.[18] Our passage, moreover, is loosely modelled on Chariton 3.3.1–8, which serves as a 'window reference' onto the earlier instances of the *topos* (particularly the Helen story).[19] In Chariton, the citizens of Syracuse discover that Callirhoe's tomb has been robbed: a pitiable

---

[14] This rapid shift from motionlessness into action also recalls the opening tableau (Whitmarsh 2002: 117).
[15] See e.g. Ath. *Deipn.* 560b (= Duris *FGrH* 76 F2): 'the greatest wars came about thanks to women: the Trojan thanks to Helen, the plague thanks to Chryseis, the wrath of Achilles thanks to Briseis; and the so-called Sacred War thanks to another spouse, so Duris says in the second book of his *Histories*, by the name of Theano, who was abducted (ἁρπασθεῖσαν) by a Phocian.'
[16] For ἁρπαγή and cognates in Herodotus' Phoenician and Persian *logoi*, see 1.2.1–3, 1.4.2, 1.5.2. Saïd 2012: 101–4 links these *logoi* with the wider structure of the *Histories*. For Heliodorus' use of Herodotus see Morgan 1982: 234–40, 250; Elmer 2008. The best-known examples are Ar. *Ach.* 528–9 and Cratinus' *Dionysalexandros*. On these and other possible comic references to the Trojan War see Wright 2007.
[17] 'Nor will you have escaped worrying over this problem—those of you who are men; those of you who are women this will not apply—you are yourselves the problem' (Freud 1933: 113).
[18] Cf. Fetterley 1978: xii–xiii: 'American literature is male. To read the canon of what is currently considered classic American literature is perforce to identify as male....America is female; to be American is male; and the quintessential American experience is betrayal by woman.'
[19] See Thomas 1986: 186 on window references, although Heliodorus' does not quite meet the criterion of being a 'very close adaptation of a model': it is more a general allusion to a cultural paradigm. Alvares 1997: 618 discusses the mustering in Chariton in the context of a wider sequence of associations with the Trojan War.

speech from Chaereas elicits mass lamentation,[20] and warships are sent out in search of her corpse. Chariton has the general Hermocrates lead the call to military action, just as the general Hegesias does in Heliodorus. When in our passage the servants at 4.19.1 have announced 'the theft of the girl' (τὴν τῆς κόρης ἁρπαγήν), then, they therefore not merely misrepresented the situation by obscuring the question of Charicleia's consent in the abduction, but also implicitly suggested that war was the only possible outcome. In other words, their 'announcing' (ἐξαγγειλάντων) of the event as a ἁρπαγή is also an act of generic designation: this story will now become a military one.[21] In Achilles Tatius too there is a ἁρπαγή with epic undertones, in the form of the abduction of Calligone in Book 2 (obliquely trailed by the Europa ekphrasis that announces the novel).[22]

One important intertextual resource for thickening out this discourse of war is oratory. A nocturnal assembly (νυκτερινὸν βουλευτήριον, 4.19.5)[23] of the entire polity (women and men) of the Delphians is convoked in the assembly, with a view to persuading the populace of the need for war. There are two speeches delivered: an initial one by Charicles soliciting his audience's pity and calling for avenging punishment (4.19.6–9), and a subsequent one by the general Hegesias calling the people to action (4.20–4.21.1). Both are, as one might expect, highly rhetorical in nature, and verge on the clichéd. (Calasiris' earlier, private speech to Charicles had also been rhetorically contrived, but in a stagey way that fitted the persona he was adopting.) Charicles begins his speech to the assembly with 'Perhaps, Delphians, you think that I have come before you and I have called this assembly out of a desire to denounce myself...' (4.19.6); this kind of 'perhaps it appears to you that...' gambit is familiar from the classical orators,[24] and self-accusations born of grief are found elsewhere in the novels.[25] His black clothing and the ashes on his head and face are obviously hackneyed markers of grief.[26] Hegesias' public speech to the assembled Delphians—which mirrors Calasiris' private speech to Charicles—similarly calls them to action: 'let Charicles lament now, and later too; but let *us* not be similarly deluged by

---

[20] ὅλον εἰς θρῆνον παραφερόμενον, Hld. 4.20.1 ~ θρῆνον τὸ πλῆθος ἐξέρρηξεν, Char. 3.3.7.
[21] The preponderance of πολεμ- roots in the following section is striking: πολεμίους, 4.19.2; πόλεμον, 4.19.3; πολέμοις, 4.20.1; πολεμίους, 4.20.2; πολεμικόν, πόλεμον, 4.21.2.
[22] On the epic motifs here, see Lefteratou 2018: 345–9 and Whitmarsh 2020: 205.
[23] βουλευτήριον is thus not used in the strict sense of a select 'council' (LSJ s.v.). At 4.19.6 the same gathering is also called an ἐκκλησία.
[24] Dem. *Phil.* 1.27, 3.4.
[25] Ach. Tat. 7.7. [26] Ashes and grief: e.g. Luc. *De luctu* 12; Max. Tyr. 5.7.

this man's suffering, as if carried along by the tide of his tears. Don't let the opportunity slip!' (4.20.1). There are also echoes of the impatient rhetoric of Demosthenes, specifically his calls to arms against Philip.[27] These echoes of classical oratory are of course appropriate to the classicizing setting of Heliodorus' narrative.

Another militaristic hypotext is the episode in *Odyssey* 24 where the relatives of the slain suitors gather in the *agora*, to be addressed by Eupeithes (the father of Antinous).[28] In the *Odyssey*, the μέγα ἔργον that requires avenging is murder rather than abduction, but the tropes are similar: like Charicles, Eupeithes weeps (24.425, 438), speaks of his suicidal grief (24.435–6), and engenders pity in his audience (24.438); like Hegesias, he calls upon his audience to act before it is too late (24.430–3), and warns them of the disgrace that will fall upon them if they do not avenge this crime (24.432–5).

These literary echoes serve to confirm the dominant narrative that is abroad in Delphi: that the call to war will presage a righteous retribution inflicted on the Thessalian transgressors. The rhetorical invocation of the ἁρπαγή-and-punishment scheme is, however, a simplification of the reasons for war: not just because (as we shall see in more detail in the following section) Charicleia was a willing participant but also because another reason is given for the abduction. In our passage, Charicles initially blames himself for his foster-daughter's abduction. The events are a manifestation, he suggests, of the gods' righteous wrath (μῆνις) against him: he had received a prophecy that he would lose 'the sight of the things dearest to him' (τῆς τῶν φιλτάτων ὄψεως), since he had on one occasion entered the inner sanctuary and seen 'what was not permitted' (ἃ μὴ θέμις, 4.19.3). This alternative explanation operates at the different, and partially complementary level of divine machination. Heliodorus thus invokes 'double determination' as a motivation for the elopement, in the Homeric manner (appropriately enough). There may be an allusion to the tradition that Helen's promiscuity was imposed by Aphrodite to punish Tyndareus for a ritual infraction.[29]

---

[27] The passage just cited is immediately followed by πρᾶγμα ὃ μεγίστην ἐν ἅπασιν ἔχει καὶ πολέμοις οὐχ ἥκιστα τὴν ῥοπήν, a close echo (as noted by Rattenbury and Lumb 1960: 2.34) of Dem. *Ol.* 2.22: μεγάλη γὰρ ῥοπή, μᾶλλον δὲ τὸ ὅλον ἡ τύχη παρὰ πάντ' ἐστὶ τὰ τῶν ἀνθρώπων πράγματα.

[28] *Od.* 24.420–38; cf. Feuillâtre 1966: 110.

[29] Stesichorus fr. 85 in Finglass and Davies 2015, with their comments at 319–22. On the pattern (the gods punish parents by afflicting their children) in Greek myth and folklore, see Davies 2010.

The more direct reworking, however, is of the beginning of Herodotus. The ἁρπαγή-war motif, as we have seen, is likely already to have put readers in mind of the Persian and Phoenician *logoi* that begin the *Histories*, but what Herodotus says next is also relevant. Croesus, we read, is 'the originator of the unjust acts committed against the Greeks' (τὸν... πρῶτον ὑπάρξαντα ἀδίκων ἔργων ἐς τοὺς Ἕλληνας, 1.5.3), a phrase that seems to lay the blame squarely with him. Yet Herodotus also explains Croesus' behaviour as the fulfilment of a punishment (τίσις, 1.13.2) for his ancestor Gyges' usurpation of the throne of Lydia four generations earlier. The crucial point of connection with our story is that Gyges, like Heliodorus' Charicles, also entered an interior space and saw things that were not permitted, namely Candaules' wife naked. In both episodes, then, a transgressive act of viewing within a projected inner space motivates an illicit act in a later generation, an act that leads to war.[30]

We should note in passing that the prophecy to Charicles is ambiguous: does the prediction that he will lose 'the sight of the things dearest to him' portend loss of sight or loss of what is dearest to him? Charicles himself gives no indication that he has considered the former. Readers, moreover, have already been prepared for the idea that there is a close metaphorical connection between eyesight and the objects of one's affection.[31] The oracle in our passage responds to Charicleia's better-known prophetic dream, from Book 2, of losing an eye,[32] a dream that she at the time takes to portend the loss of Theagenes ('my eye, my soul, my everything'), while Cnemon believes it means her father[33] is dead (2.16.2-6). In sum, the indications are that Charicles' interpretation is right, and that the oracle's 'losing the sight of what is dearest' means being deprived of those one loves. The hint of possible blindness, however, remains there in the background, not least because of the echoes of the blinding of Tiresias—another priest of Apollo—for witnessing τὰ μὴ θεμιτά.[34]

---

[30] On proto-novelistic elements in the Gyges and Candaules story, see Tatum 1994a.

[31] At 4.19.8 Charicles subsequently uses the phrase τῶν ἐμῶν ὀφθαλμῶν in apposition to 'Charicleia'.

[32] 2.16.1: see Winkler 1982: 115; Bartsch 1989: 99–100; Hunter 1998a: 48–9.

[33] Which of the three rivals for this title: Hydaspes, Charicles, or Calasiris? Winkler and Bartsch (previous n.) argue that Cnemon inadvertently identifies the right interpretation (albeit misunderstanding the timescale), since the dream portends the future death of Calasiris in Book 7. The ambiguity is already indicated in Cnemon's question to her: 'are your πάτερες still alive?' (2.16.5)—where the primary meaning of πάτερες seems to be 'parents' (LSJ s.v. VII.2), but of course the reader (if, admittedly, not the first-time reader) will think of her many father-figures.

[34] Call. *Hymn.* 5.78. The connection is identified by Rattenbury and Lumb 1960: 32 n. 2.

The central point, however, is that what is taken to be the divine prognostication of the cause of the potential Delphian war adds another level of complexity to the discourse of origination. It would be a war motivated both by Theagenes' immoral actions (as the Delphians judge them) and, indirectly, by Charicles' historic actions. This double-layeredness, which carries with it echoes of rich literary precedents, magnifies the event, and leads first-time readers to anticipate a war of great significance—an anticipation that will, however, be frustrated.

8.3. Questions of Consent

A ἁρπαγή narrative inevitably raises questions about agency and volition. In particular, these questions are prompted by reflections on the Ur-ἁρπαγή, the abduction of Helen. Whether she consented to go with Paris was a crucial issue, right from the very start of the Greek literary tradition. In Homer, she protests to Aphrodite that the goddess is prone to leading her around from city to city (*Il.* 3.399–405), an accusation that seems designed to mitigate her own responsibility for events. In Sappho 16, by contrast, all of the agency is said to be hers: the choice to leave her husband and family was hers alone (no mention of the Judgement). Gorgias' fifth-century *Helen* attempts to exonerate her by arguing that she was coerced into going with Paris; Euripides in his *Trojan Women* depicts her making this very point before Menelaus in an attempt to argue her innocence (940–50). In Colluthus' *Abduction of Helen* (sixth century CE), Helen apparently goes willingly, but appears in a dream to Hermione claiming coercion.[35] The precedent of Helen's ἁρπαγή and the moral questions it raises, then, guide readers to explore such questions in this passage too.

Questions of female consent remain critically important in the imperial era. In *Leucippe and Clitophon* Clinias tells his cousin Clitophon that he must use πειθώ rather than βία—while implying, like a twenty-first-century pickup artist, that 'persuasion' involves no agency on the female's part (it is simply a matter of the male applying the right seductive technique).[36] Nevertheless, we are told—in a passage that reads as shocking now—girls often pretend to be unwilling when in fact they are willing (1.10.6).

---

[35] Colluth. 372–8, with Morales 2016: 67–73.
[36] Ach. Tat. 1.10.7, with Whitmarsh 2020: 64–6. The motifs are, of course, also Ovidian (Whitmarsh 2020: 147).

Clitophon absorbs this advice and later interprets Leucippe's resistance to his kissing as a pretence (2.7.7). When Clitophon is surprised in Leucippe's bedroom, her mother raises the question of her complicity in the affair, invoking (with extraordinary callousness, from a modern vantage) the grim ancient commonplace that it would have been preferable that she had been forced rather than seduced (2.24.3).

The interest in these matters of consent and violence should be viewed in the light of historical reality. Women really were abducted, in both peace and war. The ἁρπαγή of Achilles' Leucippe has been read against the backdrop of the phenomenon identified by Judith Evans Grubbs as 'abduction marriage',[37] whereby a girl seized illegally could be treated as a legal spouse.[38] More generally, as Helen Morales has recently argued in relation to Colluthus' hexameter Ἁρπαγὴ Ἑλένης and related poems, it is an error to see themes of abduction and sexual violence as merely literary tropes:

> The *Abduction of Helen* was written approximately forty to fifty years after the Vandals sacked Rome in 455 CE. Even though we have few descriptions of the violence and, in particular, the violence towards women, the attack by the Vandals was more severe and prolonged than the attack forty-five years earlier by the Visigoths. Alaric's attack in 410 CE lasted about three days, and some accounts minimize the brutality involved, but we know that rape was used as a weapon of war and that many women were left traumatized by sexual assault.[39]

It is likely that readers of Heliodorus knew of women (and perhaps even some men) who had endured ἁρπαγή. This was, as Morales emphasizes, part of the violent reality of the world. At the same time, however, we should recognize (again with Morales) that the literary coding of ἁρπαγή was complex, and covered a variety of narratives of agency. ἁρπάζειν has violent connotations, to be sure, like the English 'grab' and 'snatch'. It is often associated with βία in the Greek tradition.[40] But while the force could assuredly be directed at the woman (as in the case of Callisthenes' abduction of Calligone in Achilles Tatius), this is not necessarily the case. In line with a common conception of rape in antiquity,[41] ἁρπαγή could be imagined to be a crime against the woman's guardian (κύριος), irrespective of her own agency and consent. In such cases, women could be 'snatched'—*from*

---

[37] Evans Grubbs 1989.   [38] Lateiner 1997.   [39] Morales 2016: 80.
[40] e.g. Isoc. *De Pac.* 8; Plut. *Reg. et imp. apophth.* 203c; Hdn. 2.2, 3, 5, etc.
[41] See Deacy and Pierce eds 1997; Omitowoju 2002.

their parents—even when they departed consensually. In such cases the complexity of the agential 'reality' behind such events (coercion can take different forms) is of course entirely lost to us, along with the vast majority of female subjectivity in Greek antiquity. But we can glimpse some of the ideological tensions, at least, in the way that abductions are reported. When Herodotus claims that the women whose abductions began the hostilities between east and west 'would not have been snatched if they had not been willing' (1.4.2: εἰ μὴ αὐταὶ ἐβούλοντο, οὐκ ἂν ἡρπάζοντο),[42] we get a flavour of the anxiety of the tortuous cultural logic that must have been required in order to reconcile the reality of female sexual agency with a heavily asymmetrical, patrilocal world in which women were almost always subject to the control of men, whether κύριοι or abductors.

Female consent was not, therefore, the factor that demarcated rape from seduction: ἁρπαγή covered both unwilling abduction and willing elopement. But this did not mean consent was a non-issue. Ancient discourse around ἁρπαγή is entirely androcentric, and pays little or no attention to the well-being of its victims; but the question of consent remained an important one. Crucially, by the time that Heliodorus was writing,[43] consent was a principle recognized in law, albeit not in the way that we would recognize it today. Constantine I enacted a decree in 320 defining *rapere* (the Latin equivalent of ἁρπάζειν) as the abduction of a girl 'whether unwilling or willing' (*invitam...vel volentem*). The full passage runs as follows:

> If any man who had not previously made a pact with the parents of a girl should snatch this girl against her will, or if he should abduct a girl who was willing, hoping to obtain protection from the consent (*responsione*) of the girl, although it was because of the fault of the frivolity and the inconstancy of her sex and judgement that a girl was altogether excluded by the ancients from conducting suits in court and from giving testimony and from all matters pertaining to courts, the consent (*responsio*) of the girl shall be of no advantage to him, as it would have been under the ancient law, but rather the girl herself shall be held liable as a participant in the crime.[44]

---

[42] In Herodotus' mind must have been, as well as real-life examples, the literary paradigm of the Phoenician slave-woman described in *Odyssey* 15, who worked in the young Eumaeus' house before eloping, apparently voluntarily, with a Phoenician trader.

[43] I assume a date later in the fourth century.

[44] *Codex Theodosianus* 9.24.1–2. This is the law that Evans Grubbs 1989 interprets as an attempt to outlaw abduction marriage. That may well have been the intention, but the law is broader in its coverage, and would have included elopement.

The Constantinian decree presents itself as supplanting a more lenient earlier law, self-consciously rejecting the view of 'the ancients' that took the girl's consent as a mitigation of the man's crime. According to the Constantinian decree, by contrast, the only difference that sexual consent makes is that it renders the girl equally culpable. The discussion of female agency is striking: the girl is simultaneously empowered by the law ('…shall be held liable…') and belittled for 'the frivolity and the inconstancy of her sex'. The law proceeds, indeed, to instrumentalize this new-found agency against the females in question. Rape victims, we read, are partially to blame, since 'they could have kept themselves chaste at home up to the time of marriage'; indeed, 'if the doors were broken by the audacity of the ravisher, the girls could have obtained the aid of neighbours by their cries and defended themselves by all their efforts' (9.24.2). The question of the girl's consent affects only the degree of her own culpability: if she is willing then she shares the blame with the rapist, whereas if she is unwilling she is less so (but still not blameless, for she could have done more to keep herself from public view or to defend herself).

This law was in place at the time Heliodorus wrote. How commonly it was called upon we do not know. Nor can we assume that Heliodorus imagines a world in which Roman law applies: his narrative is set in the classical period, and in general the romances' presentation of law is (in the words of Saundra Schwartz) 'a bricolage. It draws from a range of sources: the declamations, the Attic orators, the revival of the culture of the classical *polis*, and the experience of living under Roman rule while grappling with distinctly Roman (i.e., foreign) ways of conceptualising legal disputes.'[45] Nevertheless, as Schwartz's final point indicates, contemporary Roman law does provide some of the moral framework within which the Greek romances' agents act. So it is worth asking, in the light of the Constantinian law, whether the Delphians believe Charicleia to be an active or a passive participant. Theagenes is guilty of ἁρπαγή either way; but the Constantinian innovation was to demand that we consider also the question of the girl's consent, so as to judge her culpability.[46]

The Delphians in fact assume without question that Theagenes and the Thessalians are the culpable parties: they are said to be guilty of ὕβρις

---

[45] Schwartz 2016: 9.

[46] It is presumably a similar cultural attitude that motivates Clinias' warning to Clitophon in Achilles Tatius that seduced women often pretend to have been raped ἵνα τῇ δόξῃ τῆς ἀνάγκης ἀποτρέπωνται τῆς αἰσχύνης τὸ ἑκούσιον (1.10.6). Under Constantinian law, the 'shame' became legally actionable.

(4.19.2, 7) and—insofar as it is the ζάκορος of Artemis who has been abducted—ἀσέβεια (4.21.1), and deemed worthy of τιμωρία (4.19.2, 7, 4.20.2). Even the deceptive Calasiris pins the blame entirely on Theagenes. We could pursue them, Charicles says, 'if we knew who it was who has inflicted this grievous act of war' upon us (εἰ τίς ὁ τὸν βαρὺν τοῦτον ἐπενεγκὼν πόλεμον ἐγινώσκομεν, 4.19.3). 'The Thessalian!' replies Calasiris.[47] In the Delphians' mind, then, the decision to go to war is rhetorically legitimated by a clear assertion of culpability, criminality, and the need for retribution.

What of Charicleia? No mention is made in the assembly of the possibility that she might have been willing, but there may be an echo of the Constantinian law's victim-blaming. In addition to immediate military action, Hegesias proposes that in future the priestess of Apollo should not appear in public (ἀναφαίνειν, 4.21.1) in front of those who are engaging in the hoplite race, since it was that 'first viewing' of Charicleia that was the 'origin of the impiety' (ἀρχὴ…ἀσεβείας, 4.21.1). Unlike the Constantinian legislator, Hegesias blames the lax permissiveness of the Delphic polity rather than Charicleia herself; but the suggestion that sequestering women is part of the solution springs from the same mentality.

The Delphians' inability to countenance the attribution of blame to Charicleia is rooted partly in a wider cultural belief that minimizes the agency of women (both generally and specifically in matters of sexuality), and partly—attentive readers will conclude—in an authorial desire to characterize their response as a myopic misreading of romantic conventions. Theagenes is a romance hero of a particularly high-minded kind,[48] not a predator. In fact, immediately prior to our passage, Charicleia has extracted an oath from Theagenes that he will not make any sexual attempts upon her until she has reached her homeland—and Theagenes' only objection is that the oath unfairly implies that he would not be able to act virtuously without it (4.18.4-6). The effect of that passage is to underline just how misguided is the Delphians' view of him. Perhaps more significantly, the Delphians underestimate Charicleia herself. She is far from a passive victim: as has

---

[47] There is conceivably a distant echo here of the opening of the *Iliad*: the narrator asks who it was who brought together Agamemnon and Achilles 'to fight in strife' (ἔριδι…μάχεσθαι, *Il.* 1.8), before answering his own question: 'the son of Leto and Zeus' (*Il.* 1.9). We might also detect echoes of Herodotus 1.5.3, and the assertion (after all the debates about who began the ἁρπαγαί) that 'I will indicate him whom I myself know to have begun the unjust wrongs against the Greeks' (viz. Croesus).

[48] See e.g. Jones 2012: 154–8.

often been noted, she often takes the lead while Theagenes mopes or remains indecisive.[49] This greater agency is far from morally straightforward: as Helen Morales notes in this volume, it can associate her with sex-workers and others who are evaluated negatively by mainstream society. It is nevertheless clear that Heliodorus chooses to endow his female lead with a stronger will and more power to act than was traditional; and that the Delphians' misdiagnosis of the ἁρπαγή is one device he uses to signal that fact.

8.4. Conclusion

The passage under consideration has all the hallmarks of the beginning of a major new narrative thread. First-time readers may well have taken this to be the launching-point for an Iliadic conflict (and perhaps, as I have suggested above, the explanation for the battle scene the aftermath of which opens the novel). As so often, Heliodorus shows himself an attentive and deep reader of the prior literary tradition, drawing out the issues of motivation, agency, and volition that cluster around earlier military narratives that found their origin in acts of abduction (particularly the story of Helen and the opening of Herodotus). Yet that war never eventuates, and the reasons for this are already sown in our passage. The Delphians' haste to make war is based on a misprision, both of the events that have occurred and of the genre in which they are operating. This is not a work of epic or military history, but a romance; and so the elopement of Charicleia and Theagenes should be read in terms of the triumph of reciprocal passion rather than of Theagenes' violently unilateral imposition of his own desire. Indeed, it is in passages such as this that readers can feel the subversive force of the ancient romance, as it sets itself against the dominant social conventions of the day; for the actions of the two young lovers run counter not only to the wishes of Charicles, Hegesias, and the entire community in which Charicleia has been raised, but also to Constantinian law, according to which both parties are equally complicit in a crime of great magnitude. The radical nature of the romance is that it celebrates, and in Heliodorus' case sacramentalizes, a practice that conventional morality saw as deeply criminal. It is perhaps with this in mind that the Constantinian law proceeds to outlaw 'the stories

---

[49] See esp. Johne 1987; Egger 1999: 134–6.

(*fabulis*) and depraved exhortations (*pravis suasionibus*)' that nurses can employ to corrupt young girls, threatening the poor nurses with molten lead poured into their throats.⁵⁰ Was this additional provision intended to outlaw romances (and, indeed to belittle them by associating them with old women's tales)—precisely on the grounds that they cede too much erotic agency to the young, and particularly to young women?

---

⁵⁰ *Codex Theodosianus* 9.24.2. More discussion at Whitmarsh 2018: 3–4.

9
Calasiris on Zacynthus and His Dream of Odysseus (5.17–22)

Michael Paschalis

At the beginning of *Aethiopica* 5 Calasiris sails in secret with Theagenes and Charicleia out from Kirrha (Krissa), the port of Delphi, aboard a Tyrian merchant ship headed for Libya. The ship first proceeds under oar and later under sail;[1] once into the Corinthian Gulf it turns west, and towards sunset its passengers sight the island of Zacynthus in the distance (5.1.1–2). At this point Calasiris breaks off the story, and we hear that Nausicles has returned with a girl whom he thinks is Thisbe but is actually Charicleia. Calasiris is joyfully reunited with Charicleia and at an ensuing feast he resumes his story (5.1.3–5.16). The Phoenician ship reaches Zacynthus, where Calasiris poses as the father of Theagenes and Charicleia. The Tyrians have decided to spend the winter at Zacynthus, and Calasiris lodges at the hut of an old fisherman named Tyrrhenus near the seashore. The Tyrian merchant who owns the ship falls in love with Charicleia and asks persistently for her hand, but Calasiris puts him off with false promises. Tyrrhenus informs Calasiris that Trachinos, the captain of a pirate ship moored in a nearby bay, has fallen madly in love with Charicleia and intends to seize her together with the valuable goods the Phoenician ship is carrying. Alarmed at the news, Calasiris persuades the Tyrian merchant to depart from Zacynthus that very night, though it is still wintertime, by fabricating the story that he has a fearful local rival and promising to give him Charicleia in marriage when they reach Egypt, which has become their new destination for this very

---

[1] Coraes 1804: 167 compares *Od.* 11.639–40 τὴν δὲ κατ' Ὠκεανὸν ποταμὸν φέρε κῦμα ῥόοιο, / πρῶτα μὲν εἰρεσίῃ, μετέπειτα δὲ κάλλιμος οὖρος ('A rising swell / carried our ship down Oceanus' stream. / We rowed at first, but then a fair wind blew'; all translations of the Homeric poems are by Johnston 2007). When in 5.17.1 Calasiris resumes his narrative, picking up the voyage from the beginning, there is no mention of rowing. Coraes 1804: 182 detected a contradiction and suggested that in the first passage Heliodorus was carried away by Homeric imitation.

purpose. While asleep Calasiris dreams of Odysseus: the hero is angry at Calasiris for having neglected to pay a visit to Ithaca and honour him and predicts ordeals like the ones he went through, but also informs him of Penelope's blessing to Charicleia and promise of a happy ending to her adventures. In order to appease Odysseus' wrath, Calasiris asks Tyrrhenus to sail to Ithaca and conduct a sacrifice on his behalf. Calasiris and the couple sail out at dawn, but the Tyrian ship is caught in a violent storm that causes it to be beached on a Cretan shore. After the necessary repairs they resume their voyage, aided by favourable spring breezes. They are anxious to reach a safe haven, because their ship has been followed by what looks like a pirate boat (5.17–22).[2]

9.1. The Voyage to Zacynthus: Navigation, Realism, and Intertextual Opportunity

Chapters 5.17–22 cover the Zacynthian stop of Calasiris and his wards. The ship's approach to Zacynthus is narrated as follows (5.17.4):

"Ὑπερβαλόντες δὴ' λέγων 'τὸν πορθμὸν καὶ νήσους Ὀξείας ἀποκρύψαντες τὴν Ζακυνθίων ἄκραν προσκοπεῖν ἀμφεβάλλομεν ὥσπερ ἀμυδρόν τι νέφος τὰς ὄψεις ἡμῖν ὑποδραμοῦσαν,...'[3]

Saying, 'After passing through the straits and leaving the Pointed Islands in the distance behind us, we caught our first glimpse—though we could not be certain—of the heights of Zacynthus, barely visible on the horizon, like a vague cloud....'

The fact that Odysseus appears to Calasiris while the latter is on the island of Zacynthus takes for granted that this island is part of his Homeric kingdom (*Od.* 9.21-8). But contrary to the confused Homeric geography and the riddle of identifying the hero's native Ithaca,[4] the geography of Heliodorus is fairly accurate and can be traced based on the information provided by

---

[2] It is odd that Libya is mentioned as their destination at 5.22.8—it seems there is a mistake here.
[3] The text of Heliodorus is by Rattenbury, Lumb, and Maillon 1960; all translations of Heliodorus are by Morgan 1989c.
[4] On this issue see recently Bittlestone, Diggle, and Underhill 2005; regarding the course of the project see http://www.odysseus-unbound.org.

Strabo and on modern knowledge of the area.[5] Coming from the Gulf of Kirrha (5.1.2), the ship passed through the turbulent Calydonian straits (5.17.1 τὸν Καλυδώνιον πορθμόν), the narrowest point between Achaia and Aetolia ending in the promontories respectively of Rhion and Antirhion, and then proceeded along the coast of Aetolia and Acarnania. On the right hand its passengers saw the νῆσοι Ὀξεῖαι (= 'Pointed Islands'; modern Ὀξιά), situated near the mouth of the Acheloos river off the coast of Acarnania (Strabo 10.2.19 includes them under the general name of Echinades), and farther ahead the barely visible island of Zacynthus (Strabo 10.2.18).

The ghost of Odysseus will later voice the following complaint to Calasiris: 'All others whose ships have passed by the island of Cephallenia have paid a visit to our home and deemed it a matter of importance to learn of my renown. You, on the other hand, have been so neglectful as to grant me not even the common courtesy of a salutation, despite my dwelling in the vicinity' (5.22.2). Based on the information provided by Strabo and modern knowledge of the area, an obvious question would be if the narrative accurately locates Cephallenia and Ithaca. A ship getting across from the Gulf of Calydon to Zacynthus would have 'sailed by' (παρέπλευσαν) Cephallenia and, depending on the ship's course, its passengers might have been able to see Cephallenia at a distance on their right. The sighting of the Pointed Islands on the right suggests that the Phoenician ship did not take a course far removed from Cephallenia. Cephallenia lies to the north of Zacynthus and is separated by a strait which Strabo (10.2.18) calculates to be sixty stadia (= 11–12 km). The mention of Cephallenia is not unwarranted, because in the Catalogue of Ships (*Il.* 2.631–5) Odysseus is represented as leading a contingent of Cephallenians.[6]

Later Calasiris asks Tyrrhenus to sail over to Ithaca (διαπλεύσας εἰς Ἰθάκην) and sacrifice to the hero on behalf of himself and his wards (5.22.5). Ithaca, Odysseus' homeland, is located to the northeast of Cephallenia, from which it is separated by a strait 4–6 km wide and 20 km long. Assuming that Tyrrhenus has a sailing boat, he should have waited for favourable spring winds and calm seas in order to sail along the eastern coast of Zacynthus (his home lies near the town which faces the Peloponnese) across to

---

[5] On realism concerning geographical descriptions and background details in the *Aethiopica*, see Morgan 1982. As regards place-names and nationalities Morgan notes that seventy-seven out of seventy-nine are authentic (247).

[6] The identification of modern Cephallenia with the Homeric Ithaca and specifically with the peninsula of Παλική has been recently revived by Robert Bittlestone; see Bittlestone, Diggle, and Underhill 2005.

Cephallenia and then continue along the eastern coast of this island in order to reach Ithaca. In conclusion, the geographical information provided by Heliodorus sounds fairly accurate by ancient (Strabo) and modern standards.

The claim of Odysseus' ghost that all those who had sailed by Cephallenia in the past had not neglected to pay a visit to his 'home' (οἶκον) eager to learn of his 'renown' (δόξα) is strongly ironic from the reader's viewpoint. As a matter of fact, the most famous visit to those waters in antiquity was paid in Virgil's *Aeneid* (3.270-3) by Aeneas and his companions, whose attitude towards Odysseus was anything but friendly:

> iam medio apparet fluctu nemorosa Zacynthos
> Dulichiumque Sameque et Neritos ardua saxis.
> effugimus scopulos Ithacae, Laertia regna,
> et terram altricem saeui exsecramur Vlixi.[7]
> On the horizon we soon catch glimpses of wooded
>   Zacynthus,
> Samë, Dulichium, Neritus too, raised high on its steep cliffs.
> Far to our leeward, we hold craggy Ithaca, realm of Laërtes,
> Roundly cursing this land which had suckled the savage
>   Ulysses.[8]

The feelings of the Trojans are openly hostile towards Ithaca, because Odysseus and his countrymen owe their 'renown' to the conquest of Troy (*Od.* 1.2 ἐπεὶ Τροίης ἱερὸν πτολίεθρον ἔπερσε, 'after ravaging / the sacred citadel of Troy'), the homeland of Aeneas and his companions; as a result, they have been wandering for years in search of a new home.[9] The course of their approach to Zacynthus is accurately given. Like the passengers of the Phoenician ship in the *Aethiopica*, the Trojans sight Zacynthus first of the islands that once belonged to Odysseus, because they are coming from the Strophades lying to the south of Zacynthus.

Under the pressure of the pirate threat, Calasiris, Theagenes, and Charicleia depart in haste from Zacynthus aboard the Tyrian ship, now heading for Egypt (see 5.19.3 and 5.21.2). Since it is still winter the sailors vehemently oppose this decision (5.22.6). They are proven right because the

---

[7] The text is by Mynors 1969.   [8] The translation is by Ahl 2007.
[9] See further Paschalis 1987.

ship is soon caught in a violent storm and ends up beached on a Cretan shore (5.22.7):

Ἡμεῖς δὲ πνεύμασι βιαίοις χρησάμενοι ζάλης τε ἀπροσμάχου καὶ κλύδωνος ἀφράστου πειραθέντες ἀπολέσθαι τε παρὰ μικρὸν ἐλθόντες εἰς ἄκραν τινὰ Κρητικὴν προσωκείλαμεν, τῶν τε πηδαλίων θάτερον ἀποβαλόντες καὶ τῆς κεραίας τὸ πλεῖστον συντρίψαντες·

Buffeted by gales, lashed by a storm too violent to resist, pounded by a sea swell that words are not adequate to describe, we narrowly escaped with our lives and beached our ship on a headland on Crete, one of our rudders gone and most of our rigging smashed.

Cape Malea, on the southeast coast of Laconia, is the most likely point where this storm occurred. Apparently, the Tyrian ship crossed over from Zacynthus to the Peloponnese, sailed along its western coast and continued on its south side first round Cape Acritas and along the Messenian Gulf, and next round Cape Tainaron and along the Laconian Gulf until it reached Cape Malea.[10] This promontory was dreaded by sailors,[11] because contrary winds were a constant source of difficulty to vessels trying to round it in either direction, as the Tyrian merchants themselves had experienced earlier (4.16.7). Most importantly the promontory plays a pivotal role in the *Odyssey*: Menelaus (3.286–92), Odysseus (9.74–84 and 19.186–7 in the false story he tells to Penelope) and Agamemnon (4.514–20) are blown off course at this point, and for the first two heroes it marks the beginning of their wanderings.[12] Cape Malea lies opposite the extreme northwestern coast of Crete, and this would account for the fact that stormy seas in the *Odyssey* carry away to Crete half of Menelaus' ships and Odysseus in the false story

---

[10] On coastal navigation in the Mediterranean during Greco-Roman antiquity, see Beresford (2013) passim.

[11] Cf. Strabo 8.6.20 (trans. Jones (1927)) on Cape Malea: 'Corinth is called "wealthy" because of its commerce, since it is situated on the Isthmus and is master of two harbours, of which the one leads straight to Asia, and the other to Italy; and it makes easy the exchange of merchandise from both countries that are so far distant from each other. And just as in early times the Strait of Sicily was not easy to navigate, so also the high seas, and particularly the sea beyond Maleae, were not, on account of the contrary winds; and hence the proverb, "But when you double Maleae, forget your home" [Μαλέας δὲ κάμψας ἐπιλάθου τῶν οἴκαδε]. At any rate, it was a welcome alternative, for the merchants both from Italy and from Asia, to avoid the voyage to Maleae and to land their cargoes here.'

[12] See Heubeck, West, and Hainsworth on *Od.* 3.287; Heubeck and Hoekstra on *Od.* 9.80–1. The dangerous promontory provided the Corcyraeans with a plausible excuse for their absence from Salamis in 480 (Hdt. 7.168).

he tells to Penelope, and in the *Aethiopica* the Phoenician ship with Calasiris, Theagenes, and Charicleia.[13]

A stop on Zacynthus en route to Libya is realistic, then, just as are the other geographical and meteorological details, but it is the intertextual and metaliterary resonances which are the main explanation for the Zacynthian stop. These are revealed when Calasiris is visited by the ghost of Odysseus, although we should note that Heliodorus skilfully camouflaged his intention. He made the Odyssean background as unobtrusive as possible by incorporating it into the course and texture of the narrative: there is no flagrant violation of plausibility as, for instance, if the ship had sailed directly to Odysseus' homeland which lies outside the ship's course towards Libya. The result is that Odysseus' appearance is entirely unexpected. There is no hint whatsoever that the ship has reached an island formerly belonging to the kingdom of Odysseus or that an encounter of this sort lies ahead. Before chapter 22, the narrative is taken up with other information and developments, one of which, the amorous attraction of Trachinos to Charicleia, will determine the course of events till almost the end of Book 5.

9.2. The Heliodoran Odysseus

Here now is Calasiris' dream of Odysseus (5.22.1–3), and his request to Tyrrhenus that he sail to Ithaca in order to sacrifice to its former king (5.22.5):

Ἐπεὶ δὲ δείπνου πρὸς ὀλίγον μεταλαβόντες εἰς ὕπνον ἐτράπημεν, ὄναρ μοί τις πρεσβύτης ἐφαίνετο τὰ μὲν ἄλλα κατεσκληκὼς ἐπιγουνίδα δέ, λείψανον τῆς ἐφ' ἡλικίας ἰσχύος, ἀνεσταλμένου ζώματος ὑποφαίνων, κυνῆν μὲν τῆς κεφαλῆς ἐπικείμενος ἀγχίνουν δὲ ἅμα καὶ πολύτροπον περισκοπούμενος καὶ οἷον ἐκ πληγῆς τινος μηρὸν σκάζοντα παρέλκων. Πλησιάσας δή μοι καὶ σεσηρός τι μειδιάσας 'Ὦ θαυμάσιε' ἔφη, 'σὺ δὲ μόνος ἐν οὐδενὸς λόγου μέρει τέθεισαι τὰ καθ' ἡμᾶς, ἀλλὰ πάντων ὅσοι δὴ τὴν Κεφαλλήνων παρέπλευσαν οἶκόν τε τὸν ἡμέτερον ἐπισκεψαμένων καὶ δόξαν γνῶναι τὴν ἡμετέραν ἐν σπουδῇ θεμένων αὐτὸς οὕτως ὀλιγώρως ἔσχηκας ὡς μηδὲ τοῦτο δὴ τὸ κοινὸν προσειπεῖν, ἐν γειτόνων καὶ ταῦτα οἰκοῦντα. Τοιγάρτοι τούτων ὑφέξεις οὐκ εἰς μακρὰν τὴν δίκην καὶ τῶν ὁμοίων ἐμοὶ παθὼν αἰσθήσῃ,

---

[13] Cf. Coraes 1804: 187.

θαλάττῃ τε ἅμα καὶ γῇ πολεμίοις ἐντυγχάνων· τὴν κόρην δὲ ἣν ἄγεις παρὰ τῆς ἐμῆς γαμετῆς πρόσειπε, χαίρειν γὰρ αὐτῇ φησι διότι πάντων ἐπίπροσθεν ἄγει τὴν σωφροσύνην καὶ τέλος αὐτῇ δεξιὸν εὐαγγελίζεται....

'καὶ τήνδε δίδου τελευταίαν χάριν· θῦε διαπλεύσας εἰς Ἰθάκην ὑπὲρ ἡμῶν Ὀδυσσεῖ καὶ αἴτει τῆς μήνιδος ἀνεῖναι τῆς καθ' ἡμῶν ἣν ἀγανακτεῖν ὡς παρεωραμένος τῇσδέ μοι τῆς νυκτὸς ἐπιφανεὶς ἐξηγόρευσεν.'

After a light supper we retired for the night, but as I slept, a vision of an old man appeared to me. Age had withered him almost to a skeleton, except that his cloak was hitched up to reveal a thigh that retained some vestige of the strength of his youth. He wore a leather helmet on his head, and his expression was one of cunning and many wiles; he was lame in one leg, as if from a wound of some kind. He stood by my bed and said, with a sinister smile: 'You, my fine friend, are the only man who has ever treated us with such utter contempt. All others whose ships have passed by the island of Cephallenia have paid a visit to our home and deemed it a matter of importance to learn of my renown. You, on the other hand, have been so neglectful as to grant me not even the common courtesy of a salutation, despite my dwelling in the vicinity. But your omissions will be visited on you very soon. Ordeals like mine shall you undergo; land and sea you shall find united in enmity against you. However, to the maiden you have with you my wife sends greetings and wishes her joy, since she esteems chastity above all things. Good tidings too she sends her: her story has a happy ending....

'One final favour I ask of you: take your boat over to Ithaca and make an offering to Odysseus on our behalf. Ask him to temper his wrath against us, for he has appeared to me this very night and told me that he is angry at having been slighted.'

Of the two passages, it is mainly Calasiris' dream of Odysseus that has attracted attention. The reasons are plain and well-known: Homer's *Odyssey* is 'the principal foundation-text of romance'; Heliodorus' *Aethiopica* is 'the most explicitly Odyssean' novel; and Calasiris is the main one of three heroes who play the role of Odysseus in the novel (the other two are Charicleia and Theagenes).[14] The dream has not, however, been interpreted with attention to detail and has furthermore been discussed independently

---

[14] Morgan and Harrison 2008: 220 and 224–5.

of its context, which is the Zacynthian stop of Calasiris. Summary treatment has on occasion led to factual errors.[15]

Two points should in my view be taken into consideration for clearing the ground as regards any interpretation of Odysseus' dream. Both have already been touched upon by scholars but have not been used as interpretative tools. The first one has to do with the difference between Odysseus as an epic hero and Odysseus as a novelistic hero. After noting that this is the only instance where an epic hero plays a role in an ancient novel, Graverini goes on to clarify that 'the Trojan war is so far in time that he [Odysseus] cannot be Homer's hero anymore: he is an old man.... He is not even a man anymore: as a dream apparition, he acquires a quasi-divine status.'[16] The second point has to do with the μῆνις ('wrath') of the Heliodoran Odysseus. Montiglio reminds us that Odysseus plays here the role of the punishing god that initiates Calasiris' wanderings as Poseidon does with Odysseus in Homer's epic, but she also points out an obvious difference from the *Odyssey*:

> In Heliodorus there is no clear original fault on the lovers' part to make amends for (though Charicleia initially feels ashamed of her elopement), hence the intervention *ex machina* of Odysseus himself to tie the misfortunes which will beset the couple to Calasiris' negligence, according to the *Odyssey* pattern of 'fault-retribution'.[17]

Both considerations should be kept in mind while taking a closer look at Calasiris' dream. As Morgan notes,[18] the description of Odysseus at 5.22.1 contains a number of Homeric allusions through which the old man is identifiable as Odysseus. The withering of age evokes the disguise given to Odysseus by Athene at *Od.* 13.397–401;[19] the strong thigh comes from

---

[15] For instance, Bartsch 1989: 101 has argued that the dream's 'most immediate effect is to cause the hasty departure of Calasiris and his wards from the island...and thereby their subsequent capture by pirates', whereas the hasty departure is decided *before* the dream on account of the pirate threat to Charicleia and the ship's cargo. Tyrrhenus communicates the threat to Calasiris who in turn tricks the Tyrian merchant into accepting his plan for leaving the island that very night (5.21.1–4).
[16] Graverini 2014: 297.   [17] Montiglio 2013b: 149.
[18] Morgan 1989c: 462 n. 144.
[19] ἀλλ' ἄγε σ' ἄγνωστον τεύξω πάντεσσι βροτοῖσι· / κάρψω μὲν χρόα καλὸν ἐνὶ γναμπτοῖσι μέλεσσι, / ξανθὰς δ' ἐκ κεφαλῆς ὀλέσω τρίχας, ἀμφὶ δὲ λαῖφος / ἔσσω, ὅ κε στυγέῃσιν ἰδὼν ἄνθρωπος ἔχοντα, / κνυζώσω δέ τοι ὄσσε πάρος περικαλλέ' ἐόντε...('But come, I'll transform you, / so you'll be unrecognizable to all. / I'll wrinkle fine skin on your supple limbs, / remove the dark hair on your head, and then / dress you in rags which would make you shudder / to see clothing anyone. And your eyes, / so striking up to now, I'll make them dim').

Od. 18.66-8;[20] the leather helmet is derived from *Iliad* 10.261-5;[21] the words for 'cunning' and 'of many wiles' originate respectively in *Od.* 13.332 and 1.1;[22] and the wound in one leg comes from the boar-inflicted wound at Parnassus (*Od.* 19.392-4). The proposed origin of this last feature is not entirely satisfactory, because the incident in question did not give the Homeric hero a permanent limp as if he were the god Hephaestus. Odysseus acquired a temporary one when he was wounded in battle like other Homeric heroes (*Iliad* 19.47-50, where he is mentioned together with Diomedes). The problem with this alternative interpretation, however, is that Odysseus was not wounded in his foot, leg, or thigh but in the fleshy part of his ribs.[23] Hence Heliodorus may be combining here allusions to two different Homeric episodes.

What actually makes the Heliodoran Odysseus different from the Homeric is not just that the former is depicted as an old man and is inserted in the novelistic narrative as a dream apparition. It is principally the composite picture of Odysseus, and the extravagance and the nature of Homeric allusions that Heliodorus puts together in order to establish his identity in the eyes of Calasiris. Instead of one distinct feature that would have made Odysseus recognizable in the eyes of the character directly concerned and in the eyes of the reader, we find a collage of features that make up an almost comic portrait of the Homeric hero. In the *Odyssey* it takes only one physical feature, the boar-inflicted scar, for Eurycleia to recognize Odysseus (19.390-4):

---

[20] αὐτὰρ Ὀδυσσεύς / ζώσατο μὲν ῥάκεσιν περὶ μήδεα, φαῖνε δὲ μηρούς / καλούς τε μεγάλους τε…('Then Odysseus, / while hitching up the rags around his private parts, / exposed his fine large thighs,…'). Coraes 1804: 186 quotes further *Od.* 18.74 οἵην ἐκ ῥακέων ὁ γέρων ἐπιγουνίδα φαίνει ('judging from the thighs / that old man shows under those rags of his').

[21] ἀμφὶ δέ οἱ κυνέην κεφαλῆφιν ἔθηκε / ῥινοῦ ποιητήν· πολέσιν δ' ἔντοσθεν ἱμᾶσιν / ἐντέτατο στερεῶς· ἔκτοσθε δὲ λευκοὶ ὀδόντες / ἀργιόδοντος ὑὸς θαμέες ἔχον ἔνθα καὶ ἔνθα / εὖ καὶ ἐπισταμένως ('On his head Odysseus set / a hide cap, on the inside skilfully reinforced / with leather thongs. Outside, wild boars' white teeth / were placed here and there, strategically and well').

[22] οὕνεκ' ἐπητής ἐσσι καὶ ἀγχίνοος καὶ ἐχέφρων ('You're bold, with subtle plans, and love deceit'); Ἄνδρα μοι ἔννεπε, Μοῦσα, πολύτροπον…('Muse, speak to me now of that resourceful man…'). Coraes (1804) 186 quotes also *Od.* 10.330 ἦ σύ γ' Ὀδυσσεύς ἐσσι πολύτροπος ('You must be Odysseus, / that resourceful man').

[23] *Iliad* 19.47 τὼ δὲ δύω σκάζοντε βάτην Ἄρεος θεράποντε (of Diomedes and Odysseus) is quoted by Coraes 1804: 186, who notes, however, that only Diomedes had been wounded in the leg. Diomedes and Odysseus as well as Agamemnon who comes along were wounded in *Iliad* 11 (373-8, 434-8, 251-3, respectively); see further Edwards 1991 ad loc.

αὐτίκα γὰρ κατὰ θυμὸν ὀΐσατο, μή ἑ λαβοῦσα
οὐλὴν ἀμφράσσαιτο καὶ ἀμφαδὰ ἔργα γένοιτο.
νίζε δ' ἄρ' ἆσσον ἰοῦσα ἄναχθ' ἑόν· αὐτίκα δ' ἔγνω
οὐλήν, τήν ποτέ μιν σῦς ἤλασε λευκῷ ὀδόντι
Παρνησόνδ' ἐλθόντα μετ' Αὐτόλυκόν τε καὶ υἷας....

For suddenly in his heart
he was afraid that, when she touched him, she might see
a scar he had, and then the truth would be revealed.
She came up and began to wash her master.
She recognized the scar immediately, a wound
a boar's white tusk had given him many years ago,
when he'd gone to Parnassus, making a visit
to Autolycus and his sons.

Regardless of circumstances and conventions, the great difference between the Homeric and the Heliodoran recognition signs in number, kind and combination is worthy of particular attention. An emaciated, limping old man wearing a war helmet (!) looks like a caricature of the hero who once presented himself to the Phaeacians (*Od.* 9.19–20):

εἴμ' Ὀδυσεὺς Λαερτιάδης, ὃς πᾶσι δόλοισιν
ἀνθρώποισι μέλω, καί μευ κλέος οὐρανὸν ἵκει.

I am Odysseus, son of Laertes,
well known to all for my deceptive skills—
my fame extends all the way to heaven.

Though Odysseus' cunning is mentioned in both texts, in Homer his δόλοι are 'known to all people' and his κλέος 'extends all the way to heaven'. By contrast, the Heliodoran Odysseus is in need of visitors to come to Ithaca and 'learn of his renown' (δόξαν γνῶναι τὴν ἡμετέραν). In addition, though Calasiris has stopped and stayed for months on one of the islands of Odysseus' former Homeric kingdom, and though he will (chronologically) later align his narrating persona with Odysseus' (2.21.5),[24] he seems completely unaware of where he is. Consequently, the Homeric hero feels obliged to visit him in sleep and remind him that his home is located on a

---

[24] See Billault in this volume.

nearby island. His kingdom is now long gone, and the Heliodoran Odysseus does not even mention Ithaca by name: this forms a strong contrast with what the Homeric Odysseus says to the Phaeacians (*Od.* 9.21-4):

ναιετάω δ' Ἰθάκην εὐδείελον· ἐν δ' ὄρος αὐτῇ,
Νήριτον εἰνοσίφυλλον ἀριπρεπές· ἀμφὶ δὲ νῆσοι
πολλαὶ ναιετάουσι μάλα σχεδὸν ἀλλήλῃσι,
Δουλίχιόν τε Σάμη τε καὶ ὑλήεσσα Ζάκυνθος.

I live in Ithaca, a land of sunshine.
From far away one sees a mountain there,
thick with whispering trees, Mount Neriton,
and many islands lying around it
close together—Dulichium, Same,
forested Zacynthus.

The Heliodoran Odysseus complains to Calasiris that 'he has failed to give him even a neighbourly salutation' (μηδὲ τοῦτο δὴ τὸ κοινὸν προσειπεῖν, ἐν γειτόνων καὶ ταῦτα οἰκοῦντα). While it is true that the novel favours the everyday as opposed to the heroic, this complaint, which implicitly amounts to begging, makes of Odysseus, who had once won universal fame and admiration, an almost pitiful hero.

There is also the question of priorities. For Calasiris, departure is a more urgent matter than paying homage to Odysseus, because he has Theagenes and Charicleia to protect. And since he cannot sail to Ithaca to sacrifice to Odysseus and ask him to temper his wrath against them, he sends Tyrrhenus to do the job. Scholars have concerned themselves with the existence of a heroic cult on Ithaca,[25] but there is a more serious literary issue here: the limited significance which the novel implicitly attaches to the cult of Odysseus, given that Calasiris sends a fisherman in his place to perform the sacrifice.[26]

This last issue is directly related to the substance of Odysseus' speech. The speech is about the wrath of Odysseus for having been slighted and the consequent 'Odyssean' punishment awaiting Calasiris. The ghost of Odysseus predicts ordeals on sea and land like the ones he himself suffered. Are we to

---

[25] On the issue of the cult of Odysseus on Ithaca, see Malkin 1998: 94–119 and Currie 2005: 52–3.
[26] Bowie 2012: 264 wonders why no vows are made before this and other critical actions in the ancient novel.

assume that the power and effect of Odysseus' wrath is analogous to his weird appearance? Readers are called upon to understand what happens when μῆνις is associated with an aged Odysseus, withered almost to a skeleton and limping—no disguise at work here as in the *Odyssey*. They cannot miss the irony resulting from the contrast between a grand epic theme and the person who undertakes to carry it out, between the high and the low register. It is analogous to what was pointed out above, entrusting the appeasement of Odysseus' epic μῆνις to a humble fisherman. Finally, that this radically different Odysseus should have turned from persecuted to persecutor[27] may not be such an unexpected role reversal. His sardonic smile (σεσηρός τι μειδιάσας) may suggest meanness of character. The words Calasiris addresses to the fisherman (αἴτει τῆς μήνιδος ἀνεῖναι τῆς καθ' ἡμῶν ἣν ἀγανακτεῖν) may imply that the Homeric hero has become what his name indicates, 'a man of rage'.[28] Is it devoid of significance that we never learn if Tyrrhenus actually sailed to Ithaca and if the effort to appease the hero's anger was successful or not? If he failed to go or to appease Odysseus' wrath, how did this wrath work? Odysseus does not reappear in the *Aethiopica* but, if he did, would we anticipate an intervention on his part comparable to that of a powerful deity, like Poseidon's in the *Odyssey* or Juno's in Virgil's *Aeneid*?

It is sometimes suggested that the storm that hits the ship after departure from Zacynthus is the work of Odysseus. Without forgetting that Calasiris' viewpoint is restricted, it is nonetheless useful to keep in mind that there is no direct or indirect evidence to support this view, and also I argued above that the Phoenician ship was probably caught in the stormy conditions prevalent at Cape Malea. From a geographical and literary viewpoint it is analogous to the storm that throws Odysseus off course at *Od.* 9.79-81, which is not directly associated with some sort of divine anger.[29]

One might object that the hero's wrath works in a manner that is not immediately perceptible. Is the reader therefore expected to envisage the tacit intervention of Odysseus behind every misfortune that befalls Calasiris and the couple? And are we to dissociate the sufferings of Charicleia from those of Calasiris and Theagenes, because Penelope sends greetings to her through her husband and 'wishes her joy' (22.3 χαίρειν γάρ αὐτῇ φησι)?

---

[27] Cf. Paulsen 1992: 162.
[28] Cf. the etymology of Ὀδυσσεύς from ὀδυσσάμενος in *Od.* 19.407-9, with Rattenbury, Lumb, and Maillon 1960: 67 n. 2. As a figure of *mēnis* Odysseus would obviously recall Achilles.
[29] Cf. also Bartsch 1989: 101: 'We may take the comment on afflictions to refer to the subsequent storm in which Calasiris, like Odysseus, is shipwrecked; but the dream is so vague that it is difficult to see how its prefiguring action could be of much use to reader or character.'

Questions like these could be multiplied and the reader will remain at a loss for answers.

The truth of the matter is that the appearance of Odysseus to Calasiris and the theme of his wrath reflect the distance that separates Homer's heroic world from the novel of the imperial age. Emulation of the *Odyssey* stands at the root of Heliodorus' initiative to assign Odysseus the role of a novelistic character. On the other hand, the belated and almost forced introduction of the dream, the incongruous portrait of the Homeric hero, the assignment to a humble fisherman of the task to appease Odysseus' wrath, and the absence of any information about the outcome of the fisherman's mission, suggest that the novelist is probably undermining the Homeric theme of wrath. Odysseus' μῆνις could not have had any practical consequences for the development of the plot and indeed it did not. From this viewpoint it is a stillborn homage to Odysseus, to be left behind with the Tyrian ship's departure from the island of Zacynthus.

The reader may subsequently remember the appearance of Odysseus to Calasiris as a marker announcing the forthcoming end of the Odyssean first half of the *Aethiopica*.[30] It has also been suggested that Calasiris' dream is about literary succession, analogous to Ennius' dream of Homer at the beginning of the *Annales*.[31] This may be true but not in terms of an ordinary heroic/literary succession. The weird portrait of Odysseus, the circumstances under which he appears to Calasiris, the loss of his κλέος, his inconsequential wrath, and the assignment to a fisherman of the task of appeasing him imply that the Homeric hero's days are gone. In other words, it is not by exalting the Homeric Odysseus that Calasiris claims the succession as narrator and hero but by belittling him.

I have argued that the geographical location of Zacynthus and the route the Tyrian ship takes to reach the island are accurately described in the *Aethiopica*. Most importantly, the Zacynthian stop serves to introduce Calasiris' dream of Odysseus. The Heliodoran Odysseus is unconventional in more than one way: he feels almost obliged to appear on account of Calasiris' hasty departure; his portrait is made up of an almost comic collage of Homeric allusions; his anger for having been slighted proves inconsequential; and Calasiris makes amends by sending a humble fisherman to Ithaca to pay due honours. If this is a case of heroic/literary succession, it was designed as a reversal of classical precedents.

---

[30] Cf. Keyes 1922.   [31] Telò 2011: 604–5.

10
Life, the Cosmos, and Everything (5.26–34)

Ken Dowden

The ending of Book 5, for all its structural and thematic significance, and its exceptional writing, has not been much discussed.[1] In what follows, I first give an overview of its content and its place in the plot. Then I largely follow the sequence of the text from chapter 26 through to the end. Though the discussion will occasionally pause to draw in diverse matters such as those rare failures of consistency or clarity in the narrative, it does have a particular mission. It is concerned above all with the attitudes of characters and how they may be inscribed into a teleological ethical framework. The questions that need to be resolved are about priorities in human life, the role of human effort and the perception of forces beyond our control. Varying ethical viewpoints affect the narration and interaction of characters, and they are continually interpreting themselves and others. Intertextuality is interwoven with these issues: Homeric, sometimes tragic, and now and again Platonic resonances generally repay careful and thoughtful inspection. It is a both thoughtful and thought-provoking text.

10.1. Context

Book 5 as a whole concludes and dismantles the complex narrative structure of the first half of the *Aethiopica*. As it starts a long analeptic (flashback) narrative is in progress, which Calasiris had begun at 2.24. But, as the division between Books 4 and 5 is bridged, Calasiris' analeptic narrative is paused, and, back at the main level of narration, as even Calasiris does not

---

[1] Even Hefti 1950 has nothing to say about it.

Ken Dowden, *Life, the Cosmos, and Everything (5.26–34)* In: *Reading Heliodorus'* Aethiopica. Edited by: Ian Repath and Tim Whitmarsh, Oxford University Press. © Oxford University Press 2022.
DOI: 10.1093/oso/9780198792543.003.0010

know enough to deal with Cnemon's perplexity, the authorial narrator has to step in with an analepsis of his own (5.4-9), in a manner which Morgan has rightly described as 'completely at variance with the narrator's normal protocols'.[2] Nausicles becomes the centre of the main narrative when it returns, a character not hugely different in interpretative and moral capacities from Cnemon. Charicleia is securely restored to Calasiris, resolving one narrative problem (5.10-15), though Theagenes remains unfound, and Charicleia prays (5.15). Now, invited by Nausicles (5.16), Calasiris resumes, one last time, and across a thrilling narrative (5.17-33), most of a novel in itself, the story is brought up to the point at which the main narrative began, the scene of devastation on the Egyptian shore and the arrival of brigands at 1.1. At that point the clock hand of the main narrative, by now set at Nausicles' banquet, can once more tick forward: the banquet can end and the second half of the *Aethiopica* will be able in Book 6 to leave Nausicles and Cnemon behind, and with them Chemmis and northern Egypt.

In this chapter I discuss the second half of Calasiris' final narrative. At 5.27, the sun sets and the pirate ship holding our heroes is driven to land at a mouth of the Nile, the scene of the opening. The arch-pirate Trachinus announces his intention to marry Charicleia (5.28), and Calasiris feigns compliance (5.29). Charicleia resolves on suicide, but is dissuaded by Calasiris, who will devise a plan and (5.30) leads the deputy-arch-pirate, Pelorus, to believe that he in fact is the true object of Charicleia's affection: he should go (5.31) into the ship that is now her bridal-chamber (and off-limits on the orders of Trachinus) in order to behold this Artemis of a girl. Doing so, he returns inflamed with passion, and the quarrel begins between the two pirates. Their fight (5.32) escalates into a general battle amongst the pirates, with Theagenes and Charicleia adding judiciously to the slaughter. At the end, Theagenes defeats Pelorus in single combat. Calasiris meanwhile has retreated to a hill-top (5.33), only to witness the brigands from the opening scene (1.1) descending to capture hero and heroine. His story ends, Nausicles promises assistance in recovering Theagenes, and the symposium too ends. Calasiris leaves the group (5.34) and finds Charicleia asleep at the feet of the statue (of Hermes), exhausted and distraught. He weeps, prays, and helps her back to her rooms. And the fifth book ends.

---

[2] Morgan 2004: 529.

10.2. The Pirate's Interpretation of the Good

Aristotle comments on *ēthos* (character) that it serves to clarify the sort of moral choices we see made on the tragic stage and that conversely discourse that does not have a moral dimension cannot display character.[3] It is somewhat similar with the narrations and exchanges of Heliodorus: they test the ethical insight of narrator and of narratee, and we need to examine what sort of moral character those persons possess.

Clearest in this moral calculus are brigands and pirates, whose role in novels I have explored more fully elsewhere.[4] These exist in order to display inadequate ethics, but not unthinkingly: Heliodorus' pirates are not melodramatic villains but people who engage in meaningful discourse and can be engaged in turn in discourse by those who understand their thinking, as Charicleia and Calasiris do. This is immediately apparent at 5.26.1, where Trachinus explains to Charicleia that he has braved 'much ocean and danger' solely in order to win her. His self-vision is of himself as sacrificing much to achieve this objective, something which he believes will be received warmly by his addressee: 'take heart' he tells her, inviting her to realize that she will be mistress jointly with him of 'all this', namely the booty of the pirates.

From a Platonic or Aristotelian point of view,[5] there is no doubt that he has in some sense perceived the Good (given his recognition of the beauty of Charicleia), but like all pirates he has misinterpreted the pursuit of the Good as the quest for wealth and has mistaken booty for beauty: the divinely beautiful Charicleia is not concerned with a Good that is embodied in 'all this'. As a sort of internal narrator, Trachinus has played the narrative part consistent with piratical *ēthos*, but his mistake is to address a narratee who reads the world from the perspective of a different *ēthos*. Charicleia's response is praised by the narrator Calasiris as displaying a practical wisdom to deal with an awkward situation (one which Calasiris himself is well capable of): she chooses not to disturb his world-view, but to talk in terms of gods to be thanked and his *philanthrōpia* (clemency, humanity), apparently validating his action: now he can save 'brother' Theagenes and 'father' Calasiris too. But the pirate struggles even to rise to this limited moral level:

---

[3] ἔστιν δὲ ἦθος μὲν τὸ τοιοῦτον ὃ δηλοῖ τὴν προαίρεσιν ὁποία τις... διόπερ οὐκ ἔχουσιν ἦθος τῶν λόγων ἐν οἷς μηδ' ὅλως ἔστιν ὅ τι προαιρεῖται ἢ φεύγει ὁ λέγων (Arist. *Poet.* 6.24 (1450b)).

[4] Dowden 2013.

[5] Dowden 2013: 51–2, 58; for limited perception of the truly beautiful, see Plato *Symp.* 209e–212a (and in effect Plotinus 1.6).

Theagenes will make a good pirate,[6] and Calasiris, though a useless burden, can be used to win favour with Charicleia. This calculating response undermines any claim to god-pleasing *philanthrōpia*. But it continues consistently an *ēthos* based on *kerdos* (profit, gain), completely blind to the specific characteristics of Theagenes and Calasiris that justify their status in the novel.

10.3. The Expert's Interpretation of the Storm

A storm now arises at 5.27. At first sight this is a replay of the fine storm at Achilles Tatius 3.1-5, and there can be no doubt that Heliodorus had it before him, but they are quite different: the storm narrated by Cleitophon in Achilles is alive with drama and vividity and above all emerges as a narrative *tour de force*; that of Heliodorus has a more thoughtful narrator, Calasiris, concerned to interpret and understand events, judgmental even. Calasiris notes the time of day, σκιόφως, 'darkness-light', a *hapax* in Greek, further described, in Aeschylean mode,[7] as a 'battleground between night and day'. He is making an unusually precise scientific observation as he seeks to understand the natural world around him (its *physical* philosophy). He speculates further on the causes of the storm: perhaps the meteorological shift (τροπήν) was something to do with this time of day, or just maybe it was due to 'the will of some fortune' (τύχης τινὸς βουλήματι)—a strange phrase, containing the binary opposition of an event that was mere chance and an event that was designed by higher powers. Whatever it is, as the narrator thinks it through, attention shifts to the pirates, who are filled with 'unexpected uproar', failing in their transfer of goods from one ship to another, and without the expertise to steer a big ship. In Achilles, the helmsman gives orders and the sailors implement them (3.1.1-2, 3.3.1). But in Heliodorus the sailors are reduced to random improvisation and miscellaneous ignorant makeshifts: they cannot cope with the unexpected or build a knowledge that would allow prediction. This is how Heliodoran pirate society works: it has focused on wealth to the exclusion of knowledge and skill (even the merchants in Achilles throw their goods overboard on the helmsman's instructions, 3.2.9). The narrator, Calasiris, through his narration and

---

[6] This 'recruitment from prisoners' motif appears also at 1.19 (Thyamis).
[7] The 'battleground' translates μεταίχμιον (lit. 'space between the (opposing sets of) spears') and is used similarly metaphorically in the phrase ἐν μεταιχμίῳ σκότου ('the *metaichmion* of darkness') at Aesch. *Ch.* 64.

its speculations and analysis, shows the qualities of thought that his pirates by their nature lack.

This storm resonates both intratextually and intertextually. Within Heliodorus' text, it is the fulfilment and authoritative version of Charicleia's inventive account at 1.22 designed to mislead Thyamis. There the helmsman (who in her fictional account was not a pirate) surrenders to the violence of the storm and 'entrusts the ship to fortune (*tychē*)', something which, whilst regrettable, may indeed be, as John Morgan takes it in his translation, a case of simply recognizing the inevitable (as at Achilles 3.3.1). The Calasiran account, more definitive and not distorted by the intention to mislead, is more clearly damning: it is the lack of expertise (τὸ ἄτεχνον) of the helmsman (τοῦ κυβερνῶντος) that causes him to give up at nightfall (5.27). This in turn contrasts with the expert advice given by another helmsman, which had been placed recently at 5.17.5—doubtless in preparation for this scene.

However, what the whole discourse on lack of skill conjures up is of course Plato's celebrated analogy in the *Republic* (488a–e), where the management of the state is depicted as an effectively leaderless ship being run by the inexpert. The crew quarrel amongst themselves, do some roistering (a leading characteristic of brigands and pirates in the novel),[8] and the focus falls on their 'helmsmanship/steering' (κυβερνήσει, 488d), a matter in which they have no skill (τέχνην τούτου, 'skill in this', 488e). Thus Calasiris' analysis is at root a conversion of Achilles' storm into a Platonic one in which the behaviour of the pirates is iconic, and the presence of the heroes amidst them resonates with considerations of how the good man is to cope with life in this world, much as the trials of Odysseus, for instance in his shipboard encounter with the Sirens, had long since taken on a patina of ethical significance.[9]

10.4. The Interpretation of the Arrival and of the Celebrations

The arrival at the land of Egypt (5.27.8) seems poorly understood by all parties. The storm has somehow failed to destroy the ship and they are approaching a headland by the Heracleotic mouth of the Nile. 'We unhappy/ misfortunate people (δυσδαίμονες), without meaning to (ἀβουλήτως), set

---

[8] Dowden 2013: 50–1.   [9] Dowden 2011: 288–93.

foot on Egyptian soil'. These are interesting cues. How, then, if it was not by their own will, did they end up in Egypt? Odysseus reached 'Goat Island' in impossible conditions—night, fog, moonless—and judges that 'some god was guiding us' (*Od.* 9.142). Elsewhere, in Aeschylus' *Agamemnon* (662–4), we learn how the returning Greeks are nearly wiped out by the storm— except that the ship bearing Agamemnon unaccountably makes it through, picked out by 'a god, not a man, touching the rudder; and Fortune ($T\acute{v}\chi\eta$, in effect a variant of the $\delta\alpha\acute{\iota}\mu\omega\nu$ in $\delta\upsilon\sigma\delta\alpha\acute{\iota}\mu\omega\nu$) willingly sat, a saviour, upon our ship'. This might be mere luck (as at Achilles 3.5.1) or it might be something else that means the ship bearing Charicleia, Theagenes, and Calasiris just *happens* to reach Egypt, the necessary next stage on their travel to Aithiopia.[10] The pirates read this event badly, as Calasiris judges: these sinners ($\dot{\alpha}\lambda\iota\tau\acute{\eta}\rho\iota\omicron\iota$), a venomous word elsewhere applied to Demainete and to people falsely denounced as villains (especially Charicleia by Arsace),[11] proceed to make a *thank offering* to Poseidon for saving them, Calasiris snorts ($\delta\acute{\eta}\theta\epsilon\nu$). This is effectively sacrilege, as though gods protected pirates; and they will not come well out of this 'salvation', as the reader will realize. Calasiris' own reading is surprisingly restricted: he is now strictly the experiencing 'I', without his later knowledge, and is worrying that the three of them are now exposed to the whims of the pirates and in particular anticipating the forced marriage of Charicleia to Trachinus.

Chapter 5.28 sets the marriage in motion: Trachinus grandly deigns to inform Calasiris of his intention to wed her, and naively expects Charicleia to rejoice. And Calasiris does indeed offer maximum thanks to the gods for this turn of events, understanding his audience well. This enables him to influence the choreography of the 'wedding', which triggers (5.29) the unloading of multiple goods manufactured in Tyre and Sidon, which as John Morgan implies,[12] serves to recall the products that Paris had brought from Sidon at *Iliad* 6.289–92 'on the journey on which he brought Helen of noble father' (6.292). Charicleia, then, is Helen; Trachinus is Paris; the noble father, Zeus, is currently Calasiris; Theagenes is Menelaus, but present, and, like the Menelaus who recovers the real Helen (as opposed to the phantom

---

[10] See Dowden 1996: 280–3.
[11] Cnemon on a supposed adulterer 1.12.2; Demainete 1.14.4, 1.17.4; Charicleia as love-rival and fictionally guilty of poisoning in the eyes of Arsace and/or Cybele 7.10.5, 8.7.1, 8.9.1, 8.9.17; Theagenes in the eyes of Charicles 10.35.1.
[12] Morgan 1989c: 467 n. 148. The approach of Rattenbury-Lumb 1938: 76 n. 2 is more pedestrian.

that was at Troy), washed up by a storm in Egypt (Euripides, *Helen* 408–9).[13] But Calasiris' focus is on the contrast between the work invested in accumulating this wealth and the actions of *Tyche* in handing it over for an ἀσώτῳ συμποσίῳ, a 'dissolute symposium', where 'dissolute' is a key word in the characterization of pirates and brigands.[14] And Charicleia would sooner take her life rather than sign up to be a pirate's Helen.

10.5. Misplaced and Incongruous Visions and Priorities

It is for Calasiris to generate a plan, but once again, as with his supposition that arrival in Egypt is bad fortune, he has at this moment fallen prey to a sense of victimhood (unless his speech is to be thought tailored to the outlook of his audience, Theagenes and Charicleia): the attempt to outrun the pirates failed because of the non-cooperation of the *daimōn* (πρὸς τοῦτο μὲν ὁ δαίμων ἀντέπραξεν)—it did not work out (chance or intervention?). All he can now offer is exhortation: they should bravely enter this battle and win or die (5.29.6). Unusually therefore, the reader is left without an authoritative guide to the progress of the novel: the retrospective omniscience of Calasiris is suppressed, whether by Heliodorus or by the wily narrator, and the experiencing Calasiris appears less insightful than he might normally be. Indeed, the progress of the novel is obscured so that the reader may feel more deeply the crisis at this key point and join in the despair of the actors, something that in general is characteristic of Heliodorus' technique.[15]

The attention of Calasiris now turns to a different audience: the deputy arch-pirate, Pelorus (5.30). The adjective *pelōrios* ('enormous'), though it does describe others (notably Ajax) is twice used in the *Iliad* to describe Achilles (21.527, 22.92). In any case, Pelorus does here play the role of Achilles, and Trachinus Agamemnon, from the opening of the *Iliad*, where the two are in dispute over Agamemnon's taking of Achilles' girl, Briseis— who is in both cases, as de Temmerman acutely notes, the claimant's *geras*

---

[13] Feuillâtre 1966 also makes an interesting comparison between Charicleia shooting arrows and encouraging Theagenes at 5.32.3–5 with Helen encouraging her side from the ship at Eur. *Helen* 1602–4. On the whole, however, Feuillâtre's identification of Homeric and tragic material (1966: 105–21), though useful, is not as full and insightful as it might be, and it is detectable that the study of the novel was still in its infancy: e.g. 'pour varier le récit, Héliodore a inséré dans la narration, des descriptions, des discours, des lettres' (29).
[14] Dowden 2013: 50–1.
[15] Morgan 2003: 441, e.g. 'The omniscient author subtracts himself from most of the text'.

(prize to which they are entitled).[16] These pirates are, however, grotesque figures in comparison, and Calasiris knows which motive to appeal to, the typically piratical motive of κέρδος ('profit')—Calasiris has something 'very profitable' (κερδαλεώτατον) to say to him. This is sufficient: pirates respond to profit and lust, because that is the limit of their vision of the Good, doomed always to be at the vulgar level of Aphrodite Pandemos.[17] It seems also to be a 'vision' that underlies the events of 5.31: Pelorus is urged by Calasiris to view Charicleia in her separate position, on the ship. She will, according to Calasiris, look like Artemis, re-creating the reader's first vision of Charicleia, at 1.2.6.[18] There, Charicleia was of 'indescribable beauty' (ἀμήχανόν τι κάλλος, 1.2.1) and was offered to the viewing eyes of another set of brigands who 'were looking to κέρδος ['profit'] and to plunder' (1.1.8); simultaneously, it was the vision of her that was lifting Theagenes from a death that was perilously close.

Calasiris now offers the pirate Pelorus a staged vision of the truly beautiful with which he may return to this world and act, so illuminated. It is a divine vision not only because Calasiris says so to him, but because the narrating Calasiris describes her to us as golden and 'radiant' (καταυγάζουσαν, 5.31.2). The pirate has misconstrued a divine vision, a sort of Eleusinian initiation,[19] and returned to the equivalent of the Platonic 'Cave'—but in somewhat less than philosophical mode, as Calasiris knew he would, because Calasiris understands the weaknesses of piratical nature. The effect on Pelorus is immediate and exactly as expected (ὡς εἰκός): he is inflamed by πόθος ('longing') and ζῆλος ('eagerness'), key components of the toolkit of Love in Plato's *Symposium* (197d6–7). This is more, I think, than the conventional effect of beauty on the gaze in a love story.[20]

There is even a mystic element that we should not miss: in gazing upon *the radiant divine*, Pelorus *pries into that which is forbidden*—in this case by Trachinus, as Calasiris observes to him when edging him into this disastrous act. He has not been prepared for the awe of this moment: instead, he is set alight and driven to mad intentions as can immediately be seen on his return from his mere expression (5.31.2). This carries with it religious overtones about premature attempts to grasp the divine. The Sophia of the Gnostics, the youngest *Aeon*, charged forward to look upon Propator, God

---

[16] de Temmerman 2014: 292–3.
[17] Pl. *Symp.* 180e. On aspects of Heliodorus' treatment of 'pandemic love', see Jones 2006.
[18] As observed by de Temmerman 2014: 292.   [19] As at Plotinus 1.6.7.
[20] For a sensitive account of which, see Morales 2005: 13–15.

as 'Forefather' who is 'ungraspable to see', and 'suffered passion... supposedly of love, but actually of daring/rashness';[21] man is denounced in the *Corpus Hermeticum* for the rashness and *periergia* ('(misplaced) curiosity') with which he explores the 'mysteries' of nature.[22] Psyche, though forbidden, looks out of *curiositas* upon the radiant and golden Cupid (complete, incidentally, with Charicleia's bow and arrows, if lying on the floor);[23] and Plotinus and Porphyry will only gain union with the One rarely and through intense mental and spiritual preparation, following the paths laid out in Plato's *Symposium*.[24] Pelorus has given way to *periergia/curiositas* and only bad results can follow. And *periergia*, Latin *curiositas*, after all is what transforms Apuleius's Lucius into an ass, in contrast to his self-restraint in the final book.[25] Calasiris, ironically as a priest and a sort of mystagogue, encourages Pelorus to the premature vision that will destroy him.

In what follows Trachinus conjures up another Platonic passage. Is Pelorus not right to claim Charicleia, given that he is the first to board the 'enemy' ship? No, says Trachinus, because there is another law, that subjects must yield to their rulers (τοὺς ὑπηκόους εἴκειν τοῖς ἄρχουσι, 5.31.4). Anyone who has read the *Republic* will recognize this sentiment and the language in which it is expressed. Perhaps it is best illustrated from:

Σωφροσύνης δὲ ὡς πλήθει οὐ τὰ τοιάδε μέγιστα, ἀρχόντων μὲν ὑπηκόους εἶναι, αὐτοὺς δὲ ἄρχοντας τῶν περὶ πότους καὶ ἀφροδίσια καὶ περὶ ἐδωδὰς ἡδονῶν;

And are the greatest features of self-control, as a rule, not these: that they should be subjects of their rulers and that they themselves should be rulers of (their) inclinations to drinking sessions and sex and food?

(Pl. *Rep.* 389d)[26]

Thus roistering brigands are prone to anarchy and dissension, and Calasiris has exploited this key weakness of brigand society. Poor government results in chaos, as it did in the case of the storm and its analogue in the *Republic*

---

[21] οὐ καταληπτὸς ἰδεῖν... ἔπαθε πάθος... πρόφασιν μὲν ἀγάπης, τόλμης δέ, Irenaeus *Refutation of All Heresies* 1.1.2–1.2.1; Dowden 1998: 4–7.
[22] *Corpus Hermeticum* fr. 23.42, with Wlosok 1960: 135. [23] Apul. *Met.* 5.22.
[24] Porph. *Vita Plot.* 23.
[25] Apul. *Met.* 3.14.1, 3.24, 11.15.2; for a recent contribution to the discussion of *periergia/curiositas* in the novels, if focused on closure and meta-narrative, see Whitmarsh 2011: 185–91.
[26] See also 440d, 549a.

above. It may of course be doubted whether Trachinus is more than an ironic example of the philosopher-king: he is after all a man who can say, if Pelorus fails to comply, 'I shall smash your head in with this wine-bowl', as John Morgan beautifully over-translates it.

10.6. Epic (and Other) Associations

The *ekphrasis* of the chaotic battle (5.32) is comparable in its dynamics to Calasiris' earlier description of the storm: Calasiris immediately compares the battle to a swirling sea (5.32.1). Both battle and storm are in effect descriptions of chaos in the pirate community. The battle is incongruously decked out in epic colours: the metaphorical sea swirls around a *spilas* (σπιλάς), the sort of rock hexameter seas foam up around.[27] Metaphorical seas of people, whether in assembly or battle, are familiar in Homer's *Iliad*;[28] and the wailing (οἰμωγή) of people 'striking and being struck' (5.32.3) is the wailing of people 'killing and being killed' at *Iliad* 4.450–1.[29] Add to this that Calasiris describes Theagenes as not ἀπόλεμος ('warless'), a word that seems to be special at *Iliad* 2.201 (where it invites a scholion to explain it) and otherwise appears only in special registers; and the stroke with which Theagenes misses Pelorus' head but takes off his lower arm seems modelled on the unfortunate fate of one Hypsenor at *Iliad* 5.80–1.[30]

10.7. Refocusing

If Calasiris' vision has been generally[31] limited to his knowledge at the time, it is limited twice over by his withdrawal from the scene and reduction from a participant to an observer from a hilltop (5.32.3). It is as though he is being downgraded to the position of the reader, powerless to intervene. There are some oddities in the narrative too, probably unintentional. Why exactly is it that Calasiris cannot rejoin Charicleia?—Heliodorus seems to be struggling somewhat as Calasiris does not 'dare at night-time to get

---

[27] Coraes 1804: 193–4 cites *Od.* 5.401 and Ap. Rhod. 2.570.
[28] 2.144; 2.209; 4.422; 14.394; 15.381.
[29] Coraes 1804: 195; less fully, Rattenbury-Lumb 1938: 80 n. 3.
[30] Coraes 1804: 196; Rattenbury-Lumb 1938: 81 n. 4; Feuillâtre 1966: 111; Morgan 1989c: 471 n. 152; de Temmerman 2014: 300.
[31] At 5.31.2, I think Calasiris should be taken as speculating why Charicleia was so dressed (but see next note for de Temmerman's alternative view) and as reasoning and judging (εἰκὸς ... δῆλος) what happened to Pelorus when he beheld Charicleia.

involved with a place engaged in war' (5.33.1). And in this sequence of events, as Calasiris starts heading down from the hill at sunrise (5.33.2), what happened to the arrival of a *second* set of brigands (1.3)? Also, a little earlier, if Theagenes and Charicleia promised to do whatever Calasiris told them to do as part of his plan, what was it that he told each of them to do? If Charicleia was to dress up (to be beheld by Pelorus), in whose mind was it thought that the Delphic holy costume would be 'either an emblem of victory or something to be buried in' (5.31.2)? It sounds like a decision of Charicleia's. Even if it was Calasiris' plan somehow to create the Charicleian tableau, in what way then did Theagenes follow his instructions? By keeping out of it? By wearing a sword? By intervening on either side in the battle? It is remarkable how much interpreters of the novel are driven to *speculation* to identify elements of Calasiris' plan—unless it was Heliodorus' plan that they should.[32]

The focus is by now on Charicleia and her reaction to her plight, of which there is now only a distant knowledge (no direct contact, only observation from afar), and finally on the helplessness of Calasiris. Even if Charicleia has now been saved, that was due to the kindness of the gods and the goodwill of Nausicles—and no thanks to a Calasiris who could only lament (5.33.3). Nausicles tries to cheer up Calasiris in a practical way (we have your daughter and we will deal with your son in the morning), characteristic of his mentality. Calasiris responds politely that he would like that (βουλοίμην ἄν, 5.33.5), without investing in Nausicles' frame of mind.

10.8. Closure and Remembering the *daimonion*

Calasiris continues:

νῦν δὲ ὥρα γε διαλύειν τὸ συμπόσιον· μνήμη τοῦ δαιμονίου γινέσθω καὶ τὰς λυτηρίους τις σπονδὰς[33] περιαγέσθω.

---

[32] Meriel Jones 2007: 117–18 speculates that Charicleia's shooting of arrows was part of the plan; Koen de Temmerman 2014: 292 considers it strongly suggested that 'she was instructed by him to wear this dress as part of his plan'. A further difficulty is found at 5.19.1, where Calasiris refers to the Tyrian merchant seeking Charicleia in marriage from him on the supposition that he was her father (εἰς γάμον ὡς ἂν παρὰ πατρὸς αἰτῶν τὴν Χαρίκλειαν), but Nausicles, the addressee of Calasiris' narration does not (and must not) know that Charicleia is not a literal daughter of Calasiris. This problem recurs at 5.22.3 where Odysseus refers to 'the girl that you are taking with you' (τὴν κόρην δὲ ἣν ἄγεις) rather than 'your girl/daughter'. On this issue, see Hefti 1950: 85–6.

[33] The correction by Coraes 1804: 197, adopted by Rattenbury-Lumb 1938: 83. The transmitted τὰς λυτηρίους τῇ σπονδῇ makes no sense.

But now it is the hour to dissolve the symposium: let there be remembrance of the *daimonion* and let someone take round the dissolution/ deliverance libations. (5.33.5)

This strange utterance deserves comment. I do not have space here to deal with the fragmentary and conflicting evidence on drink-offerings in Greece and the Greek world. However, it does look as though Heliodorus is playing rather freely with these customs. He outlines a recognizable two-part evening, a meal followed by the (men-only) drinking session (the symposium, 'drinking together'). The sexes have in fact already been segregated at 5.15: the women take their meal in the temple (of Hermes) and the men outside in the precinct in front. Following the meal, the men then sing 'boarding songs' to Dionysus (sea-shanties?) and pour libations.

Generally among traditional Greeks, a preliminary offering of wine at the end of the meal, and therefore at the beginning of the symposium (as at 5.15), is usually made to the 'good *daimōn*'; and Homeric heroes who seem to be following a single-part feast, once they have 'set aside their desire for eating and drinking' give everyone a cup of wine from the mixing bowls so that they may 'begin', which evidently denotes a libation to the gods (*Iliad* 1.469–71).[34] There is also some evidence for a 'third libation', to Zeus *Sōtēr* ('Saviour'), argued by Kircher to come at the end of the symposium and so placed certainly by the *Suda* and apparently by Athenaeus.[35]

'Remembering the *daimonion*' means a closing prayer spoken over the libation and addressed to 'the divine'; though the *daimonion* sounds rather close to the good *daimōn* that belongs earlier in proceedings. To overlook 'the divine' would represent a failure to acknowledge the part the divine plays in our world and the respect it deserves. Calasiris, as a high priest, is characterized as instinctively understanding this and it is the same reason for which he attributes the finding of Charicleia in the first place to the 'kindness of the gods' (5.33.3): he is sensitive to the action of the divine. The libations are 'carried around' (5.34.1), rather following the practice of the Homeric heroes (above), and are described as λυτηρίους, which is ambiguous. The obvious meaning is the very literal one that they serve to

---

[34] Kircher 1910: 15; see also Stengel 1920: §63.
[35] Kircher 1910: 16–18. *Suda* s.v. Ἀγαθοῦ Δαίμονος (a 122) ('the ancients had the custom after the dinner to drink to the Good Daimon, and when they were about to split up to Zeus Sōter'); cf. s.v. Τρίτου κρατῆρος (τ 1024), which identifies Zeus Sōter with Zeus Teleios. Ath. *Deipn.* 1.16b unhelpfully places the libation to Zeus Teleios at the point where people 'break up (ἀναλύοντες) from *dinners*'.

dissolve the symposium, which is what Calasiris has just called for (διαλύειν). But this word is elsewhere used metaphorically rather than literally and lends a larger sense—an offering for *deliverance* (for dissolution of one's problems), as indeed Morgan translates it.[36] Prayer for deliverance is rather what one might expect from Zeus *Saviour* if only he was part of Heliodorus' religious vocabulary.

Heliodorus' impression of a closing ceremony is configured to meet the needs of his novel. So, the final contribution of Calasiris to the discourse is to reassert the divine level and the role it needs to play, one which is only dimly recognized by the practical Nausicles. The text of course validates the vision of Calasiris, not that of Nausicles. We can tell this from how Nausicles reads Charicleia: his immediate conception is that of a merchant (ἐμπορικόν τι, 5.8.3) as he recognizes he can acquire something much more valuable than the Thisbe he had paid Mitranes to find (5.8.2). He is, all the same, something different from the pirates, in whom one look arouses uncontrollable lust (Pelorus above; Trachinus at 5.20.6: 'I love her madly (μανικῶς), having seen her just once'). Nausicles is less brutish in sensing the commercial opportunity, and describes the effects of her beauty with care: Charicleia differs from Thisbe as god from man; it is the ultimate beauty; it is ineffable and can only be shown (5.10.2). This divine quality was already present in her first appearance, a showing to the reader at 1.2: her ἀμήχανον ... κάλλος ('indescribable beauty', 'beauty that is impossible to grasp') refers in effect to the ineffability that Nausicles now identifies. This is where the account in Plato's *Symposium* of the 'complete and epoptic' (210a) version of love and beauty fits in. *Epopteia* is the level of initiation at the Eleusinian Mysteries that allows you to behold whatever it was that was 'shown' there. In the *Symposium* (esp. 211a) this is a vision of the eternal, and divine (211e), beauty distilled of all imperfections and all particulars, an exercise in ineffability.

This vision is dwelt on to some extent by the Middle Platonist Albinus/Alcinous (*Handbook* 10.2-3) but is most conspicuously taken up by Plotinus in his chronologically first treatise, *Ennead* 1.6 'On the Beautiful'. Pirates would do well to read 1.6.8, exhorting us to flee beauty in its embodied forms. We need to 'attain the vision of indescribable beauty as if it rested inside a consecrated shrine, not venturing outside so that someone profane might see'. The phrase κάλλος ἀμήχανον ('impossible beauty'), if Heliodorus

---

[36] There is some argument for this position in Rattenbury-Lumb 1938: 83 n. 2.

belongs in the fourth century,[37] could even be drawn from Plotinus himself, but it is more straightforward to recognize this expression as deriving from Plato's *Republic* 509a6 ('you are talking about ἀμήχανον κάλλος'),[38] where the solar brilliance of the form of the Good, sole source of beauty and truth, is under discussion. Doubtless, Plotinus will not have been the only Platonist interested in this passage. Also at issue in Plotinus 1.6.8 is the image of Odysseus (cf. Heliodorus 5.22) and his role in conceptualizing the 'flight to the fatherland', i.e. the quest of the soul, like Charicleia, to return ('flee', Pl. *Tht.* 176b1) to its proper home.

10.9. Statue, Conceptions of Divinity, Resignation

Which brings us to the final chapter of the book (5.34), where it is the statue that attracts attention. Heliodorus rarely mentions an actual statue of a god:[39] he does it here at 5.34.1, and at 7.8.7. The two scenes are linked. Here Charicleia has gone into the temple's inner sanctum (ἄδυτον) and is found by Calasiris 'προσπεφυκυῖαν to the footsteps of the statue'. This is a very strong verb, denoting growing on something or closely sticking to something, like (literal) parasites or snails.[40] 'Footsteps', rather poetically, denotes the feet of the statue as if the aim was to prevent the god from going further without paying attention to one's cause. Turning to 7.8.7, it is now Calasiris (witnessed amongst others by Charicleia) who has prostrated himself before the statue, 'προσφύς (a different part of the same verb) to the footsteps of the statue'. Charicleia had prayed at length at the statue and eventually fallen asleep. Calasiris stays clinging to the statue for a very long time, then formally prays; his longer prayer 'to the goddess' comes (after another feast) at 7.11.3; then he dies—possibly it was what he prayed for (7.11.4). These prayers seem to be, one way or another, for deliverance. The characters recognize that it exceeds their mortal ability to 'turn events to the better', as Calasiris expresses it in his request to 'the god' at 5.34.2. Even at the

---

[37] As argued by Dowden 2006: 255–6.
[38] And/or *Symposium* 218e; cf. also *Republic* 615a. Less interesting use at Philostratus the Younger, *Imagines* 863 O. Elsewhere in Heliodorus at 2.30.6; in Plotinus at 2.9.17, 5.5.3, 5.8.3, 5.8.8. It is a favourite expression of John Chrysostom (fifteen times).
[39] People can be like a statue of a god (1.7.2, 2.33.2, 10.9.3) and pluralities of statues can emerge in the text (3.13.3, 9.12.3, 10.6.3).
[40] Snails: Herondas F 11 Cunningham; leeches: Galen 8.265 Kühn.

conclusion of the earlier dinner, Charicleia had been praying (no god specified) for the safety of Theagenes (5.15.3).

The object of prayer is interestingly neutral. Charicleia clings to a statue which we know from earlier must be of Hermes. Earlier she has prayed without Heliodorus finding any need to specify who to. In Book 7, Calasiris will pray to 'the goddess', namely, but without naming her, Isis. Only Rhodope, the carnal temptress of Calasiris back at 2.25, seems to think she is dealing with a personal goddess, to judge by the way 'she was continually worshipping/cultivating the goddess with multi-talent sacrifices and dedications' (τὴν θεὸν συνεχῶς ἐθεράπευε θυσίαις τε καὶ ἀναθήμασι πολυταλάντοις, 2.25.2). Meanwhile, back at 5.33.5 Calasiris offers a libation not to the Good Daimon or to Zeus Soter but to the *daimonion* ('the divinity'). Whilst a Nausicles specially honours Hermes, for the authoritative figures within the novel the divine forces are more abstract. Isis is mentioned eleven times in the novel: six occasions refer to 'the temple of Isis';[41] in one, Calasiris hams up his evil eye act with a 'by Isis!' and in another his profession is 'prophet of Isis';[42] at the beginning Charicleia is taken as Artemis or maybe 'the native Isis', and late in the novel we learn that Isis is the land and Osiris the Nile;[43] two remaining passages refer to Isis entrusting Charicleia to Thyamis in his dream.[44] Of all these scenes only Thyamis' dream has any religious potential and that seems conformed to his mentality and status in Book 1. Calasiris nowhere detects the hand of the goddess (he does not even have the right hair to be a follower of Isis).[45] Were it not her statue there, he would not be praying to her. But both Charicleia and Calasiris will still cling like leeches to the statue (whichever god it is of) and still have the sense that the statue focuses communication with the divine.

Once again, Heliodorus seems to have reinterpreted a scene from an earlier novel: Chariton's novel ends with Callirhoe face to the feet of the statue of a clearly personal, and named ('thank you, Aphrodite', 8.8.15), goddess; Aphrodite is never to separate Callirhoe from Chaereas (8.8.16); and the novel closes. Here the prayer of Calasiris is for a better closure, just as Charicleia's prayer (cf. 5.15 *fin.*) had been to be reunited with Theagenes; and the half-book closes by marking the distance that the second half must traverse to achieve true closure.[46]

---

[41] 1.18.4, 2.25.2; 2.31.5, 2.32.1, 7.2.2, 7.8.5. See also the analysis at Dowden 2006: 254–5.
[42] 3.11.1, 3.11.2.   [43] 1.2.6, 9.9.4.   [44] 1.18.4, 1.30.4.
[45] Calasiris has Neoplatonic flowing locks, not Isiac baldness (Morgan 1982: 250).
[46] I am very grateful to Ian Repath for observing this parallel and raising the issue of closure.

144 LIFE, THE COSMOS, AND EVERYTHING (5.26–34)

The fifth book, perhaps more than others, has rolled out horror and despair. There is a real sense of *aporia* as the half-way point in the novel is reached. It is right that the human characters (other than Nausicles) should be least confident in their own skills at this point: even Calasiris resorts to self-recrimination. This is when they consider that it is now for the gods to help. The divine can offer sedatives: sleep for Charicleia and, presently, death for Calasiris. But they can also unaccountably turn an impossible situation 'to the better'.[47]

The short sixth book will represent something of a *katabasis* and drive forward the momentum of the novel and the sense of a divinely determined pattern that humans must race to keep up with.

10.10. Appendix on 'Butness'

5.34 *fin*. It is interesting that Book 5 ends with a strong, final, focus on Charicleia, marked by the Greek word μέν (on the one hand). Book 6 then starts with the adversative focus on Calasiris δέ (on the other hand). Bekker's edition (Leipzig 1855) even printed the end and the beginning in one single paragraph, disregarding the book-division (which however must surely go back to Heliodorus himself). Something similar happens across Books 8 and 9, where the Persian scene is summed up (so this is what these people μέν were doing) before sweeping into (Book 9) events at Syene (δέ).[48] And the old Egyptian woman who has raised her dead son lies dead (μέν) at the end of Book 6, leaving Calasiris (δέ) and Charicleia to resume their journey at the beginning of Book 7. It is slightly different at the beginning of Book 5, where the city of Delphi (μέν) and Calasiris who has run from it (δέ) are *both* at the beginning of Book 5 (and similarly at the beginning of Book 2). This shift of focus, facilitated

---

[47] John Morgan was long a religio-sceptic in interpreting Heliodorus. The most fundamental issue, as he saw it (1978: xlviii–lvi), was the sheer variety of language for religious forces (from god to fortune) and the inconsistency with which they seemed to be applied. He preferred to see a narrative 'unifying function' that 'does not genuinely pervade the texture of the romance' (lix)—religion is in effect a form of narrative impressionism. In recent years the picture has become, as indeed it is, more complex and he has become interested, e.g., in implicit hostility to Christianity (Morgan 2005: 318), in the picture of Emesene solar religion that results from the comparison with Philostratus' *Life of Apollonius* (Morgan 2009, cf. 2007: 40–1 and Dowden 2015: esp. 9–11), and he acknowledges a framework of thought in the *Aethiopica* that is drawn from Plato's *Phaedrus* (Morgan 2012a: 575–6; 2015: 190–1). And see now the remarks on 'the *Phaidros* model' in Morgan and Repath 2019.

[48] Morgan 1978: 1 compares this with the last two books of Thucydides.

by the Greek language, must underlie the *butness* of new books. *At regina* at the outset of *Aeneid* 4 is the most memorable precedent: presumably the *sic* (so, thus) of *sic pater Aeneas* at the end of Book 3 is a disguised Greek μὲν οὖν (so on the one hand). This may also underlie the more problematic so-called 'inceptive' *At* with which Apuleius rather perversely *begins* the whole of his *Metamorphoses*.

11
On the Road Again (6.1–4)

Silvia Montiglio

11.1. Keep Going!

Book 6 begins the second half of a novel neatly divided into two parts. Calasiris has completed his retrospective narrative, ending with the massacre that explains the novel's opening scene; the last libation has been poured; and the party has broken up. We might be inclined to close the book and take a break. But the author wants us to read on, and thanks to a number of smart tricks he indicates that what is coming is as exciting as what we have read so far. How does he goad us to read on? How does he persuade us that we should not pause, not even now that a major portion of the narrative has come to a close and two main puzzles, Charicleia's origin in addition to the novel's enigmatic beginning, have been solved?

The first paragraph of Book 6 describes a scene of nocturnal restlessness. Calasiris and Cnemon, who are the guests of Nausicles in Chemmis, retire to the men's quarters but cannot sleep: 'the rest of the night passed more slowly than they wished but more quickly than they thought it would, since the greatest part of it had been spent in feasting and in the telling of stories whose length cannot satiate (ἀπροσκορὲς μῆκος)'. To start a book with a sleepless night is one effective way of keeping the readers awake along with the characters. We instantly think of Homeric precedents: the beginning of *Iliad* 2, with Zeus launching his plan while everyone else is slumbering, or of *Iliad* 10, where Agamemnon is beset by nocturnal agitation. Comparable episodes occur also at the opening of *Odyssey* 15 and 20, at climactic junctures: Telemachus cannot sleep when he is about to start off on his return journey, and Odysseus tosses and turns on the eve of the slaughter.

The novelist, however, outdoes Homer in building up anxiety, in that he piles an episode of nocturnal restlessness on top of another such episode. Book 5 ends with Charicleia retiring to her room and lying down next to Nausicles' daughter, but 'sleeplessly dealing with her present cares' (τὰς παρούσας ἀγρυπνίᾳ διετίθετο φροντίδας). Readers will contrast this novelistic ending with the Homeric pattern of wrapping up books in sleep (*Iliad* 1, 7, 9; *Odyssey* 5, 7, 14, 16, 18, 19). Heliodorus does not follow this epic formula for any of his book endings, several of which are nocturnal, as in Homer, but none of which is restful.[1] Action tends to continue through the night and to spill over from one book to the next, building a bridge. At the main transition, however, the bridge is created not neutrally, by ongoing action, but by a double paroxysm of sleeplessness, further emphasized by prior movements toward rest. First Charicleia then her friends withdraw to their night quarters. This fosters an expectation of sleep, which is instantly countered, with the result that we also stay alert and look forward to travelling on. While sleep functions as a caesura or a blank space, sending us the message, 'take a break with the characters', this accumulation of nocturnal restlessness has the opposite effect: it undermines the sense of an ending and urges us to turn the page.[2]

Heliodorus further entices the readers by paying indirect compliments to his narrative. In fact, the main reason his restless characters can after all cope with the night is the charm of the stories that have entertained them: long stories, yet so enchanting that there could not be enough of them. We are cued not to feel sated by their length (ἀπροσκορὲς μῆκος) but on the contrary to be hungry for more. The immediate reference is to Calasiris' extensive tale, which begins in Book 2 and ends with the end of Book 5; but of course that tale is Heliodorus', who this time as on other occasions draws our attention to the compelling artistry of his novel.[3] Here its driving force is evoked as the narrative takes off again. We are reminded that what we have read so far was so engrossing that we cannot possibly stop reading.

The excitement that animates Heliodorus' restless characters translates into the haste with which the action begins. In spite of the delightful entertainment, the night is still too long, and Calasiris and Cnemon do not even wait until dawn but leave their room still at night to seek Nausicles. They beg him to tell them where Theagenes might be and to take them there 'as quickly as possible' (ὡς ὅτι τάχιστα). No other book of the novel starts with such a show of impatience if the characters are in no foreseeable danger. The hastened departure of Charicleia, Theagenes, and Calasiris

---

[1] *Pace* Keyes 1922: 45—who argues that Heliodorus, like Homer, ends books with night and rest—sleep never appears in the novel's nocturnal book endings (1, 4, 5, 6, 7, 10).
[2] For further discussion of sleep and sleeplessness in this passage, see Montiglio 2015: 249–53.
[3] See also e.g. 4.4.2–3; 5.1.4.

from Delphi at the opening of Book 5 is motivated by urgency (the trio is eloping), and the hurried movements that begin Books 7, 8, and 9 are likewise justified by external circumstances (war emergencies). By contrast, at the beginning of Book 6 the only reason characters are in a hurry is that they cannot wait. Their eagerness to leave is yet another cue to the readers: do not slow down!

Another feature of this book opening that keeps readers up and going is the repeated countenancing of expectations, ending with a typically Heliodorean deferral of the action, the search for Theagenes, that gives impulse to the episode and to the second half of the novel. At the outset of the journey, Nausicles expresses his absolute confidence of finding the hero quickly ('[he] promised her [Chariclea] that they would come back instantly with Theagenes', 6.1.1), but this certainty is put in doubt right away by Calasiris' reading of an omen. As soon as they leave, the three men see a crocodile creeping from their right to their left and plunging into the Nile with great strength: 'the others took the sight as nothing unusual or troublesome, except Calasiris, who said that it indicated some obstacle along the road' (6.1.2). The readers, who by now know that Calasiris is a good interpreter of signs, are alerted that the search for Theagenes might turn out to be less simple than expected. But before they can learn more, the issue of his recovery is pushed to the backstage altogether by Cnemon's display of fearfulness (he is scared out of his wits and almost runs away at the mere sight of the crocodile's shadow), which causes Calasiris to make fun of him and to explain how he panicked just at hearing the name of a dead woman on the night when Nausicles came back from his expedition bringing Chariclea with him: '"And if I did not fear to distress him or scare him, I would tell this name, to make you laugh more, Nausicles". And at once he added: "Thisbe"' (6.1.4). Cued by Calasiris, the readers anticipate that Nausicles will laugh. But the opposite happens: he becomes serious and pensive while Cnemon bursts into loud laughter. He calls this development 'a complete reversal of conditions' ($\pi\acute{a}\theta o\upsilon\varsigma$ $\mu\epsilon\tau\acute{a}\sigma\tau a\sigma\iota\varsigma$, 6.2.1), drawing attention to a signature trait of Heliodorus' novel, filled as it is with sudden reversals of emotions.[4] A bantering exchange ensues, then Cnemon recapitulates his story, and finally the trio comes across an acquaintance of Nausicles, who expounds his own predicament as the love-slave of an unloving and tyrannical mistress, Isias. It is, unexpectedly, from this personage, and after

---

[4] For the pattern, see e.g. also 2.6.1: Theagenes recovers from despair while Cnemon faints.

the narrative has long deviated from the initial issue of finding Theagenes, that characters and readers learn that he is elsewhere, that a new expedition is needed. To prepare for it, the three men return to Chemmis. The sequence ends back where it started. Yet, its small but concentrated turns have taken the readers on a fun journey.

11.2. Cnemon on Stage

At the almost exact centre of the sequence is Cnemon's story, which he tells at Calasiris' request. Its narration is another pointer that gestures to the transition between the first and the second part of the novel, this time by urging us to read not onwards but backwards. For the presentation of Cnemon's story conjures up previous incidents with numerous neat correspondences. Most obviously and broadly, it is counterbalanced by the telling of Calasiris' story, which ends when the novel reaches its midpoint. The roles are switched: Cnemon, the main audience to Calasiris' story, now tells his to oblige the older man, as he had promised to do 'another time' when first Calasiris had asked him who he was, and he had postponed telling his story in order to hear Calasiris' own (2.26.3). Furthermore, Calasiris blames Cnemon for dodging his request just as he himself had admitted to having evaded Nausicles' earlier. When Calasiris is about to begin his narrative, he tells Cnemon that he wished his host were there because he had often asked for his story, and he had always found excuses not to tell it (2.23.6). Now that he has complied (in Book 5), he reproaches Cnemon for having postponed the narration of his own story time and again, 'with various evasive strategies' (ποικίλαις...διαδύσεσιν, 6.2.2).

The two episodes are also marked by verbal repetitions. Nausicles urges Calasiris to speak as follows: 'The story of your wanderings, if you would wish to tell it, would be the best accompaniment (ἄν...παραπέμποι) to the feast...this story which, as you know, you have often postponed telling me (πολλάκις μοι διελθεῖν...ὑπερθέμενος)' (5.16.2). Calasiris seems to remember these words when it is his turn to urge Cnemon: 'the account that you have often promised to tell me (πολλάκις μοι διελθεῖν) but have always postponed (ὑπερθέμενος)..., now it would be the right time to tell it. You would do Nausicles a favour and you would lighten the hardship of our journey, accompanying (παραπέμπων) it with your story' (6.2.2).

This strikingly rich cluster of verbal echoes at a relatively short interval audibly ties the two episodes of story-telling together, creating a symmetrical and mirror-like relationship between the end of the novel's first part and the beginning of the second. Coming back from his mission, Nausicles had asked Calasiris, 'who is this stranger' (5.1.6)? And Calasiris had answered, 'a Greek. You'll know the rest another time'. This is the 'other time'. And again, Calasiris had asked Cnemon (5.2.2), 'who is Thisbe?' 'How do you know her?' And Cnemon had said, 'you'll know the rest afterwards, when I tell you my story' (5.2.3). Now that 'afterwards' has come. By harking back to the last book of novel's first part, Heliodorus smooths over the transition to the second.

But there is a major difference between Calasiris' story and Cnemon's: the latter is not in the first person but is a recapitulation, presented in the third person and in indirect speech.[5] When Calasiris resumes his tale, he sums up the part that he has already recounted to Cnemon (5.16.5), but then he narrates afresh, while 'Cnemon told in a summary everything that he had previously narrated to Theagenes and Charicleia'. The summary, however, is a thorough one, covering one full page in the *Belles Lettres* edition. The presence of a substantial recapitulation at this juncture further underlines the position of Book 6 as the novel's new beginning by a subtle intertextual reference to Chariton's main narrative transition. Heliodorus has imitated it. Like his novel, Chariton's is neatly divided into two parts, and might have been so even materially.[6] The opening of Chariton's Book 5 falls at the exact middle of the novel, just as the opening of Book 6 does in Heliodorus. Both beginnings also launch a journey (Chariton's almost), which gives the narrative a fresh impetus. And Chariton introduces Book 5 with a half-page long recapitulation: 'How Callirhoe, the most beautiful of women, was married to Chaereas, the most beautiful of men [*et cetera, et cetera*] I have illustrated in the previous part'. Heliodorus follows the earlier novelist also by inserting a long summary at the restart of his narrative.[7]

Heliodorus, however, does not follow Chariton in that the recapitulation with which he begins his novel's second half is not in the authorial voice but, though reported, in a character's. This is consistent with the more refracted narrative style of the *Aethiopica*, which interweaves its characters'

---

[5] Similar recapitulations can be found in 2.2.1, 2.14.2, 5.10.1–2, 7.24.2, 8.1.6–7, 9.12.2.
[6] Goold 1995: 231 records the view according to which *Callirhoe* filled two rolls, with Book 5 beginning the second.
[7] Reitzenstein 1906: 95–6, followed by Schmeling 1974: 49, and partially by Whitmarsh 2009: 39, divides Chariton's novel into five acts, in the style of New Comedy (Act 1 = Books 1–3.2; Act 2 = Books 3.3–4; Act 3 = Books 5–6; Act 4 = Book 7; Act 5 = Book 8). Even if we endorse these divisions, Book 5 stands in the middle, at the beginning of Act 3.

stories and often borrows both their voices and their points of view, whereas Chariton's narrator more generally adopts an external and panoramic perspective. The two recapitulations in his novel (at the beginning of Books 5 and 8) are given from this authorial vantage point. Conversely, in Heliodorus all of them are in the voice of a character.[8] Only shorter references to previously narrated events ('we have already said this', 'you will remember'), which do not contain summaries, are in Heliodorus' voice (5.4.3; 5.8.2).[9]

The recapitulation in Book 6 is by far the most extensive in the novel. Its length stresses its function, noted above, as a counterpart to Calasiris' story. The summary also differs from all the others because it is not meant to help the readers follow what is going on. Typically recapitulations are closely connected to present happenings: so, for instance, when Cnemon summarizes how he led Chariclea down to the innermost part of the cave (2.2.1), the readers are given enough background to suspect that the dead woman eventually discovered at the cave's entrance is not she; Thermouthis recapitulates his valiant attack on the enemy and his dealings with Thisbe to explain how he ended up looking for her (2.14.2-3); the reminder of Cnemon's and Thermouthis' journey from the cave in search for Thyamis (5.4.3) serves to refresh the readers' memory about the circumstances that led the protagonists to be alone in the cave, from which they make plans to escape; and Achaemenes' summing up how Theagenes was taken from his hands (7.24.2) is directly connected with, that is, it explains, the hero's enslavement by Arsace.[10] By contrast, the recapitulation of Cnemon's story has no tie with the actions at hand, but serves to inform characters still ignorant of its contents. While all those present at the beginning of Book 6 know Calasiris' story, neither Nausicles nor Calasiris has yet heard Cnemon's. By filling them in, he ties up a loose thread and closes a chapter, as it were.

Cnemon's recapitulation is closural also because it prepares for his imminent exit. He gets to be on stage for the last time as the chief protagonist of the beginning of Book 6. His mode of presence there gives the readers yet another snapshot of his main characteristic, which he has displayed throughout the novel: cowardliness. At the sight of the crocodile's shadow, not even the real thing, he almost flees. This spurs Calasiris to rehearse a previous episode, when Cnemon, at hearing just the name of Thisbe, spent a

---

[8] See 2.2.1 (Cnemon); 2.14.2 (Thermouthis); 5.10.2 (Nausicles); 5.16.5 (Calasiris); 7.24.2 (Achaemenes); 8.1.6-7 (Achaemenes); 9.12.2 (the citizens of Syene).

[9] One exception is 9.13.2-3, where Heliodorus retells Oroondates' treacherous actions; but the retelling is not introduced as a summary.

[10] See also 5.8.2; 5.10.1; 8.1.6-7; 9.12.2.

night in terror, roaming all over Nausicles' house. But the readers will also be reminded of other such demonstrations of fearfulness: his headlong flight after dumping Thermouthis (2.20.3), or his shrinking away from the sight of Thisbe's corpse (2.7.3). Calasiris was not present at those events; but he unwittingly conjures the latter one up by verbal echoes, which Heliodorus puts into his mouth to underscore the parallel. On discovering Thisbe's body, Cnemon 'fled from a woman, and a dead one at that' (τὴν γυναῖκα, νεκρὰν καὶ ταύτην, ὑποφεύγων, 2.7.3). In Calasiris' account, he is still all a-trembling if one only mentions the name of 'a woman, and a dead one at that' (γυναικὸς καὶ ταύτης νεκρᾶς, 6.1.4). Now that we are about to leave him, we get a last summary portrayal of him. 'Cnemon in a nutshell': thus we could title the description of his reactions to the appearance of the crocodile's shadow and the evocation of his past fears.

11.3. Narrative Withheld

The deuteragonist of the episode is Nausicles. He leads the journey, knows the character they meet en route, and heartens the other men after they discover that Theagenes has been taken away. Nausicles is in the spotlight also when Calasiris mentions Thisbe's name ('to make you laugh'), which triggers his unexpected reactions, carefully recorded (6.2.1). The prominence allotted to him, as to Cnemon, foreshadows his upcoming exit from the plot. And, again like Cnemon, he will soon get to be on stage to reveal details of his story (6.8.1). For the time being, however, Nausicles keeps it to himself. Once Cnemon finishes his recapitulation, he 'turned over many thoughts. He pondered whether he should recount his adventures with Thisbe or should postpone (ὑπερθέσθαι) the story to another time. In the end, and with difficulty, he refrained' (6.3.1).

To withhold stories temporarily is a hallmark of Heliodorus' narrative technique. Calasiris and Cnemon had done so repeatedly, and Nausicles once before, when he had announced that he would give an account of his mission in search of Thisbe but on the morrow (5.1.7). On those occasions the readers are as ignorant as the characters. In contrast, when Nausicles decides not to speak at the beginning of Book 6, they know the detail that he keeps to himself, namely that he was the lover of Thisbe (see 2.24.1–3). Nausicles' untold story is the first one in the novel that does not need to be explicated for the readers to gain information.

True, something similar happens already in Book 2, when Cnemon, though shaken by emotion at hearing Calasiris mention Thisbe (2.24.1), then

Thyamis (2.25.7), manages to restrain himself. The readers understand why each time he has shown signs of agitation; they know that he is acquainted with both, whereas Calasiris does not. In those episodes, however, the emphasis does not fall on Cnemon's decision to withhold his narrative but on his desire to keep on listening to Calasiris': 'he forced silence on himself to hear the rest of the story' (τῶν ἑξῆς ἕνεκεν, 2.25.7), because he is well aware that Calasiris is curious about his own (2.21.5; see also 2.24.2). Calasiris' inquisitiveness causes Cnemon, the insatiable audience, to be wary of saying anything that might push the other to ask him about himself.

When Nausicles remains silent in Book 6, on the other hand, he is not the listener to someone else's story and he has not even been asked to tell his own. His reticence withholds information only from the characters, who are not even aware of his decision to keep his peace. For the novelist discloses it only to the readers, whereas both groups are aware of Nausicles' earlier intention to postpone his account (5.1.7). This difference highlights the growing gap of knowledge between characters and readers that marks the second half of the novel. Starting with Book 5, we are generally better equipped than the characters to understand what is going on.[11] In keeping with the more explanatory style that Heliodorus adopts as his narrative unfolds, the first sequence of the novel's second part contains a suppressed story that does not leave us in ignorance.

More characters after Nausicles decide not to tell their stories or thoughts, but their choice, just as his in Book 6, does not withhold knowledge from the readers. On the contrary, the reticent characters themselves or, alternatively, the authorial narrator, detail the information that is not given to other characters. Achaemenes' resolve to keep quiet about his dealings with Theagenes follows a soliloquy from which we learn something that the surrounding characters do not know: that it was he who was taking Theagenes to Oroondates when Thyamis seized him (7.16.2–3).[12] Charicleia's decision not to reveal her happy thoughts to Theagenes (8.17.1) comes together with their revelation to the readers. No mystery is created. And again Charicles' prudent choice not to tell the truth about Charicleia's

---

[11] Fusillo 1989: 128–32 demonstrates this increased authorial guidance by contrasting the extensive introduction of Arsace in Book 7 with the unexplained appearance of the protagonists in Book 1. Although the novelist keeps withholding information when we would need it to fully understand an event happening before our eyes (for instance, we are not told about the magic properties of Charicleia's ring before she springs onto the fire but only after she is saved: see Morgan 2003: 441), it is undeniable that we are more rarely puzzled in the novel's second half. Morgan 1989b: 105 calls it, at least in part, 'an omniscient third-person narrative'. See also Kruchió 2018b: 155–7; 160–1.

[12] On the exceptionally informative content of Achaemenes' soliloquy, see Hefti 1950: 107.

origins to Hydaspes (10.36.1) keeps nothing hidden from us. The thick concentrations of half-spoken truths and held-back confessions in the final stretch of the novel[13] is geared to defer the resolution, the expected happy ending,[14] but none of these silences leaves the readers wondering. Nausicles' reticence inaugurates this trend.

11.4. Connecting Narratives

The discovery that Theagenes is not where he was supposed to be surprises both characters and readers, and not simply because no one knows that Theagenes was taken away, but also from the manner in which the revelation comes about: unexpectedly and tangentially, as it were, from the casual encounter with the lover of Isias. This episode, like the earlier appearance of the crocodile, is not free-standing but directly connected to the main plot. This connectivity is typical of Heliodorus' handling of multiple narrative threads, including digressions. They tend to be integrated into the main narrative, even when they satisfy the reader's curiosity about the exotic and the spectacular: for instance, the appearance of a giraffe in Meroe spurs not only a lengthy description (10.27) but also Theagenes' athletic feat (10.28.1–4); Calasiris' account of the sources and the floods of the Nile kindles Charicles' interest and ultimately prompts him to tell his story (2.28.1–29.1); the procession in honour of Neoptolemus, narrated in a leisurely fashion, leads to the protagonists' first encounter and falling in love (3.5.4–6); and even descriptions of armies or military tactics (8.16.4; 9.15; 9.19.3–4), though they diverge from the plot, fit the subject matter at hand, war.[15] In sum, in Heliodorus 'there is, by comparison with some other novels, a marked absence of non-functional digressions.'[16]

The most apt comparandum is *Leucippe and Clitophon*, which deploys digressions exuberantly, regardless of whether and how deeply relevant they

---

[13] See 10.18.2; 19.2; 21.3; 29.3–4; 32.4; 33.1.
[14] See Morgan 1989a: 313, 315–16. For the same reason, both times Charicleia is about to speak clearly about the nature of her relationship with Theagenes (10.22.1 and 29.5–30.1), something prevents her, and when she finally does (10.33.4), the narrative focus switches to another scene.
[15] More aloof from the main narrative is the explanation of the mysteries of the Nile at 9. 9–10.
[16] Morgan 2003: 440–1. Rommel's 1923: 59–64 discussion of Heliodorus' digressions is an exercise in *Quellenforschung*. A helpful treatment of the scholarly positions on digressions in the novels is Whitmarsh 2011: 235–42.

are to the plot.[17] Thus, the corresponding appearance of a crocodile in this novel inspires a much longer account, which, additionally, remains hanging at the end of a book (4), while the next begins with an abrupt shift of focus ('We sailed three days and arrived in Alexandria') and with no further mention of the beast. Another such description, of a phoenix, likewise hangs loose at the end of a book (3),[18] while the first line of the next likewise moves back to the plot ('Having heard of the enemy's forces, the general decided...'). It is true that the detailed description of a hippopotamus (4.3.2–5) is motivated by the speaker's desire to keep eyeing Leucippe as long as possible; but the following account of the elephant's marvellous features and habits has at best an associative connection with the previous digression: it is spurred only by the might of the hippopotamus, almost comparable to the elephant's.[19] In contrast, the brief appearance of the crocodile in Heliodorus works as a springboard to demonstrate and expound Cnemon's fearfulness. This in turn prompts the mention of Thisbe, which in turn results in the recapitulation of Cnemon's story.[20]

The conversation with Isias' lover is not a digression. It is not a description but an intervening episode. Like a digression, however, it has the effect of interrupting the main narrative. Nausicles says it: the encounter with his acquaintance is one more reason he does not tell his story, which would have complemented Cnemon's. The intervening episode is meaningful beyond the immediate events, for it highlights the purity of the protagonists' love by inviting comparison with the unhealthy life of a man enslaved to an unloving mistress.[21] But the episode, like the plunge of the crocodile, also has instant relevance in that it provides new information about Theagenes.[22]

---

[17] See again Whitmarsh 2011: 242–6, for an overarching treatment. For specific interpretations, see Bartsch 1989 and Morales 2004: 96–151 (the latter on sententious pronouncements). Morales (98) points out that the term 'digression' is inadequate, because passages so called differ in nature and function. Indeed, the list of Achillean and Heliodorean digressions in Bartsch (12–13) does not contain *sententiae*, the main focus of Morales. I use the term 'digression' in its standard sense and for convenience.

[18] Morales 2004: 190–4, though, argues for parallels between the description of the phoenix and of Leucippe.

[19] 4. 3. 5. See Whitmarsh 2011: 244.

[20] We could also compare the descriptions of Charicleia and Theagenes (3.3–4) and of an amethyst (5.13–14), which elicit a strong emotional response from characters in the main narrative, whereby they are integrated into it, with those, in Achilles Tatius, of a sacred bowl (2.3) and of Calligone's necklace and dress (2.11), which remain inconsequential.

[21] See Morgan 1989b: 107.

[22] The episode also fills the readers in about Thyamis, who disappeared from the narrative at the end of Book 1. From Nausicles' acquaintance we learn that he has become the leader of the band that had captured him then. See Morgan 1989b: 106.

The unexpected encounter forces the travellers and the plot to reorient their movement.

11.5. Stupefied Silences

The unexpectedness of the revelation about Theagenes' whereabouts is brought into stark relief by the characters' response: 'As they heard this, they stood for a long time agape (ἀχανεῖς ἐπὶ πλεῖστον εἰστήκεσαν) at the unforeseen failure of their expectations (6.4.1). At last (ὀψέ) Nausicles revived them, telling them that they should not give up their enterprise completely on account of a passing stroke of bad luck', but instead they should return to Chemmis to prepare for another journey. The three men's paralysed silence creates a counterpoint with the agitation of Isias' lover, who rushes off (παρέτρεχεν), still speaking, while they cannot either speak or move.

This prolonged speechlessness aligns the episode with major happenings in the novel, which likewise meet with thunderstruck silences. Stupefaction is a shared feature of novelistic poetics.[23] Heliodorus grafts it on the theatricality of his novel, filled with spectacles that leave the audience dumbfounded.[24] Whether it responds to a scene markedly theatrical or not, the silence described by ἀχανής always reacts to startling sights: Charicleia and Theagenes are ἀχανεῖς at seeing an armed host coming toward them (5.6.1), Cnemon, then Thermouthis, at discovering the dead Thisbe (2.5.3; 2.12.4), Charicles at his first encounter with the inconceivably beautiful Charicleia (2.30.6), the people of Memphis as they watch Calasiris' recognition (7.7.4), and Persinna at discovering the band she had exposed with her daughter (10.13.1). These are all culminating episodes, truly *coups de théâtre*, including the revelation that initiates Charicleia's recognition. We can add the end-point of the recognition scene itself (10.15.1), which features Hydaspes, at last persuaded of Charicleia's identity, standing immobile (ἐφεστάναι), seized with wonder (θαῦμα).

The episode in Book 6 is not as climactic or startling. It is the only one in which the agape silence does not respond to a marvellous or petrifying spectacle but to a piece of (admittedly surprising) information. The response

---

[23] On the strong emotional responses of novelistic internal audiences, see Kaimio 1996 on Chariton (reworked by Tilg 2010: 138–40); Graverini 2010: 9–12, especially on Apuleius.

[24] See Marino 1990: 210.

seems out of proportion compared to the other instances. As Nausicles points out, the disappointing news will only cause a second start, another journey: more of the same rather than a dramatic reversal. I think that Heliodorus has introduced this silent paralysis in order to underline the effects of the first meaningful unexpected turn in the novel's second part, so as to keep the readers riveted to his narrative now that it is taking off again. The second half of this breath-taking novel, he intimates, starts with yet another *coup de théâtre*: a *coup de théâtre* not so much in reality as *because I am telling you so* by using a stock formula that normally describes the typical response to such coups. Please, respond accordingly! The careful second-time reader is even cued to endow this incident with the same emotional impact as perhaps the most astounding episode in the novel: Persinna's discovery of the band.

The shocked silence in Book 6 has an even stronger impact than Persinna's, not emotionally but as far as its consequences for the plot. It is a silence that paralyses all the participants. Typically this is not the case. When first Cnemon, then Thermouthis are struck dumb at discovering the dead Thisbe (2.5.3; 2.12.4), Theagenes is revived (in the first episode), and he and Cnemon are talking (in the second), causing Thermouthis to hear their voices and move toward them; the people of Memphis are spectators, not actors, in the scene that strikes them with amazement (7.7.4); Persinna is the only one to be incapacitated by her emotion (10.13.1); and while Hydaspes is seized with wonderment at recognizing Charicleia (10.15.1), Sisimithres, who knows the facts, remains calm, as he does when Charicles becomes speechless at the sight of the girl's beauty (2.30.6). As a consequence of these only 'partial' paralyses, the action does not come to a standstill. At the most, it stops for a minute, the time the spotlight falls on the silent character. The same happens in other episodes of astonishment. In several of them only some of the characters are prey to it;[25] and when all are, they recover and speak or move, or alternatively they can think and speak in spite of their bewilderment.[26] In the episode in Book 6, on the other hand, for the action to resume there is need of one character's exhortation, and even that character comes out of his petrified silence only 'late'. The closest parallel is at 5.6.1, where likewise the characters struck dumb take a long time (ὀψέ, again) to resume speaking; but in that instance they recover by themselves, without the help of whipping words.

---

[25] See 1.12.3–4; 5.2.1–2; 5.11.2–3.
[26] See 1.2.5–6; 2.23.2; 3.5.5; 5.6.1; 10.13.3–4; 10.35.2–36.1.

The sequence 'prolonged silence broken by whipping words' connects the episode of Book 6 to incidents in the *Iliad* in which an upsetting speech causes a silent paralysis until one character, at last (ὀψέ, as in Heliodorus), solves the impasse by a forceful rebuttal. In two of the Homeric parallels the silence that responds to a proposal signals resistance to it but inability to rebuke it. At *Iliad* 7.398–9, the offer is the return of Helen, with added gifts. At *Iliad* 9.29–31, it is leaving Troy. In the context of traditional stories, these proposals are unacceptable because they would introduce innovations that could not accommodate the fundamentals of the story: Helen cannot be returned and Troy cannot be abandoned because it 'must' be sacked for the myth to hold. The intervention that at last breaks the silence to reject the proposal reasserts the traditional story.

Heliodorus twists the meaning of the silence and of its resolution to make them fit the non-traditional subject matter of his narrative, and to play mind games with readers whose horizon of expectations is conditioned by their familiarity with the novelistic genre. The three men's silence does not react to a proposal, marking its unacceptability and yet their inability to come up with a viable option; rather it risks blocking the plot. In the two Homeric episodes there would be an alternative, though untenable in traditional terms, to the current state of affairs: the Greeks would leave Troy, with or without Helen. In the novel the news of Theagenes' whereabouts simply stops the characters from acting. And they would do nothing at all without Nausicles' intervention. While in Homer failure to reject the proposal would threaten the mythic plotline, in Heliodorus failure to break the silence would thwart the plotline that was advancing the story to the expected happy ending. Nausicles, therefore, opposes not an alternative option (such as to accept Helen back, or to leave Troy) but inaction, urging the others not to abandon their enterprise. At the restart of his novel Heliodorus sketches a potential short-circuit, titillating the readers' imagination with the generically impossible prospect of renouncing the search for the hero.[27] And by removing the threat, he soothingly restores generic norms and also gives the new beginning the added impetus that comes from overcoming a paralysis.

---

[27] Heliodorus is fond of suggesting such short-circuits in the second half of the novel: see Morgan 1989a: 304 and 1989b: 103.

11.6. Conclusions

The crucial role of Nausicles in solving the silent impasse is consistent with his prominence at the beginning of Book 6. He might also have his own interests in mind. For he is the one to whom finding Theagenes matters the least. It is easy for him, having never met the captured hero, to say, 'let's go back home—to my home—and take it from there'. Readers might have expected Calasiris to play the heartening role in this scene, in his capacity as a divinely inspired wise man, who can read signs from heaven (as in this very episode). Furthermore, he has guided the couple on their journey from Greece to Egypt. Faced with the substitution of the priest with the merchant, the second-time reader, who knows that Nausicles is about to leave the stage for good, will take his words of encouragement as an exit strategy. The movement back home provides him with a way out.

But the movement backward has another function: it revitalizes the enterprise. Instead of continuing, the journey will start all over again. It will also be 'longer' ($\pi\lambda\epsilon\iota\text{ova}$), and it will be accompanied by 'good hope' ($\dot{\alpha}\gamma\alpha\theta\dot{\eta}\nu\ldots\dot{\epsilon}\lambda\pi\iota\delta\alpha$, 6.4.2). This detail both rounds off the episode as a unity and looks ahead to the next one. When the three men took off, they left Chariclea behind, all excited with 'hopes' ($\tau o\hat{\iota}s\ \dot{\epsilon}\lambda\pi\iota\zeta o\mu\dot{\epsilon}\nu o\iota s$, 6.1.2) for a good outcome; and now that they return, Nausicles fills them with hope about the outcome of the new journey. The circle is completed. Hope, however, is a forward-looking emotion, and as such it also causes the movement to continue onward: 'It was not without the hands of the gods that they had come across that acquaintance. By the news he gave them they were guided sure-handedly ($\chi\epsilon\iota\rho\alpha\gamma\omega\gamma\eta\theta\hat{\eta}\nu\alpha\iota$) where they had to seek Theagenes, aiming ($\tau\epsilon\iota\nu o\nu\tau\alpha s$) their journey with impetus ($\tau\dot{\eta}\nu\ \dot{o}\rho\mu\dot{\eta}\nu\ \tau\hat{\eta}s\ \pi o\rho\epsilon\iota\alpha s$, literally "the impetus of the journey"), as to a target, straight to the village of the Herdsmen' (6.4.2). As the episode reaches its close, Heliodorus energetically launches the travellers on with renewed determination and an unfailing aim. Arrow-like, they are now 'stretching' toward the future: $\tau\epsilon\iota\nu o\nu\tau\alpha s$, 'aiming for', or 'straining for', is the episode's last word.

Readers strain as well, and look ahead to the next adventure. Once again, they do not put the book down. Heliodorus begins and ends the first episode of his novel's second part with pictures of excited movement, which incite the readers to 'move on'. He thus kindles, even endorses, intense emotional responses to the text. Taking the lead from the restless characters who set out before dawn on their journey, this novel's consumers are spurred to feel overeager themselves to start on a new adventure. They enjoy the ride's unexpected turns, and even when they end back where they started, they excitedly look forward to the next trip, 'reaching' toward it.

The centrepiece of the episode, however, the retelling of Cnemon's story, does not keep the readers on their toes, because they already know it. As I have suggested, the main function of its rehearsal is to tie together the two halves of the novel by harking back to Calasiris' performance in a number of details, which we are challenged to unearth. We are also called upon to appreciate Heliodorus' increasingly more explanatory style of narration when we measure the consequences of Nausicles' decision to keep quiet about himself against other such episodes of reticence in the novel's first half. In short, we are asked to engage with the text intellectually as well as emotionally; to reflect on shifts in narrative styles or on the functions of digressions and interwoven episodes; to read carefully enough to catch the numerous subtle intratextual and intertextual allusions scattered in the episode and also its meta-literary qualities, detectable in the compliments Heliodorus pays to his narrative by intimating that it will never satiate us or that its twists and turns—how wonderfully stunning!—strike everyone dumb. The episode demonstrates that Heliodorus' novel can be fully savoured only by a reader who is both highly literate and emotionally involved, both discriminating and voraciously enthusiastic.[28]

---

[28] On the intellectual sophistication and the emotional involvement expected of Heliodorus' ideal reader, see, respectively, Winkler 1982: 140–4 and Morgan 1989b: 106; 1991: 96–7. Most recently Palone 2020 has argued in favour of a strong emotional participation.

12
Charicleia's Dark Night of the Soul (6.8–11)

David Konstan

Among the greatest trials that the heroes and heroines of the Greek romantic novels experience is their separation from one another, with the accompanying anxiety that the other may no longer be alive. In the novels by Chariton, Xenophon of Ephesus, and Achilles Tatius, the separation occurs early in the narrative, and the protagonists are only fully reunited near the end. Longus' *Daphnis and Chloe* has a different structure, but the principal apartness, due to the onset of winter, occurs in the third book, that is, at the midpoint of the story. So too in Heliodorus' *Aethiopica*: for all their sufferings over the course of the first five books, Charicleia and Theagenes have mainly been together; it is only in the middle of the fifth book that they are parted, but much of the remainder of that book is taken up with Calasiris' narration of the events leading up to the opening scene in the novel, in which we see the couple mysteriously stranded on the beach, with no indication of who they are or how they got there. So it is only in Book 6 that Charicleia is shown responding to the absence of Theagenes.

Charicleia's despair is intense: she locks herself in her room (at this stage in the action, she and Calasiris are guests in the home of the merchant Nausicles), tears her clothing, smashes the lamp, throws herself upon her bed, and sobs and wails until she is wholly exhausted and falls into a swoon, from which she does not awaken until Calasiris bangs at her door the following morning, alarmed that she has not yet emerged. The violence of her reaction is remarkable, even in the hyper-emotional world of the novels, but it is highlighted all the more by contrast with her earlier self-control in grim situations. When Calasiris encounters her, dishevelled, half-naked, her swollen eyes 'indicating her mad state before she fell asleep' (6.9.1), he rebukes her for her failure to master her circumstances, and declares, 'I don't even recognize you now, you who were always noble and restrained

David Konstan, *Charicleia's Dark Night of the Soul (6.8–11)* In: *Reading Heliodorus'* Aethiopica.
Edited by: Ian Repath and Tim Whitmarsh, Oxford University Press. © Oxford University Press 2022.
DOI: 10.1093/oso/9780198792543.003.0012

and used to know how to endure fortune' (6.9.3). Charicleia is suitably chastened, although she feels that Theagenes' absence, and her fear that he may be dead, go some way to excusing her desolation. Nevertheless, Calasiris manages to restore her confidence, or at least to give her some hope of finding Theagenes, and at his prompting she comes up with the plan of disguising themselves as beggars and proceeding to the village of Bessa, where they have reason to believe that the bandit Thyamis, in reality the son of Calasiris, has taken him.

Clearly, this episode is meant to be taken as a turning point in the action, and it is signalled as such in various ways. First, there is its position in the narrative. The first half of the novel is marked by a complex pattern of suspense gradually relieved by a series of stories that are effectively flashbacks, filling in parts of the history of the couple that up to this point have been obscure; at the end of Book 5, Calasiris has related the final details, those leading up to the opening scene of the novel, and from this moment onwards the temporal movement is linear, from Nausicles' house in Chemmis (the modern Akhmim) to Bessa and Memphis and finally through southern Egypt and on to Meroe, the capital of Ethiopia, where Charicleia will be reunited with her true parents. What is more, by concluding the first half of the story with a lengthy recital of past events by Calasiris, Heliodorus alludes to the structure of the *Odyssey*, which similarly closes the first twelve of twenty-four books with Odysseus' recital of his adventures. Like Odysseus when he lands, at the beginning of Book 13, on Ithaca, Calasiris and Charicleia will assume the guise of beggars.[1]

This is not, in fact, the first time that Charicleia has taken to her bed: she did so also at the moment of the original infatuation, with a severe case of lovesickness that she tried to conceal from her foster-father, Charicles (3.7–9, 18, 4.10). At that time, it was Calasiris who diagnosed the problem correctly, when the doctors were at a loss. Her present crisis thus echoes her earlier condition, and in this way too serves to round off the first part of the narrative, which proceeds, albeit in a zigzag way, from the time she fell in love with Theagenes to the moment when she is parted from him. To be sure, the separation is not a resolution of the plot, but rather a second starting point; Charicleia will soon be reunited with Theagenes in Memphis, where the couple will experience further obstacles to their happiness because of Arsace's passion for Theagenes. The larger narrative trajectory

---

[1] Paulsen 1992: 163.

that frames the tale of love, separation, and reunion—that is, the discovery of Charicleia's true identity and her formal marriage to Theagenes—will only achieve its denouement in the final book of the novel. But the low point of Charicleia's emotional life coincides with the conclusion to a parallel story or subplot that is woven into the text, namely that of Cnemon.

What triggers Charicleia's grief in this episode is not just the absence of Theagenes but the celebration that is going on in the house of the wedding between Cnemon and Nausicles' daughter, Nausicleia, which serves as a counterpoint to Charicleia's misfortune. With the consummation of this union, Cnemon, Nausicles, and Nausicleia will disappear entirely from the story. Thus the middle of the novel witnesses not only the nadir of Charicleia's and Theagenes' fortunes, but also a happy ending to the secondary plot line. However, the resolution of Cnemon's story, and with it that of Nausicles, does not conform to the pattern that governs the story of the protagonists, whether in the *Aethiopica* or any of the other Greek romantic novels; and the difference sheds light on the nature of the principal love story.

Cnemon marries Nausicleia as a result of a series of substitutions. Cnemon had sailed to Egypt in search of Thisbe, a slave in the house of Cnemon's father who had conspired against both men and had, in the meantime, run off with Nausicles, who became enamoured of her when he was on a business trip to Athens. Cnemon had been taken captive by Thyamis and his band, and so fell in with Theagenes and Charicleia. Thyamis killed Thisbe, in the mistaken belief that she was Charicleia, whom he had jealously locked in a cave so that no one else might have her. In fact, a letter was discovered with Thisbe's body, in which she professed her love for Cnemon. The upshot is that Nausicles does not get Thisbe, Thisbe does not get Cnemon, and Cnemon does get a girl who until now has played no part at all in the novel, in an arrangement that is eminently practical—the wealthy merchant promises to restore the fortunes of the poor Athenian—but can hardly be regarded as a love match (6.8.1–2). Heliodorus has offered an alternative paradigm to the romantic plot that the novels celebrate, and brings it to a close at just the point at which Charicleia is most desperate and, with Calasiris' support, recovers the will and determination to seek out Theagenes.

Calasiris appeals to Charicleia to come up with a stratagem to render their expedition safe, since, as he puts it, 'You seem to be frightfully clever (δεινή) at figuring out devices for evading and delaying attackers' (6.9.7). His words cheer Charicleia up a bit, though she suspects that he may be teasing her, and she in fact does propose a plan, namely to disguise themselves as paupers. True, she had done this once before, at Theagenes' recommendation, and there too in order that her beauty not attract unwelcome attention—an anxiety that is not uncommon in the novels. But this time the plan is her own, and marks a new stage in her independence, initiative, and growth as a character. As Koen de Temmerman observes, as a result of Calasiris' compliment 'Charicleia for the first time in the entire narrative is encouraged to suggest a stratagem herself *in the presence of Calasiris* rather than merely following or imitating his advice'.[2] Although she has a native astuteness and nobility of character, Charicleia develops over the course of the novel; as de Temmerman argues, her qualities are 'indirectly shown *not* to be merely static, generically typical characteristics but rather the results of a mental change involving self-knowledge, self-esteem, and external influence'.[3]

Character development is not to be taken for granted in ancient novels, or for that matter in classical literature generally. When Bakhtin proposed his notion of the chronotope, that union of time and space that in his view varied with, and in part constituted, the several literary genres, he affirmed that the Greek romances, in contrast to the modern novel, virtually lacked the temporal dimension, which was entirely subordinated to the spatial. The protagonists are driven to every corner of the Mediterranean world, but when they are reunited, they remain, according to Bakhtin, exactly as they were. Nothing has changed, and all of their adventures may be bracketed as a timeless interlude, since the hero and heroine do not develop as a result of them. As Gary Saul Morson, a renowned expert on Bakhtin, puts it:

> The crucial point to note about the adventures in a Greek romance is that they 'leave no trace' (FTC, p. 94). They affect nothing, and, for all the difference they make, might just as well not have happened....Hero and heroine do not change, mature, grow, or even age biologically as a result of their adventures....The entire action of the Greek romance, in other words, takes place in 'an extratemporal hiatus between the two moments in biographical time' (FTC, p. 90). It is a time of 'pure digression' rather than of 'real duration,' that is, the time is opposite to what we find in the nineteenth-century novel, where experience changes people.[4]

---

[2] de Temmerman 2014: 269.   [3] de Temmerman 2014: 310.
[4] Morson 1990: 376–7. The quotations from Bakhtin are from the essay 'Forms of Time and of the Chronotope in the Novel: Notes toward a Historical Poetics' = Bakhtin 1981 (on Bakhtin

It is often assumed, indeed, that not just the novelists but the ancient Greeks and Romans generally tended to regard character as stable rather than mutable. Of course, human beings learn over the course of a lifetime, and may come to control their native dispositions, but one could usually discern in the child the traits that would mark the self: profound transformations of temperament, of the sort that we might think of as conversions, were rare and rarely described. Glenn Most has addressed the radical contrast between modern and ancient ways of explaining character formation.[5] Having first provided, by way of illustrating the modern approach, a summary of Salman Rushdie's novel, *Fury*, in which the protagonist discovers the source of his uncontrollable rages in the sexual abuse to which he was, as a child, repeatedly subjected by his stepfather, Most observes: 'no one in antiquity ever even hints that Achilles' notoriously excessive anger might have been the result of his having had an unhappy childhood—the very notion that some Greek or Roman might have even imagined making such a suggestion is ludicrous.'[6] Most wittily notes the material that Greek mythology would have provided for such an explanation: the early separation of Achilles' parents, his disguise as a girl on the island of Scyrus, and so forth. Nevertheless, Most observes, when the Greeks and Romans 'imagined Achilles as a child, they imagined him as being just like the adult Achilles, only rather smaller.'[7] And this is in general the principle that the ancients applied when investigating the relationship between childhood and adult character formation: not a violent episode that is later repressed but manifests itself in symptoms, the cause of which is obscure to the agent and to others—what Most calls the 'traumatic model'—but rather an essential continuity, in which character traits already visible in childhood endure without change or else become accentuated over time. This latter pattern Most dubs the 'continuous model.' As he writes:

> Even in political biography, like Plutarch's..., there is, despite the emphasis upon the importance of education in forming character, surprisingly little attention paid, if any, to the great man's childhood.... Alcibiades...displayed already on the playground the very same mixture of charm and vice that made him notorious as an adult.... 'He was once hard pressed in

and the novel, see now Branham 2019). Cf. de Temmerman 2014: 18: 'in Greek novel scholarship, one of the most frequent claims about the protagonists is that their characters are static' (with ample bibliography).
[5] Most 2009.   [6] Most 2009: 448.   [7] Most 2009: 449

wrestling, and to save himself from getting a fall, set his teeth in his opponent's arms, where they clutched him, and was like to have bitten through them. His adversary, letting go his hold, cried, "You bite, Alcibiades, as women do!" "Not I," said Alcibiades, "but as lions do".

(IV.5–6)[8]

We may be inclined to see the opponent's reproach as striking home, inasmuch as it anticipates a certain ambiguity in Alcibiades' sexuality for which he was notorious as an adult. His younger contemporary Xenophon remarks that 'Alcibiades was pursued by many dignified women on account of his beauty', and was courted by men as well on account of his allies and abilities.[9] Plutarch himself, in his *Life*, observes: 'Of his beauty, nothing, surely, needs to be said, except that it flourished in each age and season of his body, and rendered him lovely and pleasant as a boy, a lad, and a man.'[10] Athenaeus remarks in connection with a painting of Alcibiades that his beauty surpassed that of all the women.[11] Nevertheless, on this reading, too, Alcibiades betrays already in childhood a trait that continues into his mature life.

That ancient accounts of character development were not usually built around the Freudian model of repressed traumas and moments of sudden enlightenment does not mean that character was viewed as static: continuity allows for change, as Most himself allows, and the biographers made much of education. In an important study of Plutarch's view of character, Tim Duff asks 'how did Plutarch see education as actually working? What is its relationship to adult character?'[12] Duff begins by examining Plutarch's *Life of Themistocles*, and suggests that it 'contains within it a tension between two models for understanding the relationship of education to adult character. The first approach sees character as in the process of *being formed* in childhood, and education as affecting the way in which character develops; the second approach sees character as constant and unchanging, and as *revealed* in childhood behaviour and in attitude to education'.[13] In his essay *On Moral Virtue*, Plutarch emphasizes the importance of habituation, and Duff dubs this a 'developmental model'.[14] This latter paradigm allows for the considerable and abiding influence of inborn dispositions. Hence, the two models 'are not as contradictory as they first appear',[15] since precisely because people have 'certain innate leanings,' it is the function of education

---

[8] Most 2009: 451.   [9] Xen. *Mem.* 1.2.24.   [10] Plut. *Alc.* 1.4.
[11] Ath. *Deipn.* 12.534e.   [12] Duff 2008: 1.   [13] Duff 2008: 1.
[14] Duff 2008: 2.   [15] Duff 2008: 20.

to correct these, as all the philosophical schools in antiquity affirmed. Nevertheless, the 'static/illustrative model of character is...the norm in the *Lives*,[16] and the developmental model occurs 'in contexts where philosophical modes of thinking are dominant', most especially when there is reference or clear allusion to Plato.[17]

Heliodorus would seem, then, to be in tune with ancient philosophical interpretations of moral development, insofar as he represents Charicleia's character as, in de Temmerman's words, not 'merely static' but as undergoing 'a mental change involving self-knowledge, self-esteem, and external influence.'[18] This is far from the abrupt illumination of Most's 'traumatic model,' but it does allow that Charicleia, and also Theagenes, learn something from their sufferings and experiences, and so are not wholly fixed in a timeless universe of 'pure digression.' Yet I believe that there is in fact something more involved in Charicleia's emotional and moral collapse, and to illustrate why, let me take up two elements in the subsequent narrative that suggest that it is more of a pivotal moment than it may seem.

As we have seen, Charicleia's first action after she is chastised by Calasiris and recovers her poise is to propose that she and Calasiris disguise themselves so as to avoid possible harassment during their journey to Bessa. Their disguises are very effective: so much so, that when they finally do find Theagenes, he fails to recognize Charicleia and, as she tries to embrace him, he thrusts her away and actually strikes her, in the belief that she is a vagabond (7.7). It is only when Charicleia whispers the code names and word they had agreed upon, in the event they should be separated, that Theagenes realizes his mistake. Silvia Montiglio, in her study of recognitions

[16] Duff 2008: 21.
[17] Duff 2008: 22. Gill 2006 sees Plutarch's approach to biography as reflecting a specifically Platonic and Aristotelian model of the self, according to which 'the full development of virtue and happiness depends on a combination of the right kind of inborn nature, upbringing (conceived as habituation), and rational reflection' (205); thus, in Plutarch, 'Stability of character is a product of the interplay of inborn nature, education, and environmental influences' (419). By contrast, Gill holds that Senecan tragedy presents us with characters who are subject to 'internal conflict,' in line with a Stoic and Epicurean conception of the self as 'a psychophysical and psychological unit or structured whole' (3).
[18] de Temmerman 2014: 310. Cf. Whitmarsh 2011: 106: 'The second-century romances, then, are *transformative*.... Achilles' Callisthenes, notably, starts out as a rogue rapist, but ends up changing his personality entirely: 'everyone marvelled at his sudden transformation from a worse character to an entirely excellent one.' A subtler example is Longus' Lampis, who is 'forgiven' for his actions, implying contrition (Long. 4.38.2). At a subtler level still, Achilles and Longus fill their romances with embedded narratives of mythical metamorphosis, which reinforce towards the thematic centrality of the transformation theme.' Whitmarsh argues further that 'not only are the characters metamorphosed by their experiences, but also we as readers are promised our own far-reaching transformative event' (p. 129).

in the Greek and Roman novels, observes that earlier, in precisely the scene in which they decide on these signs, Heliodorus comments that 'should they arrive in the same place, it would be enough merely for the one to be seen by the other, for no amount of time was enough to dull the passionate tokens in their souls' (5.5.2).[19] Montiglio notes the Platonic sources of this ideal, which appears still more vividly in the description of their original enamourment, in which love is represented as a kind of recollection: 'As soon as the young pair saw one another they loved one another, as if the soul at the first meeting recognized its own likeness and ran to what was its own in worth' (3.5.4–5). Montiglio perceives an ideological tension in Theagenes' subsequent failure to see through Charicleia's humble appearance:

> on the one hand, the extraordinary beauty of the heroine, joint with the exaltation of reciprocal love at first sight typical of the novel, and, in this particular novel, the rendition of that motif in Platonic terms, calls for immediate recognition between lovers. But on the other, since the perfect love exalted in the novel only exists among the elites and since the elites of the time show uttermost care for their self-presentation and appearance, recognition, even between lovers, apparently needs visible evidence of social status. Charicleia's improper outfit and filthy face deceive the noble descendant of Achilles, no matter how keen his love.[20]

So too, Jason König affirms that 'Theagenes fails to recognize Charicleia partly because her beggarly appearance is incompatible with his view of what a properly brought up young lady ought to look like.'[21]

These are no doubt valid observations, but I would like to suggest that Theagenes' failure to recognize his beloved may reflect the fact that she has in some sense changed, not only at the level of her superficial aspect but also more deeply, and that he needs a cue established at an earlier moment in the narrative to realize that this is the Charicleia he loves. One sign that characters in the Greek novels do change as a consequence of their experiences is precisely that they cease to be recognizable. At the end of the *Ephesiaca* of Xenophon of Ephesus, the hero and heroine, after having been separated and suffered numerous misadventures, arrive simultaneously at the island of Rhodes. There first Habrocomes, and then Anthia, encounter

---

[19] Montiglio 2013a: 118.   [20] Montiglio 2013a: 120–1.
[21] König 2008: 132, cited by Montiglio 2013a: 121 n. 67.

their still faithful slaves, Leuco and Rhode; only a year has passed, but the slaves recognize neither of their masters (5.10.9; 5.12.3), for their trials have transformed their appearance. And then, after each has been informed that the other is nearby, the couple meet: 'As they saw one another, they immediately recognized each other, for this is what their hearts desired' (5.13.3). With that last, tacked on clause Xenophon spares the reader the poignancy of a reunion marred by misrecognition, but makes it plain that Habrocomes and Anthia know each other on sight only because each has been informed in advance of the presence of the other. They only saw through the changes that time and suffering had wrought because they wished it—and because each knew in advance who the other was. This is not, I think, a reflection simply of the limitations of the elite, who are blinded by marks of squalor and poverty, but a sign that the characters really are not the same as they were at the beginning, even if it is the case that their original beauty soon shines forth and excites the wonder once again of the Rhodians. The folk-tale format of the novels may require that the consequences of misery and misfortune be camouflaged, but at the crucial moment the text lays bare the truth that Habrocomes and Anthia are no longer what they were: the time during which the protagonists were apart is not a mere digression, as Bakhtin would have it.[22]

There is a similar moment in Achilles Tatius' novel, when the hero, Clitophon, is accompanying Melite, a woman who is passionately in love with him, around her estate in Ephesus, and they come upon a girl bound in chains, with her head shaved, full of grime, working in the field. Melite perceives the woman's noble bearing, despite her fallen condition, and Clitophon even notes that 'she seemed to have something of Leucippe' (5.17.7), the heroine of the novel who has been reduced to this miserable state. Clitophon believed that Leucippe was dead, but in fact it is she, as Clitophon learns when she sends him a letter revealing her identity. There is much that is witty in Achilles Tatius' novel, and we can read all kinds of ironies into Clitophon's self-confessed error. But once again, there is a suggestion, I believe, of the kind of alterations that time and hardship can wreak, which make us other than what we were before. It is thus not just education and training that condition our identities, but the harsh experiences of life.[23]

---

[22] On character development in Xenophon, see Konstan 1994; Tagliabue 2012.
[23] Cf. Laplace 1991.

The case of Charicleia is not precisely the same as that of Habrocomes and Anthia or of Leucippe, since her altered guise is deliberately assumed, but I think it too gestures at or symbolizes a deeper change in her nature. In Heliodorus' narrative the misrecognition follows just a few chapters after Charicleia's despair and subsequent recovery of confidence. Can Heliodorus be hinting that Charicleia's psychologically devastating episode really was a kind of turning point for her?

The second feature that suggests to me the possibility that Charicleia's mortification signifies a transition of some sort is the scene that immediately follows upon it in Book 6. As the camouflaged pair set out for Bessa, teasing each other lightheartedly about their costumes and entreating the *daimōn* that has beset them to set this as the limit of their trials, Heliodorus announces in advance that they are out of luck, because as they are approaching the village they come across a scene of carnage: they can see that there has been a war, but they are at a loss as to who the combatants might have been. The panorama recalls the opening of the novel, in which bandits come across a scene of slaughter and are similarly puzzled; there is a sense of a new beginning to the narrative, as Charicleia and Calasiris make their way in search of Theagenes. But before they can proceed, they encounter an old woman who explains the events to them—they learn among other things that Theagenes is now en route to Memphis—and then performs a ritual to resuscitate her dead son and question him about her other son's fate. The risen corpse condemns her evil art, as does Calasiris, and informs her that her son will not return and that she will die by the sword, adding that she has compounded her crime by performing the nefarious rites in the presence of two witnesses. The revenant concludes his forbidden revelations with a prediction concerning Charicleia, 'a young woman agitated by love and wandering over virtually the entire earth for the sake of her beloved, with whom, after thousands of toils and thousands of dangers she will, at the farthest limits, be joined for life in a brilliant and royal fortune' (6.15.9–10). Here again there is a sign of a new beginning, of the sort that might seem better suited to the novels by Chariton, Xenophon, and Achilles Tatius, where the protagonists are separated for the larger part of the story. What is more, the bizarre necromancy, which echoes similarly infernal scenes in the sixth book of Lucan's *Civil War* and the fourth book of Statius' *Thebaid* (and no doubt others in the Greek tradition), creates the kind of liminal moment that harks back to the epic catabases, from the *Odyssey* to the *Aeneid* and beyond, that tend to mark the midpoint in the hero's journey and the commencement of a new phase and clearer sense of destiny.[24] The resonance with the *Odyssey* is all the more noticeable in that the hellish interview is associated, although in reverse order, with the assumption of a beggarly disguise.[25]

Already in Book 4 of the *Aethiopica* Charicleia was infused with a new sense of pride in her birthright (τὸ φρόνημα διανιστᾶσα πλέον τῷ γένει) when Calasiris, having deciphered the script on the sash that served as her birth token, revealed that she was in fact the daughter of the monarchs of Ethiopia (4.11-12). Later in her journey, she increasingly acquires a sense of her special fate. When she is saved from the pyre by the magical stone in her keeping, she opines that her deliverance is owing to 'some miraculous and divine benefaction' or perhaps a punishment, 'unless it is some wonder-working on the part of a *daimōn* that is casting us into lowest depths and rescuing us again from our helplessness' (8.10.2)—a view that Theagenes rejects as impious (8.11.1), but which captures well the ups and downs of their fortunes and suggests that their moments of despair may well be a kind of test or rite of passage. Charicleia, however, attempts to cheer Theagenes up with an optimistic interpretation of his prophetic dream the night before (cf. 9.2.2, where again she tries to lift Theagenes' fallen spirits).

To conclude: although I do not mean to revive Reinhold Merkelbach's view of the ancient Greek novels as allegories of mystical rites of initiation,[26] which has been out of favour pretty much since the time it was published, I nevertheless believe that the authors of the novels, like those of all other literary genres, could avail themselves of imagery and symbolism derived from religious cults and related rituals. As John Morgan observes in his splendid commentary on Longus' *Daphnis and Chloe*: 'Longus has staged a story of transition, which we can describe as initiation, rite of passage, or simply growing up.'[27] Charicleia experiences her deepest abjection at the

---

[24] Parkes 2013: 253; Ganiban 2007: 65. It is conceivable that Heliodorus knew Lucian's comic essay, *Peri penthous* or *On Mourning*, in which a recently deceased youth awakens to remonstrate with his father for his unseemly and unnecessary grief; see Konstan 2013: 139-51. There is a similar scene in Apuleius' *Metamorphoses*, 2.25-8, in which a dead man roused from the bier protests at being resuscitated and argues with his own wife about the circumstances of his murder; see Slater 2007.

[25] Allegorical interpreters of Homer saw Odysseus' arrival in Ithaca as a turning point in the epic, symbolized for example by the architecture of the cave of the nymphs at the beginning of Book 13; see Lamberton 1983 and Brisson 2004: 81-5. The Cynics made much of Odysseus' disguise, seeing in his beggarly attire a model of their own humble style; cf. ps.-Diogenes *Epistle* 34.3.4-5 (the collection dates to the Roman Empire, though individual letters may well have been circulating considerably earlier); Montiglio 2011: 69-70.

[26] Merkelbach 1962.

[27] Morgan 2004a: 13.

midpoint of the *Aethiopica*, and falls into a profound stupor from which she has to be awakened by Calasiris. Her affliction is reminiscent of the moment of her original enamourment, and coincides with the happy conclusion of the subplot involving Cnemon's romantic fortunes. After she recovers, Charicleia manifests a new independence in respect to Calasiris, who conspicuously defers to her wisdom, and she proposes the stratagem of disguising themselves, a natural image for the assumption of a new identity: indeed, so profound is her outer transformation that she will prove unrecognizable to her own beloved Theagenes. Still in costume, Charicleia and Calasiris witness an unholy necromancy, in which the dead man foretells a happy ending to Charicleia's wanderings; this prophecy from the nether world, the liminal space par excellence, embraces the entirety of the couple's adversities, and so serves to launch the narrative anew. Henceforward, Charicleia becomes ever more confident that she and Theagenes are destined for better things. All these elements converge to suggest that Charicleia's breakdown and humiliation are indeed, as she later suspects, meant to be read as part of fortune's plan for her, and that she must gain the fortitude to carry on after her lapse into despair.

Let us not be put off by the assumption that the Greeks tended to view character as pre-formed and unchanging, save perhaps insofar as education might temper the extremes of innate dispositions. Education itself, in fact, could be envisioned as a kind of *rite de passage*, in the term made popular by Arnold van Gennep; Sophie Lalanne has indeed argued that the Greek novels are parables of the transition from childhood to adult roles, mediated by the journey through a liminal adventure space.[28] The Greeks and Romans could in fact imagine more extreme conversions of character, in the form, for example, of sudden conversions to philosophy such as that of Polemo, of whom Diogenes Laertius reports that he was so dissipated as a youth that he always carried money to pay for sexual favours, even going so far as to store coins on the grounds of the Platonic Academy. And yet, after bursting into the Academy while Xenocrates was delivering a lecture, he was wholly converted and eventually became head of the school himself (4.16). Suetonius tells of a remarkable change in the character of Titus, who as a youth was outstanding in both his mental and physical abilities, but when he rose to co-regent of Rome with his father Vespasian, he proved to be so cruel and dissolute 'that practically no one ever entered upon imperial rule

---

[28] Lalanne 2006.

with so negative a reputation and everyone more opposed' (*Life of Titus* 6). And yet, as soon as he assumed sole rulership of the empire, he again underwent a total change; as Suetonius writes: 'He took nothing from any citizen and abstained, if anyone ever did, from what belonged to another; he did not even accept permissible and traditional offerings, and yet he was inferior to no one before him in munificence' (7), and in the end he turns out to be the best-loved Caesar of them all.[29] Closer, perhaps, to the episode in Heliodorus, Plutarch describes, in his essay *On Those Who Are Punished Slowly by the Divinity*, how a certain Thespesius died, witnessed the punishments in the afterlife, and returned a reformed man: Plutarch calls it 'an unbelievable transformation'.[30]

Charicleia's transformation is nowhere near as radical or abrupt as these. Education takes time, 'real duration', in the Greek novels as much as in the nineteenth-century Bildungsroman. But the gradual alteration of character may be compressed, at a crucial turning point in the narrative, and take the symbolic form of a passage through a death-like trance from which one emerges with newfound strength and faith. I believe that the episode of Charicleia's breakdown, in which, as Heliodorus puts it, 'a mist and dizziness (ἀχλύς τε καὶ ἴλιγγος) overcame her and darkened the intellectual part of her soul' (6.9.1), represents such an emblematic condensation. It is an elegant variation on an ancient trope ('trope' here also in its primitive sense of 'turn'), and is among the structural devices that divide the first and second halves of the *Aethiopica*.

---

[29] Suet. *Tit.* 6, 7. See Konstan 2009: 447–62; Tatum 2014.   [30] Plut. *De sera* 563D.

13
Epic into Drama (7.6–8)*

Richard Hunter

In Book 7 of the *Aethiopica*, Calasiris' son Thyamis, assisted by Theagenes, is compelled to engage in single combat with his brother Petosiris outside the walls of the city for the position of high priest at Memphis; bloodshed is, however, averted by the sudden arrival of the real high priest, their father, whom his sons do not at first recognize, and then by the dramatic appearance of Charicleia who is reunited with her beloved Theagenes. Joyous celebration follows and, once proper piety has been observed, Calasiris resigns the priesthood and confers it upon Thyamis. Events inside and outside the city are carefully watched by Queen Arsace, burning with desire for Theagenes and cruelly jealous of anyone physically close to him, particularly Charicleia.

The thick (even by Heliodorus' standards) literary texture of this passage has long been acknowledged. The deadly race outside the city between Thyamis and Petosiris is modelled on that between Achilles and Hector around the walls of Troy in *Iliad* 22; single combat between two brothers evokes also the story of the 'Seven against Thebes' and casts Calasiris in the role (*inter alios*) of Oedipus, with perhaps particular memories of Euripides' *Phoenissae*, a very popular tragedy throughout antiquity.[1] The sudden arrivals of Calasiris and Charicleia are explicitly compared to scenes and motifs of drama by the narrator, who fills his description with what are clearly intended to sound like 'technical' terms of the criticism of drama (7.6.4–5, 7.7.4, 7.7.4, all cited below);[2] recognition is a motif shared by epic (most notably, of course, the *Odyssey*) and drama, both tragedy and comedy. Ian Rutherford has, moreover, suggested that this passage has an analogue in the Egyptian demotic narrative of the Inaros-Petubastis Cycle, in which a *calasiris*, a kind of Egyptian warrior, intervenes in a combat; if correct, a

---
* I am grateful to Tim Whitmarsh for his helpful suggestions on an earlier draft of this paper.

[1] Cf. Cribiore 2001; on Heliodorus' use of Euripides here, cf. e.g. Fusillo 1989: 41–2; Montiglio 2013a: 115–16.

[2] The theatricality of this scene has long been discussed in the Heliodoran bibliography, but cf. esp. Marino 1990: 204–9.

reader knowing this material would find yet another layer of 'meaning' in Heliodorus' narrative.[3]

Heliodorus' reworking of the race in *Iliad* 22, a reworking which reminds us that this scene really might end in bloodshed, is very detailed at the level of both diction and motif, and it will be useful first briefly to set out how the novelist has littered his text with Homeric 'fragments'.

The race περὶ τὸν κύκλον τοῦ ἄστεως, 'around the circuit of the city' (7.6.2), is modelled on the Homeric race, ἄστυ πέρι, 'around the city' (*Il.* 22.173). ὥρμησεν, 'launched himself', of Thyamis' attack on Petosiris picks up ἐπόρουσε, 'sprang at', of Achilles at *Il.* 22.138 and, particularly, οἴμησε, 'darts', of the hawk attacking the dove in the simile describing Achilles' pursuit of Hector at *Il.* 22.140; this latter verb is indeed glossed in the exegetical and the D-scholia to the Homeric passage, as many of Heliodorus' readers will have known, as ὥρμησεν.[4] Petosiris' response to Thyamis' pursuit is immediately to seek to flee within the city, whereas, at Achilles' attack, Hector had immediately taken to flight away from the city-gates (*Il.* 22.136–7). Petosiris' subsequent attempts to reach safety inside the city are repulsed by those guarding the gates and those on the walls, whereas Hector's subsequent attempts to gain safety are cut off by Achilles (*Il.* 22.194–8); τῶν ἐπὶ τοῦ τείχους μὴ παραδέχεσθαι καθ' ὃ μέρος ὁρμήσειεν ἐπικελευομένων, 'the people on the walls gave instructions not to let him in at whatever part of the walls he fled', picks up and varies Hector's futile attempts. When Petosiris throws away his weapons so that he can run faster, we are reminded of the cowardice of the classical ῥίψασπις, 'shield-abandoner', a cowardice in keeping with Petosiris' frightened reluctance to take part in the duel at all (7.5.3); in Homer too there is a marked difference between 'the one fleeing' and 'the one pursuing' (*Il.* 22.157–8), but in Homer Hector himself is ἐσθλός, 'a brave/ heroic man', though it is his misfortune that he is being pursued by 'a much better man'.

Petosiris' cowardice is marked in another way also. The motif of the threatening spear and the order to 'stop or be killed' (7.6.4) are taken by Heliodorus not from *Iliad* 22, but from the very similar scene in *Iliad* 10 (vv. 351–81) where Odysseus and Diomedes give chase (at night) to the fleeing Dolon.[5] That scene, which shares language (e.g. ὅτε δή... τότε δή...), motifs (note esp. 10.368 ~ 22.207), and a hunting-dog simile with *Iliad* 22,

---

[3] Rutherford 2000: 117–18.   [4] Cf. also Pl. *Ion* 535b: Ἀχιλλέα ἐπὶ τὸν Ἕκτορα ὁρμῶντα.
[5] For the similarities of the two Homeric scenes, cf. the brief remarks of Dué and Ebbott 2010: 335–6.

and which may in fact seem almost like a 'parody' of the later scene, is not (to my knowledge) known to have been linked in ancient scholarship to the pursuit of Hector, but the two scenes are so similar that Heliodorus himself may of course be responsible for the fusion. In adorning a reworking of a Homeric scene with echoes of another very similar Homeric scene, Heliodorus is using a mimetic technique familiar in Greek literature at least since the high period of Hellenistic poetry; here, however, the secondary model is not evoked merely at the level of diction and motif. The echo marks Petosiris as another cowardly Dolon; certainly, the manner in which the high priesthood had been awarded to him (7.2.4–5) shows that he would justly have deserved the name, 'Mr Deceitful'.

Petosiris manages to keep just in front, not because he is a better runner, but because Thyamis is in full armour; the Homeric model here is the famous simile of *Iliad* 22.199–201, which compares the race of Achilles and Hector to a race in a dream:

ὡς δ' ἐν ὀνείρῳ οὐ δύναται φεύγοντα διώκειν—
οὔτ' ἄρ' ὃ τὸν δύναται ὑποφεύγειν οὔθ' ὃ διώκειν—
ὣς ὃ τὸν οὐ δύνατο μάρψαι ποσίν, οὐδ' ὃς ἀλύξαι.

As in a dream, one cannot catch the one who flees—neither can the one escape nor the other catch—so, the one was unable to overtake the other in running, nor the other able to flee.   (Hom. *Il.* 22.199–201)

So too, Petosiris is always on the point of being caught, but it never happens.[6] Heliodorus notes that Petosiris' success in not being caught was 'probable', 'what you would have expected' (εἰκός, 7.6.3), by stressing that he threw away his armour in order to run unencumbered, whereas Thyamis is wearing armour. There are in fact several places in the novel where the narrator, as opposed to his characters,[7] appeals to τὸ εἰκός; this is one of the devices which create the impression that the narrator is relating events which 'actually happened', that he is not 'making it up',[8] despite the fact, as we learn at the end, that the basic premise of the novel is παρὰ τὸ εἰκός,

---

[6] We may compare the sequence at Ap. Rhod. *Arg.* 2.273–83 where the Boreads pursue the Harpies, without ever quite catching them: cf. Hunter 1993: 130–2. One of the models for that passage is the race of *Iliad* 22 (cf. vv. 189–93).

[7] Calasiris has a particular fondness for such meta-narrative comments, presumably as part of his display of control and knowledge.

[8] The principal study is Morgan 1982, who does not however discuss appeals to τὸ εἰκός.

'contrary to the probable' (10.14.5). Here, however, we may think that (once again) Heliodorus is engaging with the Homeric critical tradition.

Heliodorus of course knew that tradition, as well as the Homeric poems themselves, very well indeed.[9] The race between Achilles and Hector around the walls of Troy had attracted critical discussion from a relatively early date.[10] In Plato's *Ion* Socrates lists this as one of the highest moments of Homeric *eksplēxis* ('astonishment') and *enthousiasmos* ('transport', 535b5–6),[11] and in the *Poetics* Aristotle uses the pursuit first as an example of the ἄλογον ('irrational') and the θαυμαστόν ('marvellous') possible in epic but not drama (1460a11–17) and, then, as an example of an ἀδύνατον ('impossibility') which, nevertheless, serves a poetic purpose (1460b26). The first criticism is part of Aristotle's discussion of the differences between epic and tragedy.[12] The fourth-century critic Megaclides had condemned the whole duel as implausible and had apparently asked how Achilles was able to restrain so many thousands with just a nod (bT-scholia on *Il.* 22.36, 205–7 = Megaclides fr. 6 Janko); Aristarchus subsequently excised the dream-simile (vv. 199–201, cited above), because—so the scholia allege—the verses are weak in both language and thought, inconsistent with what is said elsewhere (notably the horse simile of vv. 162–6), and diminish Achilles' renown for speed.[13] It is also clear from the D and exegetical scholia on vv. 165 and 201–2 of Book 22 that why Achilles could not catch Hector was a Homeric 'problem', to which various solutions had been offered: Hector had the help of Apollo (cf. vv. 203–4); Achilles had not eaten and was emotionally and physically drained from Patroclus' death and his battle with the river, whereas Hector was rested and had the added incentive that his life was at stake; Achilles was not just running, but had constantly to prevent Hector heading for the city and make sure that none of the other Greeks intervened; Hector, moreover, was running on the inside near the city and so Achilles, who was running on the outside, had to run much further than Hector. Heliodorus has, in a manner (again) familiar from Hellenistic and Roman poetry, 'anticipated' critical discussion of this kind by explaining clearly why Thyamis was unable quite to catch his weaker brother. His solution of course precisely evokes that critical tradition for his readers; this is part not just of his

---

[9] Cf. e.g. Telò 1999; Hunter 2014.   [10] For what follows, cf. further Hunter 2005a.
[11] The first two such passages which Socrates identifies are Odysseus' self-revelation to the suitors and Achilles' pursuit of Hector; it is striking that both of these passages are used in this episode by Heliodorus, cf. below p. 181.
[12] Montiglio 2013a: 113 notes the Aristotelian background of Heliodorus' scene.
[13] Cf. Schironi 2018: 539.

ubiquitous engagement with Homer and the Homeric tradition but of the display of the novelist's craft. 'Probability' is indeed one criterion which, following an Aristotelian hint, may be used to distinguish novel from epic.

The D-scholia on *Il.* 22.201 report that some critics had argued that Homer had represented Achilles as worn out by all his recent efforts 'so that as in a theatre he could now arouse greater emotions (μείζονα πάθη)'. The reference to the theatre suggests that some of Homer's ancient readers felt something particularly 'theatrical' about the duel in *Iliad* 22, and there is no doubt that Heliodorus has played up that aspect of the scene. The citizens, and Arsace (one of Heliodorus' 'Helens'), who are watching from the walls—this is Heliodorus' *teikhoskopia*[14]—are compared to an audience in the theatre (7.6.4), a comparison which prepares for the rich theatrical language which follows, just as ἠθλοθέτει, 'judged', is picked up by the following βραβεύουσα, 'controlling', of Tyche's power over us; both verbs emphasize that this race potentially to the death is also indeed an athletic contest, as Homer too had done with considerable emphasis (vv. 159–66).[15] Homer had had three audiences, the Olympian gods (cf. *Il.* 22.166, θεοὶ δ' ἐς πάντες ὁρῶντο, 'all the gods were watching'), the Trojans watching from the walls, and finally the Greek army; this last is brought into play at v. 205 when Achilles is said to forbid anyone to shoot at Hector, lest his own glory be diminished. In his twelfth-century commentary on this passage, Eustathius notes (*Hom.* 1266.24–6) that the audience for the race consisted of the Greeks, 'but the theatre was not just a Panhellenion', as it was also formed from the enemy watching from the walls, and he takes this observation back to Homer's simile comparing Achilles and Hector to racing horses in vv. 162–3. Eustathius' note reminds us that the link between theatres and athletic contests, for both men and horses, was a real one, in Heliodorus' day (whenever that was) no less than in Eustathius'; that both Heliodorus and Eustathius bring out explicitly a vivid sense of (institutionalized) 'theatre' in Homer's scene, a sense which was not of course there in quite that way for Homer and archaic audiences, may simply show two acute readers reacting in similar ways to Homeric *enargeia* and therefore both drawing out similar

---

[14] This is not, of course, a *teikhoskopia* in the full 'Homeric' sense, but it is hard to resist the suggestion of this further Homeric layer; Euripides had already transferred the motif to the setting of the warring Theban brothers in the *Phoenissae*.

[15] Paulsen 1992: 261 n. 85 associates ἠθλοθέτει rather with the award of prizes at dramatic contests; this sense is obviously present also, but the 'athletic' image seems rather to prevail here.

implications from the narrative. Eustathius, however, knew Heliodorus,[16] and we should bear in mind the possibility that it was Heliodorus, along with the critical tradition, who planted the seed in the Byzantine commentator's mind.

More broadly, it is at least tempting (to say no more) to relate the very marked fusion of epic and drama in this passage, not itself of course an isolated instance in the *Aethiopica*, to the fact that Aristotle precisely uses the pursuit around the walls of Troy as one of the effects in which epic and drama differ (cf. above). For Plato and the post-Aristotelian tradition (cf. e.g. the scholia on *Iliad* 1.1), Homer was the 'first tragedian', and so those places where the difference between epic and drama was most clearly exposed assume a particular significance; Heliodorus chooses just such a moment most strikingly to highlight the interplay of the genres. The *Aethiopica* is Homeric in one way most of all: it is both epic and drama, just as Homer was.

Heliodorus ascribes the sudden arrival of Calasiris to 'something daemonic or to a stroke of the Fortune which controls human affairs' (7.6.4, cited below); the narrator's professed uncertainty (here strengthened by πως) about the force that was responsible for this amazing turn of events is a very familiar 'authorizing' strategy,[17] which—in a work of the sophistication of the *Aethiopica*—relies on an audience's willingness to share the narrator's pleasures in the devices of fiction. Here, however, where the literary texture is very thick, this device carries special force. The appeal to unspecified supernatural forces and/or to Tyche is, in part, a translation of the image of Zeus's scales, which appears at the corresponding point of the Homeric narrative (vv. 209-13), into an important aspect of causation operative within the novel (and also novels other than the *Aethiopica*), just as the timing of Calasiris' dramatic entry, 'when they had finished the third circuit', picks up the timing of Zeus reaching for his golden scales, 'when they reached the springs for the fourth time' (*Il.* 22.208). In Homer the image of Zeus's scales seals Hector's fate, whereas in the novel Calasiris' arrival will prevent both combatants from losing their life.

By Heliodorus' day the image of Zeus's scales had long since been allegorized and interpreted in several different ways and was recognized as part

---

[16] Van der Valk 1971: cvii lists two instances of citation from Heliodorus (*Hom.* 55.32-4, 160.15-16), both in the commentary on *Iliad* 1; we should perhaps add 159.25 (also on *Iliad* 1) where ἡμέρα διαγελᾷ looks like a borrowing from the very opening of Heliodorus' novel.

[17] Cf. esp. Morgan 1982.

of a particularly epic way of conceiving the relation between mortals and immortals and putting that into poetry; for later readers, Zeus's scales thus carried an almost 'programmatic' force about the nature of the epic poem in which they occurred. When Heliodorus now shifts to the language of drama and the theatre, this may again reflect a kind of generic consciousness steering a path between what we might call epic and post-epic modes:

τότε δή πως εἴτε τι δαιμόνιον εἴτε τύχη τις τὰ ἀνθρώπεια βραβεύουσα καινὸν ἐπεισόδιον ἐπετραγῴδει τοῖς δρωμένοις, ὥσπερ εἰς ἀνταγώνισμα δράματος ἀρχὴν ἄλλου παρεισφέρουσα....

At that time either something daemonic or a stroke of the Fortune which controls human affairs introduced a new tragic episode to the action, as though introducing as well the start of a new drama to compete in rivalry.... (7.6.4)

Translation is here notably difficult, but the notion of 'competition' (ἀνταγώνισμα) between dramas links the narrator's gloss upon his narrative with the athletic contest we have been witnessing: it is almost as if the narrative has seeped into the critical discourse.[18] Be that as it may, this unusual emphasis upon 'theorizing' of the narrative in terms of theatrical effects, a theorizing pointed by the 'learned' *figura etymologica* in δρωμένοις...δράματος, creates a strong sense of self-consciousness at this crucial turning-point. What sort of narrative is this? Is it indeed a cross between epic and drama, and—if so—what are its most significant, 'generic' features? This goes well beyond Heliodorus' familiar fondness for theatrical descriptions and for terminology drawn from the theatre[19] to become a kind of paraded exploration of the technique of the narrative. *Why* events happen as they do, or rather the mystery ('Fortune, Chance') of why things happen as they do, is indeed one of the most significant, marked areas of the *Aethiopica*. The race around the walls had been a δρᾶμα of one kind, but now another was to begin; the arrival of Calasiris and then Charicleia in Memphis will indeed prove to be both closural and initiatory:

τὸν Καλάσιριν εἰς ἡμέραν καὶ ὥραν ἐκείνην ὥσπερ ἐκ μηχανῆς σύνδρομόν τε καὶ οὐκ εὐτυχῆ θεωρὸν τῷ περὶ ψυχῆς ἀγῶνι τῶν παίδων ἐφίστησι....

---

[18] Tim Whitmarsh suggests to me that Heliodorus here alludes to the role of Τύχη at Chariton 8.1.2 and Achilles Tatius 1.3.3.
[19] Cf. e.g. Walden 1894; Bartsch 1989: 129–37, Marino 1990.

[Fortune] brought Calasiris on that very day and at that hour, as though from the *mēkhanē*, to join the race and be a wretched audience for his sons' race of life and death.... (7.6.5)

Calasiris arrives, part both of the unfolding drama (ὥσπερ ἐκ μηχανῆς, σύνδρομον) and of its audience (θεωρόν). ἐκ μηχανῆς, 'from the machine', suggests not just the suddenness of his arrival and the resolution it brings, as most notoriously in 'god from the machine', but also perhaps 'by some device (of the narrator)', a suggestion which is lent some support by μηχανησάμενον which immediately follows (in reference to Calasiris' 'contrivances' to avoid witnessing this terrible scene); the double sense draws particular attention to the controlling hand of the narrator at this point.[20]

Although his sons' race περὶ ψυχῆς, 'for life and death', takes us back to the Homeric model of *Iliad* 22, in which Achilles and Hector ran 'περὶ ψυχῆς of horse-taming Hector' (v. 161), the description which follows of Calasiris, πολλὰ μὲν ἀνατλάντα καὶ πάντα μηχανησάμενον φυγάς τε ἑαυτῷ καὶ ἄλας ξενικὰς ἐπιβαλόντα, 'having endured many things and tried every contrivance, including imposing exile and foreign wanderings upon himself', marks him as part πολύτλας Odysseus, part the wandering Oedipus, a position which also (again) marks the events as part epic, part tragedy. The epic is, however, shifting from *Iliad* to *Odyssey*, as recognition now becomes the dominant narrative mode, one inherited by drama from epic, and by the novel from both. Aristotle recognized that the *Odyssey* contains recognition throughout (*Poetics* 1459b15), and it is certainly Odysseus who is evoked as Calasiris strips off his disguise (7.7.2) so that his sons will recognize him, cf. *Od.* 22.1 αὐτὰρ ὁ γυμνώθη ῥακέων πολύμητις Ὀδυσσεύς, 'Odysseus of the many contrivances stripped off his rags'.[21] Odysseus' revelation will lead to the slaughter of the suitors, whereas Calasiris' appearance is to have a very different outcome. When Calasiris and Charicleia adopted their disguise in 6.11.3-4, a few details (the wallet (πήρα), a staff) were borrowed from Athena's disguising of Odysseus in *Odyssey* 13, and that circle of narrative allusion is now brought to a close: Calasiris is to be an Odysseus to the very

---

[20] The two senses, 'contrivance' and '(theatrical) machine' are closely connected; one thinks perhaps of the comic representation of Euripides' μυρίαι μηχαναί (Ar. *Thesm.* 927).
[21] The echo was identified as early as Coraes 1804: II 227. I have also wondered whether Calasiris' discarding of his staff and the slight crouch of supplication which he adopts (ὑπώκλασέ τε ἠρέμα) reworks Odysseus' cunning method of dealing with the threat of Eumaeus' dogs (*Od.* 14.30–1); the scholia gloss the Homeric σκῆπτρον δέ οἱ ἔκπεσε χειρός (14.31) as ἔρριψεν αὐτό, cf. Heliodorus' τὴν ἐν χερσὶ βακτηρίαν ἀπορρίψας.

end—he is indeed 'the father safe contrary to all expectation' (7.7.3), the father returned 'after ten years of wandering' (7.8.2).[22] It is thus natural to think here of Odysseus' reunion (through recognition) with Telemachus in *Odyssey* 16,[23] or perhaps of the reunion with Laertes in Book 24, but there are only very limited verbal pointers.[24] Rather, Heliodorus is now concerned to establish a generic scene, which directs our attention to the interplay of different models, rather than to any specific single epic scene; this is part of the change which Calasiris' arrival has wrought.

Charicleia's arrival is ἕτερον... παρεγκύκλημα τοῦ δράματος 'another entry wheeled into the drama' (7.7.4); whether or not παρεγκύκλημα was in fact a 'technical' theatrical term we cannot say, though the prefix carries some of the same resonance as in παρεισφέρουσα in the corresponding introduction of Calasiris at 7.6.4.[25] After the μηχανή, then, the ἐκκύκλημα. Charicleia recognizes her beloved from afar in accordance, so the narrator tells us, with the habitual alertness that lovers have to the beloved's presence. Theagenes, however, is (as often) rather slower on the uptake, a slowness which is not really explained, and may not have been intended to be, by the narrator's insouciant οἷον εἰκός.[26] Coraes for one was pained by finding such a scene in a novel for which he had the greatest admiration; for him this scene was ἄτεχνον... καὶ ἀπίθανον, 'sloppy and incredible... for how could Theagenes be so slow to recognize his beloved, when she had recognized him so quickly'.[27] Charicleia's instant recognition of Theagenes and the narrative stress on the effectiveness of her disguise, reinforced by the jingle of ἀληθῶς ἀλῆτιν, 'truly a wanderer' (7.7.6),[28] are in fact both ways of channelling our sympathy and attention towards her: just like the novel's internal audience of watchers, we have eyes only for her.[29] Theagenes' slap (διερράπισεν) might seem to carry this effect of narrative sympathy almost

---

[22] Some further aspects of Calasiris as Odysseus are discussed in Hunter 2014: 147–54, citing earlier bibliography.
[23] So e.g. Keyes 1922: 46–7; Paulsen 1992: 169.
[24] περιφύντες in 7.7.3 might recall περιφύς at *Od.* 24.320, but this is very little to go on, cf. περιφῦσα in 7.7.5.
[25] Very close to these passages is Cnemon's protest to Calasiris at 2.24.4, cf. Telò 1999: 82–5; Whitmarsh 2011: 234; Hunter 2014: 150–1. For the παρα- prefix we may perhaps compare παραδιδάσκειν used in the Athenian records for staging a play 'alongside' plays in competition, as most famously at *TrGF* DID A 1 for 386 BC.
[26] On this mode of explanation, cf. above p. 176–7. Heliodorus may here have in mind Clitophon's failure to recognize the abused Leucippe at Achilles Tatius 5.17.
[27] Coraes 1804: II.228.
[28] The pun may be traced back to the *Odyssey*, cf. Bowie 2013: 184 on *Odyssey* 14.125.
[29] On the recognition scene, cf. Konstan in this volume, pp. 167–8.

too far,[30] but perhaps we are to remember Menander's *Ῥαπιζομένη*, the plot of which is unfortunately entirely unknown, although it is an easy guess (cf. *Περικειρομένη*) that the female of the title was slapped by someone who either was or, as here, was destined to be her husband. Certainly, our thoughts are very soon to turn to comedy, and the whole scene is an instance of σκηνογραφικὴ θαυματουργία (7.7.7), perhaps 'the magic possible only on the stage'.[31]

It is indeed comedy which now takes over:

λέλυτο μὲν ἄθεσμος ἀδελφῶν πόλεμος καὶ ἀγὼν ὁ δι' αἵματος κριθήσεσθαι προσδοκώμενος εἰς κωμικὸν ἐκ τραγικοῦ τὸ τέλος κατέστρεφε.

The lawless war between the brothers was at an end and the contest which seemed likely to be judged in blood changed its ending from a tragic to a comic one. (7.8.1)

The ending of the ἀγών, a personal struggle for power as well as a potentially deadly duel and, as we have seen, also a struggle between epic and dramatic modes, turns out to be 'comic' rather than 'tragic'. This has traditionally been understood as a way simply of referring to 'a happy end', couched in Heliodorus' habitual theatrical language. Thomas Paulsen, however, has argued that Heliodorus rather presents us with a *Mischform*, a kind of tragicomedy, modelled on the 'melodramas' of late Euripides.[32] We know that the 'comic' endings of certain Euripidean plays had indeed attracted critical (in both senses) attention in the Hellenistic world,[33] and the events unfolding here might be thought to fit such a model, but in fact it seems much more likely that Heliodorus now wants us to think of New Comedy; what had all the makings of a tragedy now looks like its dramatic younger brother.

---

[30] Keyes 1922: 46 suggests that this is modelled on 'the buffets received by Odysseus in his own house while disguised as a beggar', but there is at least no verbal link to turn our minds in that direction.

[31] Morgan's 'this miracle of theatrical art' is an enlightening attempt to translate this difficult phrase. The emphasis clearly lies on how rapidly the situation has changed, as when a 'conjuror' or 'wonder-worker' performs; the phrase has been prepared by the previous emphasis on the θαῦμα of those watching from the walls (7.7.1, 4).

[32] Paulsen 1992: 170–1. Paulsen's claim that a 'Deus ex machina' often appears in New Comedy to bring about a 'happy end' is questionable at best. It is true that the solution to some comic problems arises from the sudden appearance of a new character, but that is rather different.

[33] Cf. e.g. Telò 1999: 86–7; Fantuzzi 2014.

Aristotle famously described as typical of comedy a plot in which 'those who are deadly enemies in the story, such as Orestes and Aegisthus, become friends and go off [together] at the end, and no one is killed by anyone' (*Poetics* 1453a36–8). This is indeed what happens when 'peace' here breaks out (7.8.1). Comedy had for centuries dramatized reconciliation as its appropriate, 'generic' ending,[34] and Petosiris and Thyamis are indeed now reconciled. Moreover, as so often at the end of a comedy, we have a happy young couple, Charicleia and Theagenes, τὸ ἐρωτικὸν μέρος τοῦ δράματος, 'the romantic part of the drama' (7.8.2), and this of course is to be repeated at the real end of the novel, of which the present scene may be taken as a foreshadowing,[35] as well as being a narrative 'false closure'. It is, of course, not only comedies which regularly end, as does this scene, with torchlit processions (cf. Aesch. *Eumenides*), but it is such a characteristic of comic endings that it is very hard not to believe that this is the generic situation which Heliodorus wishes us to imagine. The high spirits, music, cheering, clapping, and dancing of the procession (7.8.5) seem indeed precisely to evoke features very familiar from the conclusions of Menandrean comedies. The conclusion of Menander's *Samia*, as Moschion finally 'gets his girl', was not untypical:

> Δη. Χρυσί, πέμπε τὰς γυναῖκας, λουτροφόρον, αὐλητρίδα.
> δεῦρο δ' ἡμῖν ἐκδότω τις δᾷδα καὶ στεφάνους, ἵνα
> συμπροπέμπωμεν.
> Μο.   πάρεστιν ὅδε φέρων.
> Δη.   πύκαζε σὺ
> κρᾶτα καὶ κόσμει σεαυτόν.
> Μο.   ἀλλ' ἐγώ.
> Δη.   παῖδες καλοί,
> μειράκια, γέροντες, ἄνδρες, πάντες εὐρώστως ἅμα
> πέμψατ' εὐνοίας προφήτην Βακχίωι φίλον κρότον.   735
> ἡ δὲ καλ]λίστων ἀγώνων πάρεδρος ἄφθιτος θεὰ
> εὐμεν]ὴς ἕποιτο Νίκη τοῖς ἐμοῖς ἀεὶ χοροῖς.

Demeas. Chrysis, send off the women, the water-bearer, the pipe-player! Let someone bring us a torch and garlands so that we may escort the couple. *Moschion*. He's here! *Demeas*. Garland your head and smarten

---

[34] Cf. Hunter 1983: 27 n. 1.
[35] Cf. esp. the description of the celebrations in 10.38.

yourself up. *Moschion.* Certainly! *Demeas.* Pretty boys, the young, the old, grown men, all of you together now lustily grant us the applause which shows your goodwill and is dear to the Bacchic god. May Victory, the immortal goddess who sits beside him at the most glorious contests, always follow my choruses benevolently. (Menander *Samia* 730–7)[36]

Everything thus conspires to make this scene of the *Aethiopica* reminiscent of the closure of comic drama, as indeed Heliodorus told us it was.

The passage I have been following really only concludes with Calasiris' death (7.11.3–4), which puts one major episode of the novel to rest and opens another. Calasiris' death is not of course 'comic' in any sense, but it is both peaceful and mysterious; we may be reminded of the deaths of Socrates in Plato's *Phaedo* and of Oedipus in Sophocles' *Oedipus at Colonus*, both of whom (for very different reasons) know in advance when death is upon them. As Oedipus has already been firmly established as one of the models for Calasiris in this scene, it may be that Sophocles' play is indeed relevant here;[37] the Sophoclean Oedipus, for example, issues solemn instructions concerning his daughters to those who are left behind (vv. 1631–5), just as Calasiris tells his sons to look after and assist Theagenes and Charicleia (7.11.4), whom the novel has consistently painted as his 'children'.[38] Calasiris' painless exit is thus as 'dramatic' as his sudden re-appearance in 7.6.4–5; like Oedipus too, moreover, his influence will outlast his death, as Calasiris had always been the central figure moving the novel towards its destined *telos*.

---

[36] Sommerstein's commentary on these verses contains much relevant comparative material.
[37] Cf., e.g., Fusillo 1989: 42. I have in fact wondered whether the biographical tradition concerning Sophocles' own death may have played some role in shaping Calasiris'. Sophocles too was, so the biographical tradition reports, a priest and a very pious man (cf. *Vita Sophoclis* 11–12), and died either from choking on a grape or in excess of joy (χαρά) after a dramatic victory (*Vita Sophoclis* 14, T 85–91 Radt); in either case his extreme old age is said to have played a role. If there is anything to this, then the alternative suggestions of the temple-servant as to the cause of Calasiris' death (7.11.5) are not merely a typical Heliodoran device (cf. Morgan 1982: 229–32; Winkler 1982: 114–37), but also help further to shape Calasiris as a figure around whom biographical legend clusters, as it did around all the great 'classical' figures of the past.
[38] Cf. e.g. Winkler 1982: 115–17.

14
Enter Arsace and Her Entourage!
Lust, Gender, Ethnicity, and Class at the Persian Court (Books 7 and 8)

Froma I. Zeitlin

14.1. Preliminaries

The end of Book 6 ushers in a new and pivotal episode in Memphis, one that will take up most of the next two books (7 and 8). The spooky necromantic scene near Bessa (6.14–15) between a mother and her dead son, with Calasiris and Charicleia as hidden observers, yielded three prophecies on the part of the corpse: doom for the mother who had resorted to black magic tricks to revive him; a happy ending for the lover (Charicleia) in search for her beloved (Theagenes), and in between, the forecast to Calasiris concerning the imminent duel between his two sons, which if he makes haste to Memphis, he can hope to avert. Meanwhile, at the beginning of the seventh book, a new danger to the city arises in the form of Thyamis' band of brigands, who are also hastening to Memphis from Bessa, with Theagenes, rescued now from the forces of the Persian Mitranes, in tow. In the suspense of the moment, when the anticipated reunions (Calasiris and his sons; Theagenes and Charicleia) have yet to take place, Heliodorus brings on stage a new and formidable character in the person of the satrap Oroondates' wife, Arsace (7.2.1). Henceforth, Arsace's combination of tyrannical power, unbridled lust, and corrosive jealousy will pose the greatest threat to the future outcome of the couple's love. Yet, at the same time, her increasingly nefarious actions against them, once the enmity between Thyamis and his brother, Petosiris, is resolved and Calasiris has died, are critical in advancing the plot up the ladder of hierarchical power to move

Froma I. Zeitlin, *Enter Arsace and Her Entourage!: Lust, Gender, Ethnicity, and Class at the Persian Court (Books 7 and 8)* In: *Reading Heliodorus' Aethiopica*. Edited by: Ian Repath and Tim Whitmarsh, Oxford University Press. © Oxford University Press 2022. DOI: 10.1093/oso/9780198792543.003.0014

beyond the frontiers of Egypt and Persian dominance to arrive eventually at royal Ethiopia, the long-awaited goal, in the last book.[1]

In examining what transpires through this over-the-top figure of a feminine libido run wild, I hope to address several issues that might further enhance an appreciation of Heliodorus' narrative skills and ideological motives that are fully on display in the setting of the Persian court, when Theagenes and Charicleia, now on their own after Calasiris' death, reach the nadir of powerlessness in the face of the escalating coercive measures taken against them. The palace intrigues reach a new level of complexity when it comes to the varied cast of characters, their different ethnicities and social statuses. These generate plots and counterplots, deceptions and subterfuges, along with unexpected interventions that at the last moment finally result in the couple's rescue and the movement onward, although still fraught with danger, to their last and final adventures in Ethiopia.

A detailed summary of this extensive episode would take up far too much space, but before proceeding to some particulars, in broadest outline, once the affair of the two brothers is resolved at the outset, the books revolve around the prolonged confrontation between Arsace, the Persian satrap's wife and regent in his stead, and the resistance of Theagenes, her current erotic obsession, to her insistent demands. Supporting characters are Cybele, her loyal Greek servant and go-between (and probable role as Arsace's nurse), whose very life is at stake if she fails in her mission to procure the submission of Theagenes, and her son, Achaemenes, who having secretly caught a glimpse of the couple, falls in love with Charicleia. To his good fortune, as he imagines, he recognizes Theagenes as having escaped captivity from Mitranes, the Persian commander of the guards, who had previously planned to send his handsome prisoner as a slave to the Great King but himself was killed in the ensuing skirmish with Thyamis' troops. Having pretended at first that Charicleia was his sister, Theagenes is compelled finally to reveal the truth to Arsace to prevent her forced marriage to Achaemenes, and he, in revenge, goes off to Arsace's husband, Oroondates, to reveal his wife's perfidy and sing the praises of Charicleia in the hope of

---

[1] See Lowe 2000: 236 on this 'topography of power' that leads up the scale from bandit country to village, town, and city 'from the wild margin of the beach, to the semi-anarchy of the bandit swamplands, to the village of Chemmis, to the town of Bessa, to the city of Memphis, to the battlefront of Syene, to the final utopian destination of Meroe. There is thus a clear, even hyperschematic, path to be traversed from wilderness to utopia, anarchy to divine monarchy, individualism to ever greater community, poverty to fabulous wealth, the known world to the fabled.'

eventually procuring her for himself—an odd bit of illogic, one might add, if there ever was one, but essential to motivate the events that lead finally to Arsace's downfall and the rescue of the two lovers from the captivity of her palace. Oroondates, inflamed by rage (at his wife) and desire (for Charicleia) sends his trusted eunuch, Bagoas, to fetch the pair (8.1–3). But in the meantime, as a mixture of jealousy, anger, fear, spite, and thwarted desire infect the Persian hierarchy from high to low, the couple are yet to endure the worst at Arsace's hand: imprisonment, torture, false accusations against Charicleia of Cybele's murder by poison, along with the dramatic miracle of her survival in her ordeal by fire with the help of the magical *pantarbe* gem entrusted to her by her mother along with her other birth tokens, inscribed with sacred characters and endowed with mystical virtue (8.9–11).

14.2. The Multidimensional Court of Arsace

It is not my intention to offer anything like a full analysis of this book (7) nor the ensuing events in the first half of the next one (8) that detail the rising predicament of the captives and their efforts at strategies of delay, pretended acquiescence, and open resistance. Rather, I have chosen a few elements that seem to me to be worth touching on in fuller detail: issues of gender, ethnicity, hierarchies of social class, intertextual games, and narratorial analepses and closures (not necessarily in that order).

At one level, it would be easy to establish a firm morally inflected boundary between noble Greekness (Theagenes) and Persian tyranny (Arsace) and also between the two women (Arsace and Charicleia), one the sexual predator and the other the chaste virgin, whose virtue finally triumphs over evil. No doubt, at this juncture in the plot, the highlighting of opposing systems of thought and behaviour in favour of Hellenic virtue over Persian villainy speaks strongly to a familiar stereotyped dichotomy between the two, from Herodotus on. But if we add Arsace's Greek servant, Cybele, and her son (whose name, Achaemenes, however, suggests perhaps his father was Persian),[2] that line of demarcation between Greek and Persian is tempered by issues of class and status, one made all the more interesting by the transposition of a Greek model to a Persian one in the contest between Arsace and her would-be Greek lover, Theagenes. More specifically,

---

[2] See Groves 2012: 43.

the portrait of Arsace (and her helper Cybele) in the wake of the previous story of Demaenete (and Thisbe) in Athens reintroduces the Hippolytus-Phaedra plot into an entirely different setting[3] and entitles us to consider the cultural hybridity of Arsace's court and its implications beneath the strong polarities established between East and West.[4]

14.3. Portrait of Arsace

So who is Arsace? She is the wife of the satrap Oroondates and sister of the Great King, who, in her husband's absence to fight a war with the Ethiopians, is empowered by its citizens to act in his place on a strategy to save the city from its attackers. No doubt she cuts a formidable figure:

Ἡ δὲ Ἀρσάκη τὰ μὲν ἄλλα καλή τε ἦν καὶ μεγάλη καὶ συνεῖναι δραστήριος τό τε φρόνημα ἐξ εὐγενείας ὑπέρογκος καὶ οἷον εἰκὸς τὴν ἀδελφὴν βασιλέως τοῦ μεγάλου γεγονυῖαν, ἄλλως δὲ τὸν βίον ἐπίμωμος καὶ ἡδονῆς παρανόμου καὶ ἀκρατοῦς ἐλάττων.

Arsace was a tall, beautiful woman, and clever at understanding, and she was fiercely proud by reason of her noble birth, naturally enough for one who had been born the sister of the Great King. But otherwise her life was blameworthy and she had a weakness for perverted and immoderate pleasure. (7.2.1)[5]

Her physical stature and intellectual skills are typical for royalty. But she is also highly dangerous, combining power, violence, and rampant sexuality.

While Arsace joins ranks with the other so-called female *Gegenfiguren* in the novel, whose unbridled lust and deceitful sexual machinations (Demaenete, Thisbe, Rhodopis)[6] stand in stark contrast to the chaste and virginal bride-to-be, Charicleia,[7] her position as regent, with untold wealth and resources, along with her barbarian pedigree, high intelligence,

---

[3] Many have commented on this archetype; see especially Morgan 1989b, and further Morgan and Repath 2019; Owens 2020; and Morales in this volume.
[4] For a detailed exploration of these issues, see Musié 2019.
[5] Translations for the most part are drawn from Morgan 1989c.
[6] Rhodopis, the would-be seductress of Calasiris, fits a similar pattern, but one that he avoids by voluntary exile. See further below.
[7] But see Keul-Deutscher 1997 on parallels between Arsace and Charicleia in respect to expression of emotions, despite the differences in values. See also Morales in this volume for a stunning analysis of Charicleia as an *assemblage* of different traits.

and cultured cruelty, bring the unfolding of the plot to new heights of complexity—one that is a medley of Egyptian, Persian, and Greek elements. The drama of Cnemon with his father's wife, Demaenete, and her servant, Thisbe, unfolds in a strictly Greek, that is, Athenian, setting, rather than at a high court in a foreign milieu.[8] And while the Hippolytus-Phaedra paradigm is operative in both instances, the migration of the model from its more appropriate setting in Athens to a barbarian context gives evidence of an important polyphony that goes beyond the mere observation of yet another intertextual game of Heliodorus to recognize the subtleties of the author's 'creative adaptation and reinterpretation of his literary predecessors'.[9]

In fact, the extravagant scene that unfolds earlier before the walls of Memphis (adroitly analysed by Richard Hunter in this volume) is an even higher instantiation of this kind of merging and reorienting of classical Greek motifs, for which we seem to have found no precise critical language to identify either what exactly is at work or what finally is at stake here: Arsace = Helen at the walls of Troy; Thyamis and Petosiris = both Hector and Achilles, on the one hand, in their race to the death, and, on the other, Eteocles and Polyneices as the true enemy brothers. Calasiris, of course, is here the aged Oedipus, even to the point of his company with his 'daughter' Charicleia. But then, when he is dressed in rags, appearing as 'a vagrant or a madman' (7.7.1) and requiring recognition from his sons, we think also of Odysseus, the unrecognized beggar par excellence, whose figure more than once is shadowed behind Calasiris.[10] Yet, in the midst of this whirl of Greek literary references, once again Arsace remains a central figure in her machinations, both erotic and political, that brought about the enmity of the two brothers, as we shall shortly see.

14.4. Cultural Hybridity

Does this flurry of Greek literary allusions in their hybridized form among Persians and Egyptians indicate an easy assimilation of Hellenic elements

---

[8] At the same time, one may wonder whether the operative paradigm may look back still further to the Joseph and Potiphar's wife tale in *Genesis* and its Egyptian milieu, which is so important in the geography of Heliodorus' novel. But the symmetry between Deimanete's actions and those of Arsace suggests a more convenient intertextuality.

[9] Pletcher 1998: 26.

[10] See especially Elmer 2008: 413–16, who surveys the preponderance of critical attention to Odyssean allusions.

into foreign venues (and languages) so as to naturalize them? Or do such disturbances in cognitive awareness gesture to the artificial theatrics throughout that we and the internal audience must confront? For Whitmarsh, such contaminations function as a serious way of 'contesting the narratives which structure Greek society's mythic vision of itself'.[11] At the same time, as so many others have noted, Greek identity is itself hardly a stable category, especially when it comes to Charicleia, the poster girl for such confusion, marked by her Greek language, comportment, and appearance.[12]

This is a much-discussed topic, to which I have no easy solution (and it is likely that no easy solution exists). But in the case of Arsace and her entourage, it is important, I think, to draw attention to its mash-up of different linguistic and mythological elements, while remaining focused on the stereotyped extravagance of Persian power, especially located in the dual identity of Arsace as both woman and regent. In this regard, Thisbe is hardly a match for the cunning Cybele as Arsace's faithful Greek servant (originally from Lesbos, she is a ramped-up version of Phaedra's nurse); her role is made complicated further by her greedy son, Achaemenes (whose relationship with his mother may remind us of the mother-son duo in the necromancy at the end of Book 6), whose interference in the plot is in any case essential to the end of this high-pitched drama. And while, according to Cybele, Arsace professes a bias in favour of philhellenism (7.11.7; 7.14.2),[13] as the plot continues to unfold, Persian dominance is openly challenged by the other side of the Hellenic coin, embodied in the staunch heroism of Theagenes, in his resistance to Arsace's advances.

Why now at this juncture in the plot, we might ask, is a confrontation between Greek and barbarian staged, and what are its implications, especially in view of the fact that Charicleia too has an unwelcome suitor in the person of Achaemenes, the son of the Greek woman Cybele (whose name, however, is Persian, as mentioned above)?[14] The two poles of absolute

---

[11] Whitmarsh 1998: 116.
[12] On Charicleia's performative identity, see especially Whitmarsh 1998: 107–13, 122–4 and Perkins 1999: 197–201.
[13] 'Although she is a Persian by race, she is very much a Greek (ἑλληνίζει) at heart and very partial to people from that country. She is fond to a fault of Greek ways (ἦθος) and the company (ὁμιλίαν) of Greeks' (7.14.2). The double entendres here are obvious. As Groves 2012: 96 remarks: 'Even if Arsace is interested in the Greek language or Greek culture, she is primarily because she loves Greeks, and specifically Greek men'.
[14] The question of names has been treated by Jones 2006, but she confines herself to Greek names. Arsace's name, for example, has no Persian counterpoint in the historical record, but refers rather to the Parthian dynasty in Armenia. On the names chosen for Persian characters, see Robiano 2021.

power (Arsace) and abased status (Achaemenes, son of a servant) could hardly be more extreme. This is a point to which we will return.

More evidence of this cultural hybridity, however, relies on the alliance of Thyamis and Theagenes, who, after their initially hostile encounter, have eventually become friends and allies, to the extent that before the duel with his brother, Thyamis promises that, if he wins, he will take Theagenes to live with him and share all he has; if he loses, Theagenes is to become the leader of the bandits in Thyamis' stead (7.3–5).[15] At the beginning of the novel, Theagenes was his captive and Thyamis shortly became a dangerous rival for the love of Charicleia, but later, once the couple have escaped, he reappears and recaptures the hero from the Persian forces—the reason why they have now come to Memphis together. Without entering into the question of the complicated figure of Thyamis, who combines savagery with temperance, loyalty, and imprudence in his dual role as bandit and dispossessed priest (a fact we know from his own very brief report earlier in the novel, in 1.19), the arrival of the pair at the gates of Memphis ushers in the full story of the struggle for the priesthood between the brothers. This happens long after Calasiris, self-exiled lest he fall into the seductive clutches of the courtesan Rhodopis and to avoid witnessing the prophesied strife between his sons, had left the city. By rights, Thyamis, as the elder of the two, should have inherited his father's position, but was deprived of it by his brother, Petosiris', machinations, the specific details of which we now learn. Once again, it is a tale of illicit sexual desire and false accusations, but one raised to a higher degree in the merging of political and religious interests, and Arsace, we now learn, has the starring role to play in the affair.

It was Arsace, in fact, who had initially laid a lustful eye on Thyamis, and it was his own brother, Petosiris, who informed her husband, Oroondates, of Arsace's infatuation, adding a 'false insinuation that Thyamis had complied with her desires' (7.2.4). Although suspicious of his wife but without clear proof and wanting to spare the royal household from scandal, Oroondates instead managed to drive Thyamis into exile on various pretexts and installed his brother in the priesthood instead. Such, we are told, was 'past history now' ($\tau\alpha\hat{\upsilon}\tau\alpha$ $\mu\grave{\epsilon}\nu$ $\chi\rho\acute{o}\nu o\iota s$ $\grave{\epsilon}\gamma\epsilon\gamma\acute{o}\nu\epsilon\iota$ $\pi\rho o\tau\acute{\epsilon}\rho o\iota s$, 7.3.1).

But is it? Now before the gates, Thyamis and Theagenes step forward together. Thyamis reveals the truth of the story about Petosiris' scheme to disinherit him through false accusations against Arsace of adultery. On the

---

[15] Habrocomes and Hippothous in Xenophon of Ephesus represent another alliance of this sort.

one hand, Arsace is filled with rage against Petosiris and wants to plot her revenge; on the other, her erotic desire for Thyamis reawakens at her first glimpse of him. But the scenario is wonderfully complicated by her equal and even more pressing desire for Theagenes, his companion:

τὸν δὲ Θύαμιν ὁρῶσα καὶ αὖθις τὸν Θεαγένην διεσπᾶτο τὴν διάνοιαν καὶ ἐμερίζετο εἰς τὴν πρὸς ἑκάτερον ἐπιθυμίαν, ἔρωτα ἐπ᾽ ἀμφοτέροις τὸν μὲν ἀνανεουμένη τὸν δὲ δριμύτερον ἄρτι τῇ ψυχῇ καταβαλλομένη.

As she looked upon Thyamis and then upon Theagenes, her heart was rent in two, torn asunder by the desire she felt for each of them: in one case it was the revival of an old passion, in the other a new and more painful shaft piercing her heart. (7.4.2)

The two, having been rivals for Charicleia's affections at the outset of the narrative, are twinned once again, but in reverse: now both are the target of a woman's amorous designs and her lethal gaze.[16]

14.5. Gender and Ethnicity

Suzanne Lye's essay 'Gender and Ethnicity in Heliodorus' *Aithiopika*' is relevant here.[17] She argues that while both gender and ethnicity constitute 'performative' categories of identity, they are not equal in weight. In her view, ethnicity in the Arsace episode is a 'fluid category:' that is, 'something that can be consciously emphasized or hidden through language, dress, or demeanor.'[18] By contrast, 'gender is...a more fixed, fundamental, and internal attribute', with the result 'gender often trumps ethnicity in predicting and judging actions'—but only with respect to female characters.[19] We might note at the outset, however, that with the crucial exception of Charicleia,[20] a Greek in outward appearance, language, and education, but Ethiopian in

---

[16] Thyamis, one should add, remains concerned for Theagenes' welfare and makes a trip to the court to demand the couple's release, but to no avail. Yet he calls the gods to witness and departs, resolved to reveal all to the people (8.3–5). He appears once again at 8.9.15 when Charicleia is on the pyre (but unharmed) to encourage the people to save her, 'having been alerted to what was happening by the deafening tumult'.

[17] Lye 2016.   [18] Lye 2016: 236.
[19] Lye 2016: 236–7.   [20] See, however, Morales in this volume.

origin, every female figure in the text is negatively represented.[21] On the Greek side, think Demaenete and Thisbe in the Cnemon episode and the allusion to Rhodopis, the Thracian woman, who came to Egypt as a sexual predator and tempted the priest Calasiris beyond his powers to resist and so caused his voluntary exile (2.25.4). Then, consider the Egyptian woman of Bessa and her transgressive necromantic efforts in Book 6 (14–15), to end finally with the figures of the servant, Greek Cybele and her mistress, the Persian Arsace, whose full-blown portrait of shameless lust, vengeful cruelty, and desperate erotic madness, nullifies her more positive public role as representative of authority, while reinforcing the most stereotyped view of Persian despotism. In general, these women come to a bad end: either by suicide (Deimanete, Arsace) or death by mistaken identity (Thisbe in the cave) or by accident (woman of Bessa on a protruding spear, Cybele by poison meant for Charicleia). With the exception of the woman from Bessa (in a curious allusion perhaps to the Atossa scene in Aeschylus' *Persians* in which she raises the spirit of her dead husband, Darius),[22] all the others are negatively represented as engaged in transgressive erotic intrigues, whether as helpers (Thisbe, Cybele) or the subjects themselves of immoderate passion.[23] Behind these latter figures we detect glimpses of archetypal female characters of tragedy: Clytemnestra, Medea, Phaedra, and even Deianeira, all of whom destroy their menfolk and whose overt actions are determined or undermined by their sexual desires and erotic *amour propre*, whatever the provocations, or even despite resistance to them.[24]

There is no doubt that Charicleia is represented throughout the novel as a paragon of chastity (*sōphrosunē*), a stance taken by her own decision, fortified by her mother's own injunction to her inscribed on the swaddling

---

[21] Charicleia's mother is, of course, the model for chastity or *sōphrosunē*, whose actions drive the plot from the start and who plays a starring role in the last book. See further below.

[22] Like the scene in the *Persians*, the necromantic scene takes place around the time of a great battle.

[23] I omit Nausicleia, daughter of the merchant, Nausicles, who becomes the bride of Cnemon in Book 6. On the other hand, in this same book, Nausicles and Calasiris, on their way to Bessa to seek Theagenes, meet an acquaintance of Nausicles, carrying a flamingo, who is in haste to bring the bird to his mistress 'Isias, glory of Chemmis' to whom he is in amorous thrall to fulfil her every demand, frivolous or otherwise (6.3–4; see Montiglio in this volume). While his narrative function is to inform the pair that their errand is in vain (Thyamis had been there and carried off Theagenes), why should the informer be identified as a man in the power of a dominating woman? On negative views of women's sexuality, see also Olsen 2012.

[24] In fairness, it should also be pointed out that male sexual aggressors (with the exception of Thyamis) also meet a violent end: Thermouthis is bitten by a snake and dies (2.20.2); Trachinus is murdered by Pelorus (5.32.2), who, in his turn, succumbs to Theagenes' sword (5.32.6). See Papadimitropoulos 2013: 4.

band given first to Charicles and later deciphered by Calasiris. 'Honour chastity', it reads, 'in remembrance of your noble birth; it is the sole mark of virtue in a woman' (μεμνήσῃ τῆς εὐγενείας τιμῶσα σωφροσύνην, ἣ δὴ μόνη γυναικείαν ἀρετὴν χαρακτηρίζει, 4.8.7).[25] As many have pointed out, Charicleia's devotion to the moral attributes of chastity is a leading theme of the work, one that extends to the promise she exacts from Theagenes more than once to practice sobriety in the face of their passion for one another, and it comes into play in full force at the end, when both are tested in Ethiopia on the fiery grid in Book 10. It 'stretches from her girlhood as a priestess [of Artemis], during which she wished never to have to marry, to her arrival in Ethiopia' and the aftermath that leads to her recognition and ultimate union with her beloved.[26] Whether indicative of trends in later antiquity that favor asceticism, tinged with mystical elements, or whether abstinence is alternately an expression of self-identity or a conformity with social norms,[27] *sōphrosunē* marks a firm line of demarcation among the various characters, with repercussions especially for women. In the scenes we are discussing here, however, the contest is not one initially between Arsace and Charicleia but between Arsace and Theagenes. It is he, finally, who is confronted with most dangerous ordeals in his encounters with the love-besotted Arsace. In his defiance of her desires, he suffers incarceration and physical punishment after all her and Cybele's other seductive strategies fail to move him.

Arsace is surely the most villainous female among a host of other sexual predators that populate the novels, relying on the sheer power of her position to enforce her will by contrast, for example, with love-sick widows (Melite in Achilles Tatius) or a pirate's daughter (Manto in Xenophon of Ephesus). I cannot think of any other character, in fact, whether in the genre of the novel or elsewhere,[28] who either matches her wild excesses of desire, jealous rages, and nefarious intrigues, which are described at such length, or resorts, with the support of her go-between, Cybele, to so many persistent efforts to attain her goal. True, her evil machinations lead finally to Charicleia's trial by fire and the miracle of her salvation, but before then,

---

[25] The word includes not only chastity but self-control, temperance, and modesty.
[26] Groves 2012: 89.
[27] See Anderson 1997 for a full discussion of the term and Bird 2020 on its importance in the Greek novels; Hani 1978 on mystical and religious elements; Haynes 2003: 70–2 on femininity; and Ormand 2010 for subtle analysis especially of the scenes in Book 10.
[28] I include here Roman authors such as Juvenal, Martial, and Apuleius.

Heliodorus goes to extravagant lengths to narrate Arsace's increasing desperation in fluctuations of moods and escalations of coercive behaviour.

14.6. Social Status and Class Resentment: Achaemenes

Nevertheless, while Arsace—consumed by twin emotions of jealousy and lust—claims the central role in these Persian chapters, what of her enablers? That is, in particular, the dual roles of mother and son, Cybele and Achaemenes, who are her servants? Each partakes (albeit ambiguously) in the Greek-Persian divide, as also the one between genders (and even age), but a focus on them at this juncture introduces the matter of class, a topic generally understudied in the novel.[29] At stake are the fortunes of both Theagenes and Charicleia and their own confused status: both are nobly born but are in the awkward situation of being strangers-guests-captives-prisoners at the Persian court, a situation which leaves them vulnerable and defenceless.[30] It is not unusual in ancient prose fiction, of course, that one or both of our elite couple, having fallen on hard times, are reduced in the matter of class, whether as captive, prisoner, or actual slave.[31] This split between circumstance (or appearance) and actual status allows for a divided vision: that which their captors envision in their ability to use their power of domination against them and the private resistance that allows the reader to share in their inner thoughts. As Whitmarsh 2011 remarks:

> There are at least two ways of interpreting such situations. On the one hand, we could take them as socially conservative, marking perversions of the protagonists' 'true' social identities compromised at the outset and reclaimed at the end. Yet it is equally open to us to take them as evidence for the permeability of social boundaries and the fragility of status, a reminder to the novels' readers that they are all only one kidnapping away from social ruin.[32]

---

[29] See the few pages in Whitmarsh 2008: 84–6. He is mostly concerned with the question of elite readership and of the influence of popular culture on story-telling.
[30] As the narrator observes: 'Fate was delivering them like willing captives into the hands of their foe, imprisoning, by a semblance of kindness and hospitality, two young people, strangers in a foreign land and unsuspecting of what lay in store for them. For thus it is that a life of wandering imposes on travelers sojourning in foreign parts a lack of awareness that is tantamount to blindness' (7.12.2).
[31] e.g. Chaereas in Chariton, Leucippe in Achilles Tatius.
[32] Whitmarsh 2011: 86.

True enough, but Heliodorus manipulates these categories to complicate matters even further, as the plots and counterplots of Cybele and her son Achaemenes (in Books 7 and 8) put them at odds with the couple and eventually with one another.

Let me pause for a moment on the social roles of slaves or servants of masters and mistresses in the Greek novel. The role of the older female loyal servant, as previously observed, looks back to Phaedra's nurse and her role as a go-between in Euripides' *Hippolytus*. Plangon in Chariton might be another case in point, although her efforts on behalf of Callirhoe are initially meant to help her master, Dionysius, and she also has her own self-interest at heart.[33] Cybele, of course, has a much larger part in the proceedings. An intimate confidante of Arsace and accustomed to facilitating her lust for younger men, she resorts to every stratagem, ranging from seductive persuasion to deadly threats in order to gain the desired results.[34] Male characters in the novel, on the other hand, are more likely to be helped by devoted clever servants, a trope that looks back to New Comedy.[35]

Achaemenes, son of Cybele, does not fit this pattern or any other appropriate to his class. Ignored by most commentators, his actions and reactions regarding both his mother and the couple constitute almost diabolical strokes of plot manipulation, in both senses of the word. Inquisitive, shrewd, greedy, vengeful, resentful of his status as a slave, he is a would-be bridegroom in a wholly unsuitable match.[36] At the level of the

---

[33] I omit Thisbe from consideration in this context, despite her original efforts to abet Deimanete's pursuit of Cnemon, because she is young and becomes part of the erotic intrigue herself, although see further below on the role of Achaemenes as a would-be lover above his class. However, on Thisbe and Cybele as initially trusted servants who turn out to be anti-confidantes to their mistresses, see Egger 1990: 113–17, who points out the lack of solidarity among females in Heliodorus, unlike e.g. in Chariton.

[34] At the same time, on a symbolic level, the slave-master divide is complicated from the start as Arsace's political domination is countered by enslavement to erotic passion, a common trope from elegy on. See also Morgan and Repath 2019 as well as Montiglio 2019 and Owens 2020, who offers the idea that Calasiris fulfils the role of the *callidus servus*, so that on his disappearance from the scene, the couple is truly on their own and forced upon their own resources.

[35] e.g. Phocas for Dionysius, Artaxates for Artaxerxes in Chariton; Satyros for Clitophon and Sosthenes for Thersander in Achilles Tatius. See also Haynes 2003: 125–30, on both female and male slaves. On the absence of loyal servants to both Chariclea and Theagenes, so typical of the novel, see the excellent arguments of Montiglio 2019.

[36] Erotic rivals proliferate in all the romance plots (including Longus), and jealousy is a rampant motive, one that looks to revenge. These include would-be lovers of both high and low station (noblemen, satraps, kings; pirates and brigands) but never a slave (with the exception of Sosthenes in Achilles Tatius). At the same time, Thisbe, like Achaemenes in reverse, also looks to rise above her class in her liaison with Cnemon, and even better, with the wealthy merchant (Nausicles)—a not unfamiliar trope, however, in the tale of a *hetaera* and a respectable lover.

narrative, he constitutes the liaison between the palace and the battlefield, having served under Mitranes at Bessa, and he was personally charged with taking the prisoner Theagenes to Oroondates before he had to flee for his own life as the sole survivor of Persian defeat. We meet him first by hearsay—when his mother, having succeeded in bringing Theagenes and Charicleia into a secluded room in the palace, enjoins the doorkeeper, having locked the door, to forbid entry by anyone, even her son, adding the lie to tell him that she has taken the key with her. An inauspicious prelude to their relationship. Not to be daunted, however, Achaemenes, once arrived, peers through the keyhole, and, at one stroke, the fateful intrigue begins: he falls in love with Charicleia at first glance and thinks he recognizes Theagenes as his escaped prisoner. The first leads to his subsequent demand for Charicleia as his bride in return for helping his mother, and the second to the later revelation of Theagenes' identity, marking him as a slave of the court, like Achaemenes himself. Once Theagenes reveals Charicleia as his would-be bride, not his sister, and Arsace breaks the solemn promise she made to Achaemenes, he plots his revenge, as cited above—to reveal Arsace's infatuation to her husband, Oroondates,[37] as a scheme to eventually win Charicleia for himself. At his disappearance, both his mother and Arsace suspect the worst, and they are right, and subsequently, once the eunuch Bagoas, at Oroondates' command, sets off to free the couple, Arsace commits suicide and Achaemenes remains under Oroondates' mistrustful surveillance as they set off together for Syene.

His end in Book 9 is an ignominious one: it takes place after the Ethiopians win the battle there. Achaemenes discovers what happened at Memphis in his absence. Fearing that his part in Arsace's suicide would be discovered, he decides it is safest to kill Oroondates:

…τρῶσαι δὲ καιρίαν ἀποτυχόντος. Ὑπέσχε γε μὴν αὐτίκα τὴν δίκην πρός τινος τῶν Αἰθιόπων τόξῳ βληθείς, ἀναγνόντος μὲν τὸν σατράπην καὶ περισῴζειν, ὡς προστέτακτο, βουλομένου, ἀγανακτήσαντος δὲ τὸ ἄδικον τοῦ ἐγχειρήματος, εἰ τοὺς ἐναντίους τις ὑποφεύγων χωροίη κατὰ τῶν φιλίων, τὸν καιρὸν τῆς τύχης εἰς ἐχθροῦ ἄμυναν, ὡς ἐῴκει, θηρώμενος.

However, he failed to strike a mortal blow, and his misdeeds were instantly punished by a fatal shot from one of the Ethiopian archers, who not only recognized the satrap and wanted to save him from death, as had been

---

[37] A replay of Petosiris' previous machinations against Thyamis.

ordered, but was also much affronted by the criminality of a man in flight from the enemy attacking his own side and welcoming such an extremity in order to settle what appeared to be a personal score. (9.20.5–6)

Achaemenes, loyal only to his own interests, and forever scheming to advance himself at the expense of his masters, predictably meets with his just desserts. But his activities are crucial, as we have seen, to the sinister developments at the Persian court.

But what interests me most in the story of Achaemenes is the relationship between him and Theagenes, who, denounced now to Arsace as her slave just like himself, hears of Charicleia's betrothal to Achaemenes, and soon endures the other's taunts and threats (7.24–5.1). 'What can we do? What plan can we devise', cries Theagenes to Charicleia, 'to frustrate these abhorrent unions between Arsace and me and Achaemenes and you?' (7.25.6). Pretending to acquiesce in his surrender to Arsace, Theagenes is determined to save Charicleia, for 'apart from other considerations, it would be quite wrong [unlawful?] for a woman who takes such pride in the high nobility of her birth to become the wife of one born and bred to slavehood' (τὴν εὐγενείᾳ τῇ μεγίστῃ κομῶσαν οἰκότριβι συνοικεῖν ἀθέμιτον, 7.26.3). The ace up his sleeve, of course, is that she is not his sister, as they had thought, but his bride-to-be, which compels Arsace to nullify her promise to Achaemenes. Theagenes had engineered a clever plot, in expectation that his confidences to Arsace (in the presence of Cybele) would be betrayed to Achaemenes:

...ὡς σφόδρα χρὴ προσδοκᾶν καὶ ἐπιβουλεύσειν τῇ Ἀρσάκῃ τὸν Ἀχαιμένην, ἄνδρα δοῦλον μὲν τὴν τύχην (ἀντίθετον δὲ ὡς ἐπίπαν τῷ κρατοῦντι τὸ κρατο ὑμενον), ἀδικούμενον δὲ καὶ εἰς ὅρκους ἀθετούμενον ἐρῶντα δὲ καὶ ἄλλους ἑαυτοῦ προτετιμῆσθαι πυθόμενον, συνειδότα δὲ τὰ πάντων αἴσχιστα καὶ παρανομώτατα καὶ οὐδὲν εἰς τὴν ἐπιβουλὴν πλάσασθαι δεόμενον...ἀλλὰ καὶ ἐκ τῶν ἀληθῶν ἔχοντα πρόχειρον τὴν ἄμυναν.

His hope was that Achaemenes would go so far as to form hostile designs against Arsace: he was a man born to slavery (and a man subject to a master tends to hate the master to whom he is subject); a man wronged, a solemn pledge to whom had been set at nought; a man in love who had discovered that another had been preferred to himself; a man with intimate knowledge of the most illicit and immoral goings-on, who had no need to invent falsehoods with which to attack Arsace...but had only to reveal the truth to exact his vengeance. (7.26.10)

In Achaemenes' eyes, however, his status at the court trumps Theagenes' new condition as a slave. Now a cupbearer at Arsace's table, Theagenes infuriates the other by his haughty bearing, promoted above the heads of others who serve at banquets, to say nothing of Achaemenes' resentment at his intimacy with their mistress. Distraught finally at the news that his promised betrothal to Chariclea is annulled, he cries to his mother: 'Am I not worthy to wed my own fellow slave?' (Οὐκ εἰμὶ ἄξιος γαμεῖν ὁμόδουλον ἐμαυτοῦ; 7.28.2). Cybele is equally incensed by Arsace's failure to honour her oath and, for the first time, she reveals to her son her innermost thoughts:

Δι' ἡμᾶς...καὶ τὴν ἡμετέραν παράνομον περὶ Ἀρσάκην εὔνοιαν τε καὶ πίστιν. Ἐπειδὴ γὰρ ἐκείνην καὶ τῆς ἑαυτῶν ἀσφαλείας προτιμήσαντες καὶ τὴν ἐκείνης ἐπιθυμίαν καὶ τῆς ἡμετέρας σωτηρίας ἐπίπροσθεν ἀγαγόντες ἅπαντα καθ' ἡδονὴν συνεπράξαμεν, ἅπαξ που παρεισελθὼν εἰς τὸν θάλαμον ὁ γεννάδας οὗτος καὶ λαμπρῶς αὐτῆς ἐρώμενος καὶ μόνον ὀφθεὶς ἀναπέπεικε παραβῆναι μὲν τοὺς πρὸς σὲ γεγενημένους ὅρκους ἑαυτῷ δὲ κατεγγυᾶν τὴν Χαρίκλειαν, οὐκ ἀδελφὴν ἀλλὰ μνηστὴν εἶναι διατεινόμενος.

We ourselves are to blame...we and our loyal service to Arsace in an unlawful cause. We esteemed her above our own safety; we thought her lust more important than our own lives; we served her pleasure devotedly; and the result is that this noble fellow, this wonderful lover of hers, has had to worm his way into her chamber just once for the mere sight of him to induce her to break all the oaths she swore you and to pledge Chariclea to him, because now he claims that she is not his sister, but his bride to be.

(7.28.2-3)

Nowhere else in the ancient novel do slaves play such a commanding role in the plot and nowhere else are we privy to their self-awareness in the airing of their grievances against their masters. Cybele recognizes all too well the immoral actions in which she has been involved. At the same time, Achaemenes cannot distinguish between 'born a slave' and slave by circumstance, and despite Theagenes' argument that Chariclea is not a slave, he persists in the notion that she is. On the one hand, Theagenes' scorn for those born into slavery is hardly limited to his personal perceptions, but is conditioned by the assumptions of his class. On the other, he correctly divines the chain of circumstances that will lead Achaemenes to betray his mistress to her husband in revenge for the insult to him. And in fact, this is how Book 7 ends: 'Anger, jealousy, love, and disappointment combined to goad him [Achaemenes] to fury: emotions capable of turning anyone's mind, let alone a savage's' (ὑπ' ὀργῆς ἅμα καὶ ζηλοτυπίας καὶ ἔρωτος καὶ ἀποτυχίας οἰστρηθείς, ἱκανῶν καὶ ἄλλον τινὰ διαταράξαι πραγμάτων, μή τί γε δὴ βάρβαρον, 7.29.1). Off he rides on what the text calls his rash and unconsidered errand to Oroondates.

In conclusion, it is not entirely clear how to account for the detailed portrait of Achaemenes and gauge the larger significance of his activities other than to the furtherance of the plot. On the one hand, we are witness to scenes of the intrigues at the Persian court (with Cybele in the starring role) and get a glimpse of the motives and feelings of the folks 'downstairs'. They are slaves, fearful of their lives in the face of their mistress's untrammelled emotions, but also resentful of their involvement in behaviour they deem to be immoral and unjust. Theagenes may outwit Achaemenes and scorn him as one born in slavery; but he too acknowledges that the other is a man like any other, one who is motivated by the same human emotions as many others, whether slave or free.

In the conflict between Greek and Persian values that dominates at court, these scenes give Theagenes the opportunity to assert his noble manhood as a prelude to the heroic role of a look-alike Achilles he is eventually to play in Ethiopia, even as it enhances his erotic *persona* for the first time through Arsace's mad desire for him.[38] Add, too, the point that the dire situation that faces both Theagenes and Charicleia also gives them the opportunity to confront their increasing hardships by themselves without the protection of Calasiris. But, in the process, Achaemenes, as the rival suitor for Charicleia's hand, not only sustains the contrast between slave and free (as between hero and rogue), but enlarges our perspective on that uneasy dialogue.

Arsace remains, of course, the focalizing figure of these scenes at the Persian court. Herself a kind of hybrid Persian philhellene, occupying dual roles as erotic subject and political regent, both mistress and slave to unbridled passion, she caps the novel's engagement with gender and power that in her case looked back to Thyamis and forward to Theagenes in a

---

[38] For many, as for Groves 2012: 34, 'Theagenes, on the whole, has a less well developed personality and a less memorable role in the novel than Charicleia. He is often the passive and despondent one, quick to give up and slow to learn to trust in providence.' Books 7 and 8 tell us otherwise. But see de Temmerman 2014: 258–88, who gives a detailed analysis of Theagenes in the light of his rhetoric as a means of characterization.

dizzying set of complexities of plots and counterplots. Her ultimate defeat after the melodramatic failures of her resentful enablers opens the way to the confrontation between Persian and Ethiopian forces, which leads at last along the Nile through Syene to the end of the journey at Meroe. While new ordeals await the couple (capture, trials, sacrifice, and more), the dangers of erotic aggression and tyrannical rule are over.

15
Sending the Reader Round the Bend (8.14–17)

Ian Repath

15.1. Content and Context

After most of two books centred on Memphis, ruled by Arsace in the absence of her husband, the satrap Oroondates, the captive Charicleia and Theagenes are enabled to escape (although they still wear chains), by Bagoas, the eunuch whom Oroondates has dispatched for this very purpose.[1] They are put on horses and, accompanied by Bagoas and a band of Persians, ride all night towards Thebes, until, when it becomes too hot the next day, they stop at a bend in the Nile; here, a messenger tells them the news of Arsace's suicide. When the heat abates, they set off for Thebes, riding all night again to try to get there before Oroondates departs. En route, however, they meet a soldier, who tells them that he has already left for Syene, and so they change course accordingly. Near Syene, they are ambushed by Ethiopians, and, after some fighting, Bagoas, Charicleia, and Theagenes are captured, although the protagonists are willing for this to happen. The Ethiopians make enquiries, and decide to present all three to their king, which they do at the beginning of Book 9.

This section of the novel marks an important moment of transition. It comes after the episode in Memphis, characterized by Persian depravity and the victimization of the protagonists, and contains a definitive resolution of that episode. A significant amount of travel takes place, as the distance between Memphis and Syene, in reality roughly 550 miles, is telescoped into two nights' riding. It is followed by the arrival of the protagonists at the edge of Ethiopian territory and their introduction to the king. The first-time reader, of course, has to play a game of expectation and inference about

---

[1] See also Zeitlin in this volume.

what might happen next, a game which is particularly relevant at such a juncture: s/he can, given the contents of what has preceded, be confident that Charicleia and Theagenes will reach Ethiopia and, in view of generic conventions, can presume that they will have a happy ending.[2] How this will come about, on the other hand, and what surprises the author has in store, can be known only by reading on into the final books, but, in this section, there are several ways in which Heliodorus provides clues and hints to encourage his reader actively to anticipate and imagine what might come next. At the same time, this section looks backwards, to events just occurred and, I will argue, wider aspects of what has gone before. Although this section has received hardly any scholarly attention, there are intratextual and intertextual connections to be made, and metaliterary aspects to explore. My main focus will be on the description of the bend in the Nile, but first I want to trace how the characters themselves react and what they anticipate in this section, and to consider how Heliodorus intertwines several aspects of his plot, conjures different possibilities for the ensuing narrative, and manipulates his reader's expectations.[3]

15.2. The Characters' Perspectives and Reader's Expectations

The protagonists think they are being taken away to death (8.13.3–5), although Bagoas' intention is to follow his orders and take them to Oroondates, who was in Thebes when he sent him on his mission (8.2.3). The disjunction in expectations is emphasized when, resting at the bend in the Nile, Bagoas tries to persuade Charicleia and Theagenes to eat: they refuse in view of their impending (they believe) death, but are persuaded by Bagoas' assurances (8.14.4). Their expectations are now in line with the eunuch's, although the reader, while given no indication, can assume that they are less enthusiastic about this than the eunuch. This forward-looking aspect is changed in the next chapter, when a messenger tells Bagoas something (8.15.1). Heliodorus momentarily builds suspense about what is reported, before Bagoas then relates it to the protagonists: the message is that Arsace has hanged herself (8.15.2). She did this because of her own

---

[2] On Heliodorus' sophisticated management of his reader's expectations, see Morgan 1989a.
[3] It is fitting, in the context of this volume, that, with the exception of a few comments by Plazenet 1995: 14, only John Morgan 2012a: 567–8 has paid more than passing attention to this section.

expectations of what would happen: 'choosing to die by her own hand rather than wait for a death she could not hope to avoid, for she would not have escaped punishment by Oroondates and the Great King: either her throat would have been slit, or else she would have lived out the rest of her life in abject degradation' (8.15.2).[4] This twofold unrealized potential future highlights the dangers that might confront the protagonists, since it is to Oroondates that they are being conveyed, and he had written to Arsace that he would send them on to the Great King (8.3.1): there is a real possibility at this stage that Heliodorus will inflict more Persian immorality on them, with a reader of Chariton in particular recognizing the potential hierarchy of ever more powerful love-rivals. Bagoas tries to give his charges confidence, and he does this with an eye to the future: 'to make the young couple well disposed towards himself' (8.15.3). We are then told these words stem from his own joy that Arsace is dead, since he did not approve of her behaviour, and from his hope ($\dot{\epsilon}\lambda\pi\dot{\iota}\zeta\omega\nu$) to curry favour with his master, by bringing him a peerless young man for his retinue and a young woman to be his new wife (8.15.4). The reader is thus given a direct indication of a potential narrative danger to come. The protagonists' focus, on the other hand, is rather more retrospective: their relief at the news about Arsace outweighs any worries about the future (8.15.5).

When they set off again, Bagoas hopes to reach Oroondates still in Thebes (8.15.6), but, in the first of two significant coincidences, they meet a soldier who relates that the satrap has left for Syene, that he himself has been dispatched to rally troops to assemble at Syene, and that Syene may already have fallen to the Ethiopian army (8.15.7). There are, then, three threads to the action which are more-or-less concurrent: the journey of Bagoas and his prisoners, which is what the narrator focuses on; Arsace's suicide in Memphis and the journey of the messenger; and Oroondates' departure for Thebes. The reporting of the latter two by secondary narrators to Bagoas enables Heliodorus to move events at a considerable pace in this section.

Bagoas and company then head for Syene (8.15.7), but, in another significant coincidence, are suddenly attacked by Ethiopians: the narrator himself here recounts analeptically a fourth set of simultaneous events, detailing how the Ethiopian advance-party had got far ahead of the rest of their force and stopped to secure a position from which to ambush the enemy (8.16.1). This they do, taking Bagoas and the protagonists captive (8.16.2–7).

---

[4] I have used Morgan's translation (1989c) throughout, with some adaptations. All references are to the *Aethiopica*, unless specified otherwise.

Theagenes and Chariclea do not want to abandon the injured Bagoas, since his kindness leads them to expect (ἐλπισθέντα) more (8.16.7), but the main reason for their surrender is that this seems to be the fulfilment of the dream Theagenes had at 8.11.3, a dream which he had interpreted to mean their death, but which now seems to be realized literally.[5] Theagenes, in indirect speech, calls this 'their destiny' (πεπρωμένον) and argues that it is right to 'trust to the uncertainties of fortune (ἀδηλοτέρᾳ τύχῃ) rather than the certain dangers (τοῦ προδήλου…κινδύνου) posed by Oroondates' (8.16.7); he reflects the view that they are being handed over to the Ethiopians 'by a kinder fate' (χρηστοτέρας…τύχης) when answering their questions through an Egyptian interpreter (8.17.3). Chariclea, however, although she does not tell Theagenes her thoughts, 'knew now that Destiny (τῶν εἱμαρμένων) was guiding her steps' and 'felt sure (εὔελπις) that their fortune was about to take a turn for the better' (8.17.1).

The Ethiopians are now in control and decide what will happen: they will present all three to their king (8.17.3–4).[6] The book closes with an emphatically encouraging prolepsis:

Καὶ ἦν ὥσπερ ἐν δράματι προαναφώνησις καὶ προεισόδιον τὸ γινόμενον· ξένοι καὶ δεσμῶται τὴν σφαγὴν ὀλίγῳ πρόσθεν τὴν αὑτῶν ἐν ὀφθαλμοῖς ταλαντεύσαντες οὐκ ἤγοντο πλέον ἢ προεπέμποντο ἐν αἰχμαλώτῳ τύχῃ πρὸς τῶν ὀλίγον ὕστερον ὑπηκόων δορυφορούμενοι.

The scene was like a preface and introduction in a drama:[7] strangers in a foreign land, prisoners in chains who a short time earlier had been haunted by a vision of their own violent death, were now being not so much led as escorted in captive state, guarded by those who were a short time later to be their subjects. (8.17.5)

The section's complex and changing interplay of time and reaction and expectation is encapsulated in this passage,[8] although in a deliberately misleading way. The reader is given a direct indication of what will happen in

---

[5] See Morgan 1989a: 304–5.

[6] The first-time reader may even wonder whether the Ethiopian king will fall in love with Chariclea.…See Webb in this volume.

[7] The words translated by 'preface' (προαναφώνησις) and 'introduction' (προεισόδιον) appear to be technical terms; their precise meaning is obscure, but their general tenor is clear enough. See Morgan 1989a: 305 n. 12, and cf. Paulsen 1992: 224 n. 5, with further references.

[8] Morgan 2007a: 497–8.

the end, and this seems to corroborate the protagonists' new-found confidence. On the other hand, the close of this book is likened to a beginning, which both excites anticipation for what is to come and suggests that the end will not be easily reached. It is implied also that the prospect of a violent death, which dominated much of Book 8, has been obviated by their transfer to Ethiopian control. This makes all the more shocking the subsequent revelation, made by the Ethiopian king (9.1.4), that they are to become human sacrifices.

This section, then, looks both forwards and backwards, as one episode ends and another is about to begin. There are four strands of narrative, each involving different characters, interwoven with typical Heliodoran intricacy, as one is cut off and the other three are about to converge. The expectations of the characters are explored: these affect, if they do not straightforwardly determine, what the reader expects, until a final, explicit, narratorial intervention which suggests both that there is significant action to come and that things are now proceeding to a close. It is, therefore, especially mischievous of the author that this combination of drama and resolution does not take place for another book, as most of Book 9 is taken up with warfare.

15.3. The Setting in the Bend

The place where the characters rest after travelling overnight from Memphis is described as follows. A bend in the Nile enclosed an area:

...πολλοῦ μὲν λειμῶνος οἷα δὴ διαρρεομένου τοῦ παντὸς ἀνάπλεων πολλὴν δὲ πόαν καὶ χιλὸν ἄφθονον ἐνδαψιλεύσασθαι κτήνεσι νομὴν ἀπαυτοματίζοντα δένδρεσί τε περσέαις καὶ συκομόροις καὶ ἄλλοις τοῖς Νείλου συννόμοις φύλλοις ἐπηρεφῆ τε καὶ κατάσκιον·...

...which, the whole tract being well watered, was covered in a lush meadow and produced, unworked by human hand, a rich profusion of grass and herbiage, where animals could graze to their hearts' content beneath a shady canopy of Persea trees, sycamores, and other plants whose natural habitat is the banks of the Nile.   (8.14.3)

At one level, there is no need for such a detailed description: the reader must, therefore, take time to consider what significance it might have. In the first place, it has, as Morgan describes, a symbolic function: 'it is a haven opposed to the torture and imprisonment from which the lovers have just been liberated. Its natural simplicity similarly stands in contrast to the Persian luxury which they have just left.[9] The latter point is highlighted by the inclusion of Persea trees: they reflect the Persian episode which has just finished and replace oppression with shelter. The second main point Morgan makes is connected with the trees, since he argues that 'the location with running water, thick grass and trees immediately recalls the setting of Plato's *Phaedrus*, except that the plane trees canonical in such evocations have been replaced by the Persea'.[10] The descriptions of the setting of the *Phaedrus* (229a–b and 230b–c) were so popular, and evocations of them were so pervasive, that Heliodorus could even substitute the plane trees and still rely on his reader recognizing the hypotext.[11] Morgan suggests that 'The Platonic connotations are underlined by the presence of the horses': part of the reason for stopping is to allow their horses to rest (8.14.2). This combination of setting and horses enables the reader to appreciate another symbolic function of this setting: as Morgan puts it, 'We are thus primed to recall the erotic mythology of the *Phaedrus*, and to interpret Arsace's deviant sexuality in the light of the Phaedran myth of the soul's chariot'.[12]

These observations can be developed. As Morgan notes, this is the location where, in the next chapter, the news of Arsace's death is reported.[13] A messenger arrives at the meadow (λειμῶνος, 8.14.3) where there is pasturage (νομήν, 8.14.3) on a horse which is streaming with sweat (ἰδρῶτι...καταρρεόμενον τὸν ἵππον, 8.15.1). This reinforces the presence of horses, and may recall the horses of the chariot-teams of the soul, which endure 'sweated exertion' (ἱδρὼς ἔσχατος, *Phdr.* 248b2) in order to try to reach the plain of truth for 'the pasturage from the meadow there' (νομὴ ἐκ τοῦ ἐκεῖ λειμῶνος, 248b–c). This encourages us to reflect on the position of the protagonists, whose horses have presumably grazed in the meadow in the bend: they are striving for their goal, which is to reach the moral and philosophical high ground of Ethiopia and enjoy faithful and happy marriage. Their journey is one that few can make and requires perseverance and self-control, and this setting is a proleptic microcosm of Meroe, a place described by Heliodorus as an extremely large and exceptionally fertile

---

[9] Morgan 2012a: 567; cf. Plazenet 1995: 14.   [10] Morgan 2012a: 567–8.
[11] See Trapp 1990 for the popularity of the Platonic passages, and Repath 2010 and 2011 for their evocation in earlier novels.
[12] Morgan 2012a: 568, alluding to Socrates' second speech (*Phdr.* 243e–57b).
[13] Morgan 2012a: 567.

island bordered by the Nile and its branches (10.5).[14] Much more direct is an allusion to tragedy which follows soon afterwards, something foreshadowed by Bagoas and his men 'making the trees their tent' (σκηνὴν τὰ δένδρα ποιησάμενος, 8.14.4): the word translated by 'tent', which transliterates into English as 'scene', can also mean 'stage-building', and Heliodorus' reader has been trained from almost the very beginning of the novel to pick up on theatrical terminology.[15] Bagoas, passing on the news to the protagonists, says: 'Arsace is dead. She fastened a choking noose' (τέθνηκεν Ἀρσάκη βρόχον ἀγχόνης ἁψαμένη, 8.15.2). As is clear and well known, this is a paraquotation of the chorus in Euripides' *Hippolytus* reporting Phaedra's suicide to Theseus: 'She fastened and hung a choking noose' (βρόχον κρεμαστὸν ἀγχόνης ἀνήψατο, 802). The fact that Bagoas' Greek is supposed to be poor (8.15.3) means that this allusion should be understood as an intrusion by the author and therefore something requiring particular consideration. While Arsace is very different from the Phaedra in the version presented in the play alluded to, the Phaedra of literary tradition in general was strongly associated with a lack of sexual self-control.[16] The allusion to Phaedra in a place which recalls Plato's *Phaedrus* juxtaposes, intertextually and indirectly, the depraved and uncontrollable desires of Arsace with the chaste and mutual love of the protagonists.[17]

Another detail which connects this *locus amoenus* with the setting of the *Phaedrus* is too obvious for Morgan to comment on: the shade (*Phdr.* 229b, 230b). However, its presence here becomes more important when one compares the previous point in the primary narrative when a setting by the Nile was in focus: 2.21.[18] There, Cnemon draws close to the Nile and encounters

---

[14] There may also be a verbal prolepsis here, since the area enclosed by the Nile at 8.14.3 is described as 'an inland bay' (ἠπειρωτικόν τινα κόλπον), with ἠπειρωτικόν ('inland') anticipating that Meroe is described as being the size of a continent (ἤπειρον, 10.5.2).

[15] See Walden 1894; on the metaliterary force of such terminology, see Morgan 2012a: 574–5.

[16] At the same time, the author may, through the precise allusion, be evoking some sympathy for a woman whom he has afflicted with such a character and such a fate. For discussion of the intertextuality with Euripides, see Pletcher 1998 and Morales in this volume. Bird 2019 discusses other instances of intertextuality with Euripides' *Hippolytus*.

[17] For more detailed analysis of this contrast in the *Aethiopica* based on word-play between Phaedra and *Phaedrus*, see Morgan and Repath 2019, which builds on Morgan 1989b in particular.

[18] The only places the Nile is mentioned by name in the primary narrative between 2.21 and 8.14 are: 6.1.2, where Nausicles, Cnemon, and Calasiris see a crocodile while walking along its banks; 6.3.2, where an acquaintance of Nausicles refers to the Nile flamingo he is carrying; and 8.1.2, where the capture of the Nile city Philae by the Ethiopian king is narrated in an analepsis. At the second and tertiary levels, the Nile is mentioned at 2.26.5 (oracle greeting Calasiris at Delphi), 2.28 (Calasiris answering questions about the Nile), 2.29 and 31 (Charicles' narrative), and 5.27.7 (Calasiris narrating the landing in Egypt).

an old man, walking up and down beside the riverbank. Billault, in this volume, draws attention to elements of Plato's *Phaedrus* in this meeting, including the reversal of the Phaedran situation when Calasiris says: 'let us leave these banks of the Nile and the Nile, for a spot scorched by the sun's noon is not a pleasant place for listening to long tales' (ὄχθας...Νείλου τάσδε καὶ Νεῖλον ἀπολίπωμεν, οὐ γὰρ ἡδὺ μακροτέρων διηγημάτων ἀκροατήριον τόπος ἡλίου μεσημβρίᾳ φλεγόμενος, 2.21.6). The lack of shade makes this place unpleasant and emphasizes the idyllic nature of the setting at 8.14, where the shade is an essential component. One of the benefits of shade is that it is cooling and enables breath to be taken, and the setting at 8.14 is not only a metaphorical breathing space after the episode in Memphis, but a literal one, too, since Bagoas and his men have decided 'to get their breath back and give their horses a breather' (ἀναπνεῦσαι μὲν αὐτοὶ ἀναπνεῦσαι δὲ καὶ τὴν ἵππον, 8.14.2). This aspect is emphasized by the fact the messenger arrives 'fighting for breath' (πνευστιῶν, 8.15.1); his announcement that Arsace has stopped her own breath means that now even death might seem sweet (ἡδύ, 8.15.5) to the protagonists. The narrator then states that: 'By now the late afternoon was relaxing and making it easier to breathe, and cooling things down so that traveling was possible again' (δείλης οὖν ὀψίας ἤδη πρὸς τὸ εὐπνούστερον ἀναχεομένης καὶ πρὸς τὸ βάσιμον τὴν ὁδοιπορίαν ἐπιψυχούσης, 8.15.6). All of this, and in particular this last comment, picks up a detail from Socrates' enthusiastic description of the spot for his and Phaedrus' conversation: 'the freshness of the place is welcome and extremely pleasant' (τὸ εὔπνουν τοῦ τόπου ὡς ἀγαπητὸν καὶ σφόδρα ἡδύ·...*Phdr.* 230c1-2). It is characteristic of Heliodorus' allusivity to distribute elements of the intertext—the conduciveness to breathing and the pleasantness—in such an unobtrusive and subtle way.

What makes shade important is, of course, the sun and the heat it generates: references to this punctuate our section. The decision to rest is taken at about the third hour, when they could no long bear 'the scorching heat of the sun blazing from the summer sky of Egypt' (τῆς τε ἡλιακῆς ἀκτῖνος τὸν φλογμὸν οἷα δὴ θέρους ὥρᾳ καὶ κατ' Αἴγυπτον, 8.14.2). The point at which they are about to leave and the messenger arrives is later in the day: 'The intolerable midday heat was now beginning to abate: the sun was no longer beating down directly overhead, but its rays fell aslant as it began to sink in the west' (ἤδη δὲ τῆς ἄγαν μεσημβρίας χαλώσης οὐκέτι κατὰ κορυφὴν ἡλίου πλάγια δὲ καὶ ἀπὸ τῶν δυσμικωτέρων βάλλοντος, 8.15.1). The relative cool of the evening when they do set off is stressed at 8.15.6 (quoted above). There are two points I want to make about this. The first is that this pattern reflects the mentions of time of day in the *Phaedrus*: it with begins with references to Phaedrus' activities since dawn (ἐξ ἑωθινοῦ, 227a, 228b); before Socrates' second speech, Phaedrus suggests that they not go until the heat (τὸ καῦμα) passes, since it is midday (μεσημβρία), but go when it is cooler (ἀποψυχῇ) (242a); after his speech, they decide to stay and converse while the cicadas sing in the heat (ἐν τῷ πνίγει) in the middle of the day (ἐν μεσημβρίᾳ) (258e–259a); and, near the end of the dialogue, Phaedrus suggests they go because the heat (τὸ πνῖγος) has become milder (279b). Not only is the setting a shelter from heat in both texts, but the relationship between staying in the spot and the relative heat of the sun is the same. This would hardly be significant in itself, but, given the other allusions to the *Phaedrus*, and since the description of Heliodorus' *locus amoenus*, like Socrates' second speech, is bracketed by references to the sun's heat, it does suggest that Heliodorus wants his reader not only to consider the meaning of the symbolic function of the setting by the Nile but also to do so by relating it and what happens there to Plato's dialogue, and to the erotic mythology of the soul's chariot in particular.

The second point concerning the sun and its heat is a metaliterary one. From the sunrise at the very beginning of the novel to the self-identification of the author at the very end as 'one of those descended from Helios, the son of Theodosius: Heliodorus' (τῶν ἀφ' Ἡλίου γένος, Θεοδοσίου παῖς Ἡλιόδωρος, 10.41.4), the sun (*hēlios*) has the special role in this text of reflecting its author.[19] In this light, the unbearable Egyptian heat from the sun at 8.14.2 represents the extreme and desperate suffering inflicted by the author on the protagonists at Memphis, especially the attempted burning of Charicleia on the pyre (8.9). On the other hand, before mounting it, Charicleia prayed to the rising sun (8.9.11–12),[20] and it is no coincidence that she was miraculously unharmed by the flames: the author not only torments his central couple, but preserves them, too.[21] At 8.14, the author has

---

[19] See Whitmarsh 2005a: 99–100 on this aspect of the opening, and Bartsch 1989: 142–3 on the identity of Helios/Apollo with Heliodorus. See also Bowie, in this volume, on the sun at 1.5.2. If the original reader did not encounter the author's name until the very end of the novel, then this metaliterary angle would be fully activated only in retrospect. See also Whitmarsh and Repath in this volume on the end of the novel.

[20] Cf. Theagenes' invocation of the sun at 7.26.3.

[21] As Charicleia herself well describes at 8.10.2: her deliverance from the pyre was miraculous, but their misfortunes suggest they are being oppressed by a greater power, 'unless it is the divinity's way of working miracles to plunge us into the extreme and then deliver us from the impossible'.

fashioned a refuge and given them a rest from his own embodiment in the text, and the report of Arsace's death, which removes one danger at least, coincides with the lessening of the sun's heat: this is symbolic of Heliodorus removing some of the metaphorical heat from his protagonists. This forms a contrast with 2.21, where the effect of the sun's heat symbolizes the despondent state to which the author has reduced Calasiris. That chapter was very much concerned with beginnings—the introduction of a new character and the promise of his narrative[22]—and the contrast with it provided by 8.14–15 suggests that this later section can be seen as the beginning of the end of the novel. In fact, the sun is not mentioned in connection with heat again: as the protagonists escape the dangers in Egypt and approach Ethiopia, the sun becomes all-illuminating (9.22.4)[23] and, in the final book, is mentioned only as the god Helios. The only other mention after 8.15 encourages this reading. While for the protagonists 'the sun was no longer beating down directly overhead, but its rays fell aslant as it began to sink in the west' (οὐκέτι κατὰ κορυφὴν ἡλίου πλάγια δὲ καὶ ἀπὸ τῶν δυσμικωτέρων βάλλοντος, 8.15.1), when the Persian forces advance against the Ethiopian in Book 9, we are told that the 'sun was not long risen and was casting its rays full on the Persians' faces' (ἄρτι γὰρ ἀνίσχοντος ἡλίου καὶ τὴν ἀκτῖνα κατὰ πρόσωπον τοῖς Πέρσαις ἐπιβάλλοντος, 9.14.1). The phrase translated 'fell aslant' (πλάγια...βάλλοντος) finds its antithesis in 'casting...full on the Persians' faces' (κατὰ πρόσωπον τοῖς Πέρσαις ἐπιβάλλοντος): the use of a compound of the same verb in the same form enhances this contrast. Just as the sun ceases to oppress the protagonists but is directly opposed to the enemies of the Ethiopians, so Heliodorus begins to remove the obstacles to the former reaching their goal and will ensure that a major source of antagonism, past and potential, is defeated.

There is still a long way to go, of course, and the very presence of a *locus amoenus* suggests this, too, especially because of its intertextual nature. The descriptions of the setting of the *Phaedrus* come near the beginning of the dialogue, and this is reflected in many evocations of it, not least in the novelistic tradition which culminates with the *Aethiopica*. In Chariton, as the pirates take Callirhoe away from her tomb in Sicily, they stop opposite Attica, at a place with a spring and a meadow (*Callirhoe* 1.11.4–5): they let

---

[22] See Billault in this volume.
[23] There the sun shines directly overhead, as it was no longer doing at 8.15.1: the same phrase, κατὰ κορυφήν, is used, but oppressive heat is not mentioned, no doubt because the Ethiopian king is the focus of the narrative.

Callirhoe rest (ἀναπαύσασθαι) from her journey there, just as the Persians, seeing that the riding has affected Charicleia in particular, stop to let her refresh herself (ἀναψύξαι, 8.14.2). This juncture in Chariton sees the pirates' decision to take her to Miletus, where the rest of her adventures begin. Longus' pastoral novel is full of descriptions of the countryside, but two particularly important ones are the grove with its many trees and spring in the prologue (*Daphnis and Chloe* pr. 1), whose initiatory importance does not need discussion here, and the cave with its watered meadow on whose grass the infant Chloe is found at the very beginning of her story (*D&C* 1.4).[24] Achilles Tatius provides no fewer than three such descriptions in his first book: there is the shady, watered meadow in the description of the painting of the abduction of Europa (*Leucippe and Clitophon* 1.1.3–6); the grove with its trees and stream where Clitophon is taken to tell his story (*L&C* 1.2.3); and the tree-lined garden of Clitophon's father's house (*L&C* 1.15), where the young man begins his seduction of Leucippe. All three are starting-points, and the meadow and garden resemble each other also in that they are enclosed, protected spaces, but ones from which the young women respectively are removed, albeit in different ways. These other novelistic settings suggest that the setting in the bend of the Nile at 8.14 is not only a place of respite from what has gone before, but also a significant starting-point; the precedents in Achilles Tatius in particular may lead the reader to expect that Charicleia will be the focus of what will happen next, with abduction a possibility, and the erotic threat of Oroondates also enhanced.[25] As the reader will soon discover, however, it will be both protagonists (and Bagoas) who will be captured, by Ethiopians. Before considering this, though, there is another side to the bend in the Nile that I want to address.

15.4. The Bend in the Nile

Like the setting it encloses, the bend has intertextual and metaliterary aspects, the former of which take us to the *Phaedrus* again. After Phaedrus' reaction to Socrates' second speech, the latter says: 'Phaedrus, you don't know that the expression "pleasant bend" comes from the long bend in the

---

[24] The two are in fact the same place: see Morgan 2004a: 146–7 and 153.
[25] Such settings are the sites for abduction in non-novelistic texts, too, of course: see e.g. *Homeric Hymn to Demeter* 1–14 and Mosch. *Eur.* 34–6 and 63–71; cf. Pl. *Phdr.* 229b4–d1.

Nile' (γλυκὺς ἀγκών, ὦ Φαῖδρε, λέληθέν σε ὅτι ἀπὸ τοῦ μακροῦ ἀγκῶνος τοῦ κατὰ Νεῖλον ἐκλήθη·...257d–e).[26] While there is no verbal allusion to Plato's phrase in Heliodorus,[27] the description of the setting the bend contains and the other allusions discussed above activate the intertextuality. The first point to make concerns structure. The mention of the bend in the *Phaedrus* comes in the interlude between Socrates' second speech, the last of the dialogue's speeches on love, and the discussion concerning rhetoric. In Heliodorus, the end of Book 8 in effect marks the end of the erotic dimension of the story, which includes the origin of the love of the protagonists and the desires of various love-rivals;[28] from now on, the focus of the central plot is on the identification of Charicleia and the salvation of the protagonists, and this to a large extent will depend on who says what to whom when,[29] reflecting generally the concerns of the latter part of Plato's dialogue.

The meaning of the proverbial phrase 'pleasant bend' was debated in antiquity,[30] but the explanation given by Socrates, confirmed by the wider context, is that it is an ironic phrase which means the opposite of what it says. For a sailor, a long bend is not pleasant, because of the amount of time it takes to cover a relatively short distance (as the crow flies); however, the bend in Heliodorus *is* pleasant for those riding horses, by virtue of what it encloses. Heliodorus thus reverses a phrase of reversed meaning which is used metaphorically and makes it literal and real. The reader put in mind of the passage in the *Phaedrus* (and/or who was put in mind of this proverbial phrase and was aware of this meaning of it) might then wonder whether Heliodorus is saying one thing and meaning another (as well), and I would suggest that the means of understanding the significance of this bend are provided in the description of it:

---

[26] Some editors, such as Rowe 1986: 192, exclude the clause ὅτι...ἐκλήθη as an explanatory gloss, but it is present in the second/third-century papyrus fragment which includes these lines (*P.Ant.* 77—see Yunis 2011: 171), and so, whether original or not, it may well have been in the copy which Heliodorus read.

[27] Unless we detect a pun on ἀγκών ('bend') in the mention of Arsace's 'choking noose' (βρόχον ἀγχόνης 8.15.2).

[28] There is the slight exception of the betrothal of Charicleia to Meroebus (10.24), but she is in the pavilion until 10.38, so he does not see her; rather than something genuinely erotic, this is another of the potential obstacles to the denouement in Book 10: see Morgan 1989a: 316.

[29] See Morgan 1989a: 308–18.

[30] See Thompson 1868: 84, and de Vries 1969: 184–7. My own suspicion is that even for Plato 'pleasant bend' was a proverbial phrase of unclear meaning or disputed origin and this is one reason he makes Socrates give an explanation for it.

καὶ ἦν γάρ τις ὄχθη καὶ ἄκρα τοῦ Νείλου καθ' ἣν τῆς ἐπ' εὐθὺ στάθμης τὸ
ὕδωρ ἀνακοπὲν καὶ πρὸς ἑλιγμὸν ἡμίκυκλον ἐκτραπὲν πρός τε τὸ ἀντίθετον
τῆς ἐκτροπῆς ἐπιστρέψαν οἷον ἠπειρωτικόν τινα κόλπον ἀπετέλει τὸ
περιγραφόμενον....

There was a sort of promontory in the bank of the Nile, where the water, prevented from flowing straight ahead, turned off into a semi-circular winding, until it returned to the point opposite the place where the detour began. The area thus enclosed formed, as it were, an inland bay....

(8.14.3)

The Nile in the *Aethiopica* has been the focus of a substantial amount of scholarly discussion: it provides the structure for the narrative, is symbolic of the narrative, and aspects of it are flagged up within the narrative itself for explanation and interpretation, including the allegorical.[31] Another dimension is the metaliterary,[32] and the possibility that this passage is saying something non-literal, and, specifically, metaliterary, is increased by the number of words which can be used to refer also to aspects of writing. Most obviously, what is enclosed (τὸ περιγραφόμενον) is described with a compound of γράφω, 'I write/draw', a compound used also in describing the jewel on the ring (5.13.3, 5.14.4) which Calasiris gives Nausicles and which, too, has metaliterary properties;[33] the water is 'prevented from flowing straight ahead', with 'straight ahead' (τῆς ἐπ' εὐθὺ στάθμης) containing the word στάθμη, which is a drawn line; 'where the detour began' translates a word (τῆς ἐκτροπῆς) which can be used of a 'digression';[34] and finally, 'winding' (ἑλιγμόν) is used elsewhere by Heliodorus in a context which has been interpreted by Morgan as having a metaliterary significance.[35]

---

[31] For discussions of the Nile in Heliodorus, see Winkler 1982: 151–2; Plazenet 1995: 12–14 and 20–1; Whitmarsh 1999: 24–9; Elmer 2008: 432–47; Whitmarsh 2011: 119–22 and 129–34; Morgan 2012b; and Webb in this volume.

[32] See Plazenet 1995: 20–1; Whitmarsh 1999: 25–9; Elmer 2008: 432–47; and Morgan 2012a: 576–7. None of them discusses 8.14.

[33] See Bowie 1995: 278–80, whose argument is enhanced by Heliodorus' uses of γράφω and its compounds in 5.13 and 5.14.

[34] Polybius uses it of the point from which he digressed: 4.21.12. Cf. Plato *Plt.* 267a and Dio 7.128 (pl.), where it is used of digressions.

[35] In the description of the bandit camp, there are 'paths that change direction with many windings (ἑλιγμοῖς)' (1.6.2): see Morgan 1989b: 111 on the metaliterary function of these and of the winding tunnels in the bandits' cave (1.29.1–2), a point developed at Morgan 2012a: 575–6, and, on the cave, at Morgan 2013: 236. Charicleia is saved by these 'windings' (ἑλιγμῶν, 2.2.1) from the fire which engulfs the bandits' camp. The only other use of this word in Heliodorus is found at 8.16.6 (see main text, below). Cf. Morgan 2013: 232–4, on the intertwined snakes in Charicleia's girdle (3.4.2–5).

In the first place, the use of such language, in addition to the elaborated description, draws attention to the literary artificiality of this setting.[36] In particular, I think we can see both analeptic and proleptic aspects to this metaliterary description, with the Nile important to both. The novel begins *in medias res* and with a mention of the Heracleotic mouth of the Nile (1.1.1).[37] The events which chronologically preceded the beginning of the narrative are narrated by Calasiris in Books 2–5: he relates their arrival at the Heracleotic mouth at 5.27.7 and then what took place there, bringing the reader back to the point from which s/he began. The course of the Nile at 8.14.3, as it returns to nearly the starting point of its digression, symbolizes the process Heliodorus made his reader undergo, which, while long, contained an abundance of pleasant reading. Moreover, mentions of the Nile frame the 'detour' of Calasiris' narrations: he and Cnemon leave it at 2.21, and return to it at the beginning of Book 6 as the linear narrative resumes, at a spot presumably not far from where they left it. The former of these passages is the counterpart and antithesis of that at 8.14.3, reflected, I would suggest, in the mention of 'the point opposite' (τὸ ἀντίθετον). Thus, the Nile's bend symbolizes the theme of digression and return which is characteristic of the narrative technique of the first half of the novel and of how the narrative and its characters may depart from, but always return to, the course of the Nile.

The transitional nature of this section as a whole and the ways in which it looks forwards suggest that the bend may be proleptic, too. First, it foreshadows in a relatively straightforward way the bend which a little later enables most of the Persians to evade the Ethiopians: 'Most of them escaped by running into the shelter of a bend in the Nile, which formed a sort of headland whose protruding banks enabled them to get out of sight of the enemy' (οἱ μὲν οὖν ἄλλοι διαδιδράσκουσιν ἑλιγμόν τινα τοῦ Νείλου καθάπερ ἄκραν ὑποδραμόντες καὶ τῷ προβόλῳ τῆς ὄχθης τὴν θέαν τῶν ἐναντίων ἀποκρύψαντες·..., 8.16.6). The repetition of words from 8.14.3 forms a strong connection between the two passages, and, in this light, the Persea trees are suggestive of the Persians who are protected by the bend. The lack of description of what this second bend encloses throws the setting at 8.14.3 into greater relief. The proleptic force does not end here, though, since the

---

[36] The metaliterary dimension is strengthened by what looks like a verbal allusion in ἐπηρεφῆ τε καὶ κατάσκιον ('shady canopy', 8.14.3) to Longus' συνηρεφὴς...καὶ κατάσκιος ('sheltered and shady' *D&C* 2.3.5), since the latter is part of Philetas' description of his garden, one of whose functions is metaliterary: see Morgan 2004a: 5, 14–15, and 178.
[37] See Bowie in this volume.

Nile plays a central role in Book 9: the bend at 8.14.3 anticipates the events at the siege of Syene, where Hydaspes, the Ethiopian king, has a trench dug in a circuit around the walls, which is then filled with water from the Nile (9.3.1–5).[38] The oxymoron of 'an inland bay' (ἠπειρωτικόν τινα κόλπον, 8.14.3) which the bend contains is reflected in the paradox of Syene becoming 'an island, an inland town surrounded by water, washed by the waves of the flooding Nile' (νῆσος...περίρρυτος ἡ μεσόγαιος τῷ Νειλῴῳ κλύδωνι κυμ ατουμένη, 9.4.2). This time, the Persea trees enclosed by the bend in the Nile prefigure the Persians in Syene, besieged by the water which surrounds them. More broadly, the episode of the siege of Syene and the ensuing battle against the Persian army is, in one sense, a narrative detour: it is prefaced by the presentation of the protagonists to Hydaspes (9.1.3), who are not even mentioned after 9.2.2 until they are presented to him again after his defeat of Oroondates and his forces (9.24.1). One of the functions of the Syene episode, then, is to enable suspense to build, and it brings the reader to a point very close to that from which it started.[39] The course of the Nile at 8.14 thus foreshadows not only the artificial bend which Hydaspes will create, but also, in a metaliterary sense, the divergence of the narrative focus away from the protagonists onto the episode which contains this bend.

15.5. Ambush, Colour, Siege, and Sacrifice

Charicleia and Theagenes are presented to Hydaspes because they are captured by Ethiopians, who have hidden in some reeds and fortified them: this assimilates them to the bandits whose habitation Heliodorus describes at 1.5–6 (see, especially, 1.6.1) and thereby enhances the potential threat they pose. The ambush recalls also the episode in Book 3 of Achilles Tatius, where the protagonists and friends are travelling (on a boat) up the Nile and are ambushed by the novelistic antecedents of Heliodorus' bandits (L&C 3.9);[40] both sets of ambushers want to take their captives to their king (εἰς τὸν βασιλέα, L&C 3.9.3—βασιλεῖ, 8.17.4). One detail in each case is

---

[38] See Webb in this volume. It is fitting that a man named after a river (in India) has such control over the Nile: see Elmer 2008: 439–40.
[39] For the reader's concerns about how the outcome of the war will affect the protagonists, see Morgan 1989a: 308.
[40] Their dwellings in the reeds of the Nile, described later (L&C 4.12.4–8), are very similar to those in Heliodorus.

particularly significant. Clitophon gives the following description of the bandits' appearance:

> The land was simultaneously full of terrifying savages. All were huge, black-skinned (not the pure black of the Indians, more as you would imagine a mixed-race Ethiopian) (μέλανες τὴν χροιάν—οὐ κατὰ τὴν τῶν Ἰνδῶν τὴν ἄκρατον, ἀλλ' οἷος ἂν γένοιτο νόθος Αἰθίοψ), bare-headed, light of foot but broad of body. They were all speaking a barbarian language.
>
> (L&C 3.9.2)

The colour of the men is part of their alarming nature for Clitophon. In Heliodorus, the Persians are alarmed by the sudden shouting, and 'recognized those appearing as Ethiopians by the colour of their skin' (ἀπὸ τῆς χροιᾶς Αἰθίοπας εἶναι τοὺς φανέντας γνωρίσαντες, 8.16.3). However, for Heliodorus' protagonists, their ethnicity is a source of encouragement (8.16.7–17.1).[41] This is the first appearance of Ethiopians in the primary narrative, and it is no accident that Heliodorus emphasizes the colour of their skin at this juncture, since it is one of the fundamental factors in the plot: in this novel, it is the fact Charicleia is white which is remarkable and which led to her mother, the Ethiopian queen, exposing her to avoid the shameful death which would result from the charge of adultery her daughter's colour (τὴν σὴν χροιάν) would bring, and to leave her daughter to the 'uncertainty of fortune, which was preferable to certain death or certainly to the name of bastard (ὀνόματος νόθου)' (4.8.6). The intertextuality with Achilles Tatius and the danger represented there may cause the reader to be more cautious than the confident Charicleia and to wonder how the central problem of the novel will be solved: will she be able to prove that she is in any way Ethiopian, let alone the Ethiopian princess?[42]

The intertextuality with Achilles Tatius operates on a larger scale, too. The day after the capture by bandits, a rider appears saying that, if there is a virgin among the captives, he is to take her away to be a sacrifice to purify

---

[41] Another contrast is that Clitophon subsequently laments that he cannot communicate with the bandits (L&C 3.10.2–3), whereas the Ethiopians have brought interpreters, and Theagenes can now speak Egyptian (8.17.2–3). Cf. the language problems at the beginning of the novel (1.3–4), when the protagonists are captured by bandits twice over. See Morgan 1982: 258–60, on this aspect of Heliodorus.

[42] At the same time, Heliodorus subtly aligns Charicleia with the Ethiopians through the focalization of Bagoas: he thinks that the former is 'irresistible in her beauty' (ἀπρόσμαχον…τὸ κάλλος, 8.15.4), and he and the other Persians recognize the latter and see that their number is irresistible (τὸ πλῆθος ὡς ἀπρόσμαχον ἰδόντες, 8.16.3).

the army; Leucippe is taken away (*L&C* 3.12). Theagenes and Charicleia will not be separated (although the first-time reader should be ever aware of this possibility), but when father and daughter are reunited (although they do not realize it), the former says they are to be victory-sacrifices (9.1.4), as long as they are proved to be virgins (9.1.5 and, for Charicleia alone, 9.25.5). After Leucippe is rescued from the bandits by the army, there is a battle between the two forces: this contains thematic and verbal similarities to the siege of Syene. Achilles Tatius' bandits live on an island (νῆσον) with a causeway, 'on either side of which the waters of the lake flowed around the city' (λίμναι δὲ τῇδε κἀκεῖσε τὴν πόλιν περιέρρεον) (*L&C* 4.12.8). Hydaspes' stratagem causes the Nile to flow all around (πανταχόθεν περιρρυείς) Syene, 'turning the space between the two walls into a lake' (τὸ μεταίχμιον τῶν τειχῶν ἐλίμναζε) and Syene into an island surrounded by water (νῆσος... περίρρυτος) (9.4.2). As part of their stratagem, the bandits posted spies with orders 'to break down the river dyke' (τὸ χῶμα τοῦ ποταμοῦ κόψαντας, *L&C* 4.14.1) to flood the causeway; opening such a dyke enables the water to be channelled (ἐποχετεύεται)[43] (*L&C* 4.14.2), and this is what happens. Hydaspes builds an earthwork (τὸ χῶμα) and 'cut an inlet for the river (στόμιον τῷ ποταμῷ διατεμών) and channelled (εἰσωχέτευσεν) the outflow into the canal formed by the two arms' (9.3.4). Later, to relieve the city, he orders his men to 'cut a second channel through the earthwork' (ἕτερον κατὰ τὸ χῶμα ἐκτέμνειν, 9.7.3). Heliodorus' siege of Syene, whether or not inspired by historical events or accounts thereof,[44] is not exactly the same as Achilles Tatius' episode (including the fact that the flooding is used by attackers, not defenders); however, there are enough similarities to enable the reader to see it as a reworking of the earlier one, but on a much grander scale, since it involves a city rather than a bandit encampment and is part of an international conflict. So, when the reader of Heliodorus encounters an ambush on the Nile by darker-skinned men and recalls the similar episode in Achilles Tatius, s/he has an intertextual hint about what may follow. Heliodorus does not disappoint, but he does reverse the order, as flooding as a battle-tactic precedes the imminent threat of human sacrifice. And just as the former is on a much larger scale, so the latter, while not carried to the same gruesome extent as Achilles Tatius', is part of the climax of the novel,

---

[43] See Gronewald 1976 on the text here.
[44] For discussion, see Lightfoot 1988; Bowersock 1994: 151–5; Morgan 2003: 418–19; Elmer 2008: 425–7; and Ross 2015.

as Sisimithres argues it should be abolished in his summative reading of the events of the final book (10.39).

15.6. Conclusion

Heliodorus ensures his reader leaves Book 8 in a simultaneously optimistic and anxious frame of mind by creating a tantalizing balance of certainty and uncertainty. We know, or think we know, that the ending will be a happy one, but there are also several suggestions and hints about what dangers lie in store for Charicleia and Theagenes, and these change with the narrative's twists and surprises. Another layer of the game is that the reader is expected to be reading this novel against previous novels, playing a game of guessing and second-guessing, interpreting the text against a background of generic conventions and specific intertextuality, in particular with Achilles Tatius. Plato's *Phaedrus* is another fundamental intertext, and at this point we can see some intertextual self-commentary by Heliodorus: the types of love in this novel can be gauged Platonically, and Heliodorus uses words, ideas, themes, and structures to give his reader a moral interpretative framework to appreciate what has gone before and anticipate what may lie ahead. Literary artificiality is brought very near the surface in this section, as Heliodorus reflects himself in the sun and its effects on the characters' activities and uses the Nile as a metanarrative symbol. The heady and sophisticated mix of narrative dynamics, plot possibilities, intratextuality, intertextuality, and metaliterary aspects makes this section of the novel characteristic of Heliodorus' genius as a writer; it also provides an example of what riches this text has in store for those who follow in the footsteps of John Morgan and his fellow pioneers in trying to read this and the other Greek novels.

16
The Siege of Syene
Ekphrasis and Imagination (9.3)

Ruth Webb

The siege of Syene is a key event in the closing books of the *Aethiopica* topographically, thematically, and in terms of the narrative structure. This contribution analyses the dynamic account of the strategy devised by Hydaspes to flood the land immediately around the city which opens the narrative of the siege. To date, this particular passage with its account of the deviation of the waters of the Nile to surround the city has attracted most attention for its similarity to the account of the siege of Nisibis by the Parthians under Shapur II in 350 CE, as related by the Emperor Julian in two panegyrics of Constantius.[1] The points of contact between the two have prompted speculation about whether Julian followed Heliodorus,[2] or whether Heliodorus was inspired by Julian,[3] in which case the *Aethiopica* cannot have been composed before the second half of the fourth century. I will not enter into this debate now except to say that the fourth-century date seems entirely reasonable.

My reading will focus on the account of the siege-works as an ekphrasis, a passage that encourages the readers to visualize what is described. In this respect, the construction of the siege-works deserves to be placed alongside other ekphrastic passages such as the opening ekphrasis, situated further down the Nile at the Delta,[4] or Calasiris' account of the procession at Delphi within his lengthy internal narration. The presentation—or presentification—of these

---

[1] Julian *Or.* 1.27b–30b and 2.2b–62c. This chapter was written with the support of a Long-term Visiting Fellowship at the Council for the Humanities and the Department of Classics at Princeton University. I would also like to thank the editors and Froma Zeitlin.
[2] Szepessy 1976.
[3] Chuvin 2004: 321–5; Bowersock 1994: 149–60; Ross 2015, with further connections to accounts of sieges in late antiquity.
[4] Lowe 2000: 237 places these two passages together for other reasons. See also Repath in this volume on 'the bend in the Nile'.

siege-works is particularly interesting as an example of a type of ekphrasis that makes an entity 'visible' by describing how it was made, the Homeric Shield of Achilles being the most famous example. First, I will follow the lead of rhetorical practice contemporary with Heliodorus and his readers in order to look at what the construction at Syene might tell us about its author, the Ethiopian king, before going on to explore some of the metanarrative and metafictional aspects of the passage.[5] This second move is encouraged by several features of the place and function of Hydaspes' works in the novel: they are situated by the Nile, which has functioned throughout as an organizational principle for the action of the novel and a key to its meaning;[6] like so many significant objects and movements in the story, they are circular in form.[7] Several features of the language, moreover, seem to place this passage within a poetic and metapoetic universe, despite the apparently prosaic subject matter (utilitarian structures made of earth) and the predominantly historiographical tone of Book 9.

16.1. The Passage and Its Context

At this point in the plot of the *Aethiopica*, Theagenes and Charicleia have been captured by the Ethiopian army during the war against Oroondates and the Persians (8.16.7). Hydaspes does not realize that he has taken his own daughter prisoner, nor do Charicleia and Theagenes know for sure at this point that their captor is really Charicleia's father. Oroondates himself takes refuge with his troops in the city of Syene, prompting Hydaspes to lay siege to it. By creating a channel around the city and linking this to the Nile, he surrounds the city with water, cutting it off and weakening its outer walls. As these walls begin to crumble, the occupants surrender but, when Hydaspes' own work collapses in its turn into a sea of mud, Oroondates manages to escape and summon help from Elephantine, leading to the battle which occupies the rest of Book 9. I will focus on the short passage describing the work undertaken by the Ethiopians at 9.3, referring to this immediate context as necessary.

The importance of Syene within the structure of *Aethiopica* in terms of topography and narrative progression is clear. It is one of the stations along

---

[5] This chapter develops, and to some extent refines, the brief analysis at Webb 2009: 182.
[6] See Winkler 1982; Plazenet 1995: 20–1; Whitmarsh 1999: 24–9 and 2011: 119–25; Lowe 2000: 237; Elmer 2008: 433–47; Morgan 2012a: 557.
[7] See Morgan 2013: 236.

the Nile that mark the couple's progress from the Delta to Ethiopia, and the detailed account of the siege and the earthworks created by Hydaspes helps to focus intense attention on place and on the city's position on the banks of the river. Situated at the boundary between Egypt and Ethiopia, Syene itself changes identity through Hydaspes' victory.[8] The city's liminal setting in geographical, cultural, and political terms also corresponds to the place of the Syene episode in the structure of the novel as a whole: at the close of the previous book, the narrator had compared the appearance of Theagenes and Charicleia in chains to the 'announcement and prologue' of a drama (8.17.5), signalling clearly that Book 9 will mark the start of a new phase of their adventures. Entry into this new phase is marked by a dramatic change of perspective as the narrator switches attention to the military situation in Syene, leaving the couple temporarily in the shadows in their new role as prisoners of the Ethiopians. As he does so, he employs a 'panoramic' focalization to recount the details of the military action undertaken by Hydaspes against Oroondates and the Persians and of its localization.[9]

John Morgan's analysis of the presentation of the end of the *Aethiopica* underlined the pivotal role of the siege of Syene as the backdrop for the reunion between father and daughter.[10] This reunion, which would have seemed wholly improbable to the reader at the opening of the novel, has been gradually prepared since the reader's discovery, via Calasiris' narrative, of Charicleia's Ethiopian origins. The path leading to narrative closure and the reintegration of Charicleia into her biological family is, of course, far from straightforward, as their status as the first foreign prisoners to be captured means that the couple are destined for sacrifice in the case of an Ethiopian victory.[11] As Morgan points out, the narrative of the siege thus provokes contradictory responses in the reader, since the defeat of Oroondates and the Persians removes a significant obstacle to a happy ending for the couple, while its corollary, an Ethiopian victory, appears to be their death warrant.

It is important to note too that the siege narrative foregrounds questions of interpretation, communication and the visual: the inhabitants of Syene, watching from their ramparts, have to decipher the intentions of Hydaspes and his men (9.3.6); when Oroondates finally decides to surrender, his first

---

[8] As Whitmarsh 2011: 129 notes 'The beginning of book 9, where Syene (modern Aswan) is surrendered to Ethiopian control, marks a significant juncture'. See also Plazenet 1995: 21.
[9] The term 'panoramic' is borrowed from de Jong and Nünlist 2004.
[10] Morgan 1989a: 308.
[11] This Ethiopian custom is mentioned by the narrator at 9.1.4, immediately after the first encounter between Hydaspes and the couple.

attempts at shooting messages across the water fail (9.5.2–3) and his men are forced to resort to gesture (9.5.3–4).[12] The readers, too, find themselves in a similar position, as the narrator holds back the explanation of Hydaspes' works until they are completed at 9.3.5: like the citizens of Syene watching from their walls (9.3.6), we see the works unfolding without at first fully understanding their purpose. The key puzzle to be solved in this book is the nature and identity of the Ethiopian king himself who now holds the couple captive and wields the power of life or death over them, the power, that is, to decide the novel's ending. Crucially, the beginning of Book 9 is the first place where 'Hydaspes' becomes more than a name for the reader. The only previous mentions of his name have occurred in Persinna's letter, which mentions Hydaspes solely in relation to female characters, as Persinna's own husband and as Charicleia's father (4.8.2; 4.8.4). After this, the name does not occur again until 9.1.2. Up until this point, the conflict between the Persians and Ethiopians has been introduced as a background story (7.1.4 and 7.29.2), and an unnamed 'king of Ethiopia' has been reported as closing in on the Persians at 8.1.1. But until 9.1.2, when the narrator casually names this king in a *de* clause balancing a mention of Oroondates, the reader has no way of knowing whether Charicleia's father is still alive and in power, whether, that is, 'Hydaspes' is identical with the 'Ethiopian king'. This doubt is shared with the protagonists, as we discover later from the couple's relief (the irony of which does not escape us) when they recognize (γνωρίζω) the name 'Hydaspes' pronounced by one of their guards. Up until that point, the narrator explains, they had been uncertain (ἀμφιβάλλω) about the current king's identity.[13]

It is therefore particularly important that, in the ekphrasis that opens the account of the siege of Syene, Hydaspes comes into his own as the agent, both grammatically (he, rather than his soldiers, is the subject of the verbs expressing speech, thought, and action) and in terms of the organization of the narrative. One result is to add the roles of 'military commander' and

---

[12] As noted by Bartsch 1989: 110. The central role in the *Aethiopica* of amphiboly and the resulting need for interpretation on the part of both characters and readers was first pointed out by Winkler 1982.

[13] Heliod., *Aeth.* 9.24.2: οἱ δὲ μιξέλληνά τινα τῶν φυλάκων ὅποι τὸ παρὸν ἄγοιεν ἠρώτων· ἐκείνου δὲ εἰπόντος ὡς βασιλεὺς Ὑδάσπης ἐπισκοπεῖ τοὺς αἰχμαλώτους 'θεοὶ σωτῆρες' ἀνεβόησαν ἅμα οἱ νέοι τοὔνομα τὸ Ὑδάσπου γνωρίσαντες, εἰς τὴν τότε ὥραν μὴ καὶ ἕτερός ἐστιν ὁ βασιλεύων ἀμφιβάλλοντες. 'They asked one of their guards, a half-Greek, where they were being taken now. When he replied that King Hydaspes was inspecting the prisoners of war, "The gods have saved us!" cried the young couple with one voice, recognizing the name Hydaspes as, up to that moment, they had been uncertain whether another ruler might be on the throne.'

'king' to those of 'father' and 'husband'. Each of these roles or functions brought with it a set of expectations of the attitudes and behaviours likely (*eikos*) to be displayed by those occupying them, and, at this point, these broad categories are all that the reader has at her disposal to fill out the almost empty vessel that is Hydaspes' name.[14] In this way, Heliodorus progressively builds up our idea of Hydaspes through an accumulation of different roles, prompting the reader to ask how their contradictions will be managed.[15]

As the last two books of the novel progress, different techniques are put in play to fill out this portrait, one of these being the account of Hydaspes' actions (*praxeis*) in Book 9, another being his speeches and choices in Book 10.[16] By presenting Hydaspes' siege-works at 9.3 though the device of the ekphrasis *tropou*, or vivid account of the way in which something is done or made, Heliodorus invites the reader to focus on the maker just as much as on the resulting creation. In the epideictic tradition familiar to Heliodorus and his contemporaries (whatever date we prefer for his work), such accounts of a ruler's military actions were a standard feature of encomia, and their presentation in the form of vivid descriptions (ekphrasis) had the added effect of making the audience into virtual witnesses of the events.[17] This meant that Julian faced a tricky challenge in his two accounts of Shapur's attempt to take Nisibis, in that Constantius' role was almost entirely defensive and reactive. His solution was to present the outcome as proof of Constantius' preparations, while his second account (*Or.* II) magnifies the importance of Constantius' defensive action by comparing it to that of the Achaean heroes defending their ships and their newly constructed wall against Hector's onslaught beginning in Book 12 of the *Iliad*.[18] We will

---

[14] Morales 2004: 67 makes a similar observation about the depiction of Leucippe in Achilles Tatius' novel.

[15] My allusion to these categories is inspired by the theory of declamation as set out by Hermogenes in his treatise on argumentation, *On Issues* 5–6 (29–30). Here, Hermogenes identifies as types of character suitable for declamation those designated by proper names (e.g. Pericles, Demosthenes); those whose names indicate a relationship (fathers, sons, etc.) and titles like 'general' or 'politician'. These characters carried with them a fixed set of characteristics making it possible to invent and to evaluate arguments about them. Many declamation themes were constructed around the conflicts between these different roles and the ethical problems posed. One example is the case of the leader who is told he must sacrifice his child to save his city from disaster (see, for example, Sopater *On the Division of Questions* 232).

[16] On the different modes of character portrayal used in the novels and their rhetorical counterparts, see de Temmerman 2010 and 2014: 33–41.

[17] See Men. Rhet. *On Epideictic* II 373.17–29; Webb 2009: 159.

[18] Julian *Or.* I.27b: 'The magnitude of your preparation revealed (ἀπέφηνεν) [the enemy's] expectations to be empty'.

return to this Homeric model after an analysis of the ekphrasis of Hydaspes' siege-works.

The works that Hydaspes is shown carrying out around the city of Syene are described in two phases. First, we are told how a circular outer wall is constructed around the city to form a type of moat around it. Then the Ethiopians join this channel to the Nile by creating a second, straight channel, down which the water rushes to fill the moat, transforming the city into an island. Where the panegyrist spelt out for his audience the conclusion to be drawn from the actions described, Heliodorus' narrator once again leaves the readers to draw any inferences about the Ethiopian king. The passage thus prompts the reader to make a transition from the perceptible phenomena described in its words to the causes of those phenomena, a mental operation that is comparable to that set in motion by the opening scene of the novel. In my analysis, I will deal with the two phases of Hydaspes' works separately, as each invites a rather different type of analysis: the first phase of the works can be explained as a vivid and practical illustration of Hydaspes' characteristics, a question that is of intense concern to the reader for the reasons outlined above; the second part, by contrast, opens up the passage to metanarrative and metafictional readings, and here the clues are as much in the language used by the narrator as in the entities (objects and actions) that exist on the level of the story.

16.2. Ways and Means

Our attention is directed to Hydaspes' action from the very first words of the account of the siege at 9.3.1: ἔπραττε δὴ οὖν <u>οὕτως</u> ('So he acted in this way').[19] The qualitative force of the adverb οὕτως is vitally important as it implies that the narrator is answering the reader's question not simply about 'what' was done (a question that could be answered in a brief statement) but 'how' Hydaspes responded to the problem posed by the Persian occupation of Syene. This detail identifies the account that follows as an ekphrasis of the *tropos*, describing how something was done or made. In these ekphraseis, objects are shown in the process of coming to be, and the actions of the

---

[19] Morgan translates 'This is what he did' which is closer to the Greek than Maillon's French translation which misses the emphasis on Hydaspes and his agency by rendering these words as 'Voici quels étaient ces travaux' ('The nature of these works was as follows'). My own translation misses the force of the imperfect which I have tried to render in the version below.

maker can be just as, if not more important than the form of the finished product; such an ekphrasis serves to make visible the gestures, decisions, and energies that are involved in the creation of a thing or situation and that remain encoded within it like the traces of a chisel on stone.

The first-century rhetorician Theon is the first to isolate this category of ekphrasis, and, significantly, the examples he cites are all connected to warfare and belong to narrative genres: the fabrication of the Shield of Achilles in *Iliad*, 18.468–617, Thucydides' accounts of the construction of walls around Plataea at 2.75–8 and of the construction of siege machines (4.100), as well as an account of a stratagem to fool the enemy used by the inhabitants of a besieged city in Ctesias' *Persian History* (Fragment 9b).[20] As John Morgan has noted, the siege of Plataea presents some similarities to Hydaspes' works, and details of terminology further encourage this identification: the term the Heliodoran narrator uses to refer to the works at 9.3.6 (*periteichismos*) is the same one used by Theon to define the construction of the walls at Plataea.[21]

The adverb οὕτως in Heliodorus' text and, above all, the details that follow show that the narrator is interested here in the construction of the siege-works as a process, a fact that is underlined by the use of the imperfect (ἔπραττε) in the introductory phrase with its sense of an action unfolding in time. The ekphrastic nature of our passage emerges more clearly when we compare it to the earlier accounts of the Ethiopian king's actions which are more akin to plain *diēgēsis* ('narrative').[22] The narrator thus invites us to visualize both the process of creation and its result and to pay attention along the way to what we are told, or to what we can deduce, concerning the thoughts and intentions of Hydaspes himself. This presentation also encourages the reader to imagine the form taken by the works as they are described

---

[20] Theon *Progymnasmata* 118. Text and English translation in Webb 2009: 197–9. Theon was probably active in the first century CE, though Heath 2002–3 argues for a fifth-century CE date on the basis of the existence of an Armenian translation of this date. This translation certainly shows that, whatever the date of composition, this version of the *Progymnasmata* was in use in late antiquity. Although Theon is the only author of *Progymnasmata* to mention the ekphrasis *tropou* explicitly, it is implicit in the subjects for ekphrasis proposed by all the authors of these manuals in that these are based on the parts of narration ('who', 'what', 'when', 'where', 'why', and 'how').

[21] Thucydides himself uses the slightly different form *periteichisis* at 2.77.2. On the similarities, see Morgan 1978: 18.

[22] The ruse which allowed him to take Philai at the beginning of Book 8, for example, is narrated very rapidly. For the contrast between an ekphrasis that explains how something was done and a *diēgēsis* that simply states what happened, see Nikolaos *Progymnasmata* 68–9; text and translation in Webb 2009: 202–5.

16.3. A Portrait of the King as a Military Leader

The beginning of the ekphrasis reads as follows:

ἔπραττε δὴ οὖν οὕτως· εἰς μοίρας <u>κατανέμει</u> τοῦ τείχους τὸν κύκλον καὶ <u>δεκάδα</u> ὀργυιῶν <u>δεκάδι</u> ἀνδρῶν <u>ἀποκληρώσας</u> εὖρός τε καὶ βάθος ὡς ὅτι πλεῖστον <u>ἀφορίσας</u> ὀρύττειν εἰς τάφρον <u>ἐκέλευσεν</u>.

He therefore undertook the following actions: he divided (lit. 'divides') the circle of the walls into sections and, allotting lengths of ten fathoms to groups of ten men, he ordered them to dig a ditch, defining their width and depth to be as great as possible. (9.3.1)

To the reader searching for clues about Charicleia's father's disposition, about 'how' he acts, Hydaspes begins to emerge here as a master of order, organization, and authority and as a careful calculator: in creating the circular wall around the city he divides the perimeter into regular sections of ten fathoms (c.60 feet), each of which is allocated to a group of ten men. The carefully ordered nature of the action is reflected both in the sentence structure and in the language with its repetition of the term δεκάς ('group of ten') in different cases. The generalized activity expressed by the verb πράττειν is thus subdivided into the actions of dividing (κατανέμειν), allotting (ἀποκληροῦν), defining or marking out (ἀφορίζειν) and commanding (κελεύειν), and the use of the 'historical period' with its participial clauses, introduced and rounded off by finite verbs, mirrors at the level of syntax the sense of predetermined structure in the actions referred to.

To these actions of Hydaspes correspond the three tasks carried out by different groups of men within each group:

οἱ δὲ ὤρυττον, ἄλλοι τὸν χοῦν ἐξεφόρουν, ἕτεροι εἰς ὀφρῦν πρὸς ὕψος ἐσώρευον, τῷ πολιορκουμένῳ τείχει ἕτερον ἀντεγείροντες.

Some were digging, others were carrying away the earth and yet others were piling it up into a high ridge, raising a second wall opposite the wall of the besieged city. (9.3.1)

It is here that the immediate aim of these actions, to encircle the city walls (though we still do not know exactly why), is first made explicit. The impression is of orderly collective activity, and the repetition of the verb ὀρύττειν, now in a finite form, underlines the way in which the order given verbally by Hydaspes just before is immediately put into action.

Next the account identifies Hydaspes' foresight (*pronoia*) as the reason why the Ethiopians encounter no opposition to their work: he has measured out the space and placed them at a sufficient distance from the city for them to be safely out of reach of any missiles fired from the walls. His thought process here is clearly expressed in the explanatory part of the sentence:

ὁ γὰρ Ὑδάσπης καὶ τούτου <u>προὐνόησε</u>, τὸ μεσεῦον τῶν δύο τειχῶν ὅσον βολῆς ἐκτὸς εἶναι τοὺς ἐργασομένους συμμετρησάμενος.

Hydaspes had thought of this in advance as well, having measured out the space between the two walls so that it was great enough for those who were going to carry out the work to be beyond the reach of missiles.

(9.3.2)

With this explanation of Hydaspes' thoughts and judgements we move to an embedded focalization that provides us with a brief glimpse of Hydaspes' assessment of his surroundings and his thought processes. This focalization also serves to underline the distinct hierarchy in operation on the Ethiopian side: the troops act, their king commands and protects them. No thoughts or individual actions are attributed to the soldiers, who remain an indistinct mass under the benevolent control of their king, a situation that contrasts with the active role of the Ethiopian people in the following book.[23] As the next sentence shows, this multitude works extraordinarily quickly and effectively. The narrator does not specify the length of time taken, saying simply that the wall 'was completed faster than it could be spoken of since there were a multitude of workers to hurry the work along for him' (τοῦτο καὶ λόγου θᾶττον ἤνυσεν ἅτε δὴ μυρίας αὐτῷ χειρὸς τὸ ἔργον ἐπισπευδούσης, 9.3.3).

So, Hydaspes' first named appearance reveals him as an organized and effective leader who plans, measures, and distributes. He is possessed of the foresight necessary to protect his troops and able, Odysseus-like, to make

---

[23] It is true that, as Morgan 2006: 57 points out, the Ethiopians are manipulated by Hydaspes' speech in Book 10; but the fact that he needs to resort to manipulation, rather than being able simply to issue a command, is significant in itself.

the best use of the resources at his disposal, in this case earth and water. Through the use of ekphrasis, the readers 'see' before their minds' eyes proof of his authority and of his concern for his people (just as Julian's audience witnessed the signs of Constantius' preparations), and this organization distinguishes him and the Ethiopian army. It may also serve to align him with the Athenians of Thucydides' narrative who construct a similar wall around the city of Nisaea (4.69.2), though the comparison serves to highlight the differences between the political organization of Hydaspes' kingdom and any kind of democracy.[24] Hydaspes is also shown to be in command of his environment. This is not just any environment, given that his strategy involves diverting the Nile itself and turning a city into an island. This portrait is traced almost entirely through the account of his actions and makes use of a mode of presentation that contrasts starkly to the manner in which the Persian army is presented later on in Book 9. Here the narrator employs a different type of ekphrasis *tropou* in order to focus entirely on the process of their arming and the appearance of the various weapons and body armour, turning the objectified Persians into an exotic spectacle.[25]

One further characteristic of Hydaspes that may be detectable here is his respect for *nomos* ('law', 'custom'). This emerges not through the account of his *actions* but indirectly through the narrator's choice of *words*, since, at the root of the verb κατανέμειν (to divide, distribute) used of his division of the circumference of the city into ten parts, is the term *nomos* ('law', 'custom'), also used at 9.1.4 of the Ethiopian practice of sacrificing the first prisoners. The verb is stressed both by its position at the beginning of the list of actions and by the use of the historic present. Hydaspes' troubled relationship with *nomos* becomes increasingly apparent as the narrative progresses. At the end of Book 9, for example, the captive Oroondates describes Hydaspes as ἐννομώτατον ('most respectful of law/custom', 9.27.2). If this can be put down to the Persian prisoner's need to create a flattering reflection of his captor, the same respect for *nomos* is in evidence throughout the action of Book 10 and is central to Hydaspes' dilemma.

---

[24] Roisman 1993: 17 characterizes this siege narrative as 'a familiar picture of Athenian busy activity and purposefulness' in contrast to the disorganization shown by the Peloponnesians. Thucydides, as well as Herodotus, thus appears to be present in the historian's stance analysed by Morgan 1982.
[25] 9.14–15. The ekphrasis of the Persians' armour is introduced with the term *tropos*. The process described in what follows is that of arming: the contrast between the impressive appearance of the Persians and the effective action of the Ethiopians continues in the battle narrative.

The ekphrasis *tropou* thus introduces the reader to one particular set of Hydaspes' qualities and characteristics—his own *tropoi* (10.10.3)—which, as Meriel Jones notes, make him a positive model for Theagenes: Hydaspes is a Hellenized Ethiopian, skilled in warfare and in stratagems.[26] Later in the siege narrative, when he decides to spare the inhabitants of Syene (9.9.2), he is also revealed as a compassionate man who has learned *andreia* and how to use it to the right degree. As the vehicle for conveying some of these qualities, the ekphrasis corresponds to common panegyric usage, and, if this were a panegyric, the interpretation could probably stop here.[27] However, the fact that this ekphrasis is found within a narrative context of unusual complexity means that the implications of Hydaspes' portrayal are at best ambiguous and even contradictory. His respect for *nomos*, in particular, serves to create the final dramatic tension, thanks to his initial claims to respect the Ethiopian *nomos* of sacrificing the first foreign prisoners.[28] An essential quality for a leader thus acquires, within the particular narrative context of the *Aethiopica*, an unambiguously negative role.

In context, then, the portrait of Hydaspes implicit in the ekphrasis is far from simple or univocal.[29] And the ambivalence of his respect for *nomos* is not the only ambiguity that emerges from the narrative content of the Syene episode. The plan to use the waters of the Nile to undermine the city walls is chosen by Hydaspes only after a first failed attempt to take the city (9.2.3). Angered by the fierce resistance from inside the city, he decides on this form of attack to ensure that not a single person escapes from it (9.2.3). By creating this impression of Hydaspes as a fierce and unforgiving warrior immediately before the account of the siege-works themselves, the narrator once again keeps the reader in a state of uncertainty as to the king's character and his treatment of his captives. The reader may no longer be in any doubt about the identity of the Ethiopian king but is still left guessing about his likely future actions.

Further questions emerge as the Syene episode unfolds and, far from destroying the city with its whole population as the narrator claims he initially intended to do, Hydaspes takes humanity and mercy to an extreme after its surrender, sparing the inhabitants and even allowing them to

---

[26] Jones 2012: 149–51.   [27] As I did at Webb 2009: 182.
[28] The terminology of law or custom (*nomos/nomimon*) is used throughout this episode. See for example 10.3.3; 10.7.6 and 7; 10.9.7. Further on in Book 9, the verb διανέμω is used of the carefully considered distribution of rewards to the troops (9.23.2).
[29] As Morgan 2006: 53 points out, this ambiguity continues in Book 10 with Hydaspes' use of a figured speech.

celebrate the festival of the Neiloa (9.9.2). In so doing he is, of course, displaying the qualities of *philanthrōpia* (9.5.4; 9.6.2) and of piety which were expected of a Roman leader.[30] Within the larger frame of the plot, however, this behaviour is quite simply and unambiguously inconsistent with Hydaspes' original aim of allowing no one to escape the city alive (9.2.3). The reader might want to see him as embodying the type of humane change of heart that made the Athenians, for example, go back on their decision to slaughter and enslave the population of Mytilene (Thucydides, 3.36–49), but the absence of any commentary by the narrator to explain this change of tactic and of heart leaves us in the dark as to the Ethiopian king's motivations. Most importantly, it contributes to the uncertainty as to which Hydaspes will decide the couple's fate (as well as leaving open the possibility that the narrator himself is being less than reliable). Will it be the vengeful soldier or the magnanimous leader of men, the strict respecter of *nomos* or the humane prince? The father or the king?[31] It may also induce us to wonder whether the inconsistency is attributable to the narrator or to his subject.

The uncertainty created here only grows as the siege goes on. Hydaspes' magnanimity turns out to have an unintended consequence: it creates the opportunity for Oroondates to escape from Syene while the inhabitants are occupied with the festivities (9.10.2–9.11.2). Here, the narrator dramatically undercuts the forethought (*pronoia*) that he had attributed to Hydaspes in the ekphrasis of the siege-works by explaining that the Ethiopians 'foreseeing nothing' (οὐδὲν προϊδομένους), had not mounted a guard and were 'sleeping without forethought' (ἀπρονοήτως καθεύδοντας) (9.10.2). The narrator does not draw our attention explicitly to these inconsistencies between Hydaspes' conduct here and at the beginning of the siege, leaving them instead for the reader to detect. This technique of veiled criticism is reminiscent of the criticism of Titus that McLaren has convincingly detected in Josephus' depiction of Titus' actions in the *Jewish War*.[32] Among the many incidents in that text that seem to point to the young commander's inexperience and lack of judgement, one in particular is reminiscent of Hydaspes' lapse: Titus' own respect for religious observance (in this case the Jewish Sabbath) allows a dangerous enemy to escape from a besieged city to

---

[30] See, for example, Men. Rhet. II, 374.27.
[31] Hydaspes' dilemma is presented in terms of a choice between these two roles at 10.17.2 in the Ethiopian people's response to Hydaspes' speech.
[32] McLaren 2005.

Jerusalem, where his actions prolong the war against the Romans with catastrophic consequences.[33]

In its own way, then, the account of the siege of Syene plays a vital role in the progressive construction of a complex and contradictory portrait of Hydaspes.[34] The effect is to create suspense and unease as the movement of the couple towards Ethiopia is delayed and the reader is left to wonder which Hydaspes will decide the couple's fate. The multiplicity of hypotexts mobilized by Heliodorus in this episode adds to the ambiguity. In addition to the general Herodotean flavour of the book,[35] there are also echoes of Thucydides: in particular, Hydaspes is associated with Greek and Athenian collaboration and organization (via the echoes of the Athenian blockade of Nisaea and of the Lacedaemonian blockade of Plataea, cited by Theon as an example of the ekphrasis *tropou*). What is more, the Ethiopian ruler is, as Elmer notes, aligned both with the fourth-century CE Parthians at Nisibis and with the Persians of Herodotus' *History*.[36] In addition to their diverging ethical associations, all these models belong to very different political systems, leaving open the further question of the type of polity that Theagenes and Chariclea will find in Ethiopia, where their fate will be decided.

The 'manner in which' the siege-works are constructed and in which the wider siege is conducted thus contributes to building up this complex portrait of a new but long-awaited character. The particular use made of the device of the ekphrasis *tropou* has another function, though: it leads to the perception of a *form* that takes shape within the fictional world of the novel.[37] Various aspects of the presentation contribute to this perception. First of all, the narrator's adoption of a distant perspective (equivalent to the panoramic 'eagle's gaze' with which the novel opens)[38] enables a synoptic view of the construction, as if it were seen from a great height. In this sense, the reader is allowed a privileged viewpoint that no human spectator could

---

[33] Jos. *BJ* 4.97–104.
[34] The switch of focalization at 9.3.6, where the narrator recounts the reactions within the city at the sight of Hydaspes' works, followed by their attempt to counter their effect by building a tunnel to divert the water away from the city, provides yet another perspective on him as aggressor to an innocent population caught up in his war with the Persians.
[35] See Morgan 1982, esp. 230 on 9.8.2.
[36] Elmer 2008: 426–7. See also Ross 2015 on Hydaspes' characterization.
[37] The care taken by the narrator of the *Aethiopica* to describe the exact size and shape of the wall built around the city contrasts with the brevity of Julian's account of the Parthian earthworks around Nisibis, and this suggests that the form of the resulting work may be significant.
[38] See Telò 2011.

achieve.[39] The careful ekphrastic account of the making of this shape in the earth and of its effect on the flow of water, diverting the river to surround the city, encourages the reader to imagine it, to form a mental image, a *phantasia*, of the work and its result. Throughout, the reader is invited to maintain a twofold imaginative effort, picturing both the process of construction and its result. The type of cognition demanded here is comparable to that required of readers of ancient technical manuals. As Courtney Roby has shown, authors of manuals describing military machines frequently urge their readers to 'imagine' the process of their construction, as if author and reader occupied a shared space.[40] Heliodorus is likewise placing before the eyes of his readers an entity that is simultaneously action and object, static and eternally fixed in the process of its coming to be.

The effects are multiple: the individual workers are eclipsed as they melt into the mass; conversely, the reader gains access, gradually, to the idea in the mind of Hydaspes. In the absence of any description of the landscape here, the works are the only feature made visible to the reader, with the result that, at this point in the novel, Hydaspes creates the narrative space within which he functions.

16.4. Figures in the Earth

The second half of the ekphrasis describes the creation of the most important part of Hydaspes' works at Syene in terms of their function: the straight channel dug between the circular ditch and the Nile, allowing the water to pour in and surround the city. Here, it is worth comparing Julian's account of the works at Nisibis which, in very general terms, mentions a circular system of dykes allowing the waters of the Mygdonius to flood the land around the city, turning it into an 'ocean'.[41] In Heliodorus' version, by contrast, the narrator draws attention to the creation of the straight channel between the circular ditch and the Nile, explaining that:

ἑτέρου τοιοῦδε ἤρχετο. τοῦ κύκλου μέρος, πλάτος ὅσον ἡμίπλεθρον, ἰσόπεδόν τε καὶ ἄχωστον διαλιπών, κατὰ τὴν ἀπολήγουσαν ἑκατέρωθεν ἄκραν σκέλος

---

[39] On the differences between the perspective of the readers and that of the characters, see Grethlein 2019.
[40] Roby 2016: 209–43 (esp. 213).   [41] Julian *Or*. 1, 27b.

ἐκ χώματος ἐπιζευγνὺς ἐπὶ τὸν Νεῖλον εἰς μῆκος ἦγεν, ἀπὸ τῶν ταπεινοτέρων ἀεὶ πρὸς τὰ ὄρθια καὶ μετέωρα σκέλος ἑκάτερον προβιβάζων.

He commenced a second part of the work which was of the following type. Having left a section of his encirclement, about half a *plethron* wide, flat and without any mounds of earth, from each of the two end points of his earthworks he extended a leg (*skelos*) linking these earthworks to the Nile, making each leg advance (*probibazōn*) progressively from the lower ground to the higher. (9.3.3)

In this way, the ditch surrounding the city is joined to the Nile, and the river's bank is breached to allow the water through. But the narrator delays mention of the point at which the water rushes through and spins out his account by telling us that the two long mounds resembled the Long Walls at Athens (9.3.4) before specifying the distance between them (a half *plethron*, or 50 feet, throughout) and their length (equal to the distance between the city and river). Only after providing these two pieces of information (which appear superfluous at first sight, except that the strict parallelism of the lines is further proof of Hydaspes' organization) does the narrator arrive at the climactic moment at which Hydaspes breaches the bank of the river and 'directs the water in':

ἐπεὶ δὲ συνῆψε τὸ χῶμα ταῖς ὄχθαις, ἐνταῦθα στόμιον τῷ ποταμῷ διατεμὼν εἰς τὸν ἀπὸ τῶν σκελῶν ὁλκὸν τὴν ἀπορροὴν <u>εἰσωχέτευσεν</u>.

When he had joined the mound to the banks, cutting an opening for the river at that point he directed the flow into the channel created by the sides.

(9.3.4)

As in the first part of the ekphrasis, the reader is invited to visualize the same phenomenon in two ways. On the one hand, we are to conceive an image of the completed form of the single channel running around the city and down to the Nile. And then there is the kinetic quality of the account of its creation, in which Hydaspes, through the manual labour of his men, creates the encirclement and then 'extends' the raised sides (or 'legs', σκελῶν, in the Greek), encouraging the reader to imagine the parallel lines in the process of stretching out to the riverbank until they meet it.

The account of the works around Syene is therefore characterized by the insistence on the straight channel joining the circle to the Nile, a channel formed by the two raised 'legs' between which the water runs. The comparison to the classical model of the Long Walls at Athens (9.3.4), in a formulation that ascribes the comparison to an unidentified observer (τις) endowed with the classical learning that marks the narrator and his ideal narratee, helps to underline the importance of this channel and its sides.

From this point, hydraulic force takes over, thanks to the downwards gradient from the river to the ditch around the city (another sign of Hydaspes' ingenuity and foresight),[42] and the subject of the verbs changes to become the water itself, rather than Hydaspes:

οἷα δὲ ἐξ ὑπερδεξίων πρὸς χθαμαλώτερον καὶ ἐξ ἀπείρου τῆς κατὰ τὸν Νεῖλον εὐρύτητος στενῷ πορθμῷ τὸ ὕδωρ ἐμπῖπτον καὶ ταῖς χειροποιήτοις ὄχθαις θλιβόμενον πολύν τινα καὶ ἄφραστον κατὰ μὲν τὸ στόμιον φλοῖσβον κατὰ δὲ τὸν ὁλκὸν ἐξάκουστον καὶ τοῖς πορρωτάτω πάταγον ἀπετέλει.

As [it was flowing] from a higher level to a lower and from the infinite breadth of the Nile, the water rushing into the narrow channel and pressed between the banks made by human hand resulted in a great and indescribable (*aphrastos*) sonorousness (*phloisbos*) at the entrance and a rumbling (*patagos*) along the channel that was audible from far away. (9.3.5)

In describing the entrance of the water into the channel formed by these 'legs', the narrator insists on the fabricated nature of this construction, telling us at 9.3.5 that the water was 'pressed between the banks made by human hand'. At the point where attention is drawn to the creative effort behind the construction, the language itself becomes noticeably poetic, as the description declares its own inadequacy to the task through the use of the poetic adjective *aphrastos* ('unutterable', 'indescribable'). And, as well as vision and the sense of movement in space, hearing is also involved in the reception of this part of the ekphrasis through the onomatopoeic evocation of the rushing water, which creates the sounds designated by the terms *phloisbos* and *patagos*. In its linguistic virtuosity, this sentence also draws attention to the productive tension that exists throughout the ekphrasis between the form that the reader's reconstructive imagination creates and the language used by the narrator to describe the shaping of that form.

The earthworks, and the straight channel in particular, are thus qualified as artificial creations, poised, like the gardens in other Greek novels, between art and nature.[43] The verbal account is capable, for the reader armed with the relevant knowledge, of alluding to other texts and anchoring

---

[42] Morgan 1989c: 538 points out that '[t]he river would be embanked to control the summer flood'.
[43] See Zeitlin 2013.

Hydaspes' works into a network of classical monuments (the Long Walls to name just one). Their effect in the world of the novel is to channel a force of nature in such a way as to direct its destructive power. The potential disruption of the water is expressed not only in the statements about the noise and its perception by distant listeners (τοῖς πορρωτάτω) but in the hyperbaton separating *phloisbos* and *patagos* from their adjectives (underlined in the Greek text above). In this way, Heliodorus the author draws the reader's attention to his verbal material as he makes the most direct attempt to simulate the sense of presence that is fundamental to ekphrasis of all types. The text thus draws attention to what I have called elsewhere the 'poetics of ekphrasis', namely the play between the creation of a sense of presence and the recognition of the impossibility of this enterprise that is ignored by pragmatic rhetoricians but richly explored in other genres.[44] If the manner in which it is presented, its own *tropos*, can be qualified as metaliterary, the form of Hydaspes' earthwork, which the reader is invited to visualize, can bear a similar interpretation that sees them as proleptic (in a suitably ambiguously manner) and metafictional.

16.5. Hydaspes' Works as a Metaliterary Artefact

The ekphrasis of Hydaspes' works thus describes, or defines, the resulting object in two complementary ways. In describing the progress of the works, the narrator speaks in terms of the raised barrier of earth built up by the Ethiopians to guide the water from river to city walls. This barrier takes the form of a single line running from the river around the city and back to the river, creating the parallel lines between city and river stressed in the account. I would like to suggest that the shape moulded in relief out of the landscape by Hydaspes and his men can be read as a figure for Charicleia's journey—out from Ethiopia, around and back to her point of origin. So it could be said that Hydaspes is—at the time and the place of his reunion with his daughter—tracing an image of her journey.[45] Here, the use of the ekphrasis *tropou* as a technique takes on a further significance in that a description of the completed works as a static feature of the landscape

---

[44] Webb 2009: 167. See also Whitmarsh 2011: 171–6.
[45] Winkler 1982: 152 suggests that the diversion of the river and its return (*nostos*) to its bed at (9.8.4) figures Charicleia's return. See Lowe 2000: 238 for a very useful chart of the protagonists' journeys.

would be less suggestive of a journey through space than is the narrative presentation with its verbs of movement. A further reading is possible, given the narrator's emphasis on the twin 'legs' advancing together towards the river: these two lines may figure the protagonists in their parallel journey. Neither of these options excludes the other: the two lines can simultaneously represent Charicleia's journey out and back and also her return, accompanied by Theagenes. Such a double reading leaves open two possible endings (Charicleia completes her circular journey alone, or with Theagenes) that both remain in play until the very last lines of the novel.

This is not all. The mingling of earth and water and the digging of channels that are part of the creation of the siege-works also have erotic implications, as is made clear a little later in the account of the Neiloa festival, when the narrator reveals that, to the initiated, the Nile is Osiris and the land is Isis. Hydaspes' works thus bring about not just a miniature instance of the Nile flood (to which Julian had compared the results of Shapur's works at Nisibis) but an encircling of the female by the male, a prefiguring of the union of Charicleia and Theagenes.[46] It seems likely, too, that there is an erotic subtext to the last phase of Hydaspes' works as he lets the waters of the Nile rush into a narrow opening between the 'legs' he has built of the female earth, an action expressed through the use of the verb εἰσωχετεύειν ('to let in by creating a channel'). Moreover, the Greek term used for the opening he makes (στόμιον) is also used of female genitalia.[47] In further support of this reading we can note that the related noun ὀχετηγός ('ditch-digger', 'irrigator') frequently occurs in an erotic context in Nonnus' *Dionysiaca*.[48] Here, the implications of Hydaspes' prefiguration of his own daughter's loss of virginity in a shape that reduces her body to legs and genitalia are disturbing and may point to an unspoken possibility in the plot, that the captor might rape his unknown captive. The various possibilities for the development of the plot that are signalled have already been envisaged by the reader, and the ekphrasis, as we have seen, leaves them open. The possibility of the rape of Charicleia has also been present throughout, but what is striking about its figuration here is that reader becomes complicit in this

[46] Heliod. *Aeth.* 9.9.4. The presence of this divine romance is signalled by Grethlein 2016: 329.
[47] See Sor. *Gyn.* 1.9–10. Whitmarsh 2010: 335 proposes a similar reading of the narrow corridor that leads to Leucippe's bedroom at Achilles Tatius, *Leucippe and Clitophon*, 2.19.
[48] Nonn. *Dion.* 7.203, 15.240 (the eye creates the channel for desire);19.261 (Eros as a metaphorical ditch-digger), 42.42 (wonder creates a channel for desire); 42. 216 and 43.34 (Bacchus and Ares respectively as creators of channels for the Erotes). At Pl. *Phdr.* 251e, the verb ἐποχετεύομαι is used in the context of a discussion of love.

act, and the imaginative consequences of the eroticized description of her by Calasiris (another father figure) at 3.4 are made explicit.

Now that we have set out on this metaliterary path, there is a further comparison to be made between our passage and the ekphrasis of the belt Charicleia wore around her breasts which was the focal point of Calasiris' description of her appearance at Delphi. Although the making of the belt, unlike the creation of the siege-works, has taken place at some moment before the start of the novel, the object itself is described as the result of the artist's actions. Both artefacts are circular and both are *hapaxes*: the creator of the belt never made another (3.4.2), and Hydaspes' works are a contingent response to a particular set of circumstances and could never be exactly repeated. That the belt has a metaliterary function as a figure for the structure of the novel has been convincingly argued by John Morgan.[49] In particular, Morgan notes the similarity between the vocabulary used by Calasiris to describe the intertwining of the serpents on the artefact and the terms used by the Byzantine critic, Michael Psellos, to convey the structural complexity of the first half of the novel.[50]

There is one aspect of the belt, however, that is particularly puzzling and that may perhaps be illuminated by comparison with Hydaspes' siege-works (strange as this comparison may seem). This is the position of the serpents' heads: whereas Psellos likens the novel's structure to a coiled up serpent which hides its head (i.e. the beginning of the story) in its coils, the account of the belt speaks of the heads of the two serpents emerging from the intertwined bodies and then hanging down on each side of her 'like a residue', 'as if they were superfluous' (ὡς περίττωμα) or, in Morgan's translation, 'as if they formed no part of the clasp'.[51] If we think purely in terms of objects and functions in the real world outside the text, a belt could hardly be more different from Hydaspes' earthworks. If we think, though, in terms of the structures and forms evoked—leaving aside material, function, and size—there are striking similarities: both involve a circular element (the wall around Syene, the intertwined bodies of the serpents) and two equal lines (the heads of the serpents, the two 'legs' of earth running back to the river).[52] In

---

[49] Morgan 2013.
[50] Psellos, *Comparison of Achilles Tatius and Heliodorus* in Dyck 1986: 93. See pp. 3–4.
[51] Hld. 3.4.3: δυοῖν γὰρ δρακόντοιν τὰ μὲν οὐραῖα κατὰ τῶν μεταφρένων ἐδέσμευε τοὺς δὲ αὐχένας ὑπὸ τοὺς μαζοὺς παραμείψας καὶ εἰς βρόχον σκολιὸν διαπλέξας καὶ τὰς κεφαλὰς διολισθῆσαι τοῦ βρόχου συγχωρήσας, ὡς περίττωμα τοῦ δεσμοῦ κατὰ πλευρὰν ἑκατέραν ἀπῃώρησεν.
[52] If this suggestion is correct, the personification of the earthworks implicit in their having 'legs' helps to strengthen the analogy with the snaky belt.

the case of the belt in Book 3, these lines are left hanging, appropriately enough at a point in the novel at which the author wants to keep his readers guessing about the narrative and geographical path to be taken by the two members of the central couple. If this reading of the heads as an allusion to the future story of the couple is correct, the narrator may have been teasing us in the earlier passage with his characterization of them as 'as if superfluous': the piece of information we most want to know (and simultaneously do not want to know, in order to spin out our pleasure) is declared to be of no interest. I would like to suggest that Hydaspes' earthworks are a counterpart whose difference reflects the different structure of the narrative at this point: where the account of the belt left the two 'loose' ends wandering, the verbal account of the raised mound around Syene has its 'ends' or rather 'legs' (*skelē*) running in a straight line directly to their *telos*.[53]

16.6. Hydaspes as Author and Creator

The form of Hydaspes' works may therefore simultaneously represent the journeys that are the basis of the story and the specific organization of their telling in the *Aethiopica*, characterized by a first, circling, half and then a (relatively) straight movement towards the end. By dividing the circuit of the walls into sections and 'allotting lengths of ten fathoms to groups of ten men' (9.3.1), Hydaspes echoes, and foretells, the structure of the ten-book novel in which he features.[54] By leaving one section open, he enacts the lack of completion and closure at this stage.[55] It is probably no accident that the term used to designate these sections, μοῖρα, placed in an emphatic position at the beginning of its clause, can be used to designate both the events that are destined to take place in accordance with fate (or the plot) and the narrative organization of a story.[56] Its use at the very beginning of the account of the siege-works may signal that Hydaspes' actions are, eventually and unbeknownst to any of the participants, to bring about the fulfilment of the

---

[53] See Lowe 2000: 23 on the 'mental models' of plots built up by readers. The strong correlation between movement through space and the passage of time in the Greek novels in general and in the *Aethiopica* in particular suggests that these models may well take the form of a diagrammatic map of the protagonists' movements.

[54] Dionysophanes' garden in Longus *Daphnis and Chloe* 4.2 is four *plethra* wide, corresponding to the four books of the novel (as noted by Zeitlin 1990: 451).

[55] On circularity and closure, see Grethlein 2016: 318.

[56] e.g. at Hom. *Od.* 4.266, where Menelaus comments on the story just told by Helen.

couple's *moira*. Hydaspes will appear, moreover, as author and as creator of figures in Book 10, as Morgan has shown in his analysis of the 'figured' speech which appears to present the arguments for sacrificing his newfound daughter while in fact aiming to achieve the opposite result.[57]

As well as bearing erotic associations, the vocabulary and images of channelling and irrigating that are so prominent in the siege-works also carry a rich set of poetic and metapoetic implications. The earliest appearance of the noun ὀχετηγός ('ditch-digger', 'irrigator') is in the struggle between Achilles and the river Scamander at *Iliad* 21.257, where the effect of the river breaking out of its banks to pursue Achilles is compared to the work of a ditch-digger.[58] This simile was well known in antiquity and was cited as an example of *enargeia* by Demetrius *On Style* 209.[59] Although Heliodorus uses the compound verb εἰσοχετεύειν, rather than the noun, when describing the flood of water being directed into the channel, a Homeric hypotext is strongly indicated at this point through the choice of the poetic word φλοῖσβος to express onomatopoeically the noise made.[60] This term is extremely rare in prose at any period and must have made the classically learned reader think of the Homeric formula πολυφλοίσβοιο θαλάσσης ('the resounding sea'), found six times in the *Iliad* and twice in the *Odyssey*. Most importantly, the channel and its creator had strong metaliterary implications, belonging as they did to a network of images for literary and rhetorical creation based on rivers and flows of water.[61] Dionysius of Halicarnassus, for example, uses the verb μετοχετεύω of the process of channelling many sources of inspiration into the author's soul for use and adaptation.[62] So, as well as figuring the movements of the hero and heroine, Hydaspes' works replay the process by which the author, Heliodorus,

---

[57] Morgan 2006. Hydaspes' figured speech is a rare example of a successful use of this risky strategy. Agamemnon's disastrous attempt to manipulate the troops at Hom. *Il.* 2.110–41 was a textbook example in antiquity; Nicias' second speech on the Sicilian expedition in which he tried to dissuade the Athenians from launching the expedition by exaggerating the resources needed (Thuc. 6.2.20–4) similarly had the reverse effect to the one intended.

[58] Achilles' battle against the river, moreover, was another *adunaton* that raised questions about the limits of poetic representation in ancient critical discourse. This episode forms the background to the conflict between Hephaestus and Scamander represented in the first of the Elder Philostratus' *Imagines*, and the questions relating to its plausibility are raised in Philostratus' *Heroicus*. See Webb 2015.

[59] The simile and its appropriateness were a subject of debate in antiquity. See Prioux 2016.

[60] See above. Dion. Thrax in *Grammatici graeci* Uhlig (part 1, vol. 1, p. 42, l. 4) identifies this term as onomatopoeic.

[61] See Worman 2015: 271–93. [62] *De imit.* fr. 31.1.1.

channelled his many heterogenous textual sources into the single work of fiction that is the *Aethiopica*.[63]

The account of Hydaspes' works is therefore far from being a simple imitation of a passage of panegyric or an attempt to confer a historiographical flavour on this part of the *Aethiopica*. Rather, it fulfils a multiplicity of functions on different levels of the text. In addition to its role in the plot it contains further levels of literary allusion and, most importantly, of metaliterary commentary that can be detected if we follow Hydaspes' lead and dig into the textual earth. There is, however, one further level that remains to be explored and that is the metafictional.

In shaping the landscape around him, Hydaspes can be seen as an unwitting figurer of the plot. But it is not just the form of his earthworks that can bear a metaliterary reading: the matter is also important. His use of earth and water may have corresponded to the actual tactics used in warfare, as Heliodorus and his readers would have been aware, but the mixing of the two aligns them with a familiar trope of the Greek novels in which liminal spaces combining the two elements play a significant role and have been convincingly identified as metafictional.[64] At Syene, the terrain where earth and water mix is the result not of geography, as at the Nile Delta, but is of Hydaspes' creation, and the immediate result of this mingling of the elements (9.4.2) will be to break down the boundaries between what is possible and impossible in normal circumstances. The 'most extraordinary spectacle' (θεαμάτων τὸ καινότατον) of ships sailing between walls, a sailor sailing over land and a ship sailing over fields (9.5.5) are the equivalent in a battle narrative of Horace's *adunata*: dolphins in the woods and boars on the waves (*Ars Poetica*, 30).[65] Hydaspes' agency, foregrounded by the form of the ekphrasis *tropou*, aligns him with the creator of fictions, the author, as suggested in relation to the story of Charicleia's birth by Morgan.[66] In the specific narrative context of the *Aethiopica*, Hydaspes' actions are thus like his engendering of a white-skinned daughter in that they take the reader into a

---

[63] See on this point Elmer 2008.

[64] In Achilles Tatius' novel (4.11–14), as at the beginning of the *Aethiopica*, it is the hero and heroine who find themselves between land and sea. There too, the flooding results from the destruction of dykes, this time as part of a defensive strategy by the Boukoloi. Ni Mheallaigh 2014: 188 suggests that the confused boundaries between land and sea in the description of Mytilene at Longus *Daphnis and Chloe* 1.1, for example, represent the confusion between reality and fiction. See also the remarks of Guez 2005.

[65] The Hymn to the Nile published by Cribiore 1995 from a papyrus of the late third or early fourth century also associates the river with *adunata*.

[66] Morgan 2013.

world in which the regular rules of plausibility no longer apply, as emerges clearly in the final scenes of the novel.[67]

The strong Homeric tinge to the vocabulary of the last part of the ekphrasis points to a further connection. Another wall created near to the edge of a body of water at a time of war and destroyed by the action of water shortly afterwards was the Achaean wall, constructed at *Iliad* 7.436–41 and compared to the walls of Nisibis by Julian in his second panegyric (*Or.* II 67a–68c). As the Achaeans pour all their effort into its construction, Zeus and Poseidon plan its destruction (Hom. *Il.* 7.459–63), and the end of their speech coincides with the poet's announcement of the completion of the Achaeans' work whose ultimate destruction is thus inscribed in its beginning.[68] And it is in their ends that the similarities between Hydaspes' earthworks and the Achaean wall are greatest. The Achaean wall is to be washed away after the end of the war by the action of water. Hydaspes' mounds of earth are washed away during the siege itself by the force of the water that builds up between them, reducing his creation to a formless sea of mud.[69] At the level of the story, this accident allows events to unfold, as Oroondates escapes to fight another day, and to delay the moment of decision for Hydaspes and the couple. At another level, Hydaspes' vanished mounds can be read as metafictional, as has been proposed for the Achaean wall by James Porter (2011) on the basis of the ancient reception of the Iliadic passage. The most intriguing of these commentators saw in the fact that the walls are said in *Iliad* 7 to be built only to be destroyed the ultimate illustration of the creative power of poetry. The comment attributed to Aristotle himself by Strabo at 13.1.36 occurs in a discussion of the situation of the site of Troy: Strabo speculates that the wall may simply never have existed, quoting Aristotle's suggestion that 'the poet who created/moulded [the wall] made it disappear' (ὁ δὲ πλάσας ποιητὴς ἠφάνισεν, ὡς Ἀριστοτέλης φησίν).[70]

---

[67] A very similar move is made at the beginning of Apuleius' *Metamorphoses*. See Webb 2017.

[68] It seems quite possible that the comparison between Hydaspes' own construction works and the length of the time it would take to tell of it in speech at *Aeth.* 9.3.3 may be an allusion to this coincidence between the time of the action or story and the time of the narration in the Iliadic account. The Achaeans build their wall in the time it takes for gods to speak about its destruction: Hydaspes' builds his faster than it takes to narrate (not an empty *topos*, but a comment on the relationship between these different categories of time and the power of narrative to impose its own temporality).

[69] The last of the possible explanations offered by the narrator at 9.8.2 is divine intervention, as in the *Iliad*. Another is an oversight on the part of some workmen who thus partially re-emerge from obscurity to bring about the end of Hydaspes' creation.

[70] The scholia contain similar readings of the passage. See, for example, the T scholia to *Iliad* 7.443–64c and bT scholia to *Il.* 7.445.

The wall is thus emblematic of the poet's ability to create entities out of thin air and to abolish them at will. In Aristotle and in the scholia, the verb πλάττειν ('to mould') is used in its common metaphorical sense of 'creating a fiction' from which derives the term *plasma*, the closest Greek term to 'fiction'.[71] Hydaspes' moulding of his walls out of the earth around Syene (rather than building them with blocks) is, in itself, an act of modelling that concretizes the metaphor for fictional creation. If Hydaspes is a figure for the author, however, he is an imperfect analogy for Heliodorus. As we have already seen, he is excluded from the classical references shared by narrator and reader, and from the knowledge of his own prisoners' identity. Above all, he is overwhelmed by the magnitude of his creation as it collapses in upon itself.

16.7. Conclusion

In the rapid creation and equally rapid destruction of Hydaspes' walls, Heliodorus lays bare his narrative strategy at this point in the novel: the creation of a series of devices to delay the climax of the story, devices that can be disposed of as soon as they have served their purpose. Far more importantly, he points to the nature of his enterprise, the creation not just of a hybrid work, artfully channelling a variety of textual rivers, but a hybrid work of fiction that draws the reader in, evoking feelings of fear, hope, and perplexity for entities that occupy the muddy middle ground between being and not being.

The fact that this point is explored in an ekphrastic passage is all the more powerful, in that such writing, as we have seen, aims precisely to draw the reader in, to make them feel as if they share the space with the characters and can see and feel their actions. By presenting Hydaspes' construction through the device of ekphrasis, Heliodorus has made us co-creators of the imaginary figure in the earth. He has also, through the process of our reading the *Aethiopica* up to the beginning of Book 9, shaped us and made us alert to the potential significance of forms, particularly when they are signalled with such clarity as this one is.[72] Fittingly for an ekphrasis *tropou*,

---

[71] See Morgan 1993.
[72] Grethlein 2019: 146–7 emphasizes the coexistence of experience and reflection in Heliodorus' text.

it is more the *processes* of reading, interpreting, and composing that are figured by Hydaspes' works. In encoding such a rich and multi-levelled commentary within what appears at first sight to be a straightforward imitation of panegyrical or historiographical prose, Heliodorus displays in action the many textual sources that run together in his novel as well as the type of reading it elicits.

17
Sphragis 1
To Infinity and Beyond (10.41.4)

Tim Whitmarsh

τοιόνδε πέρας ἔσχε τὸ σύνταγμα τῶν περὶ Θεαγένην καὶ Χαρίκλειαν Αἰθιοπικῶν· ὃ συνέταξεν ἀνὴρ Φοῖνιξ Ἐμισηνός, τῶν ἀφ' Ἡλίου γένος, Θεοδοσίου παῖς Ἡλιόδωρος.

Such an ending had the composition *The Ethiopian Events Concerning Theagenes and Charicleia*, composed by a Phoenician man from Emesa, one of those descended from Helios, the son of Theodosius: Heliodorus.

(Hld. 10.41.4)

The *Aethiopica* closes with a distinctive statement of authorial identity. Scholars have referred to this as Heliodorus' *sphragis* or 'seal', a term conventionally applied by classicists to any kind of authorial self-identification that is included within the text proper.[1] Whether it does, in fact, lie 'within the text' is, however, as we shall see the central issue it raises. Its relationship to the preceding narrative is studiedly ambiguous. These are the final two sentences in the text; but they also apparently position themselves beyond the 'ending' (πέρας) of the romance. Or should we be taking the deictic 'such' (τοιόνδε) to include the *sphragis* itself (in effect 'here ends…')?

This 'liminality' (as Loreto Núñez puts it)[2] reflects the generally ambiguous position of what Gérard Genette calls the 'paratext', namely the assemblage of textual material (title, authorial identification, publishing information, blurb) that mediates between the literary work itself and its material role as a social object:

---

[1] Kranz 1961. Further discussion at e.g. Ford 1985; Cerri 1991; Pratt 1995.
[2] Núñez 2014.

Tim Whitmarsh, *Sphragis 1: To Infinity and Beyond (10.41.4)* In: *Reading Heliodorus'* Aethiopica. Edited by: Ian Repath and Tim Whitmarsh, Oxford University Press. © Oxford University Press 2022.
DOI: 10.1093/oso/9780198792543.003.0017

'Para' is a double antithetical prefix signifying at once proximity and distance, similarity and difference, interiority and exteriority... something simultaneously this side of a boundary line, threshold, or margin, and also beyond it, equivalent in status and also secondary or subsidiary, submissive, as of guest to host, slave to master. A thing in 'para,' moreover, is not only simultaneously on both sides of the boundary line between inside and outside. It is also the boundary itself, the screen which is a permeable membrane connecting inside and outside.[3]

For Genette, the 'paratext' is liminal for the specific reason that it is composed equally of the 'peritext' (everything contained within the covers of a book) and the 'epitext' (everything on the outside, on the front and back covers). Ancient papyri did not have 'covers' in the same way, and even codices (when they were adopted) had much less paratextual appurtenance than their modern successors.[4] Nevertheless, it is clear that some of the information contained in Heliodorus' *sphragis*—the author's name and the title[5]—is of the kind that might also be displayed on the outside of an ancient book, for example on a tag (*titulus*, σίλλυβος).[6] The information might, however, equally well be found in a colophon, a statement of authorship and title at the conclusion of a text or an individual book of that text, such as *P.Colon.inv.* 3328 offers for 'Lollianus' *Phoinikika*' (A2 recto 22–3). It is thus open to question not only whether the *sphragis* is part of the *Aethiopica*, but also whether it was composed by Heliodorus at all (especially given the identification of the author in the third person).[7] Is the *sphragis*, ultimately, just the ancient equivalent of a Library of Congress record, and nothing to do with the text itself?

This seems unlikely, for reasons that we shall come to. But we should stress that even if it is not Heliodorean, it is still doing a lot of work on the author's behalf. An author and a title were not just practical devices for the purposes of archiving: they were crucial components of any literary text. As Alexander Beecroft has recently argued, it is far from self-evident that a given society will develop a concept of authorship, but ancient Greece (like

[3] Genette 1997: 1 n. 2.
[4] The sole fragment of the *Aethiopica* that survives is, as it happens, from a sixth- or seventh-century codex (*P.Amherst* 160). This is not, however, evidence that Heliodorus wrote with codex transmission in mind.
[5] The full title is τὰ περὶ Θεαγένην καὶ Χαρίκλειαν Αἰθιοπικά, a form that probably alludes to Xenophon of Ephesus' τὰ περὶ Ἁβροκόμου καὶ Ἀνθίας Ἐφεσιακά. In general on titling conventions, see Whitmarsh 2005b.
[6] Cf. *P.Oxy.* 301: 'Sophron's *Mimes about Women*'.   [7] Hilton 2012: 197.

ancient China) created a strong link between the privileged literary work and its author.[8] Authorship is required primarily in a complex, widescale literary culture in which it is impossible for readers or listeners to recover any original performative scenario. For texts to become 'classics'—by travelling beyond their original place of composition, and by long outliving their authors—the discursive construct of the author is a crucial mediator, a monumentalized trace of the original act of creation.

Heliodorus' *sphragis* offers more than simply identification of the author and a claim to ownership of the work:[9] it also gives us what Beecroft calls a 'scene of authorship',[10] a mini-biography that traces the author's journey from birth (Θεοδοσίου παῖς) to the chronologically culminating event, the author's composing (συνέταξεν) of this composition (τὸ σύνταγμα). The authorial scene at once dramatizes the act of writing of the book, turning it into an event worthy of historical record, and presses its claim for international significance. This is the kind of text that will voyage far beyond the boundaries of Emesa, one for which this trace of the compositional process substitutes for any face-to-face performance within a community.

The *sphragis* also, as has been noted,[11] positions the *Aethiopica* within the lineage of Greek novels. Chariton's *Callirhoe*, in particular, begins with an authorial self-identification, including by hometown and profession ('I, Chariton of Aphrodisias, a secretary to the orator Athenagoras, shall narrate a love story that happened in Syracuse', 1.1.1), and closes with a short *sphragis* 'Such is what I wrote (τοσάδε...συνέγραψα) concerning Callirhoe', 8.8.16). That closing sentence seems to be deliberately echoed in Heliodorus' τοιόνδε...συνέταξεν. Longus' and Achilles' (1.1-2) romances— the 'second wave' of romances, in the second (or possibly, in Longus' case, early third) century CE[12]—also begin with first-person narratives that describe how the author (or a fictional version of him)[13] came into contact with the story that he relates: Longus' narrator claims to have heard the story of Daphnis and Chloe from the interpreter of a cultic painting (*pr.*), and Achilles' to have heard that of Leucippe and Clitophon directly from

---

[8] Beecroft 2010.
[9] Although this is inevitably part of its function: Núñez 2014: 144 refers to this function as 'appropriation'.
[10] Beecroft 2010: 18.   [11] Morgan 2001; Núñez 2014.
[12] For this distinction between first-wave (Xenophon and Chariton), second-wave (Achilles and Longus), and third-wave (Heliodorus), see Whitmarsh 2011.
[13] On 'fictional autobiography', see Whitmarsh 2013a: 63-74.

Clitophon.[14] These scenes of authorship are somewhat different from Chariton's and Heliodorus', in that (i) the protagonist of the scene is not explicitly named as the author (though that identification is not discouraged); (ii) it is open to the reader to read the scene as fictional in the same way that the novel was; (iii) the scene focuses primarily on the transmission of the narrative content, not on the act of composition (though Longus' narrator does subsequently mention that 'I laboured over four books', pr. 3). Both of these authorial scenes thus perform three simultaneous operations: (a) they mimic a scene of originary, oral performance in a face-to-face context; (b) they reveal the first stage in the process whereby that epichoric oral event was translated (by an author) into what is implicitly to become a panchoric written text; (c) they problematize the relationship between that originary performance and the written text in our hands, by folding the authorial scene into the fictional space of the novel.[15]

Heliodorus' authorial scene is thus in one respect a return to the crisply informative manner of Chariton, after the extravagant sophistications of Achilles and Longus. The claim that 'Heliodorus wrote this text' is not open to suspicion in the same way that Achilles' claim to have been shipwrecked at Sidon is, or Longus' claim to have visited a cave on Lesbos (if, indeed, we are to consider these claims as in any sense at all autobiographical). At one level, this hardens the boundary between the fictional and the non-fictional. Not only does the *sphragis* mark the overstepping of the πέρας of fictionality—we are now reading words that we can reasonably take as factual and truthful—but also Heliodorus erases any possibility of mediation between the two worlds. Heliodorus does not claim to have encountered the story of Charicleia and Theagenes in a γραφή, as Longus does,[16] or to have heard it from one of the protagonists: that story exists entirely within the bounded world of the text, and within its author's imagination.

Viewed from a different angle, however, Heliodorus' *sphragis* is not external to the text. As John Hilton has observed, the distinctive phrase τῶν ἀφ' Ἡλίου γένος ('one of those descended from Helios': see below) highlights the idea of birth/descent (γένος), so thematically central to the novel proper

---

[14] On the wider interpretative issues raised by this episode, see Repath 2005. Dictys of Crete's *Ephemeris* and Antonius Diogenes' *Wonders beyond Thule* also contained similar authorship scenes (analysed in terms of 'pseudo-documentarism' by ní Mheallaigh 2008).
[15] On the play of oral and written in Achilles, see Marinčič 2007; and on the play between local and supra-local in Longus, see Whitmarsh 2013b.
[16] Cf. Xen. Eph. 5.15.2 for Anthia's and Habrocomes' γραφή 'of all that they had experienced and done'.

(which, of course, turns precisely upon the question of the circumstances of Charicleia's birth and family background).[17] Significant, too, is the word 'Phoenician' (ΦΟΙΝΙΞ, in ancient texts written of course without case differentiation), which—as Ewen Bowie has observed—is used with different meanings throughout the novel (date, date-palm, the colour red, the phoenix bird), and which (in the sense of 'palm') Theagenes adopts as a secret symbol shared with Charicleia.[18]

One more point may be made about Heliodorus' claim to a specifically Phoenician identity. As Josephine Quinn has recently noted, Heliodorus at this point, if we take his self-identification as straightforwardly autobiographical, becomes the first person in recorded history to self-describe emically as Phoenician; earlier uses of the term (outside of fictional texts) are entirely etic.[19] The claim therefore calls for some unpacking. Indeed, to describe an Emesan as 'Phoenician' would have been impossible before the late second century: this was not one of the ancient, coastal cities that classically minded Greeks would have associated with the term, principally Sidon (the only city that Homer calls 'Phoenician'), Tyre, Beirut, and Byblos. Emesa (modern Homs) is an inland city that was raised to prominence by successive Severan emperors, chiefly thanks to the influence of Julia Domna, wife of the emperor Septimius Severus, and the solar cult of Elagabal that came to Rome with her. In 194 CE, Septimius Severus created the province of Syria Phoenice (as distinct from Syria Coele to the north), a territory that included Emesa. It was only now, therefore, that Emesa began to be called Phoenician.[20] References in the works of the Emperor Julian show that it could also be referred to as 'Syrian',[21] but the sneering tone suggests that the word is being used dismissively here. 'Phoenician', by contrast, seems to have been pushed by imperial propaganda, from the Severan period, as a prestigious identity.[22] In this light, Quinn interprets the *sphragis* as continuing the games with fictions of identity and genealogy that the romance proper plays out, and exploring and exploding the (imperial) constructedness of 'Phoenician' identity—given the multiplicity of meanings of ΦΟΙΝΙΞ in the text as a whole.[23]

---

[17] Hilton 2012.   [18] Hld. 5.5.2; Bowie 1998.
[19] Quinn 2017: 135. Repath in the following chapter problematizes any autobiographical reading.
[20] e.g. Herodian refers to a woman τὸ γένος Φοίνισσα, ἀπὸ Ἐμέσου καλουμένης οὕτω πόλεως ἐν Φοινίκῃ (5.5.2). The city is Emesa, which is spelled variously.
[21] e.g. Jul. Or. 4. 154b, Caes. 313a.   [22] Quinn 2017: 148–50.
[23] Quinn 2017: 151.

Let us merely add two details to reinforce Quinn's interpretation. First, the *Aethiopica* is, of course, a deeply Homeric text, which plays repeatedly on its relationship to the *Odyssey*.[24] Heliodorus will have known, of course, that his hometown was not 'Phoenician' in Homer. The only Phoenicians who appear within the romance hail from Tyre (4.16.6)—which, while not in fact mentioned in Homer, was widely accepted by Greeks as one of the ancient, unproblematically Phoenician cities. These men are doing what 'classical' Phoenicians should be doing: sailing ships. This 'classical' (littoral-nautical) form of Phoenician identity is not represented in the *sphragis*; nor is the later (inland-solar) version within the classicizing romance. In this respect, the *sphragis* seems demarcated from the text. But perhaps there is the subtlest of hints that demarcation is, once again, deconstructable. Heliodorus refers to himself not just as Phoenician, but as ἀνὴρ Φοῖνιξ. For Homerically attuned readers, this will suggest Homer's references to Φοίνικες ἄνδρες:[25] Heliodorus has, therefore, used a Homeric phrase to describe a decidedly un-Homeric variety of Phoenician identity. More specifically, it will recall Homer's only use of the phrase in the singular, which also happens to be in the nominative:

ἀλλ' ὅτε δὴ ὄγδοόν μοι ἐπιπλόμενον ἔτος ἦλθε,
δὴ τότε Φοῖνιξ ἦλθεν ἀνὴρ ἀπατήλια εἰδώς,
τρώκτης, ὃς δὴ πολλὰ κάκ' ἀνθρώπους ἐέοργει.

But when the eighth year came circling around, then there came a Phoenician man who knew how to deceive, a greedy nibbler, who had inflicted many bad things upon people. (Hom. *Od.* 14.287-9)

In Philostratus' *Heroicus*, a text that Heliodorus knew well, this passage is evoked as an instance of anti-Phoenician slander, which paints them as rapaciously acquisitive ('you (Phoenicians)', says the vine-dresser, 'have a bad reputation as "nibblers"').[26] Additionally, the passage refers to the ἀνὴρ Φοῖνιξ as deceitful. Given that the Homeric passage is embedded within one of the deceptive Odysseus' Cretan lies, the irony generated by Heliodorus' allusion is considerable. Would Heliodorus have expected his readers to have completed the phrase ἀνὴρ Φοῖνιξ with ἀπατήλια εἰδώς? Does he thereby hint at his own slipperiness as an author?

---

[24] e.g. Whitmarsh 1998.   [25] *Il.* 23.744; *Od.* 15.415, 473.
[26] Philostr. *Her.* 1.3.

The second Phoenician point also relates to an allusion. Heliodorus' relationship with Achilles Tatius is profound (and indeed would benefit from modern, systematic study).[27] Achilles' tale is principally narrated by a Phoenician, the Tyrian Clitophon. Clitophon introduces himself early on: 'my family is from Phoenicia, Tyre is my fatherland, my name is Clitophon' (ἐμοὶ Φοινίκη γένος, Τύρος ἡ πατρίς, ὄνομα Κλειτοφῶν, 1.3.1), a self-identification that is distantly evoked in Heliodorus' own: both follow the same order (Phoenician identity/city/name), and both contain a prominent use of γένος. Clitophon's tale, however, is in fact a secondary narration embedded within a primary narration delivered by an unnamed visitor to Sidon. This narrator, as we have already noted, is likely to have been identified by ancient readers as (perhaps a fictionalized version of) the author himself, Achilles Tatius. Achilles appears to have come from Alexandria.[28] Heliodorus' African story told by a Phoenician might therefore be seen as an inversion of Achilles' Phoenician story told by an African.

Another word highlighted in the *sphragis* that is thematically significant for the wider text is πέρας ('end'). One of the romance's dominant motifs is the inversion of Hellenocentric geography: Ethiopia, traditionally thought of by Greeks as one of the edges of the earth, becomes the centre of this story; conversely, from an Ethiopian perspective, Greece is the edge of the earth.[29] The word used by Heliodorus for this kind of geopolitical 'edge' is, precisely, πέρας. Thus the Delphian priest Charicles has a dream in which an eagle snatches up his adopted daughter Charicleia and transports her 'to the furthest edge of the world' (γῆς ἐπ' ἔσχατόν τι πέρας, 4.14.2), meaning Ethiopia. Conversely, Charicleia's true father, the Ethiopian king Hydaspes, reflects on how his daughter was taken off to the 'furthest edge of the world' (ἐπὶ πέρατα γῆς ἔσχατα, 10.16.6), meaning Greece. The end of the novel occurs at the ends of the earth, from a Greek perspective—but it is, of course, precisely that Hellenocentric perspective that Heliodorus aims to unsettle.[30]

The *sphragis*' most striking echo of the romance narrative's theme is also its most mysterious. We have already mentioned the phrase τῶν ἀφ' Ἡλίου

---

[27] The fullest account of the relationship between the two authors is, paradoxically, one that mistakenly argues that Achilles follows Heliodorus: see Neimke 1889: 22–57.
[28] This is not certain, but the MSS and the Suda (a. 4695) are univocal. For further arguments, see Whitmarsh 2020.
[29] Whitmarsh 1998, 1999.   [30] See also Zeitlin in this volume.

γένος, 'one of those descended from Helios'.[31] What exactly does this phrase mean? Altheim claimed, in the course of a general argument that the *Aethiopica* reflects the Severans' championing of the cult of the sun (*Elagabal*), that our phrase indicates the author's membership of a clan of solar priests.[32] Nothing requires this; this is a common enough kind of expression, and the parallels clearly indicate that this is a genealogical claim: Heliodorus is claiming to be one of a group of descendants from Helios.[33] But what is this group to which he belongs? The phrasing might alternatively indicate that this is probably not a family but the populace of Emesa: τῶν ἀφ' Ἡλίου γένος could be a gloss on the immediately preceding Ἐμισηνός. Emesa was, of course, 'a place from time immemorial sacred to Helios' (ἱερὸν ἐξ αἰῶνος Ἡλίου χωρίον, Jul. *Hel.* 150c). There is no direct evidence that Emesenes believed themselves to be, collectively, descendants of Helios, but the popularity of the name Samsigeramus (derived from ŠMŠ, 'sun') among the earliest rulers points to a belief that the royal family, at any rate, had solar connections;[34] these could easily have been extended, by metonymy, to the entire people. But much more significant for our purposes than the historical question is the literary one: for Heliodorus' claim of solar descent is clearly paralleled by the Ethiopians within the fictional world of the novel. On recognizing Sisimithres, Charicleia utters a prayer: 'O Sun, first ancestor of my forefathers (γενεάρχα προγόνων ἐμῶν), and you other gods and heroes who are leaders of our race (γένους ἡμετέρου καθηγεμόνες, 10.11.3).[35] Heliodorus thus constructs a parallel between Emesa and Ethiopia,[36] and indeed between his own genealogy and that of Charicleia.[37]

These echoes in the *sphragis* of the themes of the main text are suggestive rather than load-bearing. They do not directly alter the reader's interpretation of the text; rather, they gesture imprecisely to possible points of connection between the fictional and the real worlds, and gnaw away at the boundary between the two, rendering it less fixed and determinate than it had initially seemed. Some of that ambivalence, indeed, can be seen in the humble aorist verb ἔσχε ('had'), in the first sentence. The aorist is the tense that marks the events of fictional narrative. It also, evidently, marks past events in the real world, as with the *sphragis*' second aorist, συνέταξεν

---

[31] The absence of the article before γένος is noted and paralleled by Morgan 1978: 628.
[32] Altheim 1942; cf. Birchall 1996b: 63–4; Fick 2002.
[33] e.g. οἱ ἀπὸ Δευκαλίωνος τὸ γένος, Hecat. FGrH 1 F14; ἀπὸ Διὸς ἔχοντες τὸ γένος, Acusilaus FGrH 2 F43; Φαλίος Ἐρατοκλείδου Κορίνθιος γένος τῶν ἀφ' Ἡρακλέους, Thuc. 1.24.2.
[34] Ball 2016: 32–3.   [35] Hilton 1998: 6–8.   [36] Cf. Morgan 2009.
[37] See Morgan 2009 on 'solar states'.

('composed'), which fairly unambiguously refers to a true event, the fact of the novel's having been composed. But ἔσχε is different. To say 'that was the ending that my novel *had*', in the past tense, is unsettling: the ending should be a stable, permanent feature of the text. What Heliodorus has done with this verb is blend together two ideas: 'these were the culminating events' and 'this is the end of the novel'. The first belongs to the fictional world of the narrative, and the aorist is appropriate to it; the second belongs to the real world in which the text is described as an artifice created by an author. Once again, the *sphragis* seems curiously liminal.

Should we, therefore, be pushing harder at this alleged boundary between the fictional and the non-fictional? Can we see the *sphragis* as wholly part of the (fictional, ironic, crafted) novel? Certainly, there are those who have seen the authorial scene presented in *Callirhoe* as too good to be true, given that Chariton of Aphrodisias means something like 'Mr Sexy from the City of Aphrodite'. 'Heliodorus son of Theodosius' does not initially look like an obvious pseudonym.[38] A Sidonian Heliodorus is attested in Athens in a bilingual inscription, which gives the Phoenician version as '*ABDŠMŠ*, i.e. 'servant of the Sun':[39] perhaps that was also the Semitic version of our author's name? But suspicions might be raised when we consider the centrality of Helios to the romance, which is built around the symbolic opposition of light and dark, and day and night.[40] The *Aethiopica* opens at day-break at one end of the Nile, with 'the sun shining down over the hilltop' (ἡλίου τὰς ἀκρωρείας καταυγάζοντος, 1.1.1); the plot is condensed into an Apolline oracle (2.35.5), which is recalled near the end (10.41.2); and its very last word, ostentatiously delayed like the grand revelation of the solution to a puzzle, is 'Heliodorus'. Is 'Heliodorus of solar Emesa' a pseudonym?[41] Or has the symbolic centrality of Helios to the plot been concocted in order to activate the resonances of his real name? Either way, the *sphragis*, in spite of its prima facie realism, can be seen to be integral to the design of the fictional text as a whole.

The central questions raised by the *sphragis* are therefore those with which we began: how integral to the text is it, and integral how? There is, of course, the ever-present risk of overinterpretation. Perhaps these thematic connections are the product of over-inventive minds. Perhaps an autograph

---

[38] Though the most famous Theodosioi are Jewish and Christian, the name is also borne by polytheists (e.g. the Hellenistic mathematician and astrologer).
[39] *KAI* 53.   [40] Morgan 1989b: 111.
[41] Cf. Núñez 2014: 163, and Repath in the following chapter.

copy of the *Aethiopica* will one day come to light and demonstrate conclusively that the *sphragis* was not composed by Heliodorus. Perhaps a second discovery will then come to light, demonstrating conclusively that the *sphragis* was composed for purely mechanical reasons by someone who had never read the text or pondered its themes. But even leaving aside the extreme unlikelihood of such discoveries, we should resist any impulse towards conservatism, in this of all texts. The question is not whether any particular reading is really there 'in' the text, but how we as readers are going to deal with the semi-visible traces of meaning that confront us. The *Aethiopica* repeatedly lures its readers into complex hermeneutic experiments within its narrative laboratory,[42] and it warns explicitly of the dangers not just of over-[43] but also of under-interpretation.[44] In Heliodorean terms, the choice set before us is not between solid, empirical, conventional philology and unwarranted postmodern flights of fancy, but between dull inattention to detail and an obsessive desire to wring the truth out of texts.[45] We become better readers of Heliodorus both by reading more obsessively and by ironizing our own obsessions. And what better place to start doing that than at the end?

---

[42] Hermeneutics in the *Aethiopica* have of course been widely discussed for a long time: see Winkler 1982; Morgan 1989a, 1991; Hunter 1998a. These issues have recently been reenergized by a new wave of younger scholars: see Andreadakis 2016 and Kruchió 2018a, 2018b.
[43] Cf. 1.18.5, where Thyamis 'dragged the solution (of a dream) towards his own desire' (ἕλκει πρὸς τὴν ἑαυτοῦ βούλησιν τὴν ἐπίλυσιν).
[44] Cf. 2.36.2–3, where the Delphians give up on the interpretation of the oracle.
[45] Cf. Calasiris' reading of Hom. *Il.* 13.71–2 at 3.12.2–3.

18
Sphragis 2
The Limits of Reality and the End of the Novel (10.41.3–4)

Ian Repath

18.1. Historiographical Posing(?)

Χαρίτων Ἀφροδισιεύς, Ἀθηναγόρου τοῦ ῥήτορος ὑπογραφεύς, πάθος ἐρωτικὸν ἐν Συρακούσαις γενόμενον διηγήσομαι.

I, Chariton of Aphrodisias, a secretary to the orator Athenagoras, shall narrate a love story that happened in Syracuse.

(Chariton *Callirhoe* 1.1.1).

It might seem perverse to start a discussion of the ending of the last of the Greek novels by looking briefly at the beginning of what might have been the first, and, in any case, is likely to be the earliest of the ones that survive. However, this passage can help us begin to understand what Heliodorus is and is not doing. As is well known, by introducing himself by name with the first word of his text, Chariton is evoking the beginnings of works of historiography, particularly those by Herodotus and Thucydides:

Ἡροδότου Ἁλικαρνησσέος ἱστορίης ἀπόδεξις ἥδε....

This is the display of the inquiry of Herodotus of Halicarnassus....

Θουκυδίδης Ἀθηναῖος ξυνέγραψε τὸν πόλεμον....

Thucydides the Athenian wrote about the war....

The evocation of these historiographers imbues Chariton with a similar kind of authority and suggests the authenticity of the story to follow. The use of the nominative brings Chariton closer to Thucydides, who is the more directly relevant for the context of his story, but Chariton at the same time differentiates himself by using the first person rather than the third, and by referring to narration rather than writing. These differences suggest a more personal, intimate approach, which is fitting for his subject matter, love: this is in tension with the principal subjects of Herodotus and Thucydides, who both mention war as their focus.[1] However, at the very end of his novel, Chariton uses the same verb for writing as Thucydides used at his beginning:

τοσάδε περὶ Καλλιρόης συνέγραψα.
Such things I wrote about Callirhoe.

While the first person maintains the closeness of the author to his text and emphasizes his ownership of its contents, one effect of evoking Thucydides here might be to bring Callirhoe's story closer to the historical, or to present it as a kind of alternative history,[2] perhaps even to suggest that his narrative and its topic are as serious and worthy of attention as Thucydides'.

In his *sphragis*,[3] Heliodorus, like Chariton, imitates the historiographers:

τοιόνδε πέρας ἔσχε τὸ σύνταγμα τῶν περὶ Θεαγένην καὶ Χαρίκλειαν Αἰθιοπικῶν· ὃ συνέταξεν ἀνὴρ Φοῖνιξ Ἐμισηνός, τῶν ἀφ᾽ Ἡλίου γένος, Θεοδοσίου παῖς Ἡλιόδωρος.

Such an ending had the composition *The Ethiopian Things Concerning Theagenes and Charicleia*, which a Phoenician man from Emesa composed, one of those descended from Helios, the son of Theodosius: Heliodorus. (Hld. 10.41.4)

I agree with Whitmarsh (in the preceding chapter) that Heliodorus is echoing the end of Chariton here, as τοιόνδε...συνέταξεν picks up τοσάδε...συνέγραψα, but he is closer to the historiographers than his generic predecessor in that he refers to himself in the third person.[4] This imitation is part of the 'historiographical pose' which Heliodorus adopts as part of his strategy of presenting the events in his novel as 'real'.[5] The pose entails the author being the ultimate authority for the story: the source material is 'historical fact', and there is no need to 'explain' the provenance,

---

[1] See Smith 2007a: 153–5, for discussion; also Tilg 2010: 217–20 and Núñez 2014: 147.
[2] Cf. Smith 2007a: 192.
[3] I have no doubt that the *sphragis* was written by the author of the novel: see below.
[4] Morgan 1978: 627.   [5] See Morgan 1982.

or even existence, of the story.[6] Moreover, he presents himself as more detached than Chariton, as an almost neutral recorder of things that happened: Chariton's stress on the notion that he is telling a story which 'happened' ($\gamma\epsilon\nu\acute{o}\mu\epsilon\nu o\nu$) can be read as protesting too much, while Heliodorus lets the events speak for themselves. And, in comparison with Chariton's opening, stress is laid on the Ethiopianness of the protagonists' story rather than on the erotic aspect, giving it more of an ethnographic feel (although the very mention of the protagonists in what seems to amount to a title for the work indicates the nature of the preceding story).[7]

But this is only part of the picture, since Heliodorus does not reveal his identity until the end of his text, with his name being the very last, as opposed to the very first, word. He began his novel in a way which is designed to create a range of questions and puzzles and he requires the reader to navigate his whole text before providing the final answer: he does not stamp his authority on the text from the outset, but becomes one of its mysteries, in fact its ultimate mystery.[8] But Heliodorus is not simply teasing his reader, since aspects of his identity encourage connections with, and add layers to, the preceding narrative. Recent discussion has focused on various factors, often in combination, including Heliodorus' ethnicity,[9] the question of genealogy,[10] and the importance of the sun in the narrative.[11] I wish to suggest that there is another angle from which to consider the *sphragis*, which builds on ideas put forward in the preceding chapter.

In keeping himself until last, Heliodorus provides a deliberate inversion of the historiographical technique he is evoking, and a reader needs to consider the implications of this. The simultaneous imitation of Chariton complicates the process of generic affiliation and highlights the use of the historiographical pose as a fictional device. This takes on a particular slant when we consider Heliodorus' ethnic identity and the allusions to earlier texts. In her discussion of the beginnings and endings of the Greek novels, Núñez notes the connection between Heliodorus' name and the presence of the sun at the very beginning of the novel to raise the question of whether *Helio*dorus is a pseudonym;[12] she includes Heliodorus' Phoenician identity as part of the question, given the 'reputation of being liars' that that people

[6] Cf. Longus, for example.
[7] For discussion of the novel's title, see Morgan 1978: 623–7 and Whitmarsh 2005b.
[8] See Winkler 1982: 157 n. 64, and Fusillo 1997: 212–13.
[9] See Bowie 1998; and Whitmarsh 1998 and in his analysis of the *sphragis* in this volume.
[10] Whitmarsh 1998; Hilton 2012; and Morgan 2013.
[11] Whitmarsh 2005a; Morgan 2009; and Morgan 2013.
[12] Núñez 2014: 163. I will return to this question below.

had in antiquity.[13] At the root of the literary tradition of this reputation is Odysseus, who, in one of his lies, refers to a deceitful Phoenician man (Φοῖνιξ...ἀνήρ *Od.* 14.288). Closer, both chronologically and generically, to Heliodorus, Achilles Tatius' protagonist-narrator introduces himself in the following way: 'My family is from Phoenicia, Tyre is my fatherland, my name is Clitophon' (ἐμοὶ Φοινίκη γένος, Τύρος ἡ πατρίς, ὄνομα Κλειτοφῶν, 1.3.1). As Whitmarsh notes in the preceding chapter, Heliodorus follows the same order to a certain extent: Phoenician identity, city, and name (although the father's name comes next in Achilles Tatius), and γένος features prominently in each. Heliodorus' self-identification is not only an inversion of what we find in notionally 'factual' texts (and Chariton who imitates them), but makes us think of lying Phoenicians, and in particular of a mythological character who is a serial liar and of a fictional Phoenician character whose narratorial reliability is open to doubt.[14] Heliodorus' self-revelation relates to the composition of the preceding text, and the literary and intertextual games mean that the composer's reliability is brought into question. So, just at the point where he reveals the last piece of information, Heliodorus simultaneously underlines and undermines his own authority, claiming responsibility for the (presentation of the) story and suggesting to the alert reader that he cannot be trusted. But this is not a matter of 'historiographical competence', since the question of to what extent Heliodorus' version of events might be untrue is an illusion: of course it is untrue, because it is fiction. By raising doubts about his own 'reliability', which can never be interrogated, let alone assessed, Heliodorus becomes intensely metafictional.[15]

One effect of such arguments is that we can be confident that the *sphragis* is genuine: its artful arrangement, the intertextual aspects, and its contribution to how we understand the text as a whole are best understood as part of the author's creative design. I will return to issues of more general interpretation shortly, but first want to make another argument for the authenticity of the *sphragis*. The possibility that it is an addition by a scribe is rendered less likely by the fact that some manuscripts of Heliodorus contain such additions, after the *sphragis*. V has τέλος τῶν αἰθιοπικῶν Ἡλιοδώρου, ὁμοῦ βιβλία δέκα ('End of *The Ethiopian Things* of Heliodorus,

---

[13] Morales 2004: 54–6.
[14] On Clitophon, see, for instance, Morgan 2007b; de Temmerman 2014: 152–8; and Repath 2015.
[15] Birchall 1996b: 76 briefly makes such a comment with reference to the allusion to the *Odyssey*. For a similar point about the role of Longus' exegete, see Repath 2015: 48 n. 7.

ten books in all'), and Z has τέλος τῶν περὶ Θεαγένη καὶ Χαρίκλειαν αἰθιοπικῶν. ἡ Χαρίκλεια ('End of *The Ethiopian Things Concerning Theagenes and Charicleia; Charicleia*').[16] These additions strongly suggest that the *sphragis* is genuine: a copyist would not add (or copy) such a colophon if they did not think that the *sphragis* belonged to the original text they were copying—they are commenting on the end of the text as it came to them. This does not rule out an earlier scribe writing the *sphragis*, but he would have to have done so in a way which deceived later copyists, who, if the manuscripts of other novels are anything to go by, were used to the convention of such comments being added or included.[17] That such comments were added after Heliodorus' *sphragis* might strike us as odd—why say that the text has come to an end when the text already says this?—but one effect is to highlight the oddity of Heliodorus' use of *peras* as opposed to *telos*,[18] something I shall return to in the second section.

I am now, as a tribute to this volume's honorand, and with the indulgence of my co-editor, going to develop this discussion in a narratological direction. As Morgan notes, Heliodorus in his *sphragis* 'positions himself as author outside the narrative structure of the novel. His usage distinguishes him from the primary narrator, who is an element of the text that he has "composed".'[19] While Chariton both is and is not the narrator,[20] Heliodorus is not to be identified with the voice that tells the story. This separation requires a nuancing of the argument made above about the historiographical pose. Whose pose is it? It is something imposed on the narrator by Heliodorus—the narrator is telling a story that to him is real, and in doing so tells it in such a way as to be faithful to its 'reality'. When Heliodorus reveals himself, he inverts the historiographical pose, and refers to himself in a way which highlights the fictionality of what has gone before. Part of the composer's unreliability or deviousness, I suggest, stems from his use of an apparently scrupulous narrator to tell an untrue story as if it were true.[21] This could be seen as the opposite of what we find in Homer, where the

---

[16] MP have the slightly odd: εἴληφε τέρμα βίβλος Ἡλιοδώρου ('Book of Heliodorus has received end'), which looks like a gloss on the basics of the *sphragis*.

[17] The sole manuscript which contains Chariton and Xenophon of Ephesus has one for each novel, as does W in the case of Achilles Tatius, and both V and F for Longus.

[18] See Morgan 1978: 622. See Whitmarsh in Chapter 17 for a thematic significance *peras* has within the *Aethiopica*.

[19] Morgan 2004b: 523.   [20] Núñez 2014: 149 and 161–2. Cf. Doulamis 2012.

[21] The following may seem an unexpected comparison, but the situation seems to me not too dissimilar to that which we find in Lucian's *Verae Historiae*, only there the prologue-voice tells us that what will follow is untrue, before using a narrator for whom the story is true and who presents it using a historiographical pose.

story is told as real, but Odysseus' unreliability as a narrator means that we can never know the 'truth' about his encounter with the Cyclops, if it even 'happened'; and as the opposite of what we find in Achilles Tatius, where the anonymous primary narrator relates his apparently factual story, which includes (and consists almost entirely of) a narrative whose Phoenician narrator's reliability is called into question. What we find in Heliodorus is different, since it is the composer of the text who is drawing attention to his own (un)questionable authority—the fictionality of the story is highlighted from without, not from within.[22]

At the same time, the *sphragis* encourages, if not requires the reader to reconsider what they have just read. If the narrator is the construct of someone potentially unreliable, we should re-read the novel, perhaps reading against the grain, to notice emphases, omissions, and elisions, and to imagine our own renderings. For instance, we might note that the narrator allots Theagenes far less direct speech than Charicleia and ask whether this is to mask the fact he is less enthusiastic in his adherence to chastity than she is.[23] Or we might consider the *sententiae* of the narrator: Morgan points out that they suggest a Hellenocentric figure who is concerned to form a community with his narratee, and suggests that Heliodorus' Phoenicianness is potentially in tension with this.[24] Heliodorus' potential unreliability has further implications for how we approach the ethnic and cultural orientation of this novel, making issues of contestation and/or assimilation even more slippery.[25]

However, much of this implicitly presupposes something which is best approached by returning to the question of whether the self-identification is pseudonymous. The way Heliodorus describes himself would be a nicely intertextual way of signalling his pseudonymity, but who would be doing the signalling? It would have to be the author of the whole text, who had invented some or all of the details contained in the identification in the *sphragis*. But it is only a false name if the person being referred to is the author of the whole text. One could argue that there is no reason to think otherwise, but, logically, whoever it is in the text who says he wrote the preceding story is an intra-textual author, and so is part of and therefore a

---

[22] This is not to say that there are not passages in the narrative which could be read as having a metafictional aspect, but that level of meaning would belong to the author, not the narrator.
[23] See Bird 2017. [24] Morgan 2004b: 530–1.
[25] See Whitmarsh 1998 and 2011, and Morgan 2014, for different arguments on this topic; also Zeitlin in this volume.

construct of the text, belonging to an ontologically different category from the extra-textual author. This makes sense of the intertextuality, since 'Heliodorus' would be an invented character, just as Odysseus' Phoenician is an invented character and just as Cleitophon is an invented character.[26] In that sense, if Heliodorus is not the biological author's name, it is not a pseudonym, because it is not referring to the real author. And (even) if the real author was actually called Heliodorus, and if all the details were true also for Heliodorus the extra-textual author, the persona in the text is still a construct of that text, a creation of the biological author, who has made 'Heliodorus' present himself in a way which the reader can see raises certain questions.

I therefore agree with my co-editor about the curious liminality of the *sphragis* and that it is 'integral to the design of the fictional text as a whole', but the above argument means that its belonging to the real world is only apparent. This suggests a final question (for this section): what is really real? Our first, natural, reaction to the liminality of the *sphragis* is that it bridges the fictional world of the novel and the real world of the author and reader, highlighting the fictionality of the story and referring to the process of writing by the author. However, the fictional world of the novel is presented as real, whereas the reality of 'Heliodorus' is called into question. In one direction, the *sphragis* allows the fictionality of the novel-world to get a foothold in the real world, to seep into it, bringing the novel's contents ontologically closer to the reader. At the same time, it makes the reader question the relationship of the world s/he inhabits to the world portrayed in the novel. The purpose of the presentation of a fictional story as real is to engross the reader, to make them experience it, and to make them believe that, at one level, it is 'real', while knowing that it is not.[27] In his discussion of realism in Heliodorus, Morgan suggested that it 'is...an invitation to respond to events for their own sake' and that this tells against an allegorical reading.[28] But perhaps the reader, prompted by the *sphragis*, should reconsider their terms of reference: why should they think that the world that they and the extra-textual author inhabit is more real than any other world, or that the world within the text is less real than their own?

It is at this point that the historiographical pose, one of the factors in creating the realism of the narrative, can help. For the historiographers

---

[26] It also makes sense of the tenses used in the *sphragis*: see Whitmarsh in Chapter 17 for the blurring of real and fictional in this respect. And while the historiographical precedents are sufficient explanation for the use of the third person, it does fit with the point being made here.

[27] Morgan 1982 and 1993.   [28] Morgan 1982: 262–3.

imitated in the narrative and evoked in 'Heliodorus' self-identification were, whatever Aristotle might think,[29] ultimately concerned with universal truths, with concepts, behaviours, and systems which are manifested in particulars and discernible through their recurrence.[30] Such truths are, in a sense, more real than individual historical events and more worthy of attention. So, rather than being incompatible with allegorical possibilities and different layers of meaning, historiographical realism is precisely a means of suggesting such possibilities. The inversion in 'Heliodorus'' self-identification can be read as a signal that the historiographical strategy has a double purpose: to provide the fictional story with realism, and also to encourage the reader to look for more than a narrative of individual events (which in any case never happened), but for something deeper, something universally true. Despite and because of its status as fiction, the story of Charicleia is in a sense more, rather than less, real than the 'real' world, allowing it to take on a universal significance. What that significance might be is a moot point and perhaps unrecoverable, or at least at the mercy of individual readers' interpretations, but in the context of this volume it is pertinent to note that Morgan himself has become more inclined to perceive allegorical possibilities in the text, and that this sees him become part of a tradition of Heliodoran readers which goes back at least as far as the Byzantine era.[31]

18.2. The End of the Novel(?)

The phrase τοιόνδε πέρας ('Such an ending') invites the question of what kind of ending it is.[32] The following is the final sentence of the narrative that directly precedes the *sphragis*:

στεφθέντες οὖν οἱ νέοι λευκαῖς ταῖς μίτραις, τήν τε ἱερωσύνην ἀναδησάμενοι καὶ τὴν θυσίαν αὐτοὶ καλλιερήσαντες, ὑπὸ λαμπάσιν ἡμμέναις, αὐλῶν τε καὶ συρίγγων μελῳδίαις, ἐφ' ἅρματος ἵππων μὲν ὁ Θεαγένης ἅμα τῷ Ὑδάσπῃ

---

[29] *Poetics* 1451a36–b9.   [30] See Hdt. 1.5 and Thuc. 1.21.
[31] See Morgan 2009 on Emesa and solar cult, and 2012 (esp. 571–7) for a Platonic angle. Very few now would go as far as Merkelbach 1962, but at the very least Heliodorus encourages allegorical reading: see Lamberton 1986: 148–57 and Hunter 2005 in their discussions of Philip the Philosopher's allegorical interpretation of the *Ethiopica*; also Dowden 1996 (and in this volume); Most 2007; and Kim in this volume.
[32] Notwithstanding some of the argument in the previous section, in this section I refer to the author of the whole text as Heliodorus.

(ὁ Σισιμίθρης δὲ καθ' ἕτερον ἅμα τῷ Χαρικλεῖ), βοῶν δὲ λευκῶν ἡ Χαρίκλεια ἅμα τῇ Περσίννῃ, σὺν εὐφημίαις καὶ κρότοις καὶ χοροῖς ἐπὶ τὴν Μερόην παρεπέμποντο, τῶν ἐπὶ τῷ γάμῳ μυστικωτέρων κατὰ τὸ ἄστυ φαιδρότερον τελεσθησομένων.

And so the young pair, crowned with their white mitres, invested with holy office, offered the sacrifice with their own hands, and the omens were good. Then, by the light of torches, to the melodies of flutes and pipes, they—Theagenes beside Hydaspes in a chariot drawn by horses, Sisimithres in a second beside Charicles, Charicleia with Persinna in a carriage pulled by white oxen—were escorted with cheering and clapping and dancing into Meroe, where the more mystic parts of the wedding ritual were to be performed with greater magnificence. (10.41.3)

This passage has several elements, especially verbal, which reflect what has just gone before. In the first of two speeches, Hydaspes had declared 'that this couple has been joined by the laws of matrimony' (ξυνωρίδα ταύτην γαμηλίοις νόμοις) and recommended that they make a sacrifice (θυσία) and turn to religious matters (τὰ ἱερά) (10.40.2). The army 'cheered their approval' (ἐπευφήμησεν) and 'clapped their hands in thunderous applause, as if the marriage were being solemnized then and there' (κρότον τῶν χειρῶν ὡς ἐπιτελουμένοις ἤδη τοῖς γάμοις ἐπεκτύπησαν 10.41.1). In his second speech, Hydaspes addressed Helios and Selene, saying that 'since by your decrees Theagenes and Charicleia are proclaimed man and wife (ἀνὴρ καὶ γυνή), they now have the right to serve in your priesthood (ἱερατεύειν)' (10.41.1). He then placed his mitre (μίτραν), the symbol of his priesthood (ἱερωσύνης), on Theagenes' head, and Persinna's on Charicleia's (10.41.2). This led Charicles to recall the second half of the Delphic prophecy (2.35.5) concerning the young pair (τοὺς νέους 10.41.2), the last line of which said that they would wear white crowns (λευκὸν...στέμμα 10.41.2). Thus the end is strongly closural: the structure of 10.40-1 shows some ring composition, with, broadly speaking, the focus on the issue of marriage, then the priesthood, and then marriage again; likewise, the verbal repetitions in 10.41.3 to some extent mirror what they are picking up in the previous three sections. With regard to a larger scale, the twin threads consisting of the erotic and religious dimensions which underpin the narrative are closely interwoven in the final two chapters,[33] and the architecture of the

---

[33] See Morgan 1989a: 319-20. Fusillo 1997: 221-3 stresses the religious dimension of the final scene, without focusing on the final clause: I will consider this in more detail below.

whole plot is simultaneously evoked by the mention of the oracle and brought to completion.

This sense of closure is enhanced by a comparison with other Greek novels. In both Xenophon (5.15.3) and Longus (4.39.1), the narrator provides a prolepsis which encompasses the happy future lives of the protagonists; both Chariton and Achilles Tatius end their novels with prayers for the future: Callirhoe asks Aphrodite that she and Chaereas have a happy life and joint death (8.8.16), and Cleitophon relates that they prayed that his marriage and Callisthenes' be guarded by good fortune (8.19.3). There is no such looking forward in Heliodorus, suggesting that the story is complete and that there is no potential concern for the future of the characters. As Morgan puts it:

> Their story only makes moral sense if they pass the rest of their lives in a happiness so complete and so uniform as to present no purchase for narration. This is in fact a classic closed ending; no questions are left to be asked, the text closes because there is nothing more that could be told.[34]

I will come back to this point, but a comparison with those novels that end with the wedding of their protagonists further enhances the impression of closure Heliodorus achieves in the final sentence of the narrative.

The wedding in Longus is described, in the penultimate sentence of the novel, as follows:

> τότε δὲ νυκτὸς γενομένης πάντες αὐτοὺς παρέπεμπον εἰς τὸν θάλαμον, οἱ μὲν συρίττοντες, οἱ δὲ αὐλοῦντες, οἱ δὲ δᾷδας μεγάλας ἀνίσχοντες, καὶ ἐπεὶ πλησίον ἦσαν τῶν θυρῶν ᾖδον σκληρᾷ καὶ ἀπηνεῖ τῇ φωνῇ καθάπερ τριαίναις γῆν ἀναρρηγνύντες, οὐχ ὑμέναιον ᾄδοντες.

> Now, when night fell, everyone escorted them to their bedroom, some playing the pipes, some the flute, others brandishing huge torches. And when they were close to the door, they began to sing with rough and uncouth voices, as if they were breaking up the ground with forks rather than singing the marriage hymn. (Long. 4.40.1–2)

There are elements in common to both Heliodorus and Longus: the escort (παρέπεμπον ~ παρεπέμποντο), the torches (δᾷδας μεγάλας ~ ὑπὸ λαμπάσιν

---

[34] Morgan 1989a: 320; Whitmarsh 2011: 211, likewise comments that Heliodorus, like Xenophon and Longus, 'ends with nothing left to happen'.

ἠμμέναις), and the playing of pipes and flutes (οἱ μὲν συρίττοντες, οἱ δὲ αὐλοῦντες ~ αὐλῶν τε καὶ συρίγγων μελῳδίαις). The first two are hardly surprising, but the third is perhaps significant. The playing of pipes is mentioned only three other times in the *Aethiopica*, and one of those occurs in the ekphrasis of the engraving of an amethyst which is designed to encapsulate Longus' novel (5.14.2).[35] This, and the combination of the same instruments as we find at the end of *Daphnis and Chloe*, suggest direct engagement at the end of Heliodorus as well, and I think that one of the main points is that there is a significant contrast, as the harsh sounds of the singing at the wedding in Longus are replaced by harmonious noises; this is emphasized by Heliodorus' use of μελῳδία ('melody') for the music of the flutes and pipes, since it properly refers to singing.[36] This does not necessarily mean that Heliodorus found the end of Longus troubling, just that he wanted to avoid any unpleasantness of any kind.[37]

Such a competitive edge to the intertextuality can be observed in a comparison with the weddings at the end of Achilles Tatius. Cleitophon reports that they travelled to Byzantium:

> There we concluded the marriage for which we had so often prayed (τοὺς πολυεύκτους ἐπιτελέσαντες γάμους); then we voyaged to Tyre. We arrived two days after Callisthenes and found my father about to perform the sacrifices for my sister's wedding (θύειν τοὺς γάμους τῆς ἀδελφῆς) on the following day. So we were there to share with him in the sacrifices (συνθύσοντες), and to pray to the god that my marriage and Callisthenes' (τούς τε ἐμοὺς καὶ τοὺς ἐκείνου γάμους) would be overseen by good fortunes.
>
> (8.19.2–3)

The emphasis here is on the sacrifices and the prayers, absent from the end of Longus: it seems that Heliodorus is combining elements from both novels in the conclusion of his own, thereby pointing out what each of them omits in order to suggest that his corrects and supersedes them.[38] Moreover,

---

[35] For the argument, see Bowie 1995: 278–80. The other two mentions of piping occur at 3.1.5, where music accompanies the procession of sacrificial animals, and 7.8.5, where Calasiris is escorted to the temple of Isis in Memphis; see Hunter in this volume on the latter scene as foreshadowing the celebrations at the end of the novel.

[36] As noted by Morgan 1978: 620.

[37] For a reading of Longus' wedding night as problematic, see Winkler 1990: 124–6, an argument with which Morgan 2004a: 248–9 disagrees.

[38] Cf. the wedding scenes in Chariton 1.1.13–16 and Xenophon of Ephesus 1.8.1, the latter of which contains many sacrifices being made (ἱερεῖα πολλὰ ἐθύετο), and the leading of the girl

Heliodorus' protracted denouement and strongly closural ending contrast with Achilles Tatius' rapid and anti-climactic conclusion.[39] 'Such an ending' can therefore be seen as an intra-generic comment, referring to a harmonious happy finale in which all ends are tied up, the climax is satisfying, and nothing is left open to doubt.[40] Not only is it the end of Heliodorus' novel, but it is perhaps designed to be the end of the genre of the Greek novel, since surely no one could ever outdo Heliodorus?

But there *is* something still to happen in Heliodorus' story, if not in his narrative:

...τῶν ἐπὶ τῷ γάμῳ μυστικωτέρων κατὰ τὸ ἄστυ φαιδρότερον τελεσθησομένων.
...where the more mystic parts of the wedding ritual were to be performed with greater magnificence. (Hld. 10.41.3)

Just as the primary narrative starts with a genitive absolute,[41] so it ends with one, but the latter refers to something which will not be narrated. And just as the revelation of the author's name with the final word of the novel is an artful device, so the choice to conclude the narrative with a passive participle which is cognate with *telos* ('end'), but at the same time is in the future and so refers to something beyond the end, is deliberate and designed to provoke consideration. What is it that is going to happen? It is going to be both more impressive than what has just been narrated and also shrouded in mystery, kept secret from the narratee—the two comparatives are tantalizing and add to the sense of exclusion.[42] What we have been expecting, of course, is the consummation of the marriage, and a continuation of the comparison with the end of Longus confirms this idea: Longus' final sentence concerns the wedding-night of Daphnis and Chloe, a fitting end-point and climax, given the novel's plot. Matters are less clear in the case of Achilles Tatius, where the wedding is mentioned only briefly: 'There we concluded the marriage for which we had so often prayed (τοὺς πολυεύκτους ἐπιτελέσαντες γάμους); then we voyaged to Tyre' (Achilles Tatius 8.19.2). What happened is not narrated, as if it were unimportant and uninteresting, which is the last

---

to the bedchamber with torches (λαμπάδων), singing of the bridal hymn (τὸν ὑμέναιον ᾄδοντες), and cheering (ἐπευφημοῦντες). See Whitmarsh 2011: 117 (and in this volume) on Heliodorus' relationship to Xenophon of Ephesus.

[39] See, further, below.
[40] See Whitmarsh 2011: ch. 5 for a discussion of closurality in the Greek novels.
[41] See Whitmarsh 2005a for discussion.
[42] Cf. the use of τὰ μυστικώτερα at 9.10.1 to refer to the higher knowledge concerning the flooding of the Nile and the myth of Isis and Osiris, with Morgan 1978: 96.

thing it should be, both in generic terms, and in view of Cleitophon's (narrative of his) pursuit of Leucippe in the first two books in particular. I think Heliodorus alludes to and toys with Achilles Tatius, with the latter's 'concluded' (ἐπιτελέσαντες) picked up by the use of the same compound when the army react 'as if the marriage were being solemnized then and there' (ὡς ἐπιτελουμένοις ἤδη τοῖς γάμοις 10.41.1). The point is that this is not the full or real completion, just as the marriage of Achilles Tatius' protagonists is, for the reader, in a sense not fully complete. Heliodorus' game extends beyond including the premature excitement of his internal audience to then not providing the reader with the real conclusion, highlighting what is downplayed in his generic predecessor, before pointedly declining to focus on what he did not.

From this perspective, Heliodorus' comparatives are not just internal but also intertextual—what will happen will be more mystic, in that it will be neither narrated nor brushed over, and it will be better. Moreover, John Morgan and I have argued that 'with more magnificence' (φαιδρότερον) is the culmination of Heliodorus' engagement with Plato's *Phaedrus* and signifies that the love of the protagonists is even more *phaedrus* than the 'Platonic' love in the eponymous dialogue.[43] I think that the comparative is doubly intertextual, in that the story of Heliodorus' couple, including in particular its conclusion, is more in tune with Plato than his predecessors; that Heliodorus recognized their engagement with the Platonic dialogue and is commenting on it and 'correcting' it here.[44] There is no earthy sexual congress accompanied by harsh singing and no anti-climactic marriage after an unsanctioned erotic pursuit, but something more mystic, something much more like the union of the soul with the divine.

Such is the ending of Heliodorus' composition, and his choice of words is deliberate: it has reached its *peras*, which one might translate as 'limit', rather than 'ending'. It is not the point towards which the story was leading, its *telos*, but the point at which the story ceases to be told: it is not that 'there is nothing more that could be told', just that Heliodorus does not allow his narrator to tell it. This can help explain the choice of tense: 'Such a limit *had* composition' (τοιόνδε πέρας ἔσχε τὸ σύνταγμα). The aorist is used because the story is carrying on in the reader's mind, for whom the *peras* of the presphragis text is already in the past. The composition had such a limit or cut-off point, but the future participle ('were to be performed') propels the story

---

[43] Morgan and Repath 2019.
[44] See Morales 2004: 50–60 on Achilles Tatius, and Repath 2011 on Longus.

beyond it, and the contrast between the tenses encapsulates both the tension created by the premature, and arguably prudish, ending of the narrative and the tension inherent in the narrative teleology of the novel as a whole—an erotic plot in which virginity is paramount. Whether the reader continues the story in a prurient way, or in a way suggested by the language Heliodorus uses to refer to it, depends not only on personal choice but also on the conditioning provided by the preceding text and its intertextuality, which itself pulls in different directions.[45] Either way, the narrative here slips the confines of the text, further blurring the relationship between the world of the story and the world of the reader.[46]

In terms of what the text does contain, the wedding night/consummation is replaced by the *sphragis*, something made clear by a comparison with the final sentence of Longus. This perhaps suggests a kind of equation: the climax of the novel is not the anticipated sexual union of the central couple, but the revelation of Heliodorus' identity. The reader should derive more satisfaction from the discovery of this information and from its implications, than they would have from a focus on what had become virtually unnarratable: Charicleia losing her virginity. Such a claim might seem strange, but in view of the scholarly interest generated by the *sphragis*, Heliodorus may have succeeded in diverting at least some of his readers from something he himself put beyond the limit of his text. While Longus gives his readers what they want and Achilles Tatius does not, Heliodorus gives the readers something they did not even realize they wanted, at which point they realize it is the most important thing they could be told.

---

[45] See Morgan 2013 for a metaliterary reading of the erotics of the novel.
[46] Cf. ní Mheallaigh 2014: 192–4 on the end of Longus.

References

Agapitos, P. 1998. 'Narrative, Rhetoric and "Drama" Rediscovered: Scholars and Poets in Byzantium Interpret Heliodorus'. In Hunter ed. 1998b: 125–56.
Agapitos, P. 2008. 'Public and Private Death in Psellos: Maria Skleraina and Styliane Psellaina'. *ByzZ* 101/2: 555–607.
Ahl, F. trans. 2007. *Virgil: Aeneid*. Oxford.
Allen, T. W. ed. 1917. *Homeri Opera, tomus I: Iliadis libros I–XII continens*. 2nd ed. Oxford.
Allen, T. W. ed. 1919. *Homeri Opera, tomus II: Iliadis libros XIII–XIV continens*. 2nd ed. Oxford.
Altheim, F. 1942. *Helios und Heliodor von Emesa*. Amsterdam.
Alvares, J. 1997. 'Chariton's Erotic History'. *AJP* 118: 613–29.
Ameis, K. F. and Hentze, C. 1905. *Homers Ilias 5: Erläuterungen zu Gesang XIII–XV*. 3rd ed. Leipzig.
Anderson, G. 1979. 'Two Notes on Heliodorus'. *JHS* 99: 149.
Anderson, G. 1982. *Eros Sophistes: Ancient Novelists at Play*. Chico, CA.
Anderson, M. J. 1997. 'The ΣΩΦΡΟΣΥΝΗ of Persinna and the Romantic Strategy of Heliodorus' *Aethiopica*'. *CPh* 92: 303–22.
Andreadakis, Z. 2016. 'Reading for Clues: Detective Narratives in Heliodorus' *Aithiopika*'. Diss., University of Michigan.
Andújar, R. 2013. 'Charicleia the Martyr: Heliodorus and Early Christian Narrative'. In Futre Pinheiro, M. P. et al. eds, *The Ancient Novel and Early Christian Narrative: Fictional Intersections* (= *Ancient Narrative* suppl. 16): 139–52.
Bakhtin, M. M. 1981. 'Forms of Time and of the Chronotope in the Novel: Notes toward a Historical Poetics'. In *The Dialogic Imagination: Four Essays by M.M. Bakhtin*, ed. Holquist, M., trans. Emerson, C. and Holquist, M. Austin: 84–258.
Bakker, E. J. 2013. *The Meaning of Meat and the Structure of the* Odyssey. Cambridge.
Ball, W. 2016. *Rome in the East: The Transformation of an Empire*. 2nd ed. London.
Bargheer, R. 1999. *Die Gottesvorstellung Heliodors in den* Aithopika. Frankfurt am Main, Berlin, Bern, New York, Paris, Vienna.
Bartsch, S. 1989. *Decoding the Ancient Novel: The Reader and the Role of Description in Heliodorus and Achilles Tatius*. Princeton.
Baumbach, M. 1997. 'Die Meroe-Episode in Heliodors *Aithiopika*'. *RhM* 140: 333–41.
Baumbach, M. 2008. 'An Egyptian Priest in Delphi: Calasiris as *theios anēr* in Heliodorus' *Aethiopica*'. In Dignas, B. and Trampedach, K. eds, *Practitioners of the Divine: Greek Priests and Religious Officials from Homer to Heliodorus*. Washington, DC: 167–83.
Beecroft, A. 2010. *Authorship and Cultural Identity in Early Greece and China*. New York.

Beresford, J. 2013. *The Ancient Sailing Season*. Leiden and Boston.
Bianchi, N. 2006. *Il codice del romanzo*. Bari.
Bianchi, N. 2011a. *Romanzi greci ritrovati*. Bari.
Bianchi, N. ed. 2011b. *La tradizione dei testi greci in Italia meridionale*. Bari.
Billault, A. 2015. 'Holy Man or Charlatan? The Case of Kalasiris in Heliodorus' *Aithiopika*'. In Panayotakis, Schmeling, and Paschalis eds. 2015: 121–32.
Biraud, M. and Briand, M. eds. 2017. *Roman grec et poésie: dialogue des genres et nouveaux enjeux du poétique: actes du colloque international, Nice, 21–22 mars 2013*. Lyons.
Birchall, J. W. 1996a. 'The Lament as a Rhetorical Feature in the Greek Novel'. *Groningen Colloquia on the Novel* 7: 1–17.
Birchall, J. W. 1996b. 'Heliodoros *Aithiopika* 1: A Commentary with Prolegomena'. Diss., University College, London.
Bird, R. 2017. 'Virtue Obscured: Theagenes' *Sōphrosunē* in Heliodorus' *Aethiopica*'. *AN* 14: 195–208.
Bird, R. 2019. 'Heliodorus 'Charicleia and Euripides' *Hippolytus*: Surviving *Sōphrosynē*'. In Repath and Herrmann eds. 2019: 193–210.
Bird, R. 2020. *Sophrosune in the Greek Novel*. London.
Bittlestone, R., Diggle, J. and Underhill, J. 2005. *Odysseus Unbound: The Search for Homer's Ithaca*. Cambridge.
Bowersock, G. W. 1994. *Fiction as History: Nero to Julian*. Berkeley.
Bowie, A. M. 2013. *Homer: Odyssey, Books XIII and XIV*. Cambridge.
Bowie, E. 1994. 'The Readership of Greek Novels in the Ancient World'. In Tatum ed. 1994b: 435–59.
Bowie, E. 1995. 'Names and a Gem: Aspects of Allusion in Heliodorus' *Aethiopica*'. In Innes, Hine, and Pelling eds. 1995: 269–80.
Bowie, E. 1998. 'Phoenician Games in Heliodorus' *Aithiopika*'. In Hunter, R. ed., *Studies in Heliodorus*. Cambridge: 1–18.
Bowie, E. 2007. 'Pulling the Other: Longus and Tragedy'. In Kraus, C., Goldhill, S., Foley, H. P., and Elsner, J. eds, *Visualizing the Tragic: Drama, Myth, and Ritual in Greek Art and Literature. Essays in Honour of Froma Zeitlin*. New York: 338–52.
Bowie, E. 2012. 'Socrates' Cock and Daphnis' Goats. The Rarity of Vows in the Religious Practice of the Greek Novels'. In Harrison, S. J. and Frangoulidis, S. eds, *Narrative, Culture and Genres in the Ancient Novel*. Berlin: 225–73.
Bowie, E. 2015. 'Stesichorus at Athens'. In Kelly, A. and Finglass, P. eds, *Stesichorus in Context*. Cambridge: 111–24.
Bowie, E. L. 2019. *Longus: Daphnis and Chloe*. Cambridge.
Branham, R. B. 2019. *Inventing the Novel: Bakhtin and Petronius Face to Face*. Oxford.
Bremmer, J. and Erskine, A. eds. 2010. *The Gods of Ancient Greece: Identities and Transformations*. Edinburgh.
Brethes, R. 2007. '*Poiein aischra kai legein aischra*, est ce vraiment le même chose? Ou la bouche souillée de Chariclée'. In Rimell ed. 2007: 1–33.
Bretzigheimer, G. 1998. 'Die Persinna-Geschichte: eine Erfindung des Kalasiris? Überlegungen zu Heliodors *Äthiopika*, 4, 12, 1–13, 1'. *WS* 111: 93–118.
Brisson, L. 2004 *How Philosophers Saved Myths: Allegorical Interpretation and Classical Mythology*. Trans. Catherine Tihany. Chicago.

REFERENCES 273

Buchheim, T. 1989. *Gorgias von Leontinoi: Reden, Fragmente und Testimonien.* Hamburg.
Büchner, W. 1940. 'Die Penelopeszenen in der Odyssee'. *Hermes* 75: 129–67.
Bühler, W. 1976. 'Das Element des Visuellen in der Eingangsszene von Heliodors *Aithiopika*'. *WS* 10: 177–85.
Caner, D. 2010. *History and Hagiography from the Late Antique Sinai.* Liverpool.
Capettini, E. 2018. 'Charicleia the Bacchante: *Erōs* and Genealogy in Heliodorus' *Aethiopica*'. In Cueva et al. eds. 2018: 195–220.
Castrucci, G. 2017. 'Il "Romanzo di Alcesti"'. *AN* 14: 69–102.
Cavallo, G. 1996. 'Veicoli materiali della letteratura di consume: maniere di scrivere e maniere di leggere'. In Pecere, O. and Stramaglia, A. eds, *La letteratura di consumo nel mondo Greco-Latino.* Cassino: 13–46.
Cave, T. 1988. *Recognitions: A Study in Poetics.* Oxford.
Cerri, G. 1991. 'Il significato di *sphregis* in Teognide e la salvaguardia dell'autenticità testuale nel mondo antico'. *QS* 17: 21–40.
Chuvin, P. 2004. *Chronique des derniers païens: La disparition du paganisme dans l'Empire romain, du règne de Constantin à celui de Justinien.* 2nd ed. Paris.
Ciocani, V. E. 2018. 'Searching for a Foil to Charicleia: Heliodorus' *Aethiopica* and the *Homeric Hymns to Demeter*.' *Mnemosyne* 71: 58–74.
Colonna, A. 1938 *Heliodori* Aethiopica. Rome.
Colonna, A. 1960. 'Teofane Cerameo e Filippo Filosofo'. *Bollettino del Comitato per la preparazione della edizione nazionale dei classici greci e latini* n.s. 8: 25–8.
Colonna, A. 1987. *Eliodoro. Le Etiopiche.* Turin.
Conca, F. 1983. 'Le "Narrationes" di Nilo e il romanzo greco'. In Leone ed. 1983: 349–60.
Coraes, A. 1804. Ἡλιοδώρου Αἰθιοπικῶν βιβλία δέκα. 2 vols. Paris.
Corcella, A. 2010. 'Echi del romanzo e di Procopio di Gaza in Filagato Cerameo'. *ByzZ* 103: 25–38.
Corcella, A. 2011. 'Riuso e reimpiego dell'antico in Filagato'. In Bianchi ed. 2011b: 11–19.
Corcoran, S. 2000. 'The Sins of the Fathers: A Neglected Constitution of Diocletian on Incest'. *Journal of Legal History* 21.2: 1–34.
Cribiore, R. 1995. 'A Hymn to the Nile'. *ZPE* 106: 97–106.
Cribiore, R. 2001. 'The Grammarian's Choice: The Popularity of Euripides' *Phoenissae* in Hellenistic and Roman Education'. In Too, Y. L. ed., *Education in Greek and Roman Antiquity.* Leiden: 241–59.
Criscuolo, U. 1989. *Michele Psello. Autobiografia: encomio per la madre.* Naples.
Cueva, E. P. and Byrne, S. N. eds. 2014. *A Companion to the Ancient Novel.* Malden, MA, Oxford, and Chichester.
Cueva, E. P., Harrison, S., Mason, H., Owens, W. and Schwartz, S. eds. 2018. *Re-wiring the Ancient Novel.* 2 vols. Groningen.
Cupane, C. 1978. 'Filagato da Cerami φιλόσοφος e διδάσκαλος: Contributo alla storia della cultura bizantina in età normanna'. *SicGymn* n.s. 31: 1–28.
Currie, B. 2005. *Pindar and the Cult of Heroes.* Oxford.
D'Alconzo, N. 2019. 'Concepts and Conceptions: Reading *Aithiopika* 10,14,7'. In Repath and Herrmann eds. 2019: 211–32.

Davies, M. 2010. '"Sins of the Fathers": Omitted Sacrifices and Offended Deities in Greek Literature and the Folktale'. *Eikasmos* 21: 331–55.
de Jong, I. and Nünlist, R. 2004. 'From Bird's Eye View to Close-up: The Standpoint of the Narrator in the Homeric Epics'. In Bierl, A., Schmitt, A., and Willi, A. eds, *Antike Literatur in neuer Deutung: Festschrift für Joachim Latacz anlässlich seines 70. Geburtstages*. Munich and Leipzig: 63–83.
de Temmerman, K. 2010. 'Ancient Rhetoric as a Hermeneutical Tool for the Analysis of Characterization in Narrative Literature'. *Rhetorica* 28: 23–51.
de Temmerman, K. 2014. *Crafting Characters: Heroes and Heroines in the Ancient Greek Novel*. Oxford.
de Vries, G. J. 1969. *A Commentary on the* Phaedrus *of Plato*. Amsterdam.
Deacy, S. and Pierce, K. eds. 1997. *Rape in Antiquity: Sexual Violence in the Greek and Roman Worlds*. London.
Deleuze, G. and Guattari, F. 1987 *A Thousand Plateaus: Capitalism and Schizophrenia*. Trans. Massumi, B. Minneapolis.
Deleuze, G. and Parnet, C. 1987. *Dialogues*. Trans. Tomlinson, H. and Habberjam, B. New York.
Delivorrias, A. 1968. 'Die Kultstatue der Aphrodite von Daphni'. *AntP* 8: 19–31.
Derbew, S. 2022. *Untangling Blackness in Greek Antiquity*. Cambridge.
Derbew, S. F. 2018. 'The Metatheater of Blackness: Looking at and through Black Skin Color in Ancient Greek Literature and Art'. Diss., Yale University.
Dietrich, B. C. 1983. 'Divine Epiphanies in Homer'. *Numen* 30: 53–79.
Doniger, W. 2000. *The Bedtrick: Tales of Sex and Masquerade*. Chicago.
Doulamis, K. 2012. 'All's Well that Ends Well: Storytelling, Predictive Signs, and the Voice of the Author in Chariton's *Callirhoe*'. *Mnemosyne* 65: 18–39.
Dowden, K. 1996. 'Heliodoros: Serious Intentions'. *CQ* 46: 267–85.
Dowden, K. 1998. 'Cupid and Psyche: A Question of the Vision of Apuleius'. In Zimmerman, M. et al. eds, *Aspects of Apuleius' Golden Ass, Vol. 2*. Groningen: 1–22.
Dowden, K. 2005. 'Greek Novel and the Ritual of Life: An Exercise in Taxonomy'. In Harrison, Paschalis, and Frangoulidis eds. 2005: 23–35. Groningen.
Dowden, K. 2006. 'Pouvoir divin, discours humain chez Héliodore'. In Pouderon and Peigney eds. 2006: 249–61.
Dowden, K. 2010. 'The Gods in the Greek Novel'. In Bremmer and Erskine eds. 2010: 362–74.
Dowden, K. 2011. 'The Myth that Saves: Mysteries and Mysteriosophies'. In Dowden, K. and Livingstone, N. eds, *A Companion to Greek Mythology*. Malden, MA, Oxford, and Chichester: 283–300.
Dowden, K. 2013. '"But there is a Difference in the Ends …": Brigands and Teleology in the Ancient Novel'. In Paschalis and Panayotakis eds. 2013: 41–60.
Dowden, K. 2015. 'Kalasiris, Apollonios of Tyana, and the Lies of Teiresias'. In Panayotakis, S., Schmeling, G., and Paschalis, M. eds, *Holy Men and Charlatans in the Ancient Novel (AN*, Suppl. 19). Groningen: 1–16.
Dué, C. and Ebbott, M. 2010. *Iliad 10 and the Poetics of Ambush*. Washington, DC.
Duff, T. E. 2008. 'Models of Education in Plutarch'. *JHS* 128: 1–26.
Duluş, M. 2011. 'Philagathos of Cerami and the Monastic Renewal in the Twelfth-Century Norman Kingdom: Preaching and Persuasion'. In Bianchi ed. 2011b: 53–62.

Dyck, A. 1986. *Michael Psellus: The Essays on Euripides and George of Pisidia and on Heliodorus and Achilles Tatius.* Vienna.

Edwards, M. W. 1991. *The Iliad: A Commentary. Vol. 5: Books 17–20.* Cambridge.

Egger, B. 1990. *Women in the Greek Novel.* Unpubl. Diss., University of California, Irvine.

Egger, B. 1999. 'The Role of Women in the Greek Novel: Woman as Heroine and Reader'. In Swain ed. 1999: 108–36.

Elmer, D. F. 2008. 'Heliodoros's "Sources": Intertextuality, Paternity, and the Nile River in the *Aithiopika*'. *TAPA* 138: 411–50.

Evans Grubbs, J. 1989. 'Abduction Marriage in Antiquity: A Law of Constantine (*CTh* IX. 24. 1) and its Social Context'. *JRS* 79: 59–83.

Evans Grubbs, J. 2015. 'Making the Private Public: Illegitimacy and Incest in Roman Law'. In Ando, C. and Rüpke, J. eds, *Public and Private in Ancient Mediterranean Law and Religion.* Berlin, Munich, and Boston: 115–42.

Fantuzzi, M. 2014. 'Tragic Smiles: When Tragedy Gets Too Comic for Aristotle and Later Hellenistic Readers'. In Hunter, R., Rengakos, A., and Sistakou, E. eds, *Hellenistic Studies at a Crossroads.* Berlin: 215–33.

Fetterley, J. 1978. *The Resisting Reader: A Feminist Approach to American Fiction.* Bloomington.

Feuillâtre, E. 1966. *Études sur les Éthiopiques d'Héliodore. Contribution à la connaissance du roman grec.* Paris.

Fick, S. M. E. 2002. 'Heliodors Heldin Chariklea und die Vorstellungswelt der Priesterdynastie von Emesa'. In Ulf, C., and Rollinger, R. eds, *Geschlechter—Frauen—Fremde Ethnien in antiker Ethnographie, Theorie und Realität.* Innsbruck: 515–24.

Finglass, P. and Davies, M. 2015. *Stesichorus: The Poems.* Cambridge.

Finley, M. 1964. *The World of Odysseus.* London.

Foerster, R. ed. 1913. *Libanii Opera, Vol. 7.* Leipzig.

Ford, A. L. 1985. 'The Seal of Theognis: The Politics of Authorship in Archaic Greece'. In Figueira, T. and Nagy, G. eds. *Theognis of Megara: Poetry and the Polis.* Baltimore: 82–95.

Freud, S. 1933. *New Introductory Lectures on Psychoanalysis.* London.

Fusillo, M. 1989. *Il romanzo greco: polifonia ed eros.* Venice.

Fusillo, M. 1990. 'Il testo nel testo: la citazione nel romanzo greco'. *MD* 25: 27–48.

Fusillo, M. 1991. *Naissance du roman,* tr. M. Abrioux of Fusillo 1989. Paris.

Fusillo, M. 1997. 'How Novels End: Some Patterns of Closure in Ancient Narrative'. In Roberts, D. H., Dunn, F. M. and Fowler, D. eds, *Classical Closure: Reading the End in Greek and Latin Literature.* Princeton: 209–27.

Fusillo, M. 2007. '*Aethiopica* (Heliodorus, Third or Fourth Century)'. In Moretti, F. ed., *The Novel. Vol. 2: Forms and Themes.* Princeton: 131–7.

Futre Pinheiro, M. P. 1998. 'Time and Narrative Technique in Heliodorus' *Aethiopica*'. *ANRW* II.34.4: 3148–73.

Ganiban, R. T. 2007. *Statius and Virgil: The Thebaid and the Reinterpretation of the Aeneid.* Cambridge.

Garson, R. W. 1975. 'Notes on Some Homeric Echoes in Heliodorus' *Aethiopica*'. *AClass* 18: 137–40.

Gärtner, H. 1969. 'Charikleia in Byzanz'. *A&A* 15: 47–69.

Gärtner, H. ed. 1984. *Beiträge zum griechischen Liebesroman*. Hildesheim.
Garvie, A. F. 1994. *Homer. Odyssey Books VI–VIII*. Cambridge.
Genette, G. 1997. *Paratexts: Thresholds of Interpretation*. Trans. Lewin, J. E. Cambridge.
Gilhuly, K. 2009. *The Feminine Matrix of Sex and Gender in Classical Athens*. Cambridge.
Gill, C. 2006. *The Structured Self in Hellenistic and Roman Thought*. Oxford.
Goldhill, S. 2020. *Preposterous Poetics: The Politics and Aesthetics of Form in Late Antiquity*. Cambridge.
Goold, G. P. 1995. *Chariton. Callirhoe*. Cambridge, MA.
Graverini, L. 2010. 'Amore, "dolcezza"', stupore: romanzo antico e filosofia'. In Uglione, R. ed., *Lector intende: laetaberis: il romanzo dei Greci e dei Romani. Atti del Convegno Nazionale*, Turin, April 27–28. Alessandria: 57–88.
Graverini, L. 2014. 'From the Epic to the Novelistic Hero: Some Patterns of a Metamorphosis'. In Cueva and Byrne eds. 2014: 288–99.
Graziosi, B. 2002. *Inventing Homer: The Early Reception of Epic*. Cambridge.
Grethlein, J. 2015a. 'Aesthetic Experiences, Ancient and Modern'. *NLH* 46: 309–33.
Grethlein, J. 2015b. 'Social Minds and Narrative Time: Collective Experience in Thucydides and Heliodorus'. *Narrative* 23: 123–39.
Grethlein, J. 2016. 'Minding the Middle in Heliodorus' *Aethiopica*: False Closure, Triangular Foils and Self-Reflection'. *CQ* 66: 316–35.
Grethlein, J. 2017. *Aesthetic Experiences and Classical Antiquity. The Significance of Form in Narratives and Pictures*. Cambridge.
Grethlein, J. 2019. 'World and Words: The Limits to *Mimesis* and Immersion in Heliodorus' *Ethiopica*. In Grethlein, J., Huitink, L. and Tagliabue, A. eds, *Experience, Narrative, and Criticism in Ancient Greece: Under the Spell of Stories*. Oxford: 127–47.
Grethlein, J. 2021. *The Ancient Aesthetics of Deception: The Ethics of Enchantment from Gorgias to Heliodorus*. Cambridge.
Gronewald, M. 1976. 'Ein verkannter Papyrus des Achilleus Tatios (*P.Oxy.* 1014 = Achilleus Tatios IV 14,2-5)'. *ZPE* 22: 14–17.
Grosz, E. 1993. 'A Thousand Tiny Sexes: Feminism and Rhizomatics'. *Topoi* 12: 167–79.
Groves, R. B. IV. 2012. 'Cross-Language Communication in Heliodorus' *Aethiopica*'. Diss., University of California, Los Angeles.
Guez, J.-P. 2005. 'Achille Tatius ou le paysage monde'. In Pouderon, B. ed. 2005: 299–308.
Hägg, T. 2002. 'Epiphany in the Greek Novels: The Emplotment of a Metaphor'. *Eranos* 100: 51–61. Repr. in *Parthenope. Selected Studies in Ancient Greek Fiction*. Copenhagen, 2004: 141–55.
Hall, E. 1989. *Inventing the Barbarian: Greek Self-Definition through Tragedy*. Oxford.
Halliwell, S. 2002. *The Aesthetics of Mimesis: Ancient Texts and Modern Problems*. Princeton.
Halliwell, S. 2011. *Between Ecstasy and Truth: Interpretations of Greek Poetics from Homer to Longinus*. Oxford.
Hani, J. 1978. 'Le personnage de Charicleia dans les *Éthiopiques*: incarnation de l'idéal moral et religieux d'une époque'. *BAGB* 3: 268–73.

Hardie, P. 1998. 'A Reading of Heliodorus, *Aithiopika* 3.4.1–5.2'. In Hunter ed. 1998b: 19–39.
Harris, M. 2001. 'Not Black and/or White: Reading Racial Difference in Heliodorus' *Ethiopica* and Pauline Hopkins's *Of One Blood*'. *African American Review* 35: 375–90.
Harris, W. V. 2009. *Dreams and Experience in Classical Antiquity*. Cambridge, MA.
Harrison, S., Paschalis, M., and Frangoulidis, S. eds. 2005. *Metaphor and the Ancient Novel*. AN Supplementum 4. Groningen.
Harrisson, J. 2013. *Dreams and Dreaming in the Roman Empire*. London.
Harsh, P. 1950. 'Penelope and Odysseus in *Odyssey* XIX'. *AJP* 71: 1–21.
Haynes, K. 2003. *Fashioning the Feminine in the Greek Novel*. London and New York.
Heath, M. 1998. 'Was Homer a Roman?'. *PLLS* 10: 23–56.
Heath, M. 2002–3. 'Theon and the History of the *Progymnasmata*'. *GRBS* 43: 129–60.
Hefti, V. 1950. 'Zur Erzählungstechnik in Heliodors *Aethiopica*'. Diss., Universität Basel. Vienna.
Heubeck, A. and Hoekstra, A. 1988. *A Commentary on Homer's Odyssey. Vol. 2: Books IX–XVI*. Oxford.
Heubeck, A., West. S., and Hainsworth, J. B. 1988. *A Commentary on Homer's Odyssey. Vol. 1: Introduction and Books I–VIII*. Oxford.
Hilton, J. L. 1998. 'A Commentary on Books Three and Four of the *Ethiopian Story* of Heliodorus'. Diss., University of Natal.
Hilton, J. L. 2001. 'The Dream of Charikles (4.14.2): Intertextuality and Irony in the *Ethiopian Story* of Heliodorus'. *AClass* 44: 77–86.
Hilton, J. L. 2012. 'The *Sphragis* of Heliodoros, Genealogy in the *Aithiopika*, and Julian's *Hymn to King Helios*'. *Ágora* 14: 195–219.
Hopkins, P. 1905. *A Primer of Facts Pertaining to the Early Greatness of the African Race and the Possibility of its Restauration by its Descendants*. Cambridge, MA.
Hunter, R. 1983. *Eubulus: The Fragments*. Cambridge.
Hunter, R. 1993. *The Argonautica of Apollonius: Literary Studies*. Cambridge.
Hunter, R. 1998a. 'The *Aithiopika* of Heliodorus: Beyond Interpretation?'. In Hunter, R. ed., *Studies in Heliodorus*. Cambridge: 40–59. Repr. in Hunter 2008: 804–28.
Hunter, R. ed. 1998b. *Studies in Heliodorus*. Cambridge.
Hunter, R. 2004. 'Homer and Greek Literature'. In Fowler, R. ed., *The Cambridge Companion to Homer*. Cambridge: 235–53.
Hunter, R. 2005a. 'Showing and Telling: Notes from the Boundary'. *Eikasmos* 16: 179–91. Repr. in Hunter 2008: 663–77.
Hunter, R. 2005b. '"Philip the Philosopher" on the *Aithiopika* of Heliodorus'. In Harrison, Paschalis, and Frangoulidis eds. 2005: 123–38.
Hunter, R. 2008. *On Coming After: Studies in Post-Classical Greek Literature and its Reception*. Berlin.
Hunter, R. 2014. '"Where Do I Begin?": An Odyssean Narrative Strategy and its Afterlife'. In Cairns, D. and Scodel, R. eds, *Defining Greek Narrative*. Edinburgh: 137–55.
Innes, D., Hine, H., and Pelling, C. eds. 1995. *Ethics and Rhetoric: Classical Essays for Donald Russell on his Seventy-Fifth Birthday*. Oxford.
Irwin, E. 2014. 'Ethnography and Empire: Homer and the Hippocratics in Herodotus' Ethiopian *Logos*, 3.17–26'. *Histos* 8: 25–75.

Jackson, C. R. 2016. 'Fraud, Forgery, and Falsehood: Theories and Practices of Fiction in the Ancient Novel'. Diss., University of Cambridge.

Janko, R. 1992. *The Iliad: A Commentary. Vol. IV: Books 13–16.* Cambridge.

Jeffreys, E. 1998. *Digenis Akritis: The Grottaferrata and Escorial Versions.* Cambridge.

Johne, R. 1987. 'Dido und Charikleia: zur Gestaltung der Frau bei Vergil und im grieschischen Liebesroman'. *Eirene* 24: 21–33.

Johnston, I. trans. 2007. *Homer: The Iliad.* 2nd ed. Arlington, VA.

Jones, H. L. trans. 1927. *Strabo: The Geography, Vol. 4.* Cambridge, MA.

Jones, M. 2005. 'Base and Heavenly Magic in Heliodoros' *Aithiopika*'. *AN* 4: 79–98.

Jones, M. 2006. 'Heavenly and Pandemic Names in Heliodorus' *Aethiopika*'. *CQ* 56: 548–62.

Jones, M. 2007. '*Andreia* and Gender in the Greek Novels'. In Morgan, J. R., and Jones, M. eds, *Philosophical Presences in the Ancient Novel. Ancient Narrative,* Supplementum 10. Groningen: 111–36.

Jones, M. 2012. *Playing the Man: Performing Masculinities in the Ancient Greek Novel.* Oxford and New York.

Kaimio, M. 1996. 'How to Enjoy a Greek Novel: Chariton Guiding his Audience'. *Arctos* 30: 49–73.

Kasprzyk, D. 2017. 'De Pindare à Héliodore: poésie épinicique et épinicie romanesque'. In Biraud and Briand eds. 2017: 333–46.

Kerényi, K. 1927. *Die griechisch-orientalische Romanliteratur in religionsgeschichtlicher Beleuchtung.* Tübingen.

Kessels, A. H. M. 1978. *Studies on the Dream in Greek Literature.* Utrecht.

Keul-Deutscher, M. 1997. 'Heliodorstudien II. Die Liebe in den *Aithiopika*'. *RhM* 140: 341–62.

Keyes, C. W. 1922. 'The Structure of Heliodorus' *Aethiopica*'. *SPh* 19: 42–51.

Kim. L. 2010. *Homer between History and Fiction in Imperial Greek Literature.* Cambridge.

Kim, L. 2019. 'The Trouble with Calasiris: Duplicity and Autobiographical Narrative in Heliodorus and Galen'. *Mnemosyne* 72: 229–49.

Kircher, K. 1910. *Die sakrale Bedeutung des Weines im Altertum in seiner Beziehung zur Gottheit.* Giessen.

König, J. 2008. 'Body and Text'. In Whitmarsh ed. 2008: 127–44.

Konstan, D. 1994. *Sexual Symmetry: Love in the Ancient Novel and Related Genres.* Princeton.

Konstan, D. 1994. 'Xenophon of Ephesus: Eros and Narrative in the Novel'. In Morgan and Stoneman eds. 1994: 49–63.

Konstan, D. 2009. 'Reading Politics in Suetonius'. In Dominik, W. J., Garthwaite, J., and Roche, P. eds, *Writing Politics in Imperial Rome.* Leiden: 447–62.

Konstan, D. 2013. 'The Grieving Self: Reflections on Lucian's *On Mourning* and the Consolatory Tradition'. In Baltussen, H. ed., *Greek and Roman Consolations: Eight Studies of a Tradition and its Afterlife.* Swansea: 139–51.

Kranz, W. 1961. 'Sphragis: Ichform und Namensiegel als Eingangs- und Schlussmotiv Antiker Dichtung'. *RhM* 104: 3–46, 97–124.

Krauss, K. 2021. 'Heliodorus: A New Patristic Context'. *Ancient Narrative* 18 (preliminary online version).

Kruchió, B. 2018a. 'What Charicles Knew: Fragmentary Narration and Ambiguity in Heliodorus' *Aethiopica*'. *Ancient Narrative* 14: 175–94.

Kruchió, B. 2018b. 'The Dynamics of Summing up: A Metaliterary Reading of Heliodorus 10.36 and 10.39'. In Cueva, Mason, and Schwartz eds. 2018: 153–75.

Lalanne, S. 2006. *Une éducation grecque: rites de passage et construction des genres dans le roman grec ancien*. Paris.

Lamberton, R. 1983. *Porphyry on the Cave of the Nymphs*. Barrytown, NY.

Lamberton, R. 1986. *Homer the Theologian: Neoplatonist Allegorical Reading and the Growth of the Epic Tradition*. Berkeley.

Lanata, G. 1963 *Poetica pre-platonica: Testimonianze e frammenti*. Florenz.

Laplace, M. M. J. 1980. 'Les légendes troyennes dans le roman de Chariton, *Chairéas et Callirhoé*'. *REG* 93: 83–125.

Laplace, M. M. J. 1991. 'Achille Tatius, *Leucippé et Clitophon*: des fables au roman de formation'. *Groningen Colloquia on the Novel* 4: 35–56.

Lateiner, D. 1997. 'Abduction Marriage in Heliodorus' *Aethiopica*'. *GRBS* 38: 409–39.

Lavagnini, B. 1974. 'Filippo-Filagato, promotore degli studi di greco in Calabria'. *BBGG* 28: 1–12.

Lefteratou, A. 2018. *Mythological Narratives: The Bold and Faithful Heroines of the Greek Novel*. Berlin.

Lefteratou. A. 2019. 'Gemstones, Textiles and a Princess: Precious Commodities in Heliodorus' *Aethiopica*'. *CJ* 115: 1–30.

Leone, P. 1983. *Studi bizantini e neogreci: atti del IV Congresso nazionale di studi bizantini, Saggi e ricerche (Università degli Studi di Lecce. Istituto di Storia medioevale e moderna)* 7. Galatina.

Levin, D. N. 1992. '*Aethiopica* III–IV: Greek Dunces, Egyptian Sage'. *Athenaeum* 80: 499–506.

Lightfoot, C. S. 1988. 'Facts and Fiction: The Third Siege of Nisibis (AD 350)'. *Historia* 37: 105–25.

Lowe, N. 2000. *The Classical Plot and the Invention of Western Narrative*. Cambridge.

Lye, S. 2016. 'Gender and Ethnicity in Heliodorus' *Aithiopika*'. *CW* 109: 235–62.

MacAlister, S. 1996. *Dreams and Suicides. The Greek Novel from Antiquity to the Byzantine Empire*. London and New York.

Malkin, I. 1998. *The Returns of Odysseus: Colonization and Ethnicity*. Berkeley.

Manieri, A. 1998. *L'immagine poetica nella teoria degli antichi: Phantasia ed enargeia*. Pisa.

Marinčič, M. 2007. 'Advertising One's Own Story: Text and Speech in Achilles Tatius' *Leucippe and Clitophon*'. In Rimell ed. 2007: 168–200.

Marino, E. 1990. 'Il teatro nel romanzo: Eliodoro e il codice spettacolore'. *MD* 25: 203–18.

Mavrogordato, J. 1956. *Digenes Akrites*. Oxford.

Mazal, O. 1958. 'Die Satzstruktur in den *Aithiopika* des Heliodor von Emesa'. *WS* 71: 116–31. Repr. in Gärtner ed. 1984: 451–66.

McLaren, J. S. 2005. 'Josephus on Titus: The Vanquished Writing about the Victor'. In Sievers, J. and Lembi, G. eds, *Josephus and Jewish History in Flavian Rome and Beyond*. Leiden: 279–95.

Mecella, L. 2014. 'L'enigmatica figura di Eliodoro e la datazione delle *Etiopiche*'. *Mediterraneo antico* 17: 632–58.

Meijering, R. 1987. *Literary and Rhetorical Theories in Greek Scholia*. Groningen.
Merkelbach, R. 1962. *Roman und Mysterium in der Antike*. Munich.
Montiglio, S. 2011. *From Villain to Hero: Odysseus in Ancient Thought*. Ann Arbor.
Montiglio, S. 2013a. *Love and Providence: Recognition in the Ancient Novel*. Oxford
Montiglio, S. 2013b. '"His Eyes Stood as though of Horn or Steel": Odysseus' Fortitude and Moral Ideals in the Greek Novels'. In Paschalis and Panayotakis eds. 2013: 147-59.
Montiglio, S. 2015. *The Spell of Hypnos: Sleep and Sleeplessness in Greek Literature*. London.
Montiglio, S. 2019. 'They Get By without a Little Help from Their Slaves: The Exceptional Destiny of Chariclea and Theagenes'. In Panayotakis and Paschalis eds. 2019: 127-38.
Morales, H. 2004. *Vision and Narrative in Achilles Tatius' Leucippe and Clitophon*. Cambridge.
Morales, H. 2005. 'Metaphor, Gender and the Ancient Greek Novel'. In Harrison, Paschalis, and Frangoulidis eds. 2005: 1-22.
Morales, H. 2011. 'Fantasising Phryne: The Psychology and Ethics of *Ekphrasis*'. *CCJ* 57: 71-104.
Morales, H. 2016. 'Rape, Violence, Complicity: Colluthus's *Abduction of Helen*'. *Arethusa* 49: 61-92.
Morgan, J. R. 1978. 'A Commentary on the Ninth and Tenth Books of Heliodoros' *Aithiopika*'. Diss., University of Oxford.
Morgan, J. R. 1982. 'History, Romance, and Realism in the *Aithiopika* of Heliodoros'. *ClAnt* 1: 221-65.
Morgan, J. R. 1989a. 'A Sense of the Ending: The Conclusion of Heliodoros' *Aithiopika*'. *TAPA* 119: 299-320.
Morgan, J. R. 1989b. 'The Story of Knemon in Heliodoros' *Aithiopika*'. *JHS* 109: 99-113.
Morgan, J. R. 1989c. 'Heliodorus: *An Ethiopian Story*'. In Reardon ed. 1989: 349-588.
Morgan, J. R. 1991. 'Reader and Audiences in the *Aithiopika* of Heliodoros'. *Groningen Colloquia on the Novel* 4: 85-103.
Morgan, J. R. 1993. 'Make-Believe and Make Believe: The Fictionality of the Greek Novel'. In Gill, C. and Wiseman, P. eds, *Lies and Fiction in the Ancient World*. Exeter: 175-229.
Morgan, J. R., and Stoneman, R. eds. 1994. *Greek Fiction: The Greek Novel in Context*. London.
Morgan, J. R. 1995. 'The Greek Novel: Towards a Sociology of Production and Reception'. In Powell, A. ed., *The Greek World*. London: 130-52.
Morgan, J. R. 1996. 'The Ancient Novel at the End of the Century: Scholarship since the Dartmouth Conference'. *CPh* 91: 63-73.
Morgan, J. R. 1998. 'Narrative Doublets in Heliodorus' *Aithiopika*'. In Hunter ed. 1998b: 60-78.
Morgan, J. R. 2001. 'The Prologues of the Greek Novels and Apuleius'. In Kahane, A. and Laird, A. eds, *A Companion to the Prologue of Apuleius' Metamorphoses*. Oxford: 152-62.

Morgan, J. R. 2003. 'Heliodoros'. In Schmeling ed. 2003: 417–56.
Morgan, J. R. 2004a. *Longus:* Daphnis and Chloe. Oxford.
Morgan, J. R. 2004b. 'Heliodorus'. In de Jong, I. J. F., Nünlist, R., and Bowie, A. eds, *Narrators, Narratees, and Narratives in Ancient Greek Literature.* Leiden: 523–43.
Morgan, J. R. 2005. 'Le blanc et le noir: perspectives païennes et perspectives chrétiennes sur l'Ethiopie d'Héliodore'. In Pouderon ed. 2005: 309–18.
Morgan, J. R. 2006. 'Un discours figuré chez Héliodore: Comment, en disant l'inverse de ce qu'on veut, on peut accomplir ce qu'on veut sans sembler dire l'inverse de ce qu'on veut'. In Pouderon and Peigney eds. 2006: 51–62.
Morgan, J. R. 2007a. 'Heliodorus'. In de Jong, I. J. F. and Nünlist, R. eds, *Time in Ancient Greek Literature.* Leiden: 483–504.
Morgan, J. R. 2007b. 'Kleitophon and Encolpius: Achilleus Tatius as Hidden Author'. In Paschalis, M., Frangoulidis, S., Harrison, S., and Zimmerman, M. eds, *The Greek and the Roman Novel: Parallel Readings.* Groningen: 105–20.
Morgan, J. R. and Harrison, S. 2008. 'Intertextuality'. In Whitmarsh ed. 2008: 218–36.
Morgan, J. R. 2009. 'The Emesan Connection: Philostratus and Heliodorus'. In Demoen, K. and Praet, D. eds, *Theios Sophistes: Essays on Flavius Philostratus' Vita Apollonii.* Leiden: 263–82.
Morgan, J. R. 2012a. 'Heliodorus'. In de Jong, I. J. F. ed., *Space in Ancient Greek Literature.* Leiden: 557–77.
Morgan, J. R. 2012b. 'Le culte du Nil chez Héliodore'. In Bost-Pouderon, C. and Pouderon, B. eds, *Les hommes et les dieux dans l'ancien roman.* Lyons: 255–67.
Morgan, J. R. 2013. 'The Erotics of Reading Fiction: Text and Body in Heliodorus'. In Bréchet, C., Videau, A., and Webb, R. eds, *Théories et pratiques de la fiction à l'époque impériale.* Paris: 225–37.
Morgan, J. R. 2014. 'Heliodorus the Hellene'. In Cairns, D. and Scodel, R. eds, *Defining Greek Narrative.* Edinburgh: 260–76.
Morgan, J. R. 2015. 'The Monk's Story: The *Narrationes* of Pseudo-Neilos of Ankyra'. In Panayotakis, Schmeling, and Paschalis eds. 2015: 167–93.
Morgan, J. R., and Repath, I. D. 2019. 'Mistresses and Servant-Women, and the Slavery and Mastery of Love in Heliodoros'. In Panayotakis and Paschalis eds. 2019: 139–60.
Morson, G. S. 1990. *Mikhail Bakhtin: Creation of a Prosaics.* Palo Alto.
Most, G. 2007. 'Allegory and Narrative in Heliodorus'. In Swain, S., Harrison, S., and Elsner, J. eds, *Severan Culture.* Cambridge: 160–7.
Most, G. 2009. 'Emotion, Memory, and Trauma'. In Eldridge, R. ed., *The Oxford Handbook of Philosophy and Literature.* Oxford: 442–63.
Müller, M. 2015. 'Assemblages and Actor-Networks: Rethinking Socio-Material Power, Politics and Space'. *Geography Compass* 9: 27–41.
Musié, M. 2019. 'The Representation of Persians in the Ancient Greek Novel'. Diss., Swansea University.
Mynors, R. A. B. ed. 1969. *P. Vergili Maronis Opera.* Oxford.
Neimke, Ph. 1889. 'Quaestiones Heliodoreae'. Diss., Halle.
Nesselrath, H.-G. 2002. 'Homerphilologie auf der Insel der Seligen: Lukian, *VH* II 20'. In Reichel, M. and Rengakos, A. eds, *Epea Pteroenta: Beiträge zur*

Homerforschung. Festschrift für Wolfgang Kullmann zum 75. Geburtstag. Stuttgart: 151–62.
ní Mheallaigh, K. 2008. 'Pseudo-Documentarism and the Limits of Ancient Fiction'. *AJP* 129: 403–31.
ní Mheallaigh, K. 2009. 'Monumental Fallacy: The Teleology of Origins in Lucian's *Verae Historiae*'. In Bartley, A. ed., *A Lucian for our Times*. Newcastle: 11–28.
ní Mheallaigh, K. 2014. *Reading Fiction with Lucian: Fakes, Freaks and Hyperreality*. Cambridge.
Nilsson, I. 2009. 'Desire and God Have Always Been Around, in Life and Romance Alike'. In Nilsson, I. ed., *Plotting with Eros: Essays on the Poetics of Love and the Erotics of Reading*. Copenhagen: 235–60.
Nilsson, I. and Zagklas, N. 2017. '"Hurry Up, Reap Every Flower of the *Logoi!*": The Use of Greek Novels in Byzantium'. *GRBS* 57: 1120–48.
Núñez, L. 2014. 'Liminal Games: Fluidity of the Sphragis of a Novelist'. In Futre Pinheiro, M. P., Schmeling, G., and Cueva, E. P. eds, *The Ancient Novel and the Frontiers of Genre*. Eelde: 143–68.
Nünlist, R. 2009. *The Ancient Critic at Work. Terms and Concepts of Literary Criticism in Greek Scholia*. Cambridge.
Olsen, S. 2012. 'Maculate Conception: Sexual Ideology and Creative Authority in Heliodorus' *Aethiopica*'. *AJP* 133: 301–22.
Omitowoju, R. 2002. *Rape and the Politics of Consent in Classical Athens*. Cambridge.
Ormand, K. 2010. 'Testing Virginity in Achilles Tatius and Heliodorus'. *Ramus* 39: 160–97.
Otto, N. 2009. *Enargeia: Untersuchung zur Charakteristik alexandrinischer Dichtung*. Wiesbaden.
Owens, W. M. 2020. *The Representation of Slavery in the Greek Novel: Resistance and Appropriation*. London and New York.
Palone, M. 2020. *Le Etiopiche di Eliodoro: Approcci narratologici e nuove prospettive*. Stuttgart.
Panayotakis, S. and Paschalis, M. eds. 2019 *Masters and Slaves in the Ancient Novel*. Ancient Narrative Supplementum 23. Groningen.
Panayotakis, S., Schmeling, G., and Paschalis, M. eds. 2015. *Holy Men and Charlatans in the Ancient Novel*. Groningen.
Papadimitropoulos, L. 2013. 'Love and the Reinstatement of the Self in Heliodorus' *Aethiopica*'. *G&R* 60: 101–13.
Papadimitropoulos, L. 2017. 'Chariclea's Identity and the Structure of Heliodorus' *Aethiopica*'. *HSCP* 109: 209–23.
Parkes, R. 2013. 'Chthonic Ingredients and Thematic Concerns: The Shaping of the Necromancy in Statius' *Thebaid*'. In Augoustakis, A. ed., *Ritual and Religion in Flavian Epic*. Oxford: 165–80.
Paschalis, M. 1987. 'Virgil's Actium-Nicopolis'. In Chrysou, E. ed., Νικόπολις Α΄: πρακτικά του πρώτου Διεθνούς Συμποσίου για τη Νικόπολη (23–9 Σεπτεμβρίου 1984). Preveza: 57–68.
Paschalis, M., Frangoulidis, S., Harrison, S., and Zimmerman, M. eds. 2007 *The Greek and Roman Novel: Parallel Readings*. Ancient Narrative, Supplementum 8. Groningen.

Paschalis, M. and Panayotakis, S. eds. 2013. *The Construction of the Real and the Ideal in the Ancient Novel. Ancient Narrative,* Supplementum 17. Groningen.
Paulsen, T. 1992. *Inszenierung des Schicksals: Tragödie und Komödie im Roman des Heliodor.* Trier.
Peigney, J. 2017. 'Les *Éthiopiques,* roman homérique?' In Biraud and Briand eds. 2017: 295-309.
Perkins, J. 1999. 'An Ancient "Passing" Novel: Heliodorus' *Aithiopika'. Arethusa* 32: 197-214.
Pernot, L. 2004. 'La coscia di Odisseo (σ 74) ed i suoi interpreti'. In Abbamonte, G., Conti Bizzarro, F., and Spina, L. eds, *L'ultima parola: l'analisi dei testi. Teorie e pratiche nell' antichità greca e Latina.* Naples: 247-59.
Perry, B. E. 1967. *The Ancient Romances: A Literary-Historical Account of their Origins.* Berkeley.
Petridou, G. 2016. *Divine Epiphany in Greek Literature and Culture.* Oxford.
Pitcher, L. 2016. 'A Shaggy Thigh Story. Kalasiris on the *Life of Homer* (Heliodorus 3.14)'. In de Temmerman, K. and Demoen, K. eds, *Writing Biography in Greece and Rome: Narrative Technique and Fictionalization.* Cambridge: 293-305.
Platt, V. 2011. *Facing the Gods. Epiphany and Representation in Graeco-Roman Art, Literature and Religion.* Cambridge.
Plazenet, L. 1995. 'Le Nil et son Delta dans les romans grecs'. *Phoenix* 49: 5-22.
Plazenet, L. 2008. *Héliodore. L'histoire aethiopique. Traduction de Jacques Amyot.* Paris.
Pletcher, J. A. 1998. 'Euripides in Heliodoros' *Aithiopika* 7-8'. *Groningen Colloquia on the Novel* 9: 17-27.
Pohlenz, M. 1920. 'Die Anfänge der griechischen Poetik'. In *Kleine Schriften* 2. Repr. Hildesheim 1965: 142-78.
Porter, J. I. 2011. 'Making and Unmaking: the Achaean Wall and the Limits of Fictionality in Homeric Criticism'. *TAPA* 141: 1-36.
Pouderon, B. ed. 2005. *Lieux, décors et paysages de l'ancien roman de l'Antiquité à Byzance.* Lyon.
Pouderon, B. and Peigney, J. eds. 2006. *Discours et débats dans l'ancient roman.* Lyon.
Pratt, L. H. 1995. 'The Seal of Theognis, Writing, and Oral Poetry'. *AJP* 116: 171-84.
Prioux, E. 2016. 'Jardins métapoétiques: la reflexion stylistique dans les descriptions de jardins d'Achille Tatius, de Longus et de Philostrate'. In Guez, J.-P. and Kasprzyk, D. eds, *Penser la prose dans le monde gréco-romain.* Rennes: 145-64.
Purves, A. 2019. *Homer and the Poetics of Gesture.* Oxford.
Quack, J. F. 2005. 'Gibt es eine ägyptische Homer-Rezeption?' In Luther, A. ed., *Odyssee-Rezeptionen.* Frankfurt am Main: 55-72.
Quinn, J. 2017. *In Search of the Phoenicians.* Princeton.
Ramelli, I. 2002. *I romanzi antichi e il Cristianesimo: contesto e contatti.* Madrid.
Rattenbury, R. M. and Lumb, T. W. eds, and Maillon, J. trans. 1935-43. *Héliodore. Les Éthiopiques* (Théagène et Chariclée). 3 vols. Paris. 2nd ed. 1960.
Reardon, B. P. ed. 1989. *Collected Ancient Greek Novels.* Berkeley. Rev. ed. 2008.
Reitzenstein, R. 1906. *Hellenistische Wundererzählungen.* Leipzig.
Repath, I. D. 2005. 'Achilles Tatius' *Leucippe and Cleitophon*: What Happened Next?'. *CQ* 55: 250-65.
Repath, I. D. 2010. 'Plato in Petronius: Petronius *in platanona'. CQ* 60: 577-95.

Repath, I. D. 2011. 'Platonic Love and Erotic Education in Longus' *Daphnis and Chloe*'. In Doulamis, K. ed., *Echoing Narratives: Studies of Intertextuality in Greek and Roman Prose Fiction*. Ancient Narrative, Supplementum 13. Groningen: 99-122.

Repath, I. D. 2015. 'Cleitophon the Charlatan'. In Panayotakis, Schmeling, and Paschalis eds. 2015: 47-68.

Repath, I. D. and Herrmann, F.-G. eds. 2019. *Some Organic Readings in Narrative, Ancient and Modern*. Ancient Narrative, Supplementum 27. Groningen.

Rimell, V. ed. 2007. *Seeing Tongues, Hearing Scripts: Orality and Representation in the Ancient Novel*. Groningen.

Roby, C. 2016. *Technical Ekphrasis in Greek and Roman Science and Literature: The Written Machine between Alexandria and Rome*. Cambridge.

Robiano, P. 2000. 'La citation poétique dans le roman érotique grec'. *REA* 102: 509-29.

Robiano, P. 2021. 'Nommer les personnages perses dans le roman grec: les choix de Chariton, *Callirhoé*, et d'Héliodore, les *Éthiopiques*'. *Ancient Narrative* 17: 63-89.

Robinson, D. and Goddio, F. 2015. *Thonis-Heracleion in Context*. Oxford.

Roilos, P. 2005. *Amphoteroglossia: A Poetics of the Twelfth-Century Medieval Greek Novel*. Washington, DC.

Roisman, J. 1993. *The General Demosthenes and his Use of Military Surprise*. Stuttgart.

Rommel, H. 1923. *Die naturwissenschaftlich-paradoxographischen Exkurse bei Philostratos, Heliodoros und Achilleus Tatios*. Stuttgart.

Roscino, C. 2010. *Polignoto di Taso*. Rome.

Rosenzweig, R. 2004. *Worshipping Aphrodite. Art and Cult in Classical Athens*. Ann Arbor.

Ross, A. J. 2015. 'Syene as Face of Battle: Heliodorus and Late Antique Historiography'. *Ancient Narrative* 12: 1-26.

Rossi Taibbi, G. ed. 1969. *Filagato da Cerami: Omelie per ivangeli domenicali e le feste di tutto l'anno*. Palermo.

Rowe, C. J. 1986. *Plato*: Phaedrus. Warminster.

Rutherford, I. 2000. 'The Genealogy of the *Boukoloi*: How Greek Literature Appropriated an Egyptian Narrative-Motif'. *JHS* 120: 106-18.

Saïd, S. 2012. 'Herodotus and the "Myth" of the Trojan War'. In Baragwanath, E. and de Bakker, M. eds, *Myth, Truth, and Narrative in Herodotus*. Oxford: 87-105.

Sánchez Hernández, J. P. 2018. 'Merchant's Road toward the Utopia in Heliodorus' *Aethiopica*'. *Antichthon* 52: 143-60.

Sandy, G. N. 1982a. *Heliodorus*. Boston.

Sandy, G. N. 1982b. 'Characterization and Philosophical Decor in Heliodorus' *Aethiopica*'. *TAPA* 112: 141-67.

Schironi, F. 2018. *The Best of the Grammarians: Aristarchus of Samothrace on the Iliad*. Ann Arbor.

Schmeling, G. L. 1974. *Chariton*. New York.

Schmeling, G. L. ed. 2003. *The Novel in the Ancient World*. Leiden. 2nd ed. 2003.

Schmitz, T. 1997. *Bildung und Macht: zur sozialen und politischen Funktion der zweiten Sophistik in der griechischen Welt der Kaiserzeit*. Munich.

Schuchhardt, W. H. 1977. *Alkamenes: Winckelmannsprogramm der Archäologischen Gesellschaft zu Berlin 126*. Berlin.
Schwartz, S. 2007. 'From Bedroom to Courtroom: The Adultery Type-Scene and the Acts of Andrew'. In Penner, T. and Vander Stichele, C. eds, *Mapping Gender in Ancient Religious Discourse*. Leiden: 267–311.
Schwartz, S. 2012. 'The Κρίσις Inside: Heliodorus' Variations on the Bedtrick'. In Futre Pinheiro, M., Skinner, M. B., and Zeitlin, F. I. eds, *Narrating Desire: Eros, Sex, and Gender in the Ancient Novel*. Berlin: 161–80.
Schwartz, S. 2016. *From Bedroom to Courtroom: Law and Justice in the Greek Novel*. Groningen.
Segal, C. 1962. 'Gorgias and the Psychology of the *Logos*'. *HSCP* 66: 99–155.
Selden, D. 1998. '*Aithiopika* and Ethiopianism'. In Hunter ed. 1998b: 182–217.
Sheppard, A. 2014. *The Poetics of Phantasia: Imagination in Ancient Aesthetics*. London.
Sinko, T. 1906. 'De Homero Aegyptio'. *Eos* 12: 12–20.
Slater, N. 2007. 'Posthumous Parleys: Chatting Up the Dead in the Ancient Novels'. In Paschalis, Frangoulidis, Harrison, and Zimmerman eds. 2007: 57–69.
Smith, S. D. 2007a. *Greek Identity and the Athenian Past in Chariton: The Romance of Empire*. Groningen.
Smith, S. D. 2007b. 'Wonders beyond Athens: Reading the "Phaedra" Stories in Apuleius and Heliodoros'. In Paschalis, Frangoulidis, Harrison, and Zimmerman eds. 2007: 219–37.
Squire, M. 2013. 'Apparitions Apparent: Ekphrasis and the Parameters of Vision in the Elder Philostratus' *Imagines*'. *Helios* 40: 97–140.
Squire, M. and Grethlein, J. 2014. '"Counterfeit in Character but Persuasive in Appearance": Reviewing the *Ainigma* of the *Tabula Cebetis*'. *CPh* 109: 285–324.
Stechow, W. 1953. 'Heliodorus' *Aethiopica* in Art'. *Journal of the Warburg and Courtauld Institutes* 16: 144–52.
Stengel, P. 1920. *Die griechischen Kultusaltertümer*. Munich.
Stephens, S. A. 1994. 'Who Read Ancient Novels?'. In Tatum ed. 1994b: 405–18.
Stephens, S. A. 2008. 'Cultural Identity'. In Whitmarsh ed. 2008: 39–71.
Stewart, A. F. 1990. *Greek Sculpture: An Exploration*. 2 vols. New Haven and London.
Swain, S. ed. 1999. *Oxford Readings in the Greek Novel*. Oxford.
Szepessy, T. 1976. 'Le siège de Nisibe et la chronologie d' Héliodore'. *AAAHung* 24: 247–76.
Tagliabue, A. 2012. 'The *Ephesiaca* as a *Bildungsroman*'. *AN* 10: 17–46.
Tagliabue, A. 2015. 'Heliodorus's *Aethiopica* and the Odyssean *Mnesterophonia*: An Intermedial Reading'. *TAPA* 145: 445–68.
Tagliabue, A. 2016. 'Heliodorus' Reading of Lucian's *Toxaris*'. *Mnemosyne* 69: 1–23.
Tarán, L. 1992. 'The Authorship of an Allegorical Interpretation of Heliodorus' *Aethiopica*'. In *Collected Papers, 1962–1999*. Leiden and Boston: 74–108.
Tatum, J. 1994a. 'Herodotus the Fabulist'. In Picone, M. and Zimmermann, B. eds, *Der antike Roman und seine mittelalterliche Rezeption*. Basel, Boston, and Berlin: 29–48.
Tatum J. ed. 1994b. *The Search for the Ancient Novel*. Baltimore.

Tatum, J. 2014. 'Another Look at Suetonius' *Titus*'. In Power, T. and Gibson, R. K. eds, *Suetonius the Biographer: Studies in Roman Lives*. Oxford: 159–77.
Telò, M. 1999. 'Eliodoro e la critica omerica antica'. *SIFC* 17: 71–87.
Telò, M. 2011. 'The Eagle's Gaze in the Opening of Heliodorus' *Aethiopica*'. *AJP* 132: 581–613.
Thalmann, W. G. 1998. *The Swineherd and the Bow: Representations of Class in the Odyssey*. Ithaca and London.
Thomas, R. F. 1986. 'Virgil's *Georgics* and the Poetics of Reference'. *HSCP* 90: 171–98.
Thompson, W. H. 1868. *The Phaedrus of Plato*. London.
Tilg, S. 2010. *Chariton of Aphrodisias and the Invention of the Greek Love Novel*. Oxford.
Torre, C. 2011. 'Su alcune presunte riprese classiche in Filagato da Cerami'. In Bianchi ed. 2011b: 21–54.
Trapp, M. B. 1990. 'Plato's *Phaedrus* in Second-Century Greek Literature'. In Russell, D. A. ed., *Antonine Literature*. Oxford: 141–73.
Trzaskoma, S. 2005. 'A Novelist Writing "History": Longus' Thucydides Again'. *GRBS* 45: 75–90.
Van der Valk, M. 1971. *Eustathii Archiepiscopi Thessalonicensis Commentarii ad Homeri Iliadem pertinentes, Vol. 1*. Leiden.
van Mal-Maeder, D. 1991. 'Au seuil des romans grecs: Effets de réel et effets de création'. *Groningen Colloquia on the Novel* 4: 1–33.
Vernant, J.-P. 1991. 'Mortals and Immortals: The Body of the Divine'. In Vernant, J.-P. ed., *Mortals and Immortals: Collected Essays*. Princeton: 27–49.
Versnel, H. S. 1987. 'What Did Ancient Man See When He Saw a God? Some Reflections on Greco-Roman Epiphany'. In van der Plas, D. ed., *Effigies Dei. Essays on the History of Religions*. Leiden: 42–55.
Walden, J. W. H. 1894. 'Stage Terms in Heliodorus' *Aethiopica*'. *HSCP* 5: 1–43.
Walker, J. 2004. 'These Things I Have Not Betrayed: Michael Psellos' Encomium of his Mother as a Defense of Rhetoric'. *Rhetorica* 22: 49–101.
Wasdin, K. 2019. 'Sibling Romance in Heliodorus' *Aithiopika*'. *CJ* 114: 385–408.
Webb, R. 2006. 'The *Imagines* as a Fictional Text: Ekphrasis, *Apatê* and Illusion'. In Costantini, M., Graziani, F., and Rolet, S. eds, *Le défi de l'art: Philostrate, Callistrate et l'image sophistique*. Rennes: 123–41.
Webb, R. 2007. 'Rhetoric and the Novel: Sex, Lies and Sophistic'. In Worthington ed. 2007: 526–41.
Webb, R. 2009. *Ekphrasis, Imagination and Persuasion in Ancient Rhetorical Theory and Practice*. Farnham.
Webb, R. 2013. 'Mime and the Romance'. In Whitmarsh, T. and Thomson, S. eds, *The Romance between Greece and the East*. Cambridge: 285–99.
Webb, R. 2015. 'Homère dans les *Images* de Philostrate'. In Dubel, S., Favreau-Linder, A.-M. and Oudot, E. eds, *À l'école d'Homère: la culture des orateurs et des sophistes*. Paris: 203–16.
Webb, R. 2017. 'Rhetoric and Fiction'. In Macdonald, M. ed., *The Oxford Handbook of Rhetorical Studies*. Oxford: 279–88.
West, M. L. 1998–2000. *Homerus: Ilias*. Berlin.

Whitmarsh, T. 1998. 'The Birth of a Prodigy: Heliodorus and the Genealogy of Hellenism'. In Hunter ed. 1998b: 93-124.
Whitmarsh, T. 1999. 'The Writes of Passage: Cultural Initiation in Heliodorus' *Aethiopica*'. In Miles, R. ed., *Constructing Identities in Late Antiquity*. London and New York: 16-40.
Whitmarsh, T. 2002. 'Written on the Body: Ecphrasis, Perception and Deception in Heliodorus' *Aethiopica*'. *Ramus* 31: 111-25.
Whitmarsh, T. 2005a. 'Heliodorus Smiles'. In Harrison, Paschalis, and Frangoulidis eds. 2005: 87-105.
Whitmarsh, T. 2005b. 'The Greek Novel: Titles and Genre'. *AJP* 126: 587-611.
Whitmarsh, T. ed. 2008. *The Cambridge Companion to the Greek and Roman Novel*. Cambridge.
Whitmarsh, T. 2009. 'Divide and Rule: Segmenting *Callirhoe* and Related Works'. In Paschalis, M., Panayotakis, S., and Schmeling, G. eds, *Readers and Writers in the Ancient Novel*. Ancient Narrative, Supplementum 12. Groningen: 36-50.
Whitmarsh, T. 2010. 'Domestic Poetics: Hippias' House in Achilles Tatius'. *ClAnt* 29: 327-48.
Whitmarsh, T. 2011. *Narrative and Identity in the Ancient Greek Novel: Returning Romance*. Cambridge.
Whitmarsh, T. 2013a. *Beyond the Second Sophistic: Adventures in Greek Postclassicism*. Berkeley.
Whitmarsh, T. 2013b. 'Greek Novel and Local Myth'. In Futre Pinheiro, M. P., Bierl, A., and Beck, R. eds, *Intende, Lector: Echoes of Myth, Religion and Ritual in the Ancient Novel*. Berlin: 39-42.
Whitmarsh, T. 2018. *Dirty Love: The Genealogy of the Ancient Greek Novel*. New York.
Whitmarsh, T. 2020. *Achilles Tatius, Leucippe and Clitophon: Books I and II. Edited with a Commentary*. Cambridge.
Winkler, J. J. 1982. 'The Mendacity of Kalasiris and the Narrative Strategy of Heliodoros' *Aithiopika*'. *YClS* 27: 93-158. Repr. in Swain ed. 1999: 286-350.
Winkler, J. J. 1990. *The Constraints of Desire: The Anthropology of Sex and Gender in Ancient Greece*. New York and London.
Winkler, M. M. 2000-1. 'The Cinematic Nature of the Opening Scene in Heliodorus' *Aethiopica*'. *AN* 1: 161-84.
Winkler, M. M. 2014. 'Achilles Tatius and Heliodorus: Between Aristotle and Hitchcock'. In Cueva and Byrne eds. 2014: 570-8.
Witte, K. 1913. 'Homeros (1)'. In *RE* VIII, 2: cols 2188-247.
Wlosok, A. 1960. *Laktanz und die philosophische Gnosis: Untersuchungen zu Geschichte und Terminologie der gnostischen Erlösungsvorstellung*. Heidelberg.
Worman, N. 2015. *Landscape and the Spaces of Metaphor in Ancient Literary Theory and Criticism*. Cambridge.
Worthington, I. 2007. *A Companion to Greek Rhetoric*. Oxford.
Wright, M. 2007. 'Comedy and the Trojan War'. *CQ* 57: 412-31.
Yunis, H. 2011. *Plato: Phaedrus*. Cambridge.
Zaccagni, G. 1998. 'La πάρεργος ἀφήγησις in Filagato di Cerami: una particolare tecnica narrativa'. *RSBN* 35: 47-65.

Zanetto, G. 2018. 'Intertextuality and Intervisuality in Heliodorus'. *Prometheus* 44: 209–22.

Zeitlin, F. I. 1990. 'The Poetics of Eros: Nature, Art and Imitation in Longus' *Daphnis and Chloe*'. In Halperin, D. M., Winkler, J. J., and Zeitlin, F. I. eds, *Before Sexuality: The Construction of Erotic Experience in Ancient Greece*. Princeton: 417–64.

Zeitlin, F. I. 2013. 'Landscapes and Portraits: Signs of the Uncanny, Illusions of the Real'. In Paschalis and Panayotakis eds. 2013: 61–87.

Index Locorum

Achilles Tatius
  1.1-2 248
  1.1.2-13 11
  1.1.3-6 213
  1.2.1-2 76 n.14
  1.2.2 74
  1.2.3 74, 213
  1.3.1 252, 259
  1.3.3 180 n.18
  1.10.6 109, 112 n.46
  1.10.7 109
  1.12.2 60 n.28
  1.15 213
  1.18.4 16
  2.3 155 n.20
  2.7.7 110
  2.11 155 n.20
  2.19 238 n.47
  2.24.3 110
  3-5 155
  3.1-5 132-3
  3.5.1 134
  3.9 217-18
  3.10.2-3 218 n.41
  3.12 219
  3.15.5 55 n.9
  4.11-14 242 n.64
  4.12.4-8 217 n.40
  4.12.8 219
  4.14.1-2 219
  5.3.4-8 13
  5.5.2-9 13
  5.17 182 n.26
  5.17.7 169
  8.16 31
  8.19.2 267
  8.19.2-3 266
  8.19.3 265

Acts of the Apostles
  9:3 59 n.26

Acts of Andrew
  17-22 29

Acts of Paul and Thecla
  1.12.57-62 37 n.56

Aelius Aristides
  Egyptian Oration 17

Aeschylus
  Ag. 662-4 134
  Ch. 64, 132 n.7

Alcinous
  Handbook 10.2-3 141

Anna Komnene
  Alexiad
    1.5.9 61 n.30
    1.9.1 60 n.28
    1.13.9 61 n.30
    6.5.1 60 n.28
    8.5.4 60 n.28
    14.6.4 61 n.30

Apollodorus
  3.3.8 12 n.17

Apollonius Rhodius
  Arg. 2.273-83 176 n.6

Apuleius
  Metamorphoses
    2.25-8 171 n.24
    3.14.1 137
    3.24 137
    5 27
    5.22 137
    11.15.2 137

Aristophanes
  Acharnians 528-9 105 n.16
  Peace 799-801 14 n.19
  Thesmophoriazusae 927 181 n.20

Aristotle
  Poetics
    1450b 131
    1451a36-b9 263 n.29
    1453a36-8 184

Aristotle (cont.)
  1459b15 181
  1460a11–17 177
  1460b26 177
Athenaeus
  12.534e 166
  13.558a-b, c 34 n.44
  13.560b 105 n.15
  13.590e 38 n.59
Basil
  Ep. 236.2.15 59 n.24
Callimachus
  Hymn 5.78 108 n.34
Chariton
  1.1.1 248, 256
  1.1.13–16 266 n.38
  1.11.4–5 212
  2.3.7 35 n.47
  3.3.1–8 105–6
  3.4.2 16
  5 150
  5.4.3 35 n.47
  5.5.6 83 n.7
  8.1.2 180 n.18
  8.8.15 143
  8.8.16 143, 248, 257, 265
Choricius
  Op. 42.2.101 61 n.30
  Codex Theodosianus
    9.24.1–2 111–12, 114–15
Colluthus
  Abduction of Helen 372–8 109
  Corpus Hermeticum
    fr. 23.42 137
Cratinus
  Dionysalexandros 105 n.16
Ctesias
  Persian History fr. 9b 227
Demetrius
  On Style 209 241
Demosthenes
  De Chers. 77 104 n.12
  In Aristog. 1.12 104 n.12
  Ol. 2.22 107 n.27
Digenes Akrites Grottaferrata Recension
  3.284 56 n.15
  7.126 56

Dio Chrysostom
  7.128 215 n.34
Diogenes Laertius
  4.16 172
Dionysius of Halicarnassus
  De imit fr. 31.1.1 62, 241
Euripides
  Bacchae 286–97 96 n.45
  Helen
    408–9 135
    1602–4 135 n.13
  Hippolytus 802 24 n.13, 209
  Medea 1317 24 n.9, 77
  Trojan Women 940–50 109
Eustathius
  Hom. 1266.24–6 178
Gorgias
  82 B 23 DK 44
  Helen 109
Heliodorus
  In addition to chapter titles:
  1 147 n.1
  1.1 130
  1.1.1 60 n.28, 216, 254
  1.1.5 61 n.30
  1.1.8 136
  1.2 37, 141
  1.2.1 136
  1.2.4 59 n.23, 60, 64 n.41
  1.2.5–6 157 n.26
  1.2.6 56 n.14, 64 n.41, 136
  1.3 139
  1.3–4 218 n.41
  1.3.2 56
  1.4.3 34
  1.5–6 217
  1.5.2 211 n.19
  1.6.2 215 n.35
  1.7.2 37, 142 n.39
  1.7.3 68
  1.8 65, 66, 68
  1.8.4 10
  1.8.6 76
  1.8.7 24 n.9, 67, 77
  1.9.1 8, 67
  1.9.1–1.14.2 27 n.24
  1.9.1–1.18.1 20, 77
  1.9.2 25

INDEX LOCORUM 291

1.9.3 23, 24	2.8.2 47
1.9.4 23	2.8.3 50
1.10.1 8 n.6	2.8.4 43
1.10.2 24 n.9	2.10.1 47
1.11.3–12 40	2.10.1–2.14 27 n.24
1.12.2 40, 134 n.11	2.11 35 n.46
1.12.3 56 n.14, 57 n.21, 60	2.11.2 47–8, 51
1.12.3–4 157 n.25	2.12.4 156, 157
1.13.1 8	2.14.2 150 n.5
1.14.3 23	2.14.2–3 151
1.14.4 23, 134 n.11	2.14.5 60 n.29
1.14.6 24 n.9	2.14.6 28
1.17.4 134 n.11	2.16 108
1.18.3–4 84 n.12	2.16.3 83 n.9
1.18.4 8	2.17.5 70
1.18.4–5 42	2.18 70
1.18.5 255 n.43	2.19.3–20.2 70
1.19 132 n.6, 192	2.20.2 194 n.24
1.19.2 41–2	2.20.3 152
1.19–20 42	2.21 209–10, 212, 216
1.21.1 57 n.21	2.21.5 125, 153
1.21.2 42	2.22.3–4 26 n.23
1.21.3 59 n.26	2.22.4 55 n.11
1.22 34, 133	2.23.2 157 n.26
1.22.3 15	2.23.6 149
1.23.2 34	2.24 129
1.28.1–1.31.1 27 n.24	2.24.1–3 152
1.29.1–2 215 n.35	2.24.2 8, 153
1.30–1 52	2.24.4 182 n.25
1.33 52	2.25 143
2.1 52, 65, 66	2.25.1 25, 35, 36
2.1.2–3 62	2.25.2 25
2.1.3 63	2.25.4 194
2.2 52	2.25.7 153
2.2.1 150 n.5, 151, 215 n.35	2.26.3 149
2.2.1–2.9.5 27 n.24	2.26.5 209 n.18
2.3 52	2.28 209 n.18
2.3.4 62	2.28.1–29.1 154
2.4–6 60	2.29 209 n.18
2.5.1 63	2.30.3 15
2.5.2 63–4	2.30.6 156, 157
2.5.3 64 n.42, 156, 157	2.31 209 n.18
2.6.1 64, 148 n.4	2.31.1 37, 87 n.19
2.6.2 65	2.33.2 142 n.39
2.6.3 64 n.41	2.33.3–4 37
2.6.3–4 58	2.33.4 11
2.6.4 56 n.15	2.34.5 93 n.35
2.7.2 31	2.35 36 n.50
2.7.3 152	2.35.1 33 n.42
2.8 35 n.46	2.35.5 254, 264

292 INDEX LOCORUM

Heliodorus (cont.)
2.36.2-3 255 n.44
3.1.5 266 n.35
3.3-4 155 n.20
3.4 239
3.4.2-5 215 n.35
3.4.5-6 33 n.42
3.4.7 43, 46, 82 n.5
3.4.9 44
3.4.10 46
3.4.11 46
3.5.4-5 168
3.5.4-6 154
3.5.5 157 n.26
3.7-9 162
3.12.2-3 255 n.45
3.13.3 142 n.39
3.18 162
4 147 n.1
4.4.2-3 147 n.3
4.4.3 46-7
4.5.7 26 n.22
4.7.9 11-12
4.8.2 12-13, 224
4.8.4 224
4.8.6 218
4.8.7 195
4.10 162
4.11-12 171
4.13 34
4.14.2 83 n.10, 252
4.16.6 251
4.16.7 120
4.18.4-6 113
5 147 n.1, 148
5.1 34
5.1.1-2 116
5.1.2 118
5.1.3-5.16 116
5.1.4 147 n.3
5.1.6 150
5.1.7 152, 153
5.2.1-2 157 n.25
5.2.2 150
5.2.3 150
5.2.6 14
5.3.1 31
5.3.3 64 n.41
5.4-9 130
5.4.3 151

5.5.2 97, 168, 250 n.18
5.6.1 156, 157
5.6.2 57 n.21
5.7.3 34-5
5.8.2 141, 151
5.8.3 141
5.10-15 130
5.10.1 151 n.10
5.10.1-2 150 n.5
5.10.2 31, 36, 141, 151 n.8
5.11.2-3 157 n.25
5.13-14 155 n.20
5.13.3 215
5.14.2 266
5.14.4 215
5.15 130, 140, 143
5.15.3 143
5.16 130
5.16.2 149
5.16.5 150, 151 n.8
5.17-33 130
5.18.3 15
5.19.1 139 n.32
5.20.2 15
5.20.6 42, 141
5.22 142
5.22.1 84 n.12, 97
5.22.3 71, 139 n.32
5.26 34
5.26.4 35
5.27.7 15, 209 n.18, 216
5.28.1 42
5.28.1-2 42
5.31.1 37 n.55
5.32.2 194 n.24
5.32.6 194 n.24
6 147 n.1
6.1.2 209 n.18
6.3-4 194 n.23
6.3.2 209 n.18
6.7.3 52 n.1
6.11.3-4 181
6.13.5 61 n.30
6.14-15 186, 194
6.15.9-10 170
7 147 n.1, 148
7.1.4 224
7.2.1 25, 186, 189
7.2.2 24
7.2.4 192

INDEX LOCORUM 293

7.2.4–5 176
7.3–5 192
7.3.1 192
7.4.2 193
7.5.3 175
7.6.1 24 n.10
7.7 167
7.7.1 190
7.7.4 156, 157
7.7.5 56 n.14
7.8.5 266 n.35
7.8.6 24 n.10
7.8.7 142
7.9.1 25
7.9.4 24 n.11
7.9.5 47 n.20
7.10.3 59 n.26
7.10.5 33, 134 n.11
7.11.3 142
7.11.3–4 185
7.11.4 142
7.11.5 185 n.37
7.11.7 191
7.12 26
7.12.2 57 n.21, 196 n.30
7.12.7 24 n.10
7.13.1 26
7.14.2 191
7.16.2–3 153
7.19.1 25
7.20.5 24 n.11
7.24–5.1 199
7.24.2 150 n.5, 151
7.24.4 24
7.25.6 199
7.26.3 199, 211 n.20
7.26.10 199
7.28.2–3 200
7.29.1 201
7.29.2 224
8 148
8.1–3 188
8.1.1 224
8.1.2 209 n.18
8.1.6–7 150 n.5, 151 n.8 n.10
8.2.3 204
8.3–5 193 n.16
8.3.1 205
8.7.1 134 n.11
8.9 211

8.9–11 188
8.9.1 134 n.11
8.9.3 37 n.56
8.9.11–12 211
8.9.13 37 n.56
8.9.15 193 n.16
8.9.17 134 n.11
8.10.2 171, 211 n.21
8.11.1 83 n.7, 84 n.12, 171
8.11.2 82 n.5
8.11.3 206
8.11.4 100 n.55
8.13.3–5 204
8.15.2 24 n.13
8.16.4 154
8.16.7 222
8.17.1 153
8.17.2 18 n.29
8.17.5 223
9 148
9.1.2 224
9.1.3 18 n.29, 217
9.1.4 207, 219, 223 n.11, 230
9.1.5 18 n.29, 219
9.2.2 171, 217
9.2.3 231, 232
9.3.1–5 217
9.3.4 219
9.4.2 217, 219, 242
9.5.2–3 224
9.5.3–4 224
9.5.4 232
9.5.5 242
9.6.2 232
9.7.3 219
9.8.2 233 n.35, 243 n.69
9.8.4 237 n.45
9.9–10 89 n.23, 154 n.15
9.9.2 231, 232
9.9.4 238 n.46
9.10.1 267 n.42
9.10.2–11.2 232
9.12.2 150 n.5, 151 n.8, n.10
9.12.3 142 n.39
9.13.2–3 151 n.9
9.14–15 230 n.25
9.14.1 212
9.15 154
9.19.3–4 154
9.20.5–6 198–9

Heliodorus (cont.)
9.22.4 212
9.22.6 55 n.10
9.23.2 231 n.28
9.24.1 217
9.24.2 224 n.13
9.25.5 219
9.27.2 230
10 147 n.1
10.3.3 231 n.28
10.5 209
10.6.3 142 n.39
10.7.6 231 n.28
10.7.7 231 n.28
10.9.3 59 n.26, 142 n.39
10.9.7 231 n.28
10.10.3 231
10.11.3 253
10.13.1 156, 157
10.13.3–4 157 n.26
10.14.5 176–7
10.15.1 156, 157
10.15.2 33 n.42, 97
10.16.6 252
10.17.2 232 n.31
10.18.2 154 n.13
10.19.2 57 n.20, 154 n.13
10.21.3 154 n.13
10.22.1 154 n.14
10.24 214 n.28
10.24.2 58 n.22
10.25.1 41
10.27 154
10.28–10.30.6 41
10.28.1–4 154
10.29.3–4 154 n.13
10.29.5–30.1 154 n.14
10.32.3 41
10.32.4 41, 154 n.13
10.33.1 154 n.13
10.33.4 154 n.14
10.34.3 26 n.23
10.35.1 134 n.11
10.35.2–36.1 157 n.26
10.36.1 154
10.38 184 n.35, 214 n.28
10.39 220
10.40.2 264
10.41.1 264, 268
10.41.2 254, 264
10.41.4 211

Heraclitus Homericus
26.10 90
74.1 90
Hermogenes
On Issues 5–6 225 n.15
Herodian
5.5.2 250 n.20
Herodotus
1.1 256
1.2.1–3 105 n.16
1.4.2 105 n.15, 111
1.5 263 n.30
1.5.2 105 n.15
1.5.3 108, 113 n.47
1.13.2 108
2.28.2 18 n.28
2.36 75
3.19.1 18
3.19.2 18 n.29
3.23.2 18 n.29
3.23.4 18 n.29
3.25.1 18 n.29
4.196 15
5.16 17
7.168 120 n.12
9.72.1 10 n.11
9.100 15
Homer
Iliad
1 147
1.8–9 113 n.47
1.104 87 n.19
1.200 89–90
1.469–71 140
2 146
2.110–41 241 n.57
2.201 138
2.301–3 73
2.631–5 118
3.396–7 87 n.19
3.399–405 109
4.141 97
4.146 97
4.450–1 138
5.80–1 138
6.289–92 134
7 147
7.398–9 158
7.436–41 243
7.459–63 243

INDEX LOCORUM 295

9 147
9.29–31 158
9.383 93–4
10 146
10.261–5 124
10.351–81 175
10.368 175
12 225
13.71–2 81, 89, 255 n.45
13.72 85
14.30–1 181 n.21
18.468–617 227
19.47–50 124
21.3 45
21.257 241
21.415 87 n.19
21.527 135
22 174
22.36 177
22.92 135
22.136–7 175
22.138 175
22.140 175
22.157–8 175
22.159–66 178
22.161 181
22.162–3 178
22.162–6 177
22.173 175
22.189–93 176 n.6
22.194–8 175
22.199–201 176, 177
22.201 178
22.203–4 177
22.205 178
22.205–7 177
22.207 175
22.208 179
22.209–13 179
23.744 251 n.25
24.12 75 n.11
Odyssey
  1.1 124
  1.2 119
  1.3 72
  3.286–92 120
  4.266 240 n.56
  4.514–20 120
  5 147
  6–8 71

7 147
7.311–16 72
9.1–18 73
9.19–20 125
9.21–4 126
9.21–8 117
9.39 71
9.74–84 120
9.79–81 127
9.142 134
10.330 124 n.22
11.639–40 116 n.1
13 181
13.332 124
13.397–401 123
14 147
14.125 182 n.28
14.287–9 251
14.288 259
15 111 n.42, 146
15.415 251 n.25
15.473 251 n.25
16 147, 182
17.286–7 73
18 147
18.67–8 96 n.47, 124
18.74 96, 99 n.53, 124 n.20
19 147
19.186–7 120
19.390–4 124–5
19.392–4 124
19.407–9 127 n.28
19.450 96
19.509–53 14
19.518–23 14
19.547 83
20 146
20.90 83 n.9
22.1 181
22.381–9 16
22.388 18
24 107, 182
24.320 182 n.24
Homeric Hymn to Demeter
  1–14 213 n.25

Horace
  Ars Poetica 30 242

Irenaeus
  Refutation of All Heresies 1.1.2–1.2.1 137

296 INDEX LOCORUM

John of Damascus
   Second Homily on the Dormition of
      Mary 8.26 57 n.20
   Trans. 6 57
Josephus
   The Jewish War 4.97–104 233 n.33
Julian
   Caes. 313a 250 n.21
   Hel. 150c 253
   Or. 1.27b 225 n.18, 234 n.41
   Or. 1.27b-30b 221 n.1
   Or. 2 225
   Or. 2.2b-62c 221 n.1
   Or. 2.67a-68c 243
   Or. 4.154b 250 n.21
ps.-Libanius
   Declamation 40.2.20 60 n.28
Longinus
   15.1 45
   15.7 11 n.15
Longus
   Pr. 11, 248
   Pr. 1 213
   Pr. 3 249
   1.1 242 n.64
   1.4 213
   2–3 104
   2.3.5 216 n.36
   2.5.1 14 n.19
   2.15.2 15
   3.12.4 14 n.19
   3.28.1 15
   4.2 240 n.54
   4.38.2 167 n.18
   4.39.1 265
   4.40.1–2 265
Lucian
   Toxaris 13 36
   Verae Historiae
      Pr. 260 n.21
      2.20 96 n.44
Luke
   7:11–17 55
Menander
   Samia 730–7 184–5
Menander Rhetor
   On Epideictic

     II 373.17–29 225 n.17
     II 374.27 232 n.30
Michael Psellos
   Charicleia and Leukippe 40–1 60 n.27
   Chronographia
      5.40 60 n.28
      7.17 60 n.28
   Encomium
      594–5 57 n.21
      605–6 59 n.26
      936 57 n.21
      940 57 n.21
      1142–1202 60
      1156 60
      1170–1 60
      1192 57 n.21
      1362–3 60 n.29
      1493–1558 60
      1499–1506 59
      1519 59
      1523–4 58
      1525–6 57
   In Mariam Sclerenam 131–2 57
   Theologica 25 61 n.30
Moschus
   Europa
      34–6 213 n.25
      63–71 213 n.25
Nikolaos
   Progymnasmata 68–9 227 n.22
ps.-Nilus
   Narrationes
      1.8 55 n.9
      6.1 55 n.9
      7.1.1 60 n.29
Nonnus
   Dionysiaca
      7.203 238 n.48
      15.240 238 n.48
      19.261 238 n.48
      42.42 238 n.48
      42.216 238 n.48
      43.34 238 n.48
Ovid
   Ars amatoria 1.249–50 29 n.27
   Fasti 3.675–96 27
   Metamorphoses
      4.55–92 31 n.33

7.690–862 28
10.467 26 n.19

Parthenius
    Romantic Sufferings 17 28

Pausanias
    1.19.2 14
    1.24.3 12
    9.4.1–2 9–10

Philagathos of Cerami
    Homilies
        6.8–9 55
        6.8.12–13 55 n.9
        6.9.9–11 55 n.11
        6.12.4–5 56 n.14
        6.12.8 56 n.14
        6.12.8–10 55–6
        6.12.14 56
        6.16.12 56 n.14
        31.23.2 55 n.9
        37 55 n.10
        79 55 n.10

Philostratus
    Heroicus
        1.1 76 n.12
        1.3 251 n.26
    Imagines proem 4 44
    VA 6.19 46 n.18
    VS 489 76 n.13

Pindar
    fr. 123.1–6 47 n.20

Plato
    Alcibiades 2 147b 91 n.31
    Ion 535b5–6 177
    Phaedrus
        227a 211
        227a–d 73
        227a1 74
        228b 211
        229a–b 208
        229a-230a 74
        229b 209
        229b4–d1 213 n.25
        230b 209
        230b–c 208
        230c1–2 210
        242a 211
        243e–57b 208 n.12
        248b–c 208
        251e 238 n.48
        257d–e 213–4
        258e–59a 211
        279b 211
    Protagoras 380a-88e 91 n.31
    Republic
        389d 137
        440d 137 n.26
        488a–e 133
        509a6 142
        549a 137 n.26
    Statesman 267a 215 n.34
    Symposium
        180e 136 n.17
        197d6–7 136
        209e-212a 131
        210a 141
        211a 141
        211e 141
        218e 141 n.38
    Theaetetus 176b1 142

Plotinus
    Ennead 1.6 141–2

Plutarch
    Alc. 1.4 166
    Coniugalia Praecepta 144e, f 29
    De gloria Atheniensium 346f
        11 n.15
    De sera 563d 173

Pollux
    1.99–100 15–16

Polybius
    4.21.12 215 n.34

Porphyry
    Vita Plot. 23 137

Proclus
    In Rep.
        1.126–7 90
        2.238.7 90

Sappho
    fr. 16 109

Sophocles
    Oedipus at Colonus 1631–5 185

Soranus
    Gynaecology 1.9–10 238 n.47

298 INDEX LOCORUM

Stesichorus
  fr. 85 107 n.29
  fr. 174 14 n.19
Strabo
  8.6.20 120 n.11
  10.2.18 118
  10.2.19 118
  13.1.36 243
Suetonius
  Life of Titus 6–7 172–3
Theodoros Prodromos
  Rodanthe and Dosikles 7.259 60 n.28
Theon
  Progymnasmata 118 227 n.20
Thucydides
  1.1 256
  1.21 263 n.30
  2.75–8 227
  3.36–49 232
  4.100 227

  4.69.2 230
  6.2.20–4 241 n.57
Virgil
  Aeneid 3.270–3 119
Xenophon of Athens
  Anabasis 6.4.2 17
  Memorabilia
    1.2.24 166
    3.11.10–14 35 n.49
Xenophon of Ephesus
  1.3.2 35
  1.8.1 266 n.38
  2.11.10 16
  2.12.2 16
  3.4 103 n.5
  5.10.9 169
  5.12.3 169
  5.13.3 169
  5.15.2 249 n.16
  5.15.3 265

General Index

These entries supplement the chapter titles and the Index Locorum.

abduction 102, 104, 105–7, 109–11, 114, 213
Achaemenes 151, 153, 187, 188,
 191–2, 196–201
Achilles 45, 75 n.11, 80, 105, 113 n.47, 135,
 165, 174–8, 181, 190, 201, 222, 227, 241
Achilles Tatius 3, 67, 106, 110, 161, 170, 195,
 217–9, 261, 266–9
Aeschylus
 Eumenides 184
 Persians 194
aesthetics 39–40, 42–6, 48, 51
Agamemnon 120, 134, 135, 146
agency 109–15
Alcamenes (character in the
 Aethiopica) 12–15, 19, 34
Alcamenes (sculptor) 12–15
allegoresis 90–2
allegorical reading 4, 171 n.25, 215, 262–3
allusion *passim*
analepsis 129–30, 188, 205, 216
Anthia 35, 168–9, 170
anticipation (*see also* expectation) 27, 104,
 109, 127, 134, 148, 166, 186, 204,
 207, 217
apatē 43–6, 48, 51
Aphrodite
 in Aphrodisias 254
 in Chariton 143, 265
 and Helen 107, 109
 Pandemos 136
 sculpture of 14–15
Apollo 108, 113, 177
 blamed by Charicleia 65, 66
 with Artemis, in Calasiris' dream 81,
 82–3, 85
Arsace 20, 24–5, 37, 134, 151, 163, 174, 178,
 203, 204–5, 208, 209, 210, 212
Aristippus 21, 23, 25, 26–7, 35, 40, 42, 49–50
Aristotle 131, 167 n.17, 177–8, 179, 181, 184,
 243, 244, 263
Arsinoe 26–7, 29, 31, 40

Artemis 37, 81, 82
 Charicleia's affinity with/likened to 35, 37,
 130, 136, 143
 Charicleia as priestess of 102, 113, 195
 with Apollo, in Calasiris' dream 81, 82–3, 85
Athens 8, 10–11, 13, 14, 26–7, 49, 73, 105,
 189, 190, 235
authorship 54, 247–9

Bagoas 188, 198, 203, 204–6, 209, 210, 213,
 218 n.42
bandits (*see also* brigands *and* pirates) 7, 17,
 20, 34, 37, 66, 73, 170, 192, 217–9
Bessa 162, 167, 170, 186, 194, 198
biography, Homeric 81, 93–100
brigands (*see also* bandits *and* pirates) 7, 19,
 34, 36, 52, 130, 131, 133, 135, 137,
 139, 186

Calasiris 4, 11–12, 17, 25, 26, 30, 34, 36, 42,
 43–4, 49, ch. 6–14 *passim*, 212, 216, 239
Callirhoe 26, 35, 38, 105, 143, 150, 197,
 212–13, 248, 257, 265
Cape Malea 120, 127
Cephallenia 118–19
Chaereas 26, 106, 143, 150, 265
character development 164–73
characterization 21, 24, 32–4, 36, 91, 135, 140
Charias 21, 30
Charicleia *passim*
Charicles 11, 26, 37, 102, 104, 106–9, 113,
 114, 153, 154, 157, 162, 195, 252, 264
Chariton 35, 38, 103, 104, 106, 150–1, 161,
 170, 197, 205, 248–9, 254, 256–8, 259, 260
Chemmis 70, 71, 74–5, 130, 146, 149, 156, 162
Chloe 213, 248, 267
Clitophon 13, 16, 26, 63, 67, 74, 109–10, 132,
 169, 213, 218, 249, 252, 259, 262, 265,
 266, 268
closure 139, 143, 151, 180, 184–5, 188, 223,
 240, 264–7

Cnemon 8, 11, ch. 3–7 *passim*, 108, 130, ch. 11 *passim*, 163, 190
Cybele 25, 33, 187, 188–9, 191, 194, 195, 196, 197, 199, 200, 201

daimōn 65, 135, 140, 170, 171
daimonion 139–40, 143
Daphnis 15, 248, 267
Delphi 11, 37, 41, 81, 116, 144, 148, 239
Demaenete 39, 40–1, 42–3, 45, 47–8, 49–50, 51, 189, 190, 194
desire, incestuous 22–6
despair 135, 144, 161, 170–2
dream 42, 71, 80, 82–4, 86, 96, 108, 109, 143, 171, 176, 177, 206, 252

Egypt
 arrival at 133–5
 boundary of/departure from 162, 187, 212, 223
 Homer's homeland 99
 in Herodotus 8, 17, 18, 75
 journey to 20, 82, 116, 119, 159, 163
ekphrasis 9–11
Elephantine 18, 222
enargeia 178–9
epiphany 81–5, 89, 98, 100
Ethiopians 18, 41, 189, 198, 203, 205–7, 212, 217–18, 222–4, 229–30, 253
ethnicity
 Charicleia's 33
 Cnemon's 68
 Ethiopians' 218
 Heliodorus' 258
 Homer's 94–5, 100
Euripides 183
 Helen 35 n.46
 Hippolytus 30, 197
 Phoenissae 174, 178 n.14
Eustathius 91 n.32, 95 n.42, 178–9
excitement 146, 147, 159–60, 268
expectation (*see also* anticipation) 11, 17, 27, 42, 43, 65, 67, 92, 147–8, 156, 158, 199, 203–7, 225

fish 17–18

genre
 of romance 1–2, 49, 56, 59, 61, 64, 66–7, 74, 100, 103–4, 112–15, 122 158, 164, 195, 248, 267
 interplay of 27, 39, 179

Habrocomes 35, 168–9, 170
Hector 225
 fight with Achilles 174–8, 179, 181, 190
Hegesias 102, 105, 106–7, 113, 114
Helen 35, 38, 105, 109–110, 114, 134–5, 158, 190
Helios (*see also* sun) 211, 212, 253, 254, 264
Heraclitus Paradoxographus *Peri Apistōn* 34 n.44
Herodotus 188, 233
historiographical pose 222, 242, 245, 256–63
Homer *passim*, *see also* biography *and* scholia
hybridity, cultural 190–3, 201–2
Hydaspes 12–13, 41, 154, 156, 157, 217, 219, 221–45, 252, 264

intertextuality *passim*
Isis 143
 and Osiris 143, 238
 Charicleia likened to 37, 143
 in Thyamis' dream 42, 143
 temple of 25, 143

lamentation 14, 31, 73, 139
Leucippe 13, 26, 31, 63, 110, 155, 169–70, 213, 219, 268
liminality, 170, 172, 223, 242, 246–7, 254, 262
locus amoenus 209, 211, 212–13
Longus 2, 13, 161, 171, 265–9

martyr 21, 33, 37–8
Memphis 8, 42, 156, 157, 162, 170, 174, 180, 186, 190, 192, 198, 203, 205, 207, 210, 211
Menelaus 97, 109, 120, 134
Meroe 41, 154, 162, 202, 208–9, 264
metafictionality 242–3, 259
metaliterary reading 211–12, 215–7, 236–44
Michael Psellos 3, 57–60, 61–2, 64, 69, 239
Mitranes 31, 141, 186, 187, 198
mnēstērophonia 10, 11, 15, 16–17

narrative doublet 39–40, 41–2, 62–3, 68
narrative transition 147, 149–50, 203, 216
Naucratis 8
Nausicleia 163
Nausicles 31, 36, 116, 130, 139, 141, 143, 144, 146–60, 161, 162, 163, 194 n.23, 209 n.18, 215
Neoplatonism 88–92, 99, 101
New Comedy 11, 30, 39, 183–5, 197

GENERAL INDEX 301

Nile 70, 73–4, 148, 202, 203, 204, 207, 209–10, 213–17, 219, 221–3, 226, 230, 231, 234–6, 238
floods 89 n.23, 154, 238
mouth 7, 8, 130, 133, 216, 221, 242, 254
as Osiris 143, 238
sources 154

Odysseus 71–3, 74, 77, 78, 80, 83, 96, 134, 142, 146, 162, 171 n.25, 175, 181–2, 190, 229, 251, 259, 261, 262
Oroondates 8, 153, 186, 187–8, 189, 192, 198, 201, 203, 204, 205, 206, 213, 217, 222, 223, 224, 230, 232, 243

paratext 246–7
Paris 105, 109, 134
Pelorus 130, 135–8, 139, 141
Penelope 14, 83–4, 117, 120–1, 127
Persians 8–11, 203, 208, 212–13, 216–17, 218, 222–4, 230, 233
Persinna 12–13, 19, 26, 30, 156, 157, 224, 264
Petosiris 72, 174–6, 184, 186, 190, 192–3
Phaedra 20, 24, 189, 190, 191, 197, 209
phantasia 45–6, 234
Philagathos of Cerami 4, 54–7, 69
'Philip the Philosopher' 47 n.21, 100 n.56, 263 n.31
 nom de plume of Philagathos of Cerami 4, 54
Philostratus 241 n.58
Phoenician
 Heliodorus 250–2, 258–9, 261–2
Photius 2–3, 22 n.5
pirates (*see also* bandits *and* brigands) 42, 66, 116, 117, 119, 130–6, 139, 141, 212–3
Plautus 27, 39
Polygnotus 9–10, 11, 15, 17
priestess
 Charicleia 15, 21, 33, 37–8, 195
Procne, Itys, Tereus 12–14
prolepsis 206–7, 208, 216–7, 237–8, 265
prostitute 21, 22, 25, 26, 31, 33–4, 36–7, 38

rape 27, 110–12, 238
readership 1
realism, geographical 117–21
reality 81–4, 86, 87–8, 98–9
 historical 110–11

recognition 125, 131, 156, 167–8, 174, 181–2, 190, 195, 237
 misrecognition 48, 169, 170
Rhodopis 22, 25, 35–6, 38, 189, 192, 194
romance *see* genre

scholia, Homeric 45, 91, 175, 177–8, 179, 181 n.21, 243 n.70, 244
Secundus the Silent Philosopher 28–9
Selene 37, 264
separation, of protagonists 161, 162–3, 165, 167, 168, 170
silence 10, 28, 56–7, 68, 104, 153–4, 156–8
simile 18, 34, 175, 176, 177, 178, 241
Sisimithres 37, 157, 220, 253
sleeplessness 146–7
sōphrosunē 194–5
statue 9 n.9, 10, 14, 37, 130, 142–3
sun (*see also* Helios) 17–18, 73–4, 210–12, 253–4, 258
suspense 78–9, 162, 186, 204, 217, 233
Syene 18, 144, 198, 202, 203, 205, 217, 219

telos 37, 46, 185, 240, 260, 267, 268
Theagenes *passim*
Thermouthis 54, 70, 151, 152, 156, 157, 194 n.24
thigh 96–7, 99–100, 123, 124
Thisbe 54, 62, 64, 65, 67, 70, 116, 141, 148, 150, 151–2, 155, 156, 157, 163, 189, 190, 191, 194, 197
Thyamis 24, 31, 34, 41–2, 48, 49, 50, 52, 70, 72, 133, 143, 151, 153, 155 n.22, 162, 163, 174–7, 184, 186, 187, 190, 192–3, 201
Trachinus 34, 35, 41–2, 116, 121, 130, 131, 134, 135, 136, 137, 138, 141
tragedy 30, 47–8, 67, 77, 174, 177, 179, 181, 183, 194, 209
Tyrrhenus 116, 117, 118, 121, 126, 127

visual arts 9–13, 14–15
visualization 221–2, 227–8, 235

wrath 107
 Odysseus' 117, 123, 126–8

Xenophon of Ephesus 35, 103, 161, 168–9, 170, 195